Mandarins of the Future

PUBLISHING FOR THE WORLD
125 Years

THE JOHNS HOPKINS UNIVERSITY PRESS

New Studies in American Intellectual and Cultural History

Howard Brick, series editor

Mandarins of the Future

Modernization Theory in
Cold War America

Nils Gilman

The Johns Hopkins University Press
Baltimore and London

This book has been brought to publication with the assistance of the J.G. Goellner Fund of the Johns Hopkins University Press.

The Johns Hopkins University Press
2715 North Charles Street
Baltimore, Maryland 21218-4363
www.press.jhu.edu

Library of Congress Cataloging-in-Publication Data

Gilman, Nils, 1971–
   Mandarins of the future: modernization theory in Cold War America / Nils Gilman
      p.   cm.—(New studies in American intellectual and cultural history)
Includes bibliographical references and index.
   ISBN 0-8018-7399-1 (acid-free paper)
   1. United States—Intellectual life—20th century. 2. Postcolonialism. 3. Social change—Philosophy. 4. Social change—Developing countries. 5. Economic development—Philosophy. 6. Economic development—Developing countries. 7. National characteristics, American. 8. Liberalism—United States—History—20th century. 9. United States—Politics and government—1945–1989. 10. United States—Foreign relations—1945–1989. I. Title. II. Series.
   E169.12.g55 2003
   303.44'01—dc21
                                    2002156769

A catalog record for this book is available from the British Library.

Development is a treacherous river, as everyone who plunges into its currents knows. On the surface the water flows smoothly and quickly, but if the captain makes one careless or thoughtless move he finds out how many whirlpools and wide shoals the river contains.

—RYSZARD KAPUŚCIŃSKI,
Shah of Shahs, 1982

Contents

Acknowledgments

This project was conceived and researched during the Clinton years. At that time, I was struck by how much modernization theory's relentless optimism and self-congratulation reminded me of the dominant emotional tone of Clintonian America. I considered Francis Fukuyama's success in revivifying modernization theory a result of the theory's comfortable fit with the emotional-intellectual landscape of the 1990s. If "The End of History" was modernization theory redux, it made sense that this rehabilitation would take place at a time when America felt confident in its economic, political, and ideological superiority. The celebrators of globalization were the heirs of modernization theory.

Then 9-11 happened and everything changed.

Yet somehow the discourse on modernization continued the comeback it had begun with the end of the cold war. Except now the renewed discourse of modernity, instead of representing conservative self-congratulation, became the position of liberal internationalists who hoped to add some carrots to the bag of sticks that the Bush regime presented as its main approach for dealing with the post–9-11 world. The middlebrow media, doing their bit, relentlessly contrasted America's "modernity" to the barbarism of its enemies.

While many Europeans and other foreigners took this American auto-celebration to be a sign of unreflective, crude American neo-imperialism, the reality seemed to me to be that all the celebration of America's wonderful modernity was, in fact, a thin cover for a deep-seated anxiety about the state of the world and about America's role in it. That combination of anxiety and a desire to deny that anxiety by shouting to the world how great we are in turn reminded me of something else about the 1950s.

There are two pop-historical stereotypes about the 1950s, both of which alone are but half-truths, but which together reveal something profound about the period. The first half-image is of the 1950s as a time of sock hops and rock 'n' roll, renewed economic vitality, graceful acceptance of social conformity and moral rectitude, optimism about the possibility for an improved world, and above all, a smug sense of self-congratulation. This is the 1950s that conservatives today celebrate. The second half-image invokes the specter of the bomb, the scarily relentless charge of the Soviets on the one hand and McCarthy on the other, domestic racial conflicts, and international political calamities. This is the 1950s that led me to title a course I taught on the period "America in the Age of Anxiety." These two faces of the 1950s were two sides of the same coin. The relentless optimism arose as a way to ward off the ghouls of nuclear holocaust, racial and gender anxiety, and Communism. The search for a definition of a national identity and a national mission reflected a sense of anxiety about the lack of identity and the lack of mission—in apparent contrast to ideologically fanatical enemies.

This book's central argument is that modernization theory reflects both of these sides of the 1950s—both an optimism about the possibilities and pleasures of American-style modernity and a fear that the house of cards might come tumbling down. In this respect the continued post–9-11 upsurge in popularity of the discourse of modernism comes full circle. American newspapers and opinion journals of the early twenty-first century have been full of chest- (and war-drum-) pounding declarations about the superiority of American modernity. They have argued that the answer to the question "Why do they hate us?" is "Because we're modern, and they're not, and they're jealous." Reflecting on the parallels between this discourse and its antecedent a half-century earlier, it's hard not to wonder whether the pundits do not protest too much. Is it a coincidence that these declarations come at a time of economic drift, corporate scandal, stock market decline, rising crime, and a general sense of malaise? Just as they were for the modernization theorists of the 1950s, so these strident declarations of the superiority of the "modern" American way of life in the 2000s represent a way for the nation to hide its anxieties in plain sight.

This project began in a seminar entitled "The American Intellectual History of the 1950s," which I took from David Hollinger in 1992, my senior year in college. Reading Walt Rostow's *Stages of Economic Growth* and Clark Kerr's *The Uses of the University* widened my conception of the definition and role of intellectuals in the postwar United States and provided the point of departure for this book. In addition to his invaluable intellectual guidance, David always provided me with the moral support to continue with this project even when I seemed to be losing my way. Before I met David, Martin Jay lured me from my study of economics and demography into intellectual history. His celebrated work on the Frankfurt School was the impossibly high ideal I strove to emulate in this work. Gillian Hart encouraged me to consider contemporary debates in development studies, which opened me to views of the subject beyond the parochial ones of intellectual history.

The following people read drafts and commented on various versions of this book from its earliest stages to its final form: Michael Adas, Howard Brick, Robert Brugger, Sharad Chari, David Engerman, Gerald Feldman, Lars Gilman, Jesse Goldhammer, Mark Haefele, Melody Herr, Joshua Hoffman, Andy Jewett, Sarah Kennel, Eileen Kim, Bruce Kuklick, Andrew Lakoff, Michael Latham, Alex Marashian, Keally McBride, Robert Mockler, Samuel Moyn, Dorothy Ross, Jason Smith, Justin Suran, David Szanton, Margaret Weir, and others too numerous to mention. I alone, of course, am responsible for any errors of fact or interpretation.

Thanks to Monica Blank, Erwin Levold, and Tom Rosenbaum at the Rockefeller Archives; Elizabeth Andrews, Elizabeth Boucher, Lois Beattie, Jeffrey Mifflin, and Darcy Duke at the MIT Archives; Roberta Kovitz and Daniel Meyer at the University of Chicago Archives; Kerri Friedman at Washington University's political science department; and the librarians at Indiana University and the Library of Congress, who helped me track down the most stubbornly evasive sources. Just as crucial to my work as the archives were the resources made available through the JSTOR project (www.jstor.org), hosted by the University of Michigan, which has made scores of journals going back to the nineteenth century searchable over the World Wide Web, allowing near-instantaneous uncovering of linkages among scholars, journals, words, and ideas. It is no exaggeration to say that JSTOR will revolutionize the way the history of the American social sciences gets written. Special thanks go to Gabriel Almond, Robert Bellah, Donald Blackmer, Clifford Geertz, Albert Hirschman, McKim Marriot, Lucian Pye, Walt Whitman Rostow, and Neil Smelser, whose eyewitness testimonies helped me map the social and intellectual networks behind modernization theory.

This book also benefited immeasurably from the lucky fact that my father is an academic and my mother an academic editor. They read drafts and provided moral and financial support throughout. The guidance bestowed by "the family tradition" in this case supported a most modern endeavor. Nor would this book have been completed but for the generous funding of the University of California, Berkeley. Finally, my wife, Jennifer, could not have been more supportive as I sacrificed months of vacations and countless weekends over the last two years bringing this book into its current form.

Mandarins of the Future

CHAPTER 1

Modernization Theory and American Modernism

The United States is presiding at a general reorganization of the ways of living throughout the world.

—ANDRÉ SIEGFRIED, quoted in both David Potter,
People of Plenty, 1954, and Daniel Lerner,
The Passing of Traditional Society, 1958

On a steamy June morning in 1959, sociologist Edward Shils strode to the podium of a conference hall on the former Rockefeller estate in Dobbs Ferry, New York, to deliver the keynote address at a conference on the political problems and prospects of the "new states" in the Middle East, Asia, and Africa. If the scholars and policy makers in the audience were expecting to hear about the particularities of development practices in, say, the Gold Coast or India or Brazil, they were in for a surprise. For Shils's aim was as far from empirical inquiry as one could imagine. Instead, he attempted that morning to provide nothing less than a definition of *modernity,* a term borrowed from the art world and one that Shils believed provided the linchpin for understanding the ambitions of the postcolonial regions:

In the new states "modern" means democratic and equalitarian, scientific, economically advanced and sovereign. "Modern" states are "welfare states," proclaiming the welfare of all the people and especially the lower classes as their primary concern. "Modern" states are meant necessarily to be democratic states in which not merely are the people cared for and looked after by their rulers, but they are, as well, the source of inspiration and guidance of those rulers. Modernity entails democracy, and democracy in the new states is, above all, equalitarian. Modernity therefore entails the dethronement of the rich and the traditionally privileged from their positions of pre-eminent influence. It involves land reform. It involves steeply progressive income taxation. It involves universal suffrage. Modernity involves universal public education. Modernity is scientific.

It believes the progress of the country rests on rational technology, and ultimately on scientific knowledge. No country could be modern without being economically advanced or progressive. To be advanced economically means to have
an economy based on modern technology, to be industrialized and to have a
high standard of living. All this requires planning and the employment of economists and statisticians, conducting surveys to control the rates of savings and
investments, the construction of new factories, the building of roads and harbors,
the development of railways, irrigation schemes, fertilizer production, agricultural research, forestry research, ceramics research, and research of fuel utilization. "Modern" means being western without the onus of following the West. It
is the model of the West detached in some way from its geographical origins and
locus.[1]

With these words, Shils placed the question of modernity at the center of a
decades-old debate about "development." From now on, thinking about
development would have to take on not only the banausic details of how to
spur change in the postcolonial world but also the larger question of what
kind of society "development" should strive to create. With this speech, the
discourse about development would join a larger and older conversation
about the nature and definition of modernity, both at home and abroad.

In the audience that June day were most of the intellectuals who today are
collectively known as the modernization theorists: Gabriel Almond, Lucian
Pye, David Apter, Cyril Black, Bert Hoselitz, Myron Weiner, Karl Deutsch, and
Daniel Lerner, among others. Although some in the audience doubted elements of Shils's description of modernity, most agreed that Shils had crystal-
lized into an aesthetic whole the ideas about development that all of them
had been working on for the better part of a decade. Shils's aim here was to
create foundational certainty that the overall purpose of development was to
achieve modernity the world over, and that this ambition was something that
postcolonial peoples themselves desired. If his aim was to turn modernity into
a universal category "detached in some way from its geographical origins and
locus," however, Shils's definition of modernity nevertheless reflected the
time and place in which he was writing. Systematizing the social ideals of
midcentury American liberals, Shils defined modernity as social leveling to
minimize class distinctions; state-guided industrialism; an exaltation of rationalism, science, and expertise as the guide for democratic institutions; and
convergence on a consensual model of social organization based on progres-

yes- contradiction -
impossible ahistorialy

post colonialism

sive taxation and state provision of social benefits. In short, the ideal terminus of development, according to Shils and his colleagues in the audience, was an abstract version of what postwar American liberals wished their country to be.

In its broad outlines, the story of modernization theory is well known: from the late 1950s through the 1960s, modernization theory dominated American social scientific thought regarding economic, political, and social change in the postcolonial world. Rooted in the contrast between "traditional" and "modern" societies, modernization theory posited the existence of a common and essential pattern of "development," defined by progress in technology, military and bureaucratic institutions, and the political and social structure. As the newly independent states of Africa and Asia and the older states of Latin America accelerated their industrialization after World War II, American social scientists used the term modernization with increasing frequency to describe this process. By defining a singular path of progressive change, the concept of modernization simplified the complicated world-historical problems of decolonization and industrialization, helping to guide American economic aid and military intervention in postcolonial regions. Unfortunately, the story typically concludes, modernization theory was hopelessly reductionist in its conception of change abroad, fundamentally conservative in its politics, and blindly reflective of the political and social prejudices of the midcentury American Establishment. As a result, it helped lead American policy makers into terrible mistakes, most notably the Vietnam War, and was discredited by the early 1970s. By the 1980s, modernization theory had become a cliché, dismissed as a symbol of the misinformed platitudes of the Eisenhower, Kennedy, and Johnson eras, in contrast to the weary wisdom of our own age.

Like most potted histories, this story is a mixture of truth and half-truth. If modernization theory was misguided in many ways, it also signified a necessary and serious attempt to grapple with the intellectual and policy issues that decolonization raised in the context of the cold war. Understood on its own terms, modernization theory was the fruit of American social scientists' effort to build a comprehensive theory not only for understanding what was happening in postcolonial regions, but also for promoting change that would make these regions become more like "us"—and less like the Russians or the Chinese. A key theme of this book is to explore what these scholars meant by "us." Three central case studies describe how a constellation of ideas that eventually became known as modernization theory emerged out of the interactions of midcentury American scholars operating within three different kinds of institutions: an academic department, a funded research committee, and an academic think tank with strong government ties. As examinations of the social life of the mind for midcentury American academics, these case studies show how a set of ideas emerged from a conjuncture of geopolitics, the institutional growth of the academy, the compelling power of the ideal of modernization, and a healthy dose of plain old careerism. On one level, therefore, I hope that these chapters stand alone as contributions to the sociology of mid-twentieth-century American academia.

By themselves, however, these three case studies cannot provide us with a full understanding of the meaning of modernization theory and its connection to the wider intellectual life of twentieth-century America. To help contextualize modernization theory, this book also examines the images of postcoloniality that undergirded the theory. By comparing the modernization theorists' texts about development with coeval debates concerning the American national identity, this book examines how these midcentury American intellectuals defined modernity. Examining modernization theory in this light reveals postwar American liberals' peculiar combination of anxiety and confidence about American ways of organizing the world. On the one hand, the language and practice of modernization expressed a confidence that the United States *should* be a universal model for the world and a sense that the United States had a duty to promote this model. On the other hand, "modernization" arose at a moment when Americans felt both unsure about how to define themselves, and challenged by geopolitical ideological competitors. (Sociologist Robert Bellah would later describe his own early work in modernization theory as "a modern apology for liberal society and an attempt to show its relevance to the developing areas."[2]) If postwar American intellectuals consistently used the term *modernity* to express an idealized vision of the United States, then as the ideal of "America" changed, so did the content of the term *modern* in internationalist language and practice. Contrary to the widespread view that modernization theory was primarily a conservative ideology, this juxtaposition of modernization theory to other texts show that modernization theory is best understood as a manifestation of American postwar liberalism, and that its history cannot be understood apart from the fate of that liberalism. As liberal confidence about modernity declined, so too did modernization theory.

The central thread that ran through all of modernization theory was a particular rendition of the dichotomy of "the traditional" and "the modern."

LIBERALISM

According to modernization theorists, modern society was cosmopolitan, mobile, controlling of the environment, secular, welcoming of change, and characterized by a complex division of labor. Traditional society, by contrast, was inward looking, inert, passive toward nature, superstitious, fearful of change, and economically simple. All of the countries of Latin America, Asia, and Africa were unified within the single category of "traditional." Although modernization theorists were quick to note that every country was unique, their actual analyses downplayed differences between so-called underdeveloped countries. When they did draw nonlinear distinctions between underdeveloped countries, it was in spite of their theory rather than because of it.

Modernization theorists like sociologists Edward Shils and Talcott Parsons, economist Walt Whitman Rostow, and political scientists Gabriel Almond and Lucian Pye conceived of modernity as a "syndrome" that included technological advancement, urbanization, rising income, increased literacy, and the amplification of mass media. Modernization was a comprehensive and cohesive process that entailed what Max Weber had called "rationalization." As Massachusetts Institute of Technology's Center for International Studies explained, modernization "inevitably involves every area and level of the life of a society."[3] Daniel Lerner explained that he conceived of "modernization as a process with some distinctive *quality* of its own, which would explain why modernity is felt as a *consistent whole* among people who live by its rules." There was little sense that modernity might be riven by internal tensions, that modernity might contain unsavory aspects, or that modernity's various features might play themselves out very differently in different places. On the contrary, Lerner continued, the various features of modernity—he listed urbanization, industrialization, secularization, democratization, education, and media participation—"went together so regularly because, in some historical sense, they *had to* go together."[4]

The certainty that history was on their side pervaded everything the modernization theorists wrote and thought, which helps explain why modernization theory would be so useful to policy makers groping for an explanation of the United States' place and responsibilities amid the uncertainties of the postwar world. Indeed, modernization theory represents the most explicit and systematic blueprint ever created by Americans for reshaping foreign societies. More than just a system for explaining the world in a rational fashion, modernization theory constituted a metalanguage that supplied not only a sense of the "meaning" of postwar geopolitical uncertainties, but also an implicit set of directives for how to effect positive change in that dissilient world.[5] For geopolitical reasons to be explored in chapter 2, the need to "do something" for postcolonial regions was a political imperative that demanded a scientific justification. Modernization theory would provide one by trying to explain how, by learning from the history of industrialized countries, "latecomers" could bypass the various historical cul-de-sacs that had slowed the growth of these first movers. Given proper technical guidance and financial help, as well as political education and institutions, poor countries ought to be able to catch up with the rich countries. As political scientist Karl Deutsch put it in a talk given at the same conference where Shils delivered his definition of modernity, "The developing countries of Asia, Africa, and parts of Latin America may have to accomplish . . . within a few decades a process of political change which in the history of Western Europe and North America took at least as many generations; and they may have to accomplish this accelerated change almost in the manner of a jump, omitting as impractical some of the historic stages of transition through a period of near laissez-faire that occurred in the West."[6] Because it took place more or less the same way everywhere and always—in this historical past of the first world, in the present and future of the third world— modernization was a homogenizing process, the modernization theorists believed: the manifold forms of traditional life were giving way to a unitary, interlocking, and global modernity, the shape of which was already discernable in the contemporary United States. In the course of economic development," Deutsch explained, "countries are becoming somewhat less like Ethiopia and somewhat more like the United States."[7] In sum, the metanarrative of modernization would provide what Clifford Geertz would refer to as "a hopeful idiom" for activist social scientific and political programs in sore need of justification.[8]

Modernization as Modernism

"What makes 'modernization' modern," political scientist Rupert Emerson explained in 1964, "is the ability to live, to think, to produce, to organize, in substantially the same fashion as the Western countries whose imperial hold has now been almost totally broken. [For] the governing elites of Asian and African states . . . the greater emphasis is on modernization as defined by the Western model."[9] For modernization theorists, in contrast to strict economic development theorists, modernity was not just about a way of organizing economic production, but also about society and polity, cultural norms and forms. As Frank Ninkovich has observed, the modernization theorists "were just as much participants in the conceptual revolution of modernity as were avant-garde artists, litterateurs, and musicians. They understood that modernity implied a revolutionary break with traditional social and cultural forms."[10] In this sense, the modernization theorists were modernists.

Some readers will object to this characterization. Historians have tended to erect a wall between modern*ization*—the social, economic, and technological process of progressive historical change—and modern*ism,* the cultural movement that included writers like Virginia Woolf and Marcel Proust, painters like Vasily Kandinsky and Pablo Picasso, and musicians like Igor Stravinsky and Arnold Schoenberg.[11] Where modernization refers to the technological and material dimension of bourgeois society, modernism is typically described as a *reaction against* rather than a *manifestation of* modernization.[12] In a famous statement on the subject, sociologist Daniel Bell went so far as to claim there was actually a "contradiction" (in the Marxist sense) between the hardworking values required to promote economic and technical modernization and the antinomian values promoted by cultural modernism.[13] Despite these objections, I use the term *modernism* because this is how my subjects thought of themselves; they repeatedly described their political heroes as "modernizers," successful nations as "modern" ones, the culmination of development as "modernity," and the advocates of this process (including themselves) as "modernists." As conceived by the modernization theorists, modernism was not just an aesthetic phenomenon but also a form of social and political practice in which history, society, economy, culture, and nature itself were all to be the object of technical transformation. Modernism was a polysemous code word for all that was good and desirable.

As Habermas would observe in the 1980s, the modernization theorists separated the concept of modernity from its origins as a description of a specific period of European history and "stylized it into a spatio-temporally neutral model for the process of social development in general."[14] The modernism of the modernization theorists was not the modernism of Nietzsche, Kafka, or the Dadaists, but rather that of August Comte, Piet Mondrian, and Le Corbusier. Rather than a modernism of iconoclasm, madness, and irrationality, it was a modernism of order, plan, and mastery. Rejecting the emotionality and spirituality of romanticism, this form of modernism celebrated the ideals of the Enlightenment: the power of science, the importance of control, and the possibility of achieving progress through application of human will and instrumental reason. Modernists in this tradition, like the modernization theorists, saw themselves as the culmination of an Enlightenment purged of the intellectual conceits of the *philosophes*, the sanguinary hubris of the Jacobins, and the epistemological naïveté of positivism and realism. Thus the modernization theorists saw their project as the Enlightenment writ large: a welfare state based on progressive income taxation, democratic accountability, social leveling and "integration" as a solution to social conflict, technological fixes, and industrial prowess. To paraphrase Foucault, modernization theory represented a project of "total history," one that sought "to reconstitute the overall form of a civilization, the principle—material or spiritual—of a society, the significance common to all the phenomena of a period, the law that accounts for their cohesion—what is called metaphorically the 'face' of a period."[15]

Complementing modernization theory's elitism of technical expertise was its resolute antipopulism. Modernization theorists identified progress with the imposition of elite economic, social, and cultural norms onto the masses. Modernization theorists saw themselves as charged with training what communications specialist Ithiel de Sola Pool called the "mandarins of the future,"[16] whose ethic of responsibility put them beyond the questioning of the "reasonable strata" of the public. As Clark Kerr put it in 1960, "We speak to the intellectuals, the managers, the government officials and labor leaders who today or tomorrow will run their countries, now in the midst of great transformation."[17] Disdainful of anything that stood in the way of progress as they defined it, the modernization theorists hoped to short-circuit the give-and-take of politics and instead substitute fact, knowledge, and the indisputable authority of science. Unruly traditional societies had to be reorganized to make individuals subject to the epistemological control of social science and of state agencies keen to increase economic output while maintaining political order. The modernization theorists' attitude of scientific authority marginalized competing sources of knowledge and identity that provided grounds for political resistance to their social engineering. At its core lay the eidolon of rationalist modernism: total knowledge about a society free of both want and dissent, with boredom as its most threatening feature. "Ever since graduate student days," Gabriel Almond would remember late in life, "I had nurtured Weberian aspirations—to know just about everything there was to know, and to write with apodictic confidence about its meaning."[18] The modernization theorists assumed that their (scientific, expert, administrative, instrumental) approach represented the only legitimate way to conceive of postcolonial social, political, and economic problems. This conception of the "uncompleted project of modernity" left little room for the emancipatory democratic egalitarianism that Habermas has promoted as a necessary ethical foil to the Enlightenment exaltation of instrumental reason.

The Trend toward Authoritarianism

3 flavors

Despite these generalizations about conjunctions between modernization theory and a more general modernism, modernization theory also contains much variety. Some scholars emphasized economic progress, while others emphasized political, social, or psychological elements. Despite their shared belief that modernization would bring American-style health, wealth, and democracy to traditional nations, modernization theorists disagreed about how this goal would be achieved. Broadly speaking, the modernism of the modernization theorists came in three flavors: a *technocosmopolitan* flavor, which argued that modernity must be built on the foundations of tradition; a *revolutionary* flavor, which argued that modernization required a radical rupture with tradition; and an *authoritarian* flavor, which argued that this radical rupture could take place only through the force of a centralizing and omniscient state. Although these flavors to some extent competed with each other, they could coexist within individual writers or even within a single text.

Proponents of technocosmopolitanism held that modernity could and indeed had to derive from preexisting traditional forms. Technocosmopolitan or "reformist" scholars hoped (to appropriate anthropologist Paul Rabinow on French colonial practices in Morocco) to "regulate history, society, and culture by working over existent institutions and spaces—cultural, social and aesthetic—that seem to embody a healthy sedimentation of historical practices."[19] Much of the postwar writing on development—and especially the dominant interpretations of development articulated immediately before the emergence of modernization theory in the late 1950s—fell into this reformist mode. Although the reformist mode was largely replaced by revolutionary and authoritarian flavors of modernization by the late 1960s, some modernization theorists continued to believe that modernity could only be successful if rooted organically in some of the traditional practices of premodern societies. Sociologist Bert Hoselitz expressed such a view when he declared in 1966 that traditions "may have positive as well as negative effects; and, rather than leaving the whole body of ideas surrounding the analysis of tradition unsurveyed, we must make a more careful and precise study of the aspects of tradition that conduce to economic and technological progress, and of the aspects that may impede such progress."[20] Traditions that impeded progress toward modernity would have to go, but tradition itself was not all bad in the technocosmopolitan view.

As development projects began to take as their object not the palimpsest of traditional practices, but rather the "human material" itself—conceived as a universal subject whose needs, prospects, and norms could be discovered, interpreted, and fixed by science—modernization theory began to take on a more revolutionary aspect that aimed at remaking the identities of traditional people and societies. In this guise, modernization theorists wanted, as sociologist Alex Inkeles put it, to "make men modern"[21] by "freeing" them from the annoying irregularities that gender, race, "traditional" values, and autonomous opinions produced. (Samuel Huntington, in fact, suggested that "making men modern" was "the central problem of modernization."[22]) Rather than espouse the reformism of technocosmopolitanism, revolutionary modernists sought to undo older forms of social, political, and economic organization. As Arthur Schlesinger Jr. put it, modernization theory "represented a very American effort to persuade the developing countries to base their revolutions on Locke rather than on Marx."[23] As such, revolutionary modernists conceived of the state as a set of bureaus designed to deliver public services and to provide steering mechanisms for society.[24] In contrast to technocosmopolitan language and practice, which accepted history and nature as constraints within which to structure their work, revolutionary modernization theorists considered society a discrete object, from which natural, historical, and social references were to be stripped away. The state would be the instrument for imposing these changes on society. The supposed transparency of the state's motives—namely, to promote efficiency, welfare, and progress—rendered its institutional identity (or interests) analytically indistinct from society itself. The rhetoric and practice of development thus became a Trojan horse for extending the power of the postcolonial state. As modernization theorists reduced their descriptions of the state to its social functions, the institutional self-interest of the state tended to become invisible.[25]

Finally, an even more radical approach to achieving modernity developed, which sociologist James Scott has referred to as "authoritarian high modernism." Using what they regarded as scientific knowledge (but motivated also by aesthetic considerations), high modernists drafted extensive prescriptions for the "administrative ordering of nature and society." What distinguished the high modernists from the technocosmopolitan or revolutionary modernists was not so much the content of their vision of the modern, but rather their ruthless willingness to apply unrestrained state force to achieve their modernist dreams. Understood in this fashion, the category of high modernism illuminates the uncanny homologies of the centralized economic planning of the Soviet Union, the procapitalist tyranny of fascism or Nazism, and the orchestrated anarchism of the Chinese Cultural Revolution. Exemplified by the work of Lucian Pye and Walt Rostow, modernization theory would represent liberalism's entry into this hall of twentieth-century ideological horrors. As Scott concludes, "High-modernist faith was no respecter of political boundaries; it could be found across the political spectrum from left to right but particularly among those who wanted to use state power to bring about huge, utopian changes in people's work habits, living pattern, moral conduct, and worldview."[26] When hemmed in by popular parliamentary controls, these utopian impulses could spur social reform, but in the absence of political controls, such high modernism almost invariably led to disaster. In the context of an American cold war mentality that considered "developmental dictatorships" preferable to "vulnerable" democracies, the utopian impulses of American liberals all too easily degenerated into endorsing the wholesale destruction of communities and social and political groups as the necessary by-product of "forcing men to be free" in a non-Communist fashion.

Although technocosmopolitan, revolutionary, and authoritarian views all found persistent advocates among the modernization theorists throughout the postwar period, a shift of emphasis between these flavors of modernism over time may also be detected. As the three case studies will show, modernization theory became increasingly authoritarian as it moved from the abstract theory in Talcott Parsons's work, to the policy-oriented questions of Almond's "political development" school, to the actual policy recommendations of Rostow's Center for International Studies. Especially after the Communist victory in China in 1949, American scholars and diplomats perceived the need to promote a more rapid, radical vision of modernization. During the 1950s and 1960s, in the face of mounting problems in postcolonial regions, technocosmopolitanism gave way to revolutionary and authoritarian visions of modernization. The tendency to consider modernization as "the right kind of revolution" represented the intellectual equivalent of hitting the gas pedal on a skidding car: an attempt to accelerate out of a problem. As moderate solutions to development failed again and again, hard-core solutions found more and more advocates.

Conceptualizing the passage to modernity as a brief transitional period, with political instability and the concomitant threat of Communist takeover as the main risks, many modernization theorists began to suggest that the United States should promote the most rapid possible passage through this dangerous "stage of growth"—by whatever means necessary. Ultimately, this theory would justify U.S. intervention in Vietnam on the grounds that such action promoted modernization. Although early modernization theory had proclaimed the supposed synergies between democracy and modernity, as time went on, these alleged connections tended to disappear from both the language of development studies and its practice. Over the course of the 1950s and 1960s, respect for anything smacking of "tradition" steadily eroded, and the willingness to countenance dictatorial solutions in changing societies steadily increased. Whether this pattern of "hardening" represented a perversion of the liberal principles behind modernization theory or the gradual unveiling of modernism's mailed fist from the velvet glove of liberal meliorism is an open question. However one answers this question, it is evident that the intellectual history of modernization theory represents in miniature the tragedy of postwar American liberalism.

Modernization Theory and Postwar American Liberalism

Modernization theory mirrored and bolstered wider movements in postwar American thought. A central argument of this book is that modernization theory, while overtly focused on the plight of the third world, echoed and amplified unfolding American sentiments about the condition of modernity at home. To crib a label sometimes applied to a certain school of German historiography, the approach adopted in this book provides a *Primat der Innenpolitik* account of modernization theory's historical development. That is, it suggests that postwar American thought about non-Western peoples had less to do with anything intrinsic to those people than it did with Americans' understanding of their own identity. This approach helps us reconsider some debates about the import of modernization theory.

For example, the common assertion used to be that while the modernization theorists were "optimists" about the prospects for postcolonial regions,
those scholars who came later, jaded by the various "development" disasters
of the 1960s, were pessimists.[27] Revisionist scholars retorted that American
intellectuals were always pessimists about the prospects for democracy and
progress in postcolonial regions.[28] Both positions, however, presume that the
experience of the postcolonial world itself was the primary determinant of
American intellectuals' attitudes about modernity and modernization.
Although I generally agree with the view that the modernization theorists
were pessimistic about the prospects for democracy in postcolonial states
(with certain exceptions, like the indefatigably sunny Rostow), I believe that a
Primat der Innenpolitik approach can reconcile the two positions: while there
remained a fairly constant pessimism about the prospects of modernity in
postcolonial regions, American intellectuals did indeed experience a crucial
shift from optimism to pessimism about modernity itself (as opposed to the
more limited issue of its postcolonial prospects) from the 1950s to the 1970s.
This change in attitude occurred primarily in reference to the modernity *of
American society,* and only secondarily by the seeming success or failure of
postcolonial modernity. Whereas scholars in the 1950s felt good about
modernity and confident that imposing modernity on the postcolonial world
would be a good thing, by the 1970s they were dubious about modernity even
in their own homeland, and despairing about the prospect and even the desirability of postcolonial regions becoming modern.

The failure to recognize the importance of domestic sentiments about
modernity in the heart and minds of the modernization theorists has contributed to the great canard in the literature about modernization theory, the
tendency to historicize (or dismiss) it as an extension of the "totalitarian"
school of thought—in other words, as just another cold war–driven anti-
Communist screed. If it is true that modernization theory emerged as an
answer to the surging postwar geopolitical and ideological power of the Soviet
Union, we must also recognize that it turned anti-Communism from the hys-
terical red-baiting populism of McCarthy into a social-scientifically
respectable political position. It did this by promoting modernization as a
high-concept version of Americanism: materialism without class conflict, secularism without irreverence, democracy without disobedience. In the process
of making Americanism respectable by equating it with modernization, the
modernization theorists reflected on the meaning and place of the United

States in the world arena. Not surprisingly, as Americans altered their understanding of the otherness within their own society, their ideas about Others
abroad followed suit. In other words, modernization theory was as much
about defining America as it was about attacking Communism—though it is
revealing that during the 1950s (in fact, during most of the twentieth century), these two phenomena were all but inextricable.

A notable irony—though also a logical extension of the argument about
the "modernism" of modernization theory—is that although modernization
theory was anti-Communist in its overt politics, it simultaneously replicated
many of the intellectual structures of its high modernist cousin, Marxist-
Leninism.[29] To put the matter bluntly, to a peasant, the aims of postwar
Communists and liberal capitalists seemed more similar than different: both
wanted to build a centralizing, tax-collecting state charged with making its
citizens legible and docile. (Leninism differed from the authoritarian form of
modernization theory mainly in that it located political and economic
authority in the Party rather than in a scientific bureaucracy or the military,
as some modernization theorists proposed.) Acknowledging this similarity,
modernization theorists conceded that "both the United States and the USSR
represent politically modern societies."[30] Modernization theorists considered
totalitarianism and liberalism two different ways to achieve "over-all social
integration in modern industrial societies"[31] and argued that "the political
modernization process might terminate at various points along a spectrum
from democratic to totalitarian systems."[32] But this is not to say that they considered Communism or totalitarianism morally equivalent to liberalism.

To explain how the Soviet Union could be both the same ("modern") and
different from the United States ("the West"), modernization theory described
Communism as a "pathological" or "deviant" form of modernity, always hop-
ing that the Soviets would "converge" with the liberal version of modernity
extant in the West. Whereas classical Marxist analysis made eschatological
prophecies of a coming Communist utopia, the modernization theorists
instead asserted that secular, materialist utopia had already been achieved in
the supposedly postideological United States of the Eisenhower and Kennedy
years. For the modernization theorists, the whole world was destined to converge with the model of modernity limned by the contemporary United States.
Modernization theory, in this sense, was a universalist faith. But its universalism did not involve the ecumenical reconciliation of all the world's manifold
cultural, political, and economic traditions in a higher order of circulation and

exchange. Rather, it meant the imposition of "modern" (i.e., contemporary American) values on "backward societies" and the economic integration of all economies into the world capitalist system as junior members.

Another way in which modernization theory broke with the "totalitarian" school of thought is that while modernization theory regarded the Soviet system as an alternative form of modernism, it generally did not consider fascism a form of modernism. Instead, it considered it a radical mass movement opposed to modernism. Most modernization theorists, informed by the bipolar ideological order of the cold war, considered Communism and liberal capitalism the only modernist regimes. Fascism, on the other hand, resulted from "premodern residues" in countries like Japan and Germany. This account of fascism would help make modernization theory the basis for the dominant schools of postwar historiography in both Germany and Japan. In Germany, Hans-Ulrich Wehler's *Gesellschaftsgeschichte* school asserted that Germany's late industrialization had imposed an industrial infrastructure on a premodern social and political order. The disjunctures that this pattern of development created had allowed the Nazis to hijack Germany's natural development toward a liberal welfare state—a process that had been put on firm footing again only by the postwar political order.[33] Likewise, in Japan, the dominant postwar historiography claimed that the fascist period (1926-45) had derailed Japan's maturation toward liberal democracy and that the postwar order had put Japan back on the liberalizing path of the earlier Taisho period (1912-26).[34] In both the German and the Japanese case, modernization theory thus helped legitimate the American-imposed postwar liberal order.

If fascism was antimodern and Communism a pathological form of modernity, then the "normal" version was an idealized portrait of the United States. Liberal intellectuals of the 1950s wanted to direct the process of development in other nations by proposing that those nations follow the mythic American example. The modernization theorists believed they were doing the world a favor by aiding "them" to become more like "us." For the modernization theorists, modernity suggested a God-fearing but secular society in which race and gender were of little import; a privately run full-employment economy of well-paid workers, all of whom owned a house and a car and lived in a nuclear family; and a formal democratic system in which consensus existed about societal goals, the details of which would be worked out by technically trained public service elites. While arguing that modernism shared these common features, the modernization theorists also insisted that modernism did not necessarily entail cultural homogenization—"cultural differences" would survive the advent of modernity. But the scope of "culture" was very much restricted. Differences about things like the desirability of social mobility, free speech, or the inclusion of women in the public sphere would necessarily disappear in the course of becoming modern. Though the point was rarely made explicit, modernization theorists tacitly assumed that international cultural differences were going the way of ethnic differences among Americans of European extraction—assimilation toward a single national culture, with ethnicity expressed mainly in terms of the dishes served during holidays.

As this last example suggests, the modernization theorists took their ideas about the "modernity" from discourses about American national identity that were taking place at the same time as the formation of the modernization paradigm. Modernization theory's picture of modernity offered a selective synthesis of arguments drawn from several contemporaneous intellectual debates—among political scientists about the nature of democracy; among industrial sociologists about global societal convergence; among historians about the "consensual" nature of American society; and among public intellectuals about how the 1950s were witnessing the "end of ideology." By buttressing its fundamental precepts with arguments from these related debates, modernization theory not only gained credence for its own claims but also embedded these other discourses within a wider metahistorical narrative that lent them an aura of plausibility that they might not otherwise have enjoyed. The sociologists, economists, political scientists, and historians of the day read each other's work and agreed on basic issues. Instead of raising suspicions, these agreements made scholars believe that they were onto something. The role of modernization theory within this overdetermined dialectic of influence was to unify these discourses by providing an overall cognitive framework for understanding the differences between the United States (or more generally, the "first world") and the postcolonial or "third" world.

Modernization theory was thus the foreign policy counterpart to "social modernism" at home, namely the idea that a meliorist, rationalizing, benevolent, technocratic state could solve all social and especially economic ills.[35] According to sociologist Reinhard Bendix, modernization meant "the growth of the welfare state in the industrialized societies of the world, which in one way or another provides a pattern of accommodation among competing groups as well as a model to be emulated by the political and intellectual leaders of follower societies."[36] By achieving a fundamental economic and social democratization of industrial societies, the welfare state would complete the transition to modernity. The "developmental state," with its paternalist assumption of responsibility for economic growth, was the third world analog to the welfare state. In large measure the rise and decline of modernization theory mirrored the rise and decline of faith in welfare-state modernism in the United States. In other words, modernization theory as it was articulated in the 1950s and 1960s was the foreign policy counterpart to what Esping-Andersen has referred to as "the golden age of the welfare state."[37]

Although modernization theorists knew that the United States had not fully achieved this idealized modernity (the Jim Crow South was a particular problem), they believed that sooner or later, their vision of modernity was bound to succeed in imposing itself everywhere. Because they used their study of postcolonial countries as a springboard for defining America's own national identity, the modernization theorists exemplify or perhaps caricature Edward Said's proposition that the West constructs its identity in contradistinction to those of Others. As David Riesman observed in his introduction to Daniel Lerner's *The Passing of Traditional Society*, "Mr. Lerner shows that every encounter with another people is a confrontation with ourselves."[38] The obsessive search for "the" national identity by American scholars during the 1950s can thus be seen as a counterpart to modernization theory: national self-definition provided a model against which to judge third world Others and thus complemented a program of foreign aid and military-political domination. Given their need to find elements of the American national identity that would help justify their program of liberal internationalism, it is not surprising that when modernization theorists drew on the works of thinkers such as Riesman, Arthur Schlesinger Jr., or Louis Hartz, they often reduced these scholars' relatively subtle formulations regarding consensus and social conformity to insipid celebrations of the supposed virtues of the United States.

There were of course dissenters from what Hartz referred to as America's "overbearing" and "monolithic" liberalism. From the moderate right, "realist" scholars like Hans Morgenthau would admonish readers to "forget about the crusading notion that any nation, however virtuous and powerful, can have the mission to make the world in its own image." More extreme views came from organizations like the John Birch Society or the Ku Klux Klan—but these remained outside the realm of respectable political discourse and were ignored by liberals like the modernization theorists. Richard Hofstadter typified the liberal response when he dismissed these as typifying a "paranoid style."[39]

Similarly, left-oriented critiques of modernity, issued by scholars such as Paul Goodman, Stanley Milgram, Hannah Arendt, or Michael Paul Rogin, were disregarded by the liberal mainstream.[40] Marxism was, of course, beyond the pale. Leftists tended to be concerned more with domestic issues than with foreign policy. For the most part, American liberals during the first two postwar decades simply ignored nonliberal discourse about the United States' role in the world. However, as we shall see in the final chapters, the repressed voices of both left and right would eventually return with a noisy vengeance.

Because it synthesized so many elements of the liberal intellectual milieu of the 1950s, modernization theory provides us with a weather vane for tracking the changing mental climate during this period. An indelible antipopulism was the most fundamental political sentiment subtending modernization theory. To American liberal intellectuals of the 1950s—especially Jewish intellectuals like Rostow, Almond, or Shils—populism of any sort recalled jackbooted bigots in the streets. Insofar as popular groups rejected their prescriptions, modernization theorists tended to consign these people to the dustbins of both history and politics. The modernization theorists believed that bureaucracies, technical experts, and social engineers of various stripes should impose economic and political order on cities, nations, and the world. Nazism, therefore, was not a manifestation of bureaucracy and social engineering gone mad, but rather an example of populism in power. The modernization theorists may have favored democracy, but only insofar as it involved a docile demos, firmly subordinated to "responsible" managers. Technocracy rather than "people's liberation" was what modernization would ideally achieve. Despite their statist proclivities, modernization theorists were thus in an important sense antipolitical: politics was the realm of subjective messiness rather than scientific exactitude. Although personally opposed to the notion that politics could be undone by planning, Edward Shils acknowledged that American intellectuals had subscribed to "an antipolitical tradition for more than a century."[41] Drawing on a long Madisonian legacy, modernization theory deemed good governance to be *of* the people and *for* the people, but most assuredly not *by* the people.

Much of the literature on American liberalism claims that whereas prewar liberals embraced the ideal of human perfectibility and the inevitability of progress, postwar liberals stressed the ambiguity, paradoxes, and limitations of the human condition. Yet an examination of the modernization theorists shows that American liberalism displayed more continuity and complexity than this distinction suggests. Consider Shils's definition of liberalism:

Liberalism is a system of pluralism. It is a system of many centers of power, many areas of privacy and a strong internal impulse toward the mutual adaptation of the spheres rather than of the dominance or the submission of any one to the others. . . . In a liberal society, church and state are separate, but each respects the other and also exercises some influence on the other. In a liberal society, the economy is not run by the government and the government is not run by the owners or managers of the economy. . . . In a liberal society, philosophers are not kings, the intellectuals do not rule any sphere except their own, nor do businessmen, politicians or priests govern intellectual life. In a liberal society, the intellectual sphere—the universities, the press, publishing houses, scientific academies and laboratories—must possess an extensive autonomy which is respected and facilitated by the elites of the political and economic sphere.[42]

Comparing this passage with Shils's long passage on "modernism," quoted earlier, we can see that liberalism was, in effect, a synonym for the American form of modernity. As Robert Bellah put it, liberalism was "the primary ideology of modernization"[43]—and therefore the desired end point of human sociopolitical evolution. The challenge for postwar liberals was to sustain a transforming vision of the future in the absence of a classic progressive belief in the virtue of the people or an Enlightenment faith in the perfectibility of man. As we shall see, modernization theory's appropriation of coeval ideas about the national identity of the United States, about the social role of political and intellectual elites, and the end of ideology helped provide a sanguine vision of what lay at the end of the rainbow of modernization.

Modernization theory also continued prewar progressive themes that emphasized the meliorist impact of government social programs. New Deal liberals had hoped that after the war they would be able to implement enlarged domestic reform measures, such as federally guaranteed work and a national health insurance scheme. As these wider dimensions of President Harry Truman's Fair Deal fell apart amid partisan acrimony and conservative backlash, liberals found themselves unable to continue their social engineering projects at home.[44] Promoting "modernization" in countries emerging from colonialism allowed American liberals to retain their self-image as progressive reformers, even as they acquiesced to a conservative domestic agenda. The world-historical narrative of modernization theory thereby validated the domestic conservatism of American liberals: the United States was deemed a modern country, and therefore in need of little profound reform (thus legitimating conservatism at home), while postcolonial countries were considered "traditional" and therefore in need of radical change (thus legitimating progressivism abroad). Meanwhile, postcolonial countries (or rather, their leaders) were eager for economic aid and were therefore willing to assent to the radical schemes of social reform that their supposed benefactors required. The postcolonial world thus became a stage on which domestically frustrated liberals could act out their social reformist fantasies.

Tension existed between the modernization theorists' sincere desire to imagine better lives for the global masses and their increasingly authoritarian approach to achieving this vision. The various hells that postcolonial countries from Indonesia to Iraq to Colombia have entered in the last thirty years were almost always preceded and justified by well-intentioned modernizers, both liberal and Communist, who believed that they knew what was best for these lands.[45] Modernizers aimed to replicate—by force if necessary—the stable, democratic, capitalist welfare state that they believed was being created in the United States. Intrinsic to both the welfare state and the developmental state, and linking the two, was a sense of social solidarity between haves and have-nots, a sense that all members of a nation—and that all nations—owed an obligation to one another. The liberal universalism of the modernization theorists was heartfelt in this respect. They hoped to realize a New Deal on an international scale that would achieve full employment and an end to grinding poverty, embrace unionism and big business, establish inclusive governance, respect civil liberties, and promote social tolerance and equality. If many modernization theorists did not consider most postcolonial nations "ready" to embrace these values, the theorists themselves subscribed to these ideals and held them out as the heuristic. Today, in the early twenty-first century—when an ideology of consumerism, free trade, and "structural adjustment" is virtually all that the United States offers postcolonial regions—it is instructive to consider the ambitious postwar vision of what the United States could do for the postcolonial poor. The tragedy of modernization theory is that while its misleading understanding of the historical process still underpins much Western (and postcolonial) thinking about postcoloniality, its secular reformist ideals have died without being replaced by positive alternatives.

Microhistories of Modernization Theory

This volume contributes to the growing body of historical literature concerning the idea of development. Methodologically, this work attempts to map out the social networks that gave rise to an enduring terminology and set of ideas about development. It describes how "modernization" emerged out of early postwar economics, sociology, and political science to become a key concept in the American social scientific paradigm of development in the early 1960s. Chapter 2 discusses the context in which modernization theory emerged. The next chapters present close studies of how modernization theory unfolded within three academic institutions: the Harvard Department of Social Relations (DSR), the Social Science Research Council's Committee on Comparative Politics (CCP), and the Massachusetts Institute of Technology's Center for International Studies (CIS). I chose to examine these three institutions because they housed most of the key figures of modernization theory— including Walt Rostow, Gabriel Almond, and Lucian Pye. However, modernization theory was an intellectual movement with many sects, and while a remarkable percentage of the key works of modernization theory issued from scholars affiliated with at least one of these institutions, several did not, most notably David Apter's *The Politics of Modernization* (1965) and Cyril Black's *The Dynamics of Modernization* (1966).[46] Despite their lack of formal affiliation with the three institutions discussed below, however, Black and Apter were part of the same intellectual circles. Both were influenced by DSR scholar Marion Levy—Black as a colleague and friend of Levy's at Princeton, and Apter as Levy's student (Apter dedicated *The Politics of Modernization* to Levy). In addition, Apter and Black both participated in the watershed 1959 CCP meeting at Dobbs Ferry at which Shils gave his influential keynote address.

The methodological approach to these institutional case studies is grounded in a fundamental assumption about the sociology of postwar *academy* American academics, namely that the proximate cause for most arguments is a reaction to the writing of other academics. Even though modernization theory took its momentum from the entire postwar intellectual scene, specific lines of argument often represented immediate reactions to local intellectual contexts. In other words, Parsons's attempt to institutionalize his pursuit of a comprehensive theory of social action (for example) should be sought in the context of Harvard in the thirties, forties, and fifties. Likewise, the struggle over the reception of Parsonian ideas in political science should be interpreted in light of the specific personalities of the CCP. The modernization theorists were themselves aware of the importance of institutions in the formation of common viewpoints. "The success of such an institution," the CIS suggested, "is to be measured by the degree to which there emerges from the work of its

primacy of institutions

individual members something that is greater than the sum of the component pieces of its program—a characteristic approach, a distinctive set of related hypotheses, a number of shared convictions as to what it is important to work on and how the work can best be advanced."[47] By this definition, the institutions of modernization theory—the DSR, the CCP, and the CIS—were unquestionably successful institutions. Each institution developed a distinctive intellectual profile—what might be called a collective persona—with certain family resemblances to the others. These resemblances emerged partly because crucial figures—for example, Lucian Pye, Clifford Geertz, and Edward Shils—participated in more than one of these institutions, but also because contemporary circumstances encouraged them all to pursue similar approaches to the problems of development.

It is important for me to be clear about what this book is not. It is not an attempt to describe "the real" of the third world—a task impossible in any event. Nor is it a study of the application of modernization theory to the formation of foreign policy, a task that others have pursued.[48] Rather, it examines modernist ideas about development at the time of their birth, while their intellectual capillaries remained visible, before they were exposed to the harsh glare of political reality and policy compromise. I seek to describe both the local conditions for the production of these ideas, and the ambient cultural and political circumstances that made this endeavor seem not only urgent but something other than quixotic. If I am skeptical of the results, and skeptical also that success was ever possible for such a hubristic undertaking, I am also somewhat more sympathetic to the undertaking than most commentators have been. Indeed, given my initial skepticism of and even disdain for the authors I describe, it has been rather uncomfortable for me to realize my growing respect for the motives behind their ideas. For example, though Walt Rostow by the late 1960s was spending most of his time directing the killing of Vietnamese peasants, he was also more sincerely interested in improving the welfare of postcolonial peoples than the vast majority of his contemporaries. My own feeling about modernization theory (and of social modernism more generally) is thus one of melancholy; I find myself in a position of ironic resignation toward the passing of this more optimistic era.

Finally, this work is not merely a study in the sociology of intellectuals. It is also an attempt to assess the wider historical meaning—unfashionable though this concept may be—taking shape "behind the backs" of the individual participants. Although the reasons for their arguments must be sought in local institutional environments, these arguments had an undeniable impact on the wider trajectory of American history. The final two chapters of this work draw back from the microhistorical approach of the case studies to examine modernization theory's fall from grace. Chapter 6 begins by showing that there was always resistance to the liberal nostrums of modernization theory, and then describes the shockingly rapid collapse of modernization theory in the late 1960s and early 1970s under various criticisms from right and left. The final chapter interprets this collapse in reference to the emergence of postmodernism, and tracks the various successor movements that have arisen in modernization theory's wake. The demise of modernization theory had less to do with some realization of its internal incoherence than with erosion of positive feelings about modernity itself—not least because of the atrocities committed from Iran to China to Vietnam in the name of modernization.[49] With the decline of the fundamental assumption that modernity was desirable, theorizing about how to achieve modernization became beside the point. It was not so much that modernization theory was disproved in the early 1970s; it was that the questions it asked were no longer considered relevant. Whether these questions are today once again relevant remains to be seen.

CHAPTER 2

From the European Past to the American Present

> We have our philosophical persons, to make modern and familiar, things supernatural and causeless.
>
> —*ALL'S WELL THAT ENDS WELL*

It seems obvious that the past few hundred years have witnessed a portentous world historical change, a metamorphosis global in scale and unprecedented in scope. As modernization theorist Cyril Black commented in 1959, "[S]een in historical perspective, modernization is a transformation of the human condition no less fundamental than that which took place some eight or ten thousand years ago from hunting and gathering to agriculture and the formation of civilized societies."[1] It was only in the 1950s, however, that this radical transformation began to be widely described by the term *modernization,* a term that quickly became one of the most fashionable concepts in postwar American social science. This chapter describes the emergence of the term in the nineteenth and early twentieth centuries, and explains the circumstances that encouraged its acceptance as an indispensable term for postwar American social scientists.

Modernization as European History

Diffusionism is implicit in the theory of modernization: the historical changes described by the term *modernization* began sometime between the thirteenth and eighteenth centuries in Europe—even more specifically, in England[2]—and then spread to the rest of the world. Social historian Peter Stearns recently compiled a list of those interconnected trends within Western European history that suggest the coming of modernity:[3]

- more direct contact between government and individual citizens, entailing efforts to win direct loyalty from citizens through mass education, nationalism, and voting

- transformation of agricultural into industrial economies
- growth in central government and development of new state functions
- growth of bureaucracies and their training and specialization
- fundamental technological change
- new organizations at work, such as factories, larger commercial farms, and office complexes
- urbanization
- shift of social structure to rely mainly on money and education levels rather than birth and legal status
- new protest movements (e.g., trade unions)
- more overt political content to protests (e.g., socialism)
- more demands on the state by the citizens
- demand for new rights rather than restoration of past standards
- effort by elites to disseminate officially approved values and new official values
- respect for intense work
- wide promulgation, through schools and the mass media, of mobility and achievement
- praise for science as the source of truth and progress
- reason dislodging faith as the basic source of worthwhile knowledge
- leisure coming to depend less on community traditions, more on commercial outlets, self-improvement, and self-expression
- demographic shift to lower fertility, entailing changes in motives for having children and definitions of childhood
- emphasis in the family on emotional satisfaction rather than economic function
- disease fought by science rather than ritual
- more overall value placed on progress, both personal and general
- praise for women as moral agents as they exit the work force

Post-Enlightenment North Atlantic intellectuals have spent a great deal of time cataloguing and linking these traits and trends. Contributing to the taxonomy of modernity was one of the main products of nineteenth-century European social thought. Many of the greatest figures in European intellectual history made their names through their ingenious ability to connect the various dimensions of the macrohistorical quantum known as modernity: Henry Maine (1822-88) focused on the distinction between status and contract;

Ferdinand Tönnies (1855-1936) built his social theory on the contrast between Gemeinschaft and Gesellschaft; and Max Weber (1864-1920) made "rationalization" the centerpiece of his historical theory. The modernization theorists placed themselves squarely in this intellectual stream, what political scientist Lucian Pye called "that powerful tradition of Western social philosophy in which it is assumed that all societies can be classified according to a dichotomous scheme and in which all significant social and cultural changes are seen as related to the movement of a society from one category to the other."[4]

Though there always existed a conservative intellectual tradition that doubted the beneficence of these trends, most social philosophers considered them progressive. Nowhere was this truer than in the postwar United States, where historical theories emphasizing cyclicality or decline were far to seek. At least two distinct views of historical progress were in vogue in the 1950s. The first was the Enlightenment view of history as a humanly guided process. In some sense, this was less a notion of history than a historiographic justification for a normative program of change. In this ideology, human beings themselves were the primary historical agents (though sometimes guided by invisible hands or the cunning of reason). Despite their differences, Immanuel Kant, Adam Smith, and the Marquis de Condorcet all held to various versions of this progressive, humanist ideology. The second important view of the historical process, the romantic-historicist view of progress, was a nineteenth-century product that received its fullest expression in the work of Georg Wilhelm Friedrich Hegel. Hegel did not impute progress to the intentions of the actors but rather located it in the inherently rational nature of history itself. The immanent rationality of history had a progressive teleology.[5] The most influential theory of progress to emerge from the nineteenth century, however, was Karl Marx's attempt to combine these opposed views of the source of historical progress. Combining Hegel's *Geist* with Vico's *verum factum* principle, Marx claimed that historical progress was *both* inevitable *and* the result of intentional human activity. By making this argument, Marx threw down the gauntlet for all future analysts of modernity's historical progression: how could historical inevitability and human agency be combined? What these views shared was the understanding that history meant progress toward modernity, itself the culmination of the human capacity for self-realization. Changes that did not contribute to the evolution of modernity were, in Hegel's memorable phrase, "cold-blooded and meaningless . . . with no more significance than cleaving a head of cabbage or swallowing a draught of water."

Because the only historical change that mattered was progress toward modernity, one commonly finds references in nineteenth-century European texts to "traditional" societies as being outside of history, static and insignificant. The most notorious expression of this view was Marx's commentary on the British role in India. "Indian society has no history at all," Marx claimed. "What we call its history is but the history of the successive intruders who founded their empires on the passive basis of that unresisting and unchanging society. . . . England has to fulfill a double mission in India: one destructive, the other regenerating—the annihilation of the old Asiatic society, and the laying of the material foundations of Western society in Asia."[6] In other words, England's role was to give India history, by which Marx meant progress toward bourgeois modernity (and eventually, he hoped, Communism). Marx's statement typified the European view of its imperial subjects. With history defined as the advance toward modernity, the allegedly stagnant historical present of Asia and Africa was associated with the allegedly stagnant historical past of Europe's own history between the end of antiquity and the advent of modernity. The "Dark Continent" thus was covertly equated with Europe's "Dark Ages": periods and places bereft of both history and progress. Like early anthropological theory, modernization theory transposed temporal categories onto geographic categories. As anthropologist Bernard Cohn has put it, "These theories make the present of one civilization—India for example—the past of another, namely Western Europe. They locate the dominators and the dominated in one analytical scheme which is temporal."[7] Modernization theorists believed in "backwardness" in literal terms: the problem with colonial and postcolonial peoples, according to sociologist Edward Shils, was that they were literally trying to "maintain the past in the present."[8]

As the example of India's purported lack of history indicates, the advent of thought about the historicity of modernity coincided with the rapid expansion of European global power in the nineteenth century. As imperialism brought European administrators, merchants, missionaries, and social philosophies into contact with indigenous peoples throughout the globe, the radical nature of the qualitative changes Europe was experiencing became increasingly apparent. Moreover, late nineteenth-century Europeans connected the positive valuation of these domestic changes with their various imperial projects; imperialism was justified, among other reasons, because it exported (modern) European civilization. At the same time, this contact with *Others* shaped Europeans' view of themselves and their modernity. Europeans defined themselves by contrasting their own progressive modernity with their subjects' backward traditions.[9] Scientific and literary knowledge about Asia and Africa helped define and refine the particular qualities that differentiated European societies from non-European ones. "According to this paradigm," explains philosopher Enrique Dussel, "Europe had exceptional *internal* characteristics that allowed it to supersede, through its rationality, all other cultures."[10] The discourses generated from this knowledge production reinforced rising ideologies of European cultural and racial superiority. The categorical construction of enlightened modernity thus emerged from the simultaneous construction of its malformed twin: a non-European, or non-Western Other. Although modernization theory eschewed the racism of earlier colonialist discourses, it still defined modernity in contrast to an implicitly inferior "traditional" other.

Despite the invidious tendency of Europeans to define themselves and their history in contrast to non-European others, it is also important to remember that another central trend of the Enlightenment was its universalism. This tendency had important implications for the relationship between imperialism and the construction of modernity. For even as European intellectuals were defining European progress in contrast to the supposed historical lethargy of non-European others, they were also beginning to abstract the category of modernity from its Western European context and starting to understand it as a universal world-historical phenomenon. The earliest English use of the verb "to modernize," in the sense of progress toward a universal modernity, was William Thackeray's suggestion in 1860 that "[p]rinting and gunpowder tend to modernize the world."[11] Thackeray's pioneering usage pointed to the emerging popularity of a notion of modernity conceived as an ideal type toward which any society could move, rather than as the particular quality of recent European historical experience. It was the world itself, rather than some geographic or technological subsystem, which was the object of modernization. As such, European history provided a historical template that charted the future of humanity itself. Again, it was Marx who provided the earliest and clearest formulation of this perspective, in the introduction to the first German edition of *Capital*: "The country that is more developed industrially only shows, to the less developed, the image of its own future."[12] Modernization theorists would quote this phrase as one of their basic credos.[13]

The "more developed" countries of Europe of course did more than just *show* the future to their "less developed" imperial subjects. They systematically tried to impose European systems on these subjects. European languages, religions, and cultures were exported and taught abroad. European military and administrative strategies disrupted indigenous political structures. And European intrusion into local economies transformed indigenous modes of production from relatively localized affairs into extractive systems aimed at producing commodities for export by metropolitan elites, often leading to permanent dependency rather than progress. All of these events took place with the complicity of various local actors, who themselves took advantage of the imperial intrusion to advance into political and economic positions hitherto held by others. The process of collaboration meant that indigenous leaders and subjects adapted and appropriated different parts of the European systems, thereby transforming their content and meaning. Indeed, much fruitful contemporary scholarship focuses on the interactions between metropolitan and local elite strategies of domination and the native and popular efforts to resist and accommodate these strategies.[14]

Colonial and postcolonial ideas and attitudes, moreover, colored much of this resistance and accommodation. For Europeans exported not only their efficient administrative apparatus, but also those other typical products of modernity, oppositional and idealistic ideologies such as socialism and nationalism. As with the export of diseases, these ideological exports often had more far-reaching implications for the futures of colonized societies than any of the more tangible or intentional material exports. These discourses provided an intellectual foundation for the indigenous struggles for liberation, culminating in the rapid decolonization of Africa and Asia in the wake of World War II. For example, labor unions, though an invention of Western Europe, served as powerful forces for popular indigenous resistance to domination and control.[15] Modernization theorist Ithiel de Sola Pool explained: "We have in recent decades seen the impact of Western ideas on Asia and Africa. The culture and values of Asian intellectuals are increasingly the culture and values of Europe, taught them in mission and government schools. That is true even of their socialism, which is no indigenous matter but is the ideology of young students in the London School of Economics or in the University of Paris in the first decades of this century. Their anticolonialism is Western liberalism turned against the West. For good or evil European values were communicated."[16] He added, hopefully, "The same can and probably will be true for American values over the next quarter century." Like the wider category *development,* the term *modernization* stood for an ideal around which leaders and followers in postcolonial nations could unite.[17] Everywhere in the postcolonial world the idea of nationhood emerged in tandem with the concept of modernization, which brought together demands for political unity and the needs of economic development. For postcolonial leaders, the nation represented the vehicle for delivering modernity and development. Indeed, the greatest champions of modernization often turned out to be indigenous rather than metropolitan elites. As political scientist James Coleman approvingly put it in 1954, for postcolonial elites the "core of most of their programs [is] rapid modernization by a centralized bureaucratic machine."[18]

Modernization theorists would struggle to understand how these modernist ideologies functioned in societies still supposedly mired in "traditional" ways of life.[19] These postwar scholars did not doubt that studying the history of Europe would provide tools for understanding what was happening in postcolonial regions. As political scientist Gabriel Almond recalled of the early postwar years, scholars tried to understand the prospects of the postcolonial world by using "the ideas and concepts of the enlightenment and nineteenth- and early twentieth-century social theory, which had sought to make sense out of European and American modernization."[20] In other words, European history and social theory provided a means of dealing with the cognitive crisis that postwar American scholars faced as they began to try to understand the world outside the North Atlantic in a systematic, scientific manner. Indeed, modernization theory would represent itself as the direct heir of the Enlightenment crusade to establish reason, empiricism, science, universalism, progress, individualism, toleration, freedom, secularism, and the uniformity of human nature.

Modernization as a Replacement for Colonialism

Despite these antecedents in European social thought, "modernization" as a political slogan seems to have begun, ironically, in reaction to European dominance. Although the *idea* of an all-encompassing world-historical progressive process had roots in eighteenth- and nineteenth-century European thought, use of the word *modernization* to describe a political and economic program was first popularized by the Turkish dictator Kemal Ataturk (1880-1938), who made the "modernization of Turkey" one of his central political slogans. If

Thackeray had been the first to use the term to describe a general macrohistorical process, Ataturk was the first to use it to indicate a *directed* process of nation building.[21] Especially for those modernization theorists inclined toward authoritarian modernism, Ataturk's "claim to genius" was "as the first planner of social-economic development in contemporary terms."[22]

The term *modernization* indicated Ataturk's intention to turn Turkey toward a Western model of modernity as a way of revitalizing the decadent fortunes of the Turkish people who had just been defeated in World War I by the Western powers. For Ataturk, modernization implied the adoption of Western standards, such as enforced secularization; the banning of fezzes; the romanization of the alphabet; the emancipation of women (including universal suffrage and the abolition of polygamy); the straightening of highways; state-directed heavy industrialization; the adoption of French, Swiss, and Italian legal codes; and the institutionalization, at least formally, of a constitutional democracy. More than mere material increase, modernization entailed the reorientation of an entire social, political, and economic system, conceived as an integrated totality, toward norms defined by the West. (It also entailed the physical displacement, cultural domination, and at times genocidal military excursions against Greeks, Armenians, and Kurds bent on preserving their cultural particularities.) Modernization thus encompassed not only what Ataturk's near contemporary Sun Yat-sen (1866-1925) had meant when he became the first to use the term *development* in its contemporary sense[23]—namely the government-directed augmentation of the *economy*—but also the steering of *social change* toward a terminus defined by the Western example. In Ataturk's new usage, *modernization* came closer to its pure etymological derivation, indicating the movement of an entire social system toward nothing less than modernity, conceptualized as an integrated whole. Contemporary usage of the term thus emerged as an expression of burgeoning reactive nationalism in the "underdeveloped" world.

Ironically, Ataturk's adoption of this universalizing historical philosophy took place only as those same concepts were falling out of fashion in the West itself. Although from the 1920s forward, Occidental Turkey scholars on occasion adopted Ataturk's usage of the term *modernization,* Ataturk's general sense of the term did not catch on among European or American scholars or statesmen during the interwar years, in part because Europeans and Americans of the interwar period found it difficult to conceive of Western modernity as an integrated whole. The disaster of World War I had shaken the self-confidence that had fed the construction of modernity as a universalizing and beneficent historical process. Only to a non-European would the state of West European economy, society, and politics in the 1920s have seemed like an organic and completed phenomenon worthy of emulation. The cultural despair typified by Oswald Spengler's *Decline of the West* and T. S. Eliot's *The Waste Land* set the tone for European conceptions of Western modernity during the interwar period.[24] Contemporary critics of the West (including non-Westerners like Mohandas Gandhi, a notable antimodernist) stressed the half-measures and failed efforts at social change, the hesitations and tensions within the social systems, and the murderous differences between nations. In short, they focused on the incompleteness and failure of Western modernity. As a result, interwar Europeans and Americans considered a singular process termed *modernization* a rather dubious proposition.

Although during the 1920s Americans were more confident than Europeans about their national achievements, the retreat into isolationism precluded a generalized conception of "the West" on which the construct of modernization rested. Thus as the term *modernization* first began to be used in the United States in the beginning of the twentieth century, it generally referred to technical improvements in some particular element of the physical or bureaucratic infrastructure. For example, modernization could indicate upgrading of a physical plant, as in the phrase of the *American Economic Review*, which in 1912 spoke of the "modernization of the port of Bordeaux,"[25] or in the argument that the "modernization of our ocean—and Great Lakes—terminals must be along the lines followed in Hamburg."[26] The term was also used to indicate administrative streamlining, as in the modernization of an army or a system of tax collection. When agriculture was the object of modernization, it usually meant the introduction of new machine equipment or chemical fertilizers (rather than the rationalization of the agricultural labor force, as later usage would have it). But for a few isolated exceptions, the term *modernization* was never used in reference to a society as a whole before World War II. In general the term applied only to specific technical or administrative systems, not to entire social systems.

If by the 1940s the term *modernization* had already had a variegated semantic history, three factors conjoined in the decade after World War II to make modernization seem a suddenly much more seductive category to American social scientists, who would radically redefine its meaning. First was decolonization. In part as a continuation of the Wilsonian promise to assure the rights of peoples to self-determined sovereignty, and in part because it was clear that, like it or not, many lands (especially in Asia) were soon to become independent, the United States positioned itself after the war as against formal imperialism. Second was the availability of resources. The United States emerged from World War II as the dominant geoeconomic power, and both charity and the search for new markets and resources dictated that the United States attempt to help poor countries improve their economies. The impetus for such activity was given a great boost by the perceived successes of the Lend Lease Program during the war and the Marshall Plan after the war, which seemed to demonstrate that the United States could kick-start growth in impoverished economies. Finally, there was the increased influence of the Soviet Union, which presented an unprecedented ideological and economic challenge to the United States. Moreover, as the burgeoning cold war shifted its focus away from Europe and toward the former colonial areas with the Korean War, U.S. policy makers found themselves forced to confront what was happening in these regions. The response of the United States to these three conditions, in a word, was to adopt development as a mantra.[27]

Rather than support European hopes for continued empire after World War II, the United States advocated colonial peoples' right to sovereignty. A combination of political realism and ideology determined this diplomatic stance. On the one hand, despite the dreams of conservatives (and considerable fighting, especially in Southeast Asia), the European powers were too weary after the war to sustain the colonial drive. The United States realized that repressing the nationalist aspirations of colonial peoples would require insupportably large expenditures of political, diplomatic, and military energy. From its perspective, resources could better be extracted from these areas through free enterprise rather than through a formal colonial system. On the other hand, the United States found few moral reasons to support the Europeans' colonial pretensions. While continental conquest and assimilation had constituted the main American foreign policies in the nineteenth century, the American emulation after 1898 of European-style colonialism through its annexation of the Philippines had never sat well with the American public. Overt political subordination of other peoples was at odds with the republican self-image on which the country had been founded. Unlike most European imperialists, Americans did not subscribe to the idea that some ethnic or racial superiority gave them the right or indeed the obligation to rule. In general Americans greeted the release of the Philippines from the colonial yoke in 1945 with a sigh of relief rather than regret. Pointing out its reluctance to be a colonial power and its willingness to give up the Philippine colony allowed the United States to imagine itself as different from other colonizing nations, less exploitative and more interested in the welfare of its subjects. This dubious historical self-image blinded Americans to the continuities between the imperious attitudes of former imperialists (including themselves) and their own postwar ideas about the way in which development policy should be analyzed and promoted.

Although "development" was something that some colonial authorities had been advocating since the beginning of the century, American social scientists generally ignored these discourses, if their footnotes and acknowledgments are to be believed. Because postwar Americans saw themselves as radically different from the colonialists they were replacing, they saw little need to understand the colonial policies or theories of the British, French, or Dutch. Dankwart Rustow captured the typical sentiment of the modernists by observing in 1957 that "[n]ot long ago Western man ruled the world; today he studies it."[28] Indeed, the very concept of the uniformity of "traditional" societies, which was basic to modernization theory, tended to efface the significance of colonialism. American social scientists generally considered the disparate countries of the "third" world as faced with broadly similar problems, and therefore amenable to a broadly similar theoretical conceptualization and policies. The concept of "new nations" offered a unitary category of social scientific and policy analysis into which wildly different disparate national and social entities could be inserted. Hunter-gatherers in the Kalahari and the multiethnic, multilingual, multireligious Indians faced the same problems of building themselves into a coherent, unified, rational nation. In short, they all faced the problem of how to become modern. Whereas the European late colonial project aimed at maintaining differences between imperialists and colonial subjects, the American postwar modernization projects both denied and sought to undo these differences. Where modernization theory and policies echoed earlier colonial discourses, therefore, this echo was usually unwitting.[29]

It was a peculiar feature of the postwar period that leaders everywhere sought the solution to the political problem of decolonization in the economic sphere. "Economic development" became a key slogan of the postwar world because it represented the nexus between the demands of the postcolonial political leadership and the capacities of the United States. On the one *lumping social scientists + policy makers — is this accurate?*

hand, indigenous elites realized that building the typical institutions of the sovereign modernist state, such as an efficient bureaucracy and an effective military apparatus, required wealth. It was obvious that the mere departure of the colonial administrators would not bring the former colonial peoples the affluence and welfare associated with the metropole. To drum up popular support, the political leaders of these newly independent states called for development as the answer to the "revolution of rising expectations" of the indigenous masses. On the other hand, American social scientists and policy makers proposed economic improvement as a solution to the challenges of decolonization because greater prosperity was one of the few things they felt capable of providing to foreign countries. (One wild-eyed optimist even suggested that "the rate of U.S. shipments of fighting stuff at the 1944 [war] peak could provide the materials to industrialize all the backward nations of all the world in a single year"![30]) Despite a great deal of rhetoric to the contrary, the United States advocated economic development not so much for humanitarian reasons but because it perceived national resentments about poverty to be major causes of international strife. It was understood that a major cause for the rise of Hitler, and hence for World War II, had been the economic misery of the German people, compounded by nationalist resentments stemming from the onerous Versailles settlement after World War I. Many suspected that similar resentments could be brewing in the poor lands being released from colonialism. Americans worried that the political vacuum created by decolonization could make these countries susceptible to domestic instability, military adventurism, and totalitarianism. For early postwar intellectuals and leaders, industrialization was seen as the solution to, rather than the cause of, political turmoil.

ECONOMISTS

If the idea of development was the postwar response to the economic problems associated with decolonization, then development economics was the social scientific discipline that first tackled the problem. As Hans Arndt suggested, "The very fact that economists had a theory, or theories, of economic growth seemed to give them a head start over other social scientists as experts on economic development."[31] In the late 1940s, the economics profession was completing a disciplinary revolution. Marginalist microeconomics and Keynesian macroeconomics had transformed economics from a form of social criticism into a discipline geared toward empirical verification through mathematical modeling. As a result, politicians increasingly respected the prognostications and policy advice of economists.[32] The most important historical result of the newfound "scientific" legitimacy and policy orientation of economics was to encourage leaders from every point of the political compass to settle on the deliciously ambiguous concept of "economic development" as the answer to the problem of decolonization. For American social scientists, *underdevelopment* invoked poverty, agriculture, morbidity, illiteracy—in short, backwardness, a term it was meant to replace.[33] Policy makers identified development with economic growth—another ambiguous expression—with the additional implication that this economic growth would be distributed so that the masses as a whole would benefit. Depending on who was speaking (and who was listening), development could mean either increased income or increased welfare, or put another way, increased production or increased consumption. However it was defined, economic growth was something tangible and measurable, unlike "democracy" or "sovereignty" or "international respect."

The relative economic prosperity of the industrialized countries—the Great Depression notwithstanding—provided both proof that material progress was possible, and a metaphorical "book of blueprints" that nonindustrialized countries could use to design their own industrialism.[34] As a quasi-public good, the argument went, these blueprints could be had virtually free of charge and would allow countries to skip the technological dead ends that had slowed the progress of the "first movers." (The availability of these blueprints was what led Russian-born economist Alexander Gerschenkron to suggest that there were in fact *advantages* associated with what he still called backwardness.[35]) As Colin Leys has pointed out, development theory got its start as a theory about how colonial, and then later postcolonial, states could accelerate national economic growth: "The goal of development was growth; and the agent of development was the state and the means of development were macroeconomic policy instruments."[36] Regardless of their ideological stripes, advocates of development agreed that industrialism represented the only road to modernity, and that the experiences of the pioneers provided essential lessons for the latecomers to industrialization. The international economic architecture that had been set up at the end of World War II further supported this belief.

The central institutional pillars of the postwar geoeconomic order were established at the Bretton Woods Conference in 1944. Its basic framework involved fixed exchange rates, institutions to promote reconstruction and development (the World Bank and the International Monetary Fund), with the United States acting as the lender of last resort—in other words, as the financial guarantor of the system. The basic aim of Bretton Woods was to prevent the mistakes that had been made in the 1930s from recurring—competitive devaluations, punitive trade barriers, and withdrawal of states from the global economic system. The positive aim was to promote global integration through free trade. Some have argued that Bretton Woods promoted capitalist penetration of vulnerable foreign markets. It is true that getting access to former colonial markets figured in the United States' support for the Bretton Woods system. However, the system subordinated businesspeople to the authority of governments in economic decision making, the assumption being that scientifically trained elites were least likely to act either "irrationally" or out of a self-interest at odds with the interests of the social collective. Furthermore, under conditions of rapid economic growth and the social dislocations that went with it, strong government was necessary to help rein in the political passions of the masses. Political scientist Karl Deutsch spoke for all modernization theorists when he declared, "For the uprooted, impoverished, and disoriented masses produced by social mobilization, it is surely untrue that that government is best that governs least. They are far more likely to need a direct transition from traditional government to the essentials of a modern welfare state."[37] Modernization theory would therefore support a relatively statist approach to economic development.

The aims of Bretton Woods were ultimately less economic than political: the system of American-guaranteed fixed exchange rates, along with government controls on capital flows, provided the best assurances that the economic dislocations (and the concomitant political mayhem) of the 1930s would not recur. Preventing such a recurrence was the main aim of the system. As Eugene Staley commented in 1943, "Our interest is to help establish a self-running world (in which we take an appropriate part), not to try to run the world ourselves, or to withdraw and have it run into chaos again."[38] Economists agreed that the competitive devaluations and trade barriers of the early 1930s had exacerbated the problems of the worldwide depression.[39] The Bretton Woods system, while modest in its emphasis on free trade in comparison with the late twentieth century, helped the United States by opening up markets for the huge American industrial base and access to resources available from colonial and postcolonial regions. Bretton Woods's system of fixed exchange rates allowed states maximum leeway in determining internal financial arrangements while still making trade an engine of growth. Although some American conservatives were unhappy about the statist implications of Bretton Woods, one of the reasons John Maynard Keynes had favored the system was that it allowed for this sort of planning. By operating as a lender of last resort and thus guaranteeing the whole system, the United States played the crucial role in allowing state control and free trade to coexist.

A second reason why the postwar United States would countenance state planning of foreign economies was that recent domestic precedents supported the role of state planning. For advocates, planning was seen as inoculating society against more radical Communist or fascist alternatives. As political scientist Charles Merriam, founder of the Social Science Research Council and professor to Gabriel Almond, put it in 1934, "Sound and reasonable planning is the very safeguard against what many people fear, planning accompanied by violence, tyranny, by harsh repression, the working out of a blueprint in a frame, and planting it down on the soft flesh of the people. Sound planning is a way to prevent that."[40] Though thwarted at home, the technocracy movement of the 1930s provided the background for postwar development planning. More immediately, the most important examples of planning's benefits were the popular and economic successes of the Tennessee Valley Authority (TVA) and the European Recovery Program, better known as the Marshall Plan.

The Tennessee Valley had long been considered one of the most "backward" parts of the United States. Established in 1933 as one of the inaugural New Deal programs, the TVA was a grand scheme for the concerted development of the natural and human resources in the region. It aimed to control the Tennessee River, generate electricity, increase local employment, and end poverty. Within a decade, the collaboration of public and private experts had helped to turn one of the poorest regions of the United States into one of the biggest industrial growth areas in the country. In the minds of liberal American intellectuals and policy makers, the TVA became a prototype for how the state could act as a rational, benevolent enforcer of the national interest in a way that still conformed with the social democratic ethos of the time.[41] Charles Maier has observed that the successful application of economic rationality in the management of New Deal agencies like the TVA helped convince American liberals that planning could provide a way out of political strife. Looking at their own domestic situation in the 1930s and during World War II, American scientific and political leaders concluded that "by enhancing productive efficiency, whether through scientific management, industrial cooperation, or corporatist groupings, American society could transcend the class conflicts that arose from scarcity."[42] Technology and economic expansion would substitute for redistribution as solutions to conflicts over scarcity.

After the war, many Americans believed that development projects in poor countries could be implemented on the TVA model. The existence of an apparently universalizable American model of development helps explain why Americans theorists and development practitioners tended to ignore the colonial antecedents to their own projects.[43] In the eyes of its advocates, the TVA had conquered "so many of those problems which plague other regions of the world: low income, resignation to the status quo as inevitable, complacency on the part of other more favored areas."[44] Mordecai Ezekiel ended his 1947 volume *Towards World Prosperity through Industrial and Agricultural Development and Expansion* by proclaiming the need for a "Tennessee Valley Authority for the Danube Basin."[45] Proponents characterized the TVA as a collection of experts realizing the people's will. The TVA presented itself as a technical solution to social, political, and economic problems, and hence as a countermodel to Communism. As Arthur Schlesinger Jr. put it, "No people in the world approach the Americans in mastery of the new magic of science and technology. Our engineers can transform arid plains or poverty-stricken river valleys into wonderlands of vegetation and power. Our factories produce astonishing new machines, and the machines turn out a wondrous flow of tools and goods for every aspect of living. The Tennessee Valley Authority is a weapon which, if properly employed, might outbid all the social ruthlessness of the Communists for support of the people of Asia."[46] Furthermore, given the conservative backlash about domestic social planning that took place in the United States after World War II, reformist liberals had no choice but to pursue their agenda abroad. To this day, the TVA continues to hold a hallowed place in the hearts of development planners.[47]

The other important precedent for postwar development planning was the reconstruction of the European economy after World War II through the European Recovery Program (ERP), sometimes described as a "European TVA."[48] Launched by U.S. Secretary of State George Marshall in 1947 in response to the acute European fiscal and monetary crises of the two previous years, the ERP contributed $12 billion in aid to European economies over a four-year period. Although after the war, there was some discussion of permanently deindustrializing Germany (the so-called Morgenthau Plan), calmer spirits had decided that the best way to guarantee the postwar European peace was to reconstruct the industrial infrastructures of all the European nations to allow a return to prewar trade patterns.[49] For American leaders, the ERP was the solution to the so-called dollar crisis, the double economic bind caused by excess domestic industrial capacity and excess consumer demand in the United States, combined with insufficient demand and liquidity in the European markets that had consumed American goods before the war. By exporting both goods and currency, the United States hoped to head off both depression and inflation at home and abroad. Economic growth would also help guarantee pro-American, non-Communist political stability in Europe. As the European economy recovered in phoenix-like fashion, economists and politicians gave the ERP great credit for having facilitated this renaissance. Like the TVA in the United States, the ERP seemed to have solved some of the perennial state-labor-industry conflicts that had plagued Europe for a century or more. Keynesian economics seemed to promise macroeconomic tools for effective state control over the economy that did not need to involve more radical and direct interventions into the production process.

The development consensus of the postwar period rested on the belief that a mixed private-public economy, orchestrated by professional economists trained in macroeconomic theory, represented the best way to relieve the transitory and chronic poverty of much of the world's population.[50] The collapse of the Western economies during the 1930s not only had provided a crucial impetus for destabilizing the empires but also had shaken all countries, including the United States, out of dogmatic prejudices against state intervention into the economy. By demonstrating that economic aid could help build foreign markets, the ERP's perceived contribution to the European economy constituted the single most important precedent for postwar foreign aid programs.[51] Just as the European market for U.S. goods had been rebuilt, so, too, would postcolonial markets be built up to become markets for U.S. goods. The ERP helped reconstitute the multilateral world trade system whereby overseas areas, especially Southeast Asia, exported raw materials to hard currency areas. The difference, however, was that these raw materials would now be directed more to the United States rather than the old European metropole. The aim was to reconstruct Western Europe while opening overseas territories to U.S. investment and commerce.[52] All of this would be done through private commercial channels, but managed by government-sponsored technocrats.

However, American postwar economic policy did not aim merely to reconstitute prewar (or, more accurately, pre-1914) trade conditions. It also aimed to increase the overall global industrial base. Compared with the late colonial development projects formulated by Europeans, which had aimed at increasing production of locally available primary goods, postwar development economics decided that material improvement for the postcolonial countries required industrialization. Development economics claimed to supply the economic expertise necessary to achieve industrialization. Whether they favored import substitution or export-oriented specialization, early development economists and postcolonial leaders both favored industrialization.[53] Keynesian economic theory classified them both as special cases of economies with "surplus labor" trapped in a low productive equilibria. Few economists at first challenged the notion that industrializing an agricultural or extractive economy might require a different approach from that needed to revive a war-damaged industrial economy. And it was this lacuna that provided the primary theoretical opening for modernization theory.

The Postwar Context

So far this chapter has discussed the long-range background for modernization theory. The rest of this chapter discusses the more immediate postwar context of modernization theory. I begin by considering the influence of the cold war, and then take a closer look at three important contemporary intellectual movements that have only rarely been considered in relation to modernization theory. The first is the end of ideology debate, which was carried out with specific reference to the postcolonial world, thereby linking it to modernization theory. I then examine the dominant democratic theory of the postwar period, which emphasized institutional stability and the need for firm leadership by elites, thereby providing the intellectual foundation for modernization theory's discussion of the possibility for democracy in the postcolonial world. Finally, I examine the dominant historiographic trend of the period to show how modernization theory reflected and influenced ideas about American history and society being articulated by contemporary American historians. This discussion shows not only how modernization theory connected to the wider intellectual life of the postwar period, but also how these discourses were themselves, in ways that have rarely been remarked, reflections upon the difference between traditional and modern societies. As the central point of connection between these various important episodes in postwar intellectual history, modernization theory provided American intellectuals with a sense of intellectual wholeness and moral mission based on an overarching, interlocking, global conception of historical change.

The Cold War

It is often said that the United States emerged from World War II with unprecedented geopolitical power, with an undamaged economy and occupation of its Axis opponents. This dominance was no doubt real, but to many observers of the postwar scene, the rise of the Soviet Union's geopolitical influence was an even more striking outcome of the war. If decolonization established the need for development, then the invigorated clout of the USSR surely had more influence than any other single factor on the manner in which American development discourse would be articulated over the following decades. Soviet Communism is today often interpreted as a form of imperialism and the collapse of the Soviet Union as the final installment in the twentieth-century process of decolonization. During the cold war years, however, the Soviets' anti-imperialist credentials appeared unassailable, especially in contrast to America's prewar record in the Philippines and its reticence about denouncing the imperial claims of its cold war allies. Especially on the left, the Soviets were widely viewed as liberators rather than oppressors. With decolonization as the motive force behind development discourse, the Soviet Union and its developmental methods appeared to many to occupy the rhetorical high ground during the early postwar period.

Even more than the competitive propaganda campaign for the hearts and minds of postcolonial peoples, what made the Soviet Union threatening to postwar liberals was its supposed economic success. Every political leader in the postwar world knew that during the 1930s, while the capitalist economies had languished in depression, Stalin had industrialized the Russian economy while maintaining political stability.[54] Both sides in the early cold war agreed that the USSR afforded living proof that turning a poor agrarian economy into an industrial powerhouse did not require either a capitalist or a democratic approach. Furthermore, in the early postwar years it was not at all clear that the capitalist system had an inherent edge on the Communist system for promoting economic growth. American economist Holland Hunter spoke for many when he declared that the example of Soviet industrialization was "mysterious in its contours and awesome in its results."[55] Even though the Soviets were unable to compete in absolute terms with the material largesse of the United States, their exemplary economic growth lent credence to their ideological challenge to the United States. In short, the USSR posed a power-ful alternative to the democratic-capitalist model of modernity.

The apparent success of the Soviet Union in achieving rapid and sustain-able industrialization caused grave concern among American policy makers and social scientists. From the onset of the cold war, fears that the USSR was providing a better example of development than anything the West had to offer animated thinking in development circles. Leading modernization theo-rists regarded the Soviet threat as the essential starting point for thinking about development. For example, Max Millikan, director of the Center for International Studies (CIS) at MIT, argued that a "much extended program of American participation in the economic development of the so-called under-developed states can and should be one of the most important elements in a program of expanding the dynamism and stability of the Free World and increasing its resistance to the appeals of Communism. The best counter to Communist appeals is a demonstration that these same [development] prob-lems are capable of solution by other means than those the Communists pro-pose."[56] Modernization theory supported the anti-Communist policy agenda by describing why and when Communism could interrupt the capitalist for-mula of development, and by providing an alternative to the Communist model. Modernization theorists proposed technocratically managed social and economic reform as an alternative to the radical redistributions of politi-cal power and resources of Communism. The CIS's interest in "underdevelop-ment" was thus a direct and unmistakable product of the cold war.

Similar sentiments were found at the Social Science Research Council. In 1948, Bryce Wood, who would soon sponsor the Committee on Comparative Politics, suggested along with Norman Buchanan and Joseph Willitts, the director for the social sciences at the Rockefeller Foundation, that one of the main influences of the Soviet Union was its "possession of a successful system and scheme for development." In a memo proposing a new research center for the study of development, he worried, "We have not worked out any counter-plan beyond a 'finger in the dike' technique. A center [of development stud-ies] could help formulate orderly and democratic ways which could avoid a totalitarian 'x-year plan.'"[57] A decade later, Buchanan, having succeeded Willitts as director for the social sciences, would reiterate these views when he wrote to Dean Rusk that "there is no blinking the fact that the Soviet's accom-plishments in industrializing its economy in a short space of time has made an enormous impression in the underdeveloped areas."[58] Although before the war there had been concerns that federal funding for social science research could lead to government interference in the autonomy of scientists, these fears receded as the potential of federally funded research became apparent in the wake of the Manhattan project. For the government, "national security provided the fundamental rationale for government support of natural and social scientists."[59]

With the onset of the Korean War, it became clear that the main front of the cold war was swinging from Europe to the postcolonial regions. As veteran diplomat Averell Harriman put it, "The battle against Communism is in the underdeveloped countries and it's not in Europe."[60] While CIS leaders Max Millikan and Walt Rostow agreed with Harriman about the shifting geography of the cold war, they also argued that the military stalemate in the Korean War had changed the terms of the struggle. Though many in Washington believed that the lesson of Korea was that the cold war would eventually turn hot and that therefore military expansion held the only solution, Millikan and Rostow argued that Korea marked the end of Communist efforts to expand their sphere of influence by military means alone. While military subversion remained a threat, the major struggle between Communism and capitalism would henceforth be waged on an economic and ideological rather than military level. Even though Millikan and Rostow recognized the difficulties that development would entail, they felt that placing the emphasis on economics gave the United States a great advantage in its competition against the Soviets, since the United States was so much richer than the Soviet Union.[61] After the Korean War, the U.S. foreign economic aid program would become inseparable from military concerns. (Indeed, the United States would distribute most foreign economic aid under the umbrella of military assistance. One major debate would turn on how, if at all, to "link" economic and military ends—a problem American policy makers still had not solved half a century later.) Contrary to their image as febrile militarists, the modernization theorists would distinguish themselves in the late 1950s by arguing that economic, social, and political factors as much as military ones would determine the outcome of the cold war.

In the wake of the Korean military stalemate, therefore, the overriding imperative became for the United States to formulate a program capable of challenging the ideological promise and the material achievements of the Soviet system. The postcolonial world was undergoing rapid transformation regardless of whether or not the United States got involved. As Rostow put it,

"The Communist bid to win Asia by demonstrating rapid industrialization is already launched. Peking and Moscow have set the time span of the race. It behooves the Free World and especially the United States to decide promptly whether it is to observe or participate in this struggle on which so much of our destiny hinges."[62] Like it or not, the result of this "uprooting and breaking away" of traditional society meant that modernization was coming to the postcolonial world in one form or another. And the United States had better come up with proactive plans. "To rely upon automatic developments in economic and political life in [the underdeveloped countries]," Karl Deutsch observed in 1961, "would be to court mounting instability, the overthrow of existing governments, and their replacement by no less unstable successors, or else their eventual absorption into the Communist bloc."[63] Deutsch, Rostow, and other modernization theorists would develop their program in response to these political realities of the post–Korean War phase of the cold war.

Another way in which the cold war influenced the rise of modernization theory was in the way it changed the funding of the social sciences. The combination of the GI Bill, which created an instant demand for thousands of new college teachers to educate discharged American soldiers, and Washington's need for new information about areas and topics where American influence was being challenged by the Soviet Union, meant that the federal government after World War II was to embark on its most important funding of higher education since the Morrill Act of 1862. Whereas the Morrill Act had been passed to provide states with federal land for the purpose of building universities that would promote scientific agriculture, postwar federal funding of universities sought to promote industry, particularly the kind of industry that could be useful in the cold war struggle. Social scientists were quick to see that if they could make their work useful to the federal government, they would likely be able to benefit from its open pocketbook. Many social scientists considered it their patriotic duty to offer their services to their country in its hour of need, but no doubt the ability to be able to promote their careers by gaining access to government funding encouraged social scientists to pursue "useful" projects. No social scientists were more astute at judging this possibility than the modernization theorists. In this way the military-industrial complex quickly became the military-industrial-academic complex.

In addition to federal funding, an unprecedented amount of philanthropic money flowed into academic institutions in the postwar period. Before World War II, private philanthropic foundations, with few exceptions, had mostly promoted local projects, medical projects, or more or less explicitly religious projects, such as missions to China. After the war, for reasons that exceed the scope of this work, these foundations found themselves both flush with money and inclined to fund new areas. Notably the Carnegie Corporation, the Rockefeller Foundation, and, above all, the Ford Foundation became huge donors to the burgeoning social sciences. These philanthropic organizations looked at the successes they had had in funding medical research before the war—the Rockefeller Foundation, for example, had funded the development of a vaccine against yellow fever—and were receptive to charismatic social scientists like Gabriel Almond or Walt Rostow who claimed that, given similar resources, analogous advances were possible in the human sciences.

By focusing their work on poor countries, these social scientists tapped the habit within the foundations for funding projects designed to benefit "backward" regions. Since the 1920s the Rockefeller Foundation, for example, had worked in various poor countries, especially in Latin America and China.[64] After the war, this subject seemed more urgent than ever. According to historian Robert McCaughey, the Ford Foundation envisioned itself "doing for the rest of the world what the Marshall Plan had done for Europe: to provide it with the technical and administrative wherewithal to acquire a level of economic well-being that would allow the development of democratic institutions, thereby effectively eliminating the threat and the appeal of Communism."[65] This was hardly surprising, since Paul Hoffman, who had been the main administrator of the Marshall Plan, was president of the Ford Foundation from 1950 to 1953. The Ford Foundation defined development as the alleviation of "poverty and disease; the tensions which result from unequal standards of living and security; racial conflict; and the forces generated by political oppression and conflicting social theories and beliefs."[66] Positive goals were more difficult to define, but boiled down to high rates of economic growth and, to a lesser extent, democratic government.

According to Ronald Geiger, "For the potential patrons of academic social science . . . the United States was now the foremost power in the world, but it lacked basic knowledge about much of the rest of the globe. The trustees and officials of the major foundations felt the need for more social knowledge, and knowledge with greater detail, depth, and reliability, than was available through journalistic reports. With such needs in mind, they turned to the social sciences."[67] The specific aim of the foundations was to direct the social sciences to serve the needs of an emergent superpower. To receive funding, social scientific research projects presented themselves as constructing a new and useful understanding of the postwar world order. As the Rockefeller Foundation itself said, "The interest of the Rockefeller Foundation in the economic problems of underdevelopment has been manifested not only by grants to organizations in the areas themselves but also by support to centers in developed areas where the theoretical framework which must underlie positive action is most likely to be advanced."[68] For this purpose, the emergent theory of modernization seemed well suited, while studies operating from alternative definitions of development or progress found themselves systematically ignored. Even Edward Shils, who angrily dismissed the idea that funding sources could be used to establish authorial intent, had to admit, "In the social sciences, government and foundations—by their selectiveness [in funding research]—determine which fields of research will flourish, at least quantitatively, and which conceptions of society and economy will be promoted and which will be allowed to wither because of lack of support."[69] As the only non-Communist theory promoting a radical rethinking of development on the basis of a totalizing reconstruction of the postwar geopolitical and geoeconomic social order, modernization theory dovetailed with the interests of the foundations in promoting the moral and material interests of the United States in the emergent postwar world order.

The Elite Theory of Democracy

The postwar proliferation of "People's Republics," "Democratic Republics," and "People's Democracies" shocked the sensibilities of those raised in an Anglo-American political tradition that equated democracy with liberty, and that restricted the concept of freedom to the political sphere. Both the evident popularity of the Hitler regime and the Soviet Union's prestige among certain sectors of the postwar European working classes forced a reconsideration of what was meant by "democracy." Postwar theorists responded to these events by downplaying the importance of popular political participation in their definitions of legitimate democracy. "If interest, knowledge, and constant participation on the part of the mass were our criteria," Gabriel Almond explained, "we would have to write off all historic democracies as something other than democratic."[70] The foundational text for this new definition of democracy was Joseph Schumpeter's *Capitalism, Socialism, and Democracy*,[71] a work that would achieve popularity only belatedly after its publication in 1942, as the general intellectual milieu of the United States began to align with its insights.

By the early 1950s, with the cold war at its peak and a populist anti-Communist crusade taking its pound of flesh out of the American intelligentsia, Schumpeter's calls for a procedural rather than substantive definition of democracy started to find adherents among American intellectuals.

Schumpeter argued that the political theory of democracy ought to focus on democratic process instead of democratic substance. Disdainful of the notion of popular sovereignty, Schumpeter argued that neither the empirical record nor good sense suggested that democracy did or should have anything to do with rule by the people. (Attempts to achieve substantive democracy, he further warned, could only lead to socialism—something he himself ruefully considered the likely "wave of the future.") The way democracies actually worked, according to Schumpeter, was as a form of competition among elites for votes. This definition of democracy reduced popular political participation to the minimal act of voting. Whereas prewar scholars had considered low voter turnout an unfortunate sign of political apathy, postwar scholars reinterpreted nonvoting as a passive expression of *support* for the political system. Noninvolvement of the people thus became a sign of the "health" of a democracy.[72] Because modern societies were too complicated for most citizens to understand, the theory went, policy decisions had to be made by experts; under complex modern conditions, democracy could only be *representative*, never direct. Popular involvement in practical political decision making had only dangerous implications. Though a sentiment of despair about the cultural corrosiveness of "rationality" suffused *Capitalism, Socialism, and Democracy*, the modernization theorists would take from Schumpeter the positive descriptions of ideal democratic practice while occluding those elements that were pessimistic about the future or critical about modernity. Drawing on this legacy of Schumpeter, postwar American political theorists would define democracy as a process in which elites competed politely among themselves before a sedated and sober public, who, it was hoped, would not pay too much attention anyway. "That democracy is best," modernization theory implied, "in which the people participate least." Keeping the people from getting "too involved" with politics remained the abiding goal of postwar American intellectuals.[73]

Just as sociologists David Riesman and Talcott Parsons would argue that the goal of every "social system" was to secure social conformity, so political theorists argued that the goal of the "political system" was to achieve constitutional stability. Though postwar American authors gave lip service to the notion that democracy meant that the people controlled elites, such comments veiled the more fundamental opinion that power should belong to elites. "In all societies, of course, the making of specific decisions is concentrated in the hands of a very few people," Gabriel Almond and Sydney Verba explained. "Neither ordinary citizens nor 'public opinion' can make policy."[74] "The truly important policies of our great institutions," Rostow would likewise explain, "are, in the end, still made by a few men; for there is no other way."[75] The political ideal was for elites to present the masses with a limited range of potential political representatives, who would then be selected through formal democratic practices. With oblique reference to Schumpeter's distinction between the process and the ends of democracy, Rostow argued, "Democracies only work well [when] disagreements are tactical rather than strategic."[76] With substantive definitions of democracy removed from consideration (the word *social*, for instance, was almost never attached to the word *democracy*), the continuity of the democratic-constitutional political system became an end in itself.

Left at this point, procedural rather than substantive definitions of democracy had the unfortunate problem of doing little to distinguish the NATO democracies from the "people's democracies" to the East, with the lower voter turnout rates in the United States as the only evidence of the superiority of American democracy. To avoid this embarrassment, American political theorists added another term, claiming that proper democratic practice had to involve *pluralism*. Constructed as the opposite of totalitarianism, pluralism meant that political decision making did not reside in the hands of a single elite group, such as a political party or the military. Pluralism meant that various elite groups would compete for and share political power. It was "a system of many centers of powers, many areas of privacy and a strong internal impulse toward the mutual adaptation of the spheres rather than the dominance or the submission of any one to the others."[77] As French philosopher Raymond Aron said, "The fundamental difference between a society of the Soviet type and one of the Western type is that the former has a unified elite and the latter a divided elite. . . . Democratic societies, which I prefer to call pluralistic societies, are full of all the noise of public strife. . . . Government becomes a business of compromises [among elites]."[78] What pluralism decidedly did *not* mean was that "the masses" were to participate in political decision making.

The elite theory of democracy was in fact not so much a theory of *democracy* as a theory of *aristocracy* in the literal sense of that term—*aristos* meaning not a caste of nobles but rather "the best" (i.e., rule by an elite). It is no coincidence that *Democracy in America* by Alexis de Tocqueville, the first and most illustrious aristocratic theorist of democracy, returned to popularity in the postwar United States, after being out of print in the United States from 1904 to 1945.[79] Alan Kahan has argued that Tocqueville was an "aristocratic liberal" who sought a middle ground between complete democracy and absolute lawless despotism—exactly the balancing act that the modernization theorists also sought to achieve.[80] It is not hard to see why, given this definition of democracy, postcolonials often considered the United States to be in cahoots with the anciens régimes against which they were struggling. Many nineteenth-century theorists of democracy would no doubt have been surprised to learn that universal suffrage, competition between several political parties, and representative government represented "the ultimate point in democratic progress, beyond which it was impossible to venture."[81] But for the modernization theorists, since that was the extant political form in the United States, and since the United States was by definition "modern," then such arrangement indeed had to be "the ultimate point in democratic progress." Ideally, a self-disciplined and politely competitive elite would complement an ovine populace.

By the late 1950s, modernization theorists considered the United States an effective "democracy" because, they argued, its elites had never had terribly heated disagreements among themselves. In postcolonial countries, however, even nominal democracy of the sort that held sway in the West was inappropriate if significant differences existed about how the country should be run. Not only were the citizens of such countries less "sophisticated" or "rational" than those in the West, but the entire political system was undergoing rapid change in order to cope both with the relative political autonomy created by decolonization, and with the socioeconomic rearrangements attendant upon industrialization. To use Rostow's distinction, the process of "transition" was likely to produce "strategic" rather than "tactical" differences about politics. Democratic government was viable in such places only if democracy meant occasional plebiscitarian approbation of elite rule. Even as American intellectuals over the course of the 1950s became more confident about elite-led democracy at home, they became less and less sure that it was appropriate for postcolonial countries. As we will see in chapter 5, by the early 1960s, even the lip service to democracy would soon be torn away in favor of the throbbing vitality of militaristic forms of modernization. The initial flimsiness of their democratic concept helps explain why many modernization theorists would be able to rationalize their advocacy of outright military dictatorship: on an empirical level, the political declension from democracy of this sort to outright dictatorship was not very great.

In the minds of its social scientific advocates, however, the pluralist theory of democracy further distinguished itself from a simple justification of tyranny by its notion of how intellectuals would relate to the political sphere. According to scholars like Clark Kerr or Edward Shils, the political autonomy of the scientific community (rather than the political primacy of the plebes) provided the critical distinction between American and Communist notions of democracy. Whereas Soviet scientists, as French philosopher Raymond Aron put it, "feel that they lose all control over their discoveries as soon as they transmit their secrets to the generals and politicians,"[82] in the United States, scientists had helped determine how their inventions should be used. Shils believed that the scientific community constituted "a kind of social and cultural system with its own powers of self-maintenance and regulation."[83] Since different rules governed the community of scientists than governed the rest of society, politicians ought not interfere with their scientific self-regulating bailiwick. Shils argued that scientific communities should not only remain independent from political control, but as experts in social and political matters, should also be entrusted with political and social decision making. (Hence the impetus for Shils to edit the *Bulletin of the Atomic Scientists,* a journal dedicated to keeping scientists involved in nuclear policy making.) Postwar American social scientists imagined themselves as handmaidens to power, advisors whose "scientific" objectivity would help to guide political leaders toward elite "consensus." In other words, the modernization theorists wanted a semiporous relationship between political elites and social science, in which social scientists would advise and influence political leaders, without having their own activities dictated by politicians.

To see how these elitists applied their distrust for popular politics to the foreign policy arena, consider *The American People and Foreign Policy* (1950), a now forgotten work by the founder of political development theory, Gabriel Almond. Reflecting American intellectuals' early postwar paranoia about the emotional stability of the American people, this work exemplified the liberal anxieties of the late 1940s classically described by Arthur Schlesinger Jr. in *The Vital Center* (1949). The first step in achieving a genuine understanding of the political process, Almond claimed, was to jettison normative views of that

process. Almond pointed out (rightly enough) that there existed a "stratification of influence" in America.[84] Rather than question or criticize that stratification of influence (as he had during his graduate student days),[85] Almond
suggested that the point of "a democratic foreign policy in the realistic sense
. . . has been to involve a broad discussion among elites before an attentive
public." When Almond suggested that the broad discussion take place
"before" the public, he did not mean that it should take place where some
insolent member of "the mass" would be tempted to say something "unreal-
istic," but rather that the debate among elites ought to take place in newspapers and journals, rather than behind closed doors in the manner of
traditional diplomacy. Because the American people (like the Nazis whom
Almond had spent the war studying) were subject to "volatility and potential
explosiveness," Almond felt that the proper way for the "masses" to "participate" in policy making was "in indirect and primarily passive ways."
Reflecting the fears of American intellectuals in the late 1940s, and relying on
national character analyses of Margaret Mead and Clyde Kluckhohn, among
others, Almond claimed the American masses were "unstable," subject to irrational and shifting "moods"—in contrast to the cool rationality of those political elites he would later characterize with the word "modern."[86] Illogical and
volatile by nature, the masses could succumb to the splenetic zealotry and
sanguinary fanaticism of unscrupulous demagogues. Almond's stance typified
that of 1950s liberals, who "were simultaneously pleased and troubled, confident of America's ultimate virtue and stability, but increasingly concerned
about the short-range wisdom and resolve of the people."[87]

Almond called for better training and organization among American political elites by a scientifically rigorous community of political scientists. "The
containment of mass moods," Almond argued, "may be approximated
through a bettering of elite selection and training. Our efforts ought to be
directed toward the articulate points in the political structure. Both a democratic and effective foreign policy may be shaped and maintained as long as
we have trained and disciplined elites competing for influence before an
attentive public." In other words, to contain the volatility and explosiveness
of the masses, it was necessary for elites to remain unified among themselves.
Intellectuals had to help train elites to resist both the "mass moods" of the
American public and the ideological onslaught of the Soviets. Perhaps thinking of the vicious battle between the executive and legislative branches of the
American government in the late 1940s, Almond believed that the biggest

threat to the United States was potential conflict among American elites. Almond believed that a social science worthy of the name would overcome these squabbles. "It is in the social sciences in the universities that a democratic ideological consensus can be fostered and a democratic elite discipline encouraged. One of the factors responsible for the indiscipline of the democratic elites and for the persistence of ideological confusion, is the absence of a coherent theory of society and politics." The word "democratic" appeared in the passage like a mantra, but in fact added little to its content; what Almond was calling for was the creation of a creed that could unify American elites in the same way that Communist elites could rally around Leninism.[88]

While Almond would devote much of his efforts over the next decade to building such a "coherent theory" of "democratic" politics around which elites could rally, other modernization theorists would be thinking about ways to tranquilize the masses into acquiescing to this elite rule. Since direct coercion clashed with fundamental liberal tenets, considerable attention was devoted to finding ways to secure acceptance of elite rule. To appreciate this dimension of modernization theory, let us briefly consider Edward Shils's intervention into the 1950s debate over mass culture. Since the 1930s, leftists like Theodor Adorno, Leo Lowenthal, Dwight MacDonald, and Clement Greenberg had been criticizing mass culture for three basic reasons. First, they deplored mass culture's brutality and tawdriness; second, they considered mass culture an opiate that distracted the masses from the reality of their abjection, weakening their will to resist not only capitalist exploitation but also the depredations of the state; and third, they worried that mass culture was itself a mild form of totalitarianism, setting the stage for worse. In *Dialectic of Enlightenment* (1944)—which would not be translated into English until 1971—Adorno and Max Horkheimer had also criticized mass culture for being a product of the "culture industry," which, in the name of the masses, imposed a standardized culture on the masses from above. In other words, that mass culture represented the cultural dimension of capitalist modernity. As Daniel Bell concluded, the criticism of mass culture stood in for the criticism of bourgeois society.[89] Condemning American-style mass culture thus worked as a covert attack on American-style modernity itself.

For Shils, who was busy formulating the upbeat definition of modernity that would prove so influential on modernization theory (see chapters 1 and 3), the criticism of mass culture was thus an attack on that which he held most dear. Insofar as attacking mass culture constituted a guerrilla attack on modernity, mass culture had to be defended. In an essay entitled "Daydreams and Nightmares: Reflections on the Criticism of Mass Culture," he anointed himself as the defender of mass culture against the "transmogrified Marxism" of Adorno and MacDonald.[90] Mass culture was "ridiculous" and "brutal," Shils conceded, but he insisted that this was not necessarily a bad thing for society as a whole. Although alarm about what John Stuart Mill called the "brutish mass" has long been a hallmark of aristocratic liberal thought, Shils's general confidence in the American version of modernity occluded such fears. In fact, he defended mass culture for the same reason that Adorno and MacDonald attacked it—namely because it distracted the masses from political involvement and kept them contented. Shils saw mass culture as a way of "providing something for everyone" without conceding them true political power.[91] By giving the people what they wanted *culturally*, elites could avoid making concessions of a concrete *political* sort.

Shils implicitly agreed with the critics on two key substantive points— though he would differ sharply about the normative implications of these points. First, he agreed that mass culture was the "natural" product of modernity. Defending "modernity"—especially its American dispensation—required a defense of its "natural" cultural product, which Shils (and other defenders of mass culture) recognized as the outgrowth of the modern system of production and consumption. The criticism of mass culture, he claimed, "rests on a distinct image of modern man, of modern society and of man of past ages. This image has little factual basis. It is a product of disappointed political prejudices, vague aspirations for an unrealizable ideal, resentment against American society, and, at bottom, romanticism dressed up in the language of sociology, psychoanalysis and existentialism."[92] A proper image of modernity (such as the one he was busy formulating) would obviate the need to criticize mass culture, Shils implied. Second, Shils also agreed with the critics that mass culture acted as a political soporific on the masses. But whereas Adorno believed that the lack of critical thinking inherent in mass culture was the first step down the road to Auschwitz, Shils celebrated mass culture as a noncoercive means of keeping the masses from interfering with elites and intellectuals. Adopting the indulgent posture of the aristocrat, Shils in effect was suggesting that mass culture was at worst bad, certainly not evil, and in any event probably the best that could be expected either from or for the masses.

Shils's defense of mass culture also represented a covert moment in the struggle over the American reception of German social theory. In addition to defending modernity in toto, this essay also provided a tacit place for Shils's interpretation of certain key theorists of modernity, most specifically Weber. Adorno criticized mass culture as an example of the "disenchantment" of the world—a theoretical term taken from Weber's more dour moments. For Shils, however, this pessimism was the aspect of Weber's thought that he and Parsons had labored so hard to downplay in *Toward a Theory of Social Action.* As we will see in the next chapter, Parsons and Shils had spent years crafting a Weberian theory that permitted them to retain their image of American modernity as a wonderful thing. What the Frankfurt School critics proposed, by contrast, was to use Weber's (and Freud's and Nietzsche's) cultural pessimism about an administered world to criticize American mass culture. By intervening in the mass culture debate, Shils sought to exile those aspects of European social theory that were critical of modernism.[93] Mass culture in this sense represented the gilt on the iron cage of modernity, a pretty face that kept the masses in their place. These political and intellectual motives thus led Shils, an arch and Anglophilic man (though of working-class background), to the paradoxical position of defending popular tastes from the onslaughts of effete leftists, with the ulterior motive of keeping the masses from engaging directly in politics proper.

By the late 1950s Almond, Shils, and most other American liberals had put to rest their fears about the "volatility and potential explosiveness" of the American people—mass culture and consumerism had solved the problem. But those same fears remained the point of departure and never-abandoned subtext for their theorizing about postcolonial politics. Liberal American social scientists would transfer this image of the dangerous masses from the European and American working classes to the postcolonial hordes. Indeed, a postpassionate politics was seen as one of the primary things that differentiated "healthy" and "mature" democracies from the ideological politics commonly found among the politically "underdeveloped." As we will see in chapter 5, Lucian Pye claimed in his study of Malayan Communists that political passion was a pathology belonging to an anterior phase of development, one that the West had superseded but that still obtained in the postcolonial world.[94] Postwar American social scientists equated the emotional content of political modernism with a phlegmatic and zealless Reason. "Pluralistic politics," Edward Shils declared, "prohibits emotional intensity."[95] In contrast to postcolonial nations, Sydney Verba commented, "American society operates on a lower level of intensity."[96] David Riesman, too, had claimed that "other-directed" Americans were characteristically "cool" and detached from their political system, in contrast to the "hot" political passions of less advanced folks. As the modernization theorists came to believe that the "modern" (i.e., politically docile) elements of the American "political culture" had emerged victorious, they began to argue that the goal of politics in the postcolonial world was to "catch up" with the advanced state of American political culture. Modernization theory's understanding of postcolonial politics thus emerged out of dialectical reflection about American politics and American national character.

The Ends of Ideology in the Postcolonial World

The notion of the end of ideology is almost as old as the notion of ideology itself. Friedrich Engels was the first to suggest that if everyone were to become aware of his or her "real interests," then false consciousness (which Engels regarded as synonymous with ideology) would disappear and be replaced by "scientific socialism."[97] Since Engels's time, the search for a postideological age—an age in which science trumps politics—has inspired countless modernists. In the late 1950s and early 1960s, as social modernism reached its apogee in the United States, the phrase "the end of ideology" became a key signifier of that fond hope.

Like much American philosophical musing in the second half of the twentieth century, the phrase "the end of ideology" came to the United States from France. Raymond Aron used it as the coda to *The Opium of the Intellectuals,* his intervention into the postwar debate among French leftists about the purpose of socialism.[98] In this work, Aron followed Pareto in defining ideology not as "false consciousness," but instead as a religious attitude toward politics (hence "an opiate") in which "faith" and "commitment" rather than practical problem solving formed the operative sentiments.[99] Instead of following leftists like Jean-Paul Sartre and Maurice Merleau-Ponty in considering the proletariat as the revolutionary bearer of History and the harbinger of total emancipation, socialists like Aron and Albert Camus suggested that the socialist party take a more modest view of itself as the representative of the practical interests of the working classes. Aron concluded with the hope that he was living at "the end of the ideological age," in which "fanaticism" was giving way to a "tolerance born of doubt," and in which intellectuals would "teach everyone to doubt all the models and utopias, to challenge all the prophets of redemption."[100]

Aron agreed with the modernization theorists that "industrialism" meant technologically driven and elite-led convergence on a rather bland technocratic society.[101] Despite important similarities between Aron's thought and those of the American modernization theorists, however, Aron was a subtler thinker than most American modernization theorists. According to Aron, the scope and historical implications of technological change and industrial expansion exceeded the prophetic bent of social scientists. Aron argued that "one cannot remake society according to a plan," and that emancipation could never be absolute. Stressing the radical particularity of all political and social organization, Aron preached a lesson of intellectual and moral modesty in the face of the imponderable vastness and complexity of the world. Even though he agreed with the basic modernist premise that the way to "stifle the impulse toward foolish and irrational [political] hopes" was to extend "the Welfare State," he made sure to note that "India cannot model herself either on the Europe of today or on that of 1810."[102] While certain participants in the end of ideology debate (notably Daniel Bell) would retain Aron's analytical complexity and moral nuance, in the main, the end of ideology debate would not resonate in the United States as a call for political temperance, which had been Aron's main point in promoting the phrase in France.

Instead, in the United States the "end of ideology" would provide the libretto to the victory chant of a triumphant postwar American society. It would be interpreted to mean the victory of that *bien pensant* conservative center-leftism known in the postwar United States by the name of liberalism. In the United States, "the end of ideology" was mobilized not against Communist partisans (as it had been by Aron) but rather to signify, on the one hand, the disillusionment of former Trotskyists with their youthful ideological commitments and, on the other hand, the victory of elites over populist demands for political inclusion. Instead of being a relativist doctrine, the end of ideology in the United States heralded the victory of vital center liberalism over the totalitarian and populist threats of left and right. Even as modernization theorists were embracing the claim that the age of ideology was at an end, they were justifying the imposition of American values and capitalist economic practices all over the world. Just as many American readers of Sinclair Lewis's *Babbitt* had recognized Babbittry in their neighbors but not in themselves, so the modernization theorists saw only Communism in Aron's critique of ideological thinking, and nothing of their own peculiar form of liberalism.

The phrase "the end of ideology" first appeared in the United States as the title to a 1954 article by Edward Shils. Shils had picked up the phrase from Aron at that year's meeting in Milan, Italy, of the Congress for Cultural Freedom, an organization that had been formed in the early postwar period (with financial help from the CIA) to rally intellectuals worldwide against the Soviet Union's postwar ideological offensive.[103] In his article recounting the events in Milan, Shils noted that the meetings had witnessed a great deal less ideological disagreement than on previous occasions. Shils believed that a consensus had emerged (at least among the intellectuals in attendance) that some version of a democratic welfare state represented the only decent way to organize a society, and that the ideological battle against Communism was therefore essentially over. Citing Aron, Shils speculated that this consensus might have a wider import; perhaps it meant that we had reached a postideological era.[104]

Scholars such as Daniel Bell and Seymour Martin Lipset (both of whom had also attended the Milan gathering of the Congress for Cultural Freedom) were soon attempting to root Shils's and Aron's speculations in more careful analyses of contemporary social and political life in the West. In contrast to the 1930s, Bell and Lipset argued (no doubt thinking of their own youthful flirtations with Trotskyism), American intellectuals in the 1950s arrayed themselves along a much narrower spectrum of ideological positions, defined by political liberalism and a basic commitment to social welfare. There was an "agreement on fundamentals" that Lipset characterized as "conservative socialism."[105] "In the Western world," Bell stated, "there is today a rough consensus among intellectuals on political issues: the acceptance of a Welfare State; the desirability of decentralized power; a system of mixed economy and political pluralism."[106] According to Lipset, this consensus had emerged because in the United States "the fundamental political problems of the industrial revolution have been solved: the workers have achieved industrial and political citizenship; the conservatives have accepted the welfare state; and the democratic left has recognized that an increase in over-all state power carries with it more dangers to freedom than solutions to economic problems."[107] The only people who regretted any of this, Bell and Lipset suggested, were those who relied on politics for excitement, notably intellectuals and the young. Indeed, Bell claimed that the end of ideology was commensurate with the "exhaustion of political ideas," and even Aron admitted that the "real emancipation" achieved by an institutionalized welfare state was inevitably "dull."

How did the end of ideology hypothesis fit in with the intellectual culture of the United States during the 1950s? As Pierre Birnbaum pointed out, the end of ideology argument was in part the intellectual child of the behavioralist revolution in political science.[108] The greatest theoretical support for the end of ideology as a social scientific dogma came from Talcott Parsons. Revealing the influence of his professor Karl Mannheim, but forgetting his early defense of utopianism, Parsons claimed that ideology and science were epistemologically incommensurate.[109] Themselves influenced by Parsons, and smitten by the desire to elaborate a science of politics, partisans of behavioralism such as Gabriel Almond, David Easton, and Robert Dahl moved their inquiries further and further away from the traditional concerns of political theory, which they denounced as metaphysical palaver.[110] Easton and Dahl were so confident that quantitative methods would soon rule political science that they looked forward to the day when all reference to the "classics" of political theory would be relegated to intellectual history. Easton stated outright that political science ought to conform to the methodological assumptions of the natural sciences.[111] These sorts of claims on behalf of science echoed through the end of ideology literature. Lipset, for example, called for intellectuals to shift "from ideology to sociology," by which he meant value-free social science. Even if Bell did not believe that value-free science would ever be fully realized, he too believed that social science ought no longer to concern itself with normative questions—most of which had been solved—but rather with the positive question of how to achieve the universally agreed upon normative ends in the most efficient possible manner. The discourse on the end of ideology thus reinforced the belief that "healthy" political activity meant dickering about details and means rather than debating doctrines and ends. These scholars shared a fundamental vision of value-free social science replacing political disputation.[112]

The "underdeveloped" countries played a crucial role in the end of ideology argument. Indeed, I would argue that the end of ideology hypothesis emerged directly and specifically out of comparative reflections upon the differences between the "industrial" and "underdeveloped" worlds. Consider, for example, Shils's first use of the term in 1954. Although Shils wrote with his usual epigrammatic flair, he betrayed an unusual tentativeness by punctuating the title of his essay "The End of Ideology?" with a question mark. His hesitation resulted from the activities of the postcolonial (and still-colonial) intellectuals in Milan; these intellectuals had continued to make noisy ideological protests—issuing the outrageous demand, for example, that imperialist nations make reparations. Even as he celebrated Western intellectuals for having overcome ideology, he was troubled by the recognition that intellectuals from the "underdeveloped" areas had legitimate justifications for their ideological sentiments. In 1955, however, he had yet to understand modernity in a way that would allow him to explain the ideological divergence of first and third world intellectuals. In grappling with this problem over the next three years, Shils not only came up with the category of "modernity" as the keyword to describe the achievements of the West and the aspirations of the South, but also made his study of the ideology of Indian intellectuals, *The Intellectual between Tradition and Modernity* (1961), one of the first books to use the categories of tradition and modernity as its fundamental unit of analysis.[113]

Bell concurred with Shils that the intellectuals in "underdeveloped" countries represented a crucially important exception to the tendency toward decline in ideology. In contrast to an increasingly tepid American and European attitude toward politics, ideological fervor was still the norm rather than the exception among third world intellectuals. Thus Bell did not title his essay "The End of Ideology" *tout court,* but rather "The End of Ideology *in the West.*" Although ideology was a dead letter in the Western industrialized states, "the rising states of Asia and Africa" were "fashioning new ideologies with a different appeal for their own peoples."[114] And if Bell scorned first world ideologists (especially those who signed onto "the new ideology of economic development"), he pointedly did not condemn the new ideologies indigenous to the postcolonial world. Though he left the issue vague, Bell implied that ideological attitudes might be appropriate for societies undergoing "the transition." It was up to the intellectuals of the postcolonial world, Bell felt, to make sure these ideologies did not get out of hand and lead to "irresponsible" behavior. As long as these countries remained responsible, Bell suggested that the United States adopt a sympathetic attitude, regardless of the ideological posturing.

Lipset agreed with Bell that "[i]t is only the ideological class struggle in the West which is ending."[115] Echoing the psychologism of Lucian Pye (see chapter 5), Lipset argued that the anti-Western rhetoric of postcolonials was "part of their more general effort to overcome feelings of national inferiority, particularly vis-à-vis the former metropolitan ruler."[116] Given their current stage of development, ideology—by which Lipset meant fervent leftism of a Communist or socialist sort—remained appropriate for many postcolonial countries. "Ideology and passion may no longer be necessary to sustain class struggle within stable and affluent democracies, but they are clearly needed in the international effort to develop free political and economic institutions in the rest of the world." In the postcolonial world, Lipset argued, "there is still a need for intense political controversy and ideology. . . . It is necessary for us to recognize that our allies in the underdeveloped countries must be radicals, probably socialists, because only parties which promise to improve the situation of the masses through widespread reform, and which are transvaluational and equalitarian, can hope to compete with the Communists." The message of Lipset's book was that the United States should adopt a forbearing attitude toward revolutionary and anti-Western rhetoric among postcolonials, and recognize that socialism was the only available option other than Communism. Lipset called on "leftist intellectuals" in the West to recognize that gradualism, while appropriate at home, was not an acceptable doctrine abroad. Western leaders, Lipset argued, "must communicate and work with non-Communist revolutionaries at the same time as they accept the fact that ideological controversies have ended at home." Like other modernization theorists, Lipset recognized that the rhetoric of "revolution" befitted these societies; they needed "the hope implicit in revolutionary chiliastic doctrine."[117]

Going further than Bell, Lipset asserted that the divergent material conditions of the industrial and postcolonial worlds explained why ideology was ending in the first but continuing in the third world. In the long run, Lipset claimed, the universal sociohistorical phenomenon of industrial development would lead to a postideological democratization the world over. The end of ideology was the reflex, in other words, of the material conditions created by industrialism. Since the postcolonial world had yet to converge materially with the industrial nations, it was to be expected that it would remain at a lower "stage" ideologically. However, the good news was that the shape of the postideological future of the postcolonial world was already clearly in sight, right here and now in the contemporary United States. In *The First New Nation* (1963), Lipset argued that the United States could and should serve as a developmental model for the rest of the world. According to Lipset, postcolonial countries faced problems similar to those the United States had faced when it first achieved independence—economic dependency, lack of international influence, and the need to create "modern" political parties and unified central authority. Because the United States was the first country to face these problems, "perhaps its development can give us clues as to how revolutionary equalitarianism and populist values may eventually be incorporated into a stable nonauthoritarian polity."[118] There were two central assumptions in making the United States the normative developmental model. First, the solutions that the United States had found to solve its "developmental problems" were ones that every postcolonial should want to emulate; and second, if a postcolonial wanted to emulate the United States, then it would achieve the status of the contemporary United States.

Lipset argued that "a nation's values determine its political evolution."[119] In order for a society to become a healthy, modern nation, it first had to have healthy, modern values. Oddly enough, Lipset discovered that the United States had apparently always possessed these values; in other words, it had always been modern (a point he also made by noting that Americans had always been "other-directed," an argument that David Riesman himself eventually embraced).[120] In order for postcolonial nations to develop into democracies, they would therefore have to adopt "modern" or (what was by now openly acknowledged as synonymous) "American" values. Only an achievement-oriented and egalitarian value system—which was supposedly both universal and quintessentially American—could promote a healthy developmental process. Unfortunately, values were difficult to measure and even more difficult to change. Luckily, in *Political Man*, Lipset showed that there was a strong correlation between the income levels and the degree of democratic practice. From this data, Lipset concluded that the best way to promote democracy was to promote economic growth, since wealth was a prerequisite for stable democracy. Lipset's argument sanctioned support for nondemocratic developmental regimes in the name of establishing the "economic preconditions for democracy." Lipset himself admitted that the focus on economic growth as a precondition allowed social scientists to defer the political question of democracy and instead focus on economic issues. Lipset's model reduced democracy to a dependent variable, with economic growth as the independent variable.

Consensus History and Modernization Theory

Since modernization theory was, at bottom, a theory of history, it should come as no surprise that it participated in the historiographical trends of its day. Not only did modernization theory draw on contemporary historiographical practice in crafting its view of the historical process, but the influence also worked in the opposite direction, with the leading historians of the postwar period borrowing from modernization theory's structural assumptions about political and social change. Modernization theorists would use their contemporary historians' depictions of the United States to construct the "modernity" pole of the ideal-typical contrast between "traditional" and "modern" societies. But in addition to mutually influencing each other, these two intellectual movements were also both in the midst of grappling with that most characteristic of American dilemmas: how to define the United States as exceptional and unique, while in the same breath insisting that its example was universal and exemplary. In this sense, modernization theory represents the mid-twentieth-century contribution to the centuries-long (and ongoing) effort to convince the world that U.S. interests in fact are universal ones. And while most postwar American historians would conclude that the United States was a nation sui generis, the modernization theorists would chart a different course, arguing that America, in all its exceptionalist glory, could be a beacon unto the world. Indeed, in the hands of its most ambitious theorists, like Walt Rostow, America's exceptionalism was not the obstacle but in fact the very basis for the claim that America had something to offer the world by its example.

The intellectual historian John Higham coined the phrase "consensus history" in 1959 to describe what he saw as a pernicious postwar trend toward conservative historiographical thinking among historians of the United States.[121] Higham identified, among others, Louis Hartz, Clinton Rossiter, Daniel Boorstin, Ralph Gabriel, Robert Brown, Edmund Morgan, and David Potter as participating in a movement to "homogenize" the American past. These scholars, Higham claimed, argued that the old Progressive theory that social conflict was the primary motor of historical change "failed to account for the dominant role of accommodation and compromise in American history."[122] In place of the earlier views of scholars like Charles Beard or Arthur Schlesinger Sr., who had emplotted American history as an unending struggle between haves and have-nots, consensus historians substituted a story of harmonious progress. Returning to the insights of Tocqueville, who had argued that the United States' distinctiveness resulted from the absence of a feudal heritage and its concomitant lack of class conflict, these historians argued that even apparently "radical" movements had differed little from conservative movements: both sought to preserve the entrenched interests of their participants. In the absence of feudal social divisions, the United States had not suffered from great ideological disputes, and a tradition of civil political discourse had dominated its history. In short, these new historians believed that the meaning of American history was that progress could happen in the absence of serious conflict. Like Rostow, who was creating a Marxian theory of historical change with class conflict removed, consensus historians believed that class conflict was not the midwife of historical transformation but only inhibited progress.

The trend toward a consensual phrasing of American history paralleled the emergence of the elite theory of democracy. The same antipopulism we found at the root of the elite theory of democracy pervaded consensus history as well. In *The Age of Reform* (1955), Richard Hofstadter argued that populists were little more than disgruntled and atavistic losers "in the transitional stage in the history of American agriculture" who "had been bypassed and humiliated by the advance of industrialism."[123] Although Hofstadter would never have permitted himself to use the jaundiced phrase of "disease of the transition," he too believed that populism was an unhealthy derivative of the modernization process. In the same way that the modernization theorists would use it to explain postcolonial politics a few years later, Hofstadter used the terminology of "identity crisis" to explain social unrest among American farmers who found themselves caught between the older securities of agrarianism and the acquisitive and speculative ways of "the modern world."[124] "In a country where physical needs have been, by the scale of the world's living standards, on the whole well met," Hofstadter explained, underlining the materialism of his model of politics, "political life . . . is an arena into which status aspirations and frustrations are, as the psychologists would say, projected."[125] Hofstadter's essay "The Paranoid Style in American Politics" reduced political dissidence to a form of mental disturbance.[126] Like many modernization theorists, Hofstadter seemed to suggest that there was little legitimate reason for radical revolt against the modern world. Reflecting in 1968 on the correspondences between consensus history and 1950s social science, Hofstadter further explained how McCarthyism had infected the mood during the early postwar years: "The populism of the right inspired a new skepticism about the older populism of the left. While Daniel Bell was writing about the end of ideology in the West, historians were returning to the idea that in the United States, it had hardly ever begun."[127]

The historiographical starting point for a great deal of consensus history was an explicitly comparative perspective on American history. Considering the United States a concordant society made sense if one compared the United States with other countries, particularly European nations between 1914 and 1945. Consensus history was inextricably bound up with the postwar search for what made the United States different from other lands. This search for the roots of American "exceptionalism" resulted in the founding of a special domestic "Area Studies" in the form of American Studies.[128] Just as modernization theory was doing for the social sciences, so American Studies served as a historiographical substitute for Marxism.[129] The two most famous works of consensus history to highlight the exceptionalism of the United States were Daniel Boorstin's *The Genius of American Politics* (1953) and Louis Hartz's *The Liberal Tradition in America* (1955). What made the United States great, according to Boorstin, was its lack of class conflict and concomitant lack of political philosophy; instead, an instinctive conservatism had dominated all of American history. (Those who did not fit into this narrative, such as the Quakers, became Boorstin's villains.) Agreeing with Boorstin, Hartz argued that the United States lacked a history of creative political philosophy because such philosophy could only result, Hartz believed, from a reflection on conflict. Instead of generating an independent tradition of political philosophy, American political thinking constituted a long footnote to the work of John Locke. Since there had been no feudalism, there was no class struggle, and therefore the liberalism of Locke was the "natural" philosophy of America. In a memorable phrase, Hartz claimed that because Americans had been "born free," they had never really had to think about what freedom meant. The resulting "colossal liberal absolutism"[130] had destroyed the American capacity for philosophy. Even if his normative and political sentiments differed from Boorstin's, Hartz agreed with his general assessment of American history.

The influence of these scholars on the modernization theorists was acute. Rostow, for example, claimed that "Americans have not been deeply touched by the experience of the transition. They belong to a society lucky enough to be 'born free'; a society that did not have to struggle against the weight of attitudes, values, and institutions that go with a traditional society."[131] Likewise, Arthur Schlesinger Jr. clearly had Hartz's interpretation of Locke in mind when he said that modernization theory proposed that postcolonial nations should "base their revolutions on Locke rather than on Marx."[132] The consensus historians' views of American society and history as an unchanging story of conservative liberalism provided the basic vision for modernization theorists of what a healthy modern polity should look like. Reflecting late in life on his early work, Robert Bellah explained, "Modernization theory, especially in the United States, was a kind of late child of the enlightenment faith in progress. Modernization was the process that produces all the good things: democracy, abundance—in short, a good society. Like ours. I'm afraid that was a major implication of the whole idea. America and a handful of other 'advanced industrial societies' were, if not already good societies, so clearly headed in that direction that they made clear the end to which other societies, as they modernized, were tending."[133] Modernization theory imagined the end point of historical development as an idealized (and already achieved) version of the contemporary United States, and it was the more historically minded of the modernization theorists who made this move most explicit.[134]

The difficulty for the modernization theorists, however, was that most consensus historians insisted that this "exceptionalist" frame of reference made the United States an impossible act to follow. Fresh from his tell-all testimony to the House Un-American Activities Committee, Boorstin, for instance, declared, "Nothing could be more un-American than to urge other countries to imitate America. We should not ask them to adopt our 'philosophy' because we have no philosophy that can be exported."[135] Hartz, too, noted at the end of his volume that since America's liberalism stemmed from its particular historical-material base, it could never effectively export its political philosophy to countries not blessed with having been "born free." The question for the modernization theorists was how to rework the substantive claims of the consensus historians in a way that would retain their image of a benign modern America, while putting aside the claim that this benignity stemmed from irreproducible historical circumstances of American history—which would obviously not do from a policy perspective dedicated to exporting an American-style modernity. Because modernization theorists believed in what Shils called the "fundamental unity of all human beings," they would take the consensus historians' depiction of the American national character not as a definition of difference, but rather as a hopeful description of the future of "traditional" societies. The historian who would most directly confront the problem of the nonexportability of American exceptionalism was David Potter, in his 1954 classic *People of Plenty*.

Drawing on cutting-edge work in the social sciences on the concept of "national character," Potter set out to understand the conditions that had brought about "the" American national character described in the work of scholars like Margaret Mead, Karen Horney, and David Riesman. Specifically,

Potter wanted to describe what gave Americans their wonderful inclination toward democracy. The answer that Potter supplied in his title was that America's peculiar inclination toward democracy resulted from its unique wealth. Presuming that political conflict stemmed from issues of economic distribution, Potter argued that American abundance explained why the United States had experienced little conflict and why its democracy had been effective. Economic abundance explained why there was no socialism in the United States. Potter suggested that if this abundance could be exported, then there would be no need for socialism anywhere else either. Potter was creating a materialist theory of history that, like modernization theory, denied that conflict or violence had a necessary place in progressive change. That Potter's work so resonated with modernization theory made sense, since Potter claimed that the main antecedent to his argument was Walt Rostow's *The Process of Economic Growth* (see chapter 5).[136] Like so many others in the 1950s, both Potter and Rostow believed that, at the end of the day, economic growth provided the solution to political strife. In his book-length unpublished essay, "The Making of Modern America," Rostow would return Potter's intellectual favor by using *People of Plenty* to describe the final stage of the modernization process. Rostow echoed Potter's analysis of "abundance," as well as the end of ideology hypothesis, by suggesting that in the era of "high mass consumption," class conflict would disappear.[137]

Rostow wrote "The Making of Modern America" in 1958 and 1959, at the same time as he was composing *The Stages of Economic Growth*. Both were completed in 1960. "The Making of Modern America" was Rostow's attempt to apply his five-stage theory of economic development to interpret American history from the Revolution down to World War II. The monograph synthesized his thoughts about the American character with his notion of modernization. Seen in the long view, "two massive facts" could be extracted from American history; Rostow explained that "the first is the extraordinary continuity of the American experience over the classic period, a continuity which persists in many domains down to the present; the second, that as a national society the United States was a distinct success." Like other consensus historians, Rostow felt that American history could be told as a story about "relatively minor, piecemeal, compromise adaptations of a stable basic structure." Rostow echoed Potter and Riesman by claiming that the United States was a society "dominated by its domestic material pursuits and the values of individual striving and performance that went with them." Like many social theorists in the 1950s, Rostow felt that Tocqueville had understood the essence of the American national character. "Many of the characteristics isolated by recent analysts as typical of American society," Rostow claimed, "were observed by Tocqueville in the 1830s." Rostow would no doubt have agreed with Shils that "[d]espite all its internal conflicts . . . [American culture] discloses in the individual a greater sense of attachment to the society as a whole." America was a success story.

Potter's abundance hypothesis answered Hartz and Boorstin's charge that America's exceptionalism made it impossible for it to function as a workable model for export to the postcolonial world. Although Potter agreed with Boorstin and Hartz that the United States could not export its political philosophy per se, Potter argued that "America's mission" could be redefined from an export of democracy to an export of its precondition, abundance. Encouraging economic abundance, Potter said, could stand in for promoting democracy. "Democracy is the foremost by far of the many advantages which our economic affluence has bought for us. To say this, of course, is also to say that, when we propose world-wide adoption of democracy, our problem is not merely to inspire belief in it but to encourage the conditions conducive to it."[138] As with Lipset, the elitist theorists of democracy, and the modernization theorists, Potter's assumption that democracy was the natural if not inevitable result of economic abundance helped justify the deferral of democracy in poor countries. Potter's definition of democracy mirrored the formal, contentless notion of democracy that we have seen among the elitist political scientists. Because democracy was not about creating substantive egalitarianism, but was rather "a great steeplechase for the purpose of selecting a handful of winners to occupy a few enviable positions,"[139] Potter claimed that in a situation of great economic inequality, "the emotional costs" of democratic competition would be too high to permit such practices. Potter proposed, therefore, that the United States substitute the export of technology and abundance for the erstwhile and hopeless attempt to export democracy wholesale.

"A Model of Modernist Charity"

Sociologist Gilbert Rist has compellingly argued that the project of development constituted a form of modernist messianism.[140] For American proponents, development promised to exorcise the secular demons of the postwar world—poverty, Communism, and colonialism. Armed with sacramental science and technology, these emissaries of what Walt Rostow would call

"Americanism"[141] were animated not only by a proselytizing zeal but also by what historian James Patterson has described as a "self-confidence that occasionally bordered on self-righteousness."[142] In a typical outburst at a 1954 conference sponsored by the CIS, one participant explained how the aims of U.S. postwar policy toward the "underdeveloped" lands ought to be formulated: "The Soviets present to these countries a totalitarian model for their own development. We have to present them with a different model. We must not just be defensive. We must offer a framework within which the nations of Asia and Africa can develop economically as free societies. We must take our part in creating the new world which is evolving out of the upheaval in Asia and Africa. We must be missionaries."[143] Modernization theory, understood in this context, represented an addition to the long-held view of America as a "City upon a Hill," an idea first articulated by seventeenth-century Puritan minister John Winthrop, who considered America an immaculate example to the world, having left behind the sins and problems of the Old World.

Though it echoed the nineteenth-century rhetoric of Manifest Destiny, postwar American foreign policy did not aim at annexation and assimilation. The mission instead was to "modernize" the postcolonial world, to deliver its members to the secular heaven that the United States had pioneered. The aim was to spread the virtues of "the American way of life," an expansive phrase that included culture, technology, sociability, and piety. Denis Brogan, a British commentator on American life working at the CIS in 1957, observed of the contemporary intellectual climate in the United States, "The notion of 'mission' is far wider than it was; the whole world is the parish of the United States as a government and a culture. 'The American way of life,' not American Protestantism, is the creed preached and exemplified. Interest is at least as much evoked in [the] problems [of] malnutrition, technical backwardness, irrigation, mass education as in the merely strange and picturesque. The world, for selfish and less selfish reasons, must be brought near to the American standard of life, adopt American ideas and ideals."[144] Walt Rostow and Max Millikan explained that "in the largest sense," their 1957 volume *A Proposal: Key to an Effective Foreign Policy* was "designed to give fresh meaning and vitality to the historic American sense of mission—a mission to see the principles of national independence and human liberty extended on the world scene."[145] David Riesman, in his introduction to Daniel Lerner's *Passing of Traditional Society* (1958), suggested that Americans had become "apostles of modernity,"[146] and in its annual report for 1955, the CIS described its members as "crusaders."[147]

The proselytizing, missionary quality of modernization theory gives the lie to the self-definition of modernists as postideological. Indeed, Walt Rostow worried that if Communism outstripped Americanism, then "among the qualities of American society [that would be] threatened . . . would be the historic sense of American world mission, present since the nation's founding, which has given to American life much of its moral worth and distinction."[148] Asserting that there was a "sense of ideological commitment and mission built into American nationhood,"[149] Rostow argued that the missionary role had always been intrinsic to the American national style: "From its origins the United States felt within itself—and was felt by the world to have—a larger mission. . . . The transcendent quality which has long suffused American life and which still gives it a special worth is the conviction that the adventure of America has a meaning and relevance for the world as a whole. . . . The United States, child of the Enlightenment, favored adolescent of the nineteenth century, powerful but erratic youth of the first half of the twentieth century, must now confront its maturity by acting from the present forward to see the values of the Enlightenment—or their equivalents in non-Western cultures—survive and dominate in the twenty-first."[150] Late in life, he would reflect that "as individuals, most of us felt, I suspect, some kind of moral or religious impulse to help those striving to come forward through development. In that sense we were in the line that reached back a century and more to the missionaries from Western societies." Indeed, it comes as little surprise that many of the key figures associated with modernization theory were themselves children of missionaries (Lucian Pye, David Apter) or other clerics (Talcott Parsons, Harold Lasswell, Gabriel Almond).

Concerns about decolonization, poverty, and the cold war came together in Point Four of Truman's 1949 inaugural address. Emboldened by the hope that scientific planning could promote the quasi-religious mission of the United States to promote democracy and peace across the globe, Truman pledged an expanded program of financial aid and technical assistance for "the underdeveloped countries":

> We must embark on a bold new program for making the benefits of our scientific advances and industrial progress available for the improvement and growth of underdeveloped areas. . . . For the first time in history, humanity possesses the knowledge and skill to relieve the suffering of these people. The United States is preeminent among nations in the development of industrial and scientific tech-

niques. The material resources which we can afford to use for the assistance of other peoples are limited. But our imponderable resources in technical knowledge are constantly growing and are inexhaustible. . . . The old imperialism—exploitation for foreign profit—has no place in our plans. . . . Greater production is the key to prosperity and peace. And the key to greater production is a wider and more vigorous application of modern scientific and technical knowledge.[151]

Engagement with the economic problems of postcolonial countries thereby became a matter of official state policy in the United States. Truman envisioned Point Four as an extension of the Fair Deal to the rest of the world.[152] On the one hand, technical assistance was meant to provide the material support that postcolonial peoples desired. On the other hand, Truman countered the Communist appeal to the ideal of a socialist paradise with an idealized portrait of the United States and its scientific capacities. Secretary of State Dean Acheson explained that the aim of the Point Four program would be "to make clear in our own country and to all the world the purpose of American life and the purpose of the American system. That purpose is to . . . use material means to a non-material end."[153]

The ideological core of modernization theory was already present in Truman's address: the peculiarly American mix of lofty idealism and crude materialism; the emphasis on industrialization as the key of progress; the notion that there existed noneconomic conditions (and obstacles) to economic growth; the emphasis on technology as the key to economic growth; the anticolonialism; and above all, the boundless faith in the power of American scientific knowledge and goodwill to make the world a better place from a social point of view.[154] Although Point Four itself, with its limited goal of promoting economic growth through technical assistance, did not emphasize the social scientific dimension of development theory and policy, which would be the critical innovation of modernization theory, it indicated that henceforth the American government would consider development a topic of international concern. The following year Congress cemented this commitment by creating the Agency for International Development in order "to aid the efforts of the peoples of economically underdeveloped areas to develop their resources and improve their working and living conditions."[155] The era of American-led development had arrived. And as Acheson and Rostow both understood, the project of development abroad would become inseparable from a process of national self-definition at home.

The Harvard Department of Social Relations and the Intellectual Origins of Modernization Theory

Our strategy must be . . . both *global,* embracing every part of the world, and *total,* with political, psychological, economic, and military considerations integrated into one whole.

—INTERNATIONAL DEVELOPMENT ADVISORY BOARD,
Partners in Progress, 1951

As David Rockefeller's International Development Advisory Board underscored in its 1951 report to the United States Senate, by the early 1950s, American policy makers and intellectuals were increasingly cognizant of the need to develop a comprehensive strategy for understanding the problems common to those areas of the world that would soon be collected under the rubric "third world." This program needed to understand the world as a single, interconnected totality; to do so, it would have to synthesize every branch of knowledge to form a complex, comprehensive theory. Before scholars could undertake this vast, synthetic project, they needed to develop an adequate theoretical basis from which this synthesis could take place. Given the enormous empirical diversity within a category like the "third world," as well as the monumental problems that third world countries faced, scholars needed an equally enormous theoretical apparatus to determine what was going on in these various places. With the world war, cold war, and decolonization bringing the full variability of the world's peoples into plain view for the first time, American intellectuals raised in the tradition of pragmatic, theoretical modesty faced a cognitive crisis that would propel them into embracing avant-garde European social theory as a basis for understanding the third world.

It was in this context of cognitive and political crisis that intellectuals interested in problems of development in postcolonial regions began to turn to the innovative work being done at the Harvard Department of Social Relations (DSR), particularly the work of the DSR's guiding light, Talcott Parsons. Although Parsons's work had its origins in academic debates from the 1920s and 1930s and was related to the reception of European social theory in the United States, the intellectual ambition of his work made it ideally suited as a theoretical foundation for the kind of profound and totalizing reflection of the problems of the "emerging" world. This confluence of U.S. foreign policy needs and the ambitions of Parsons and his collaborators would provide the foundation for a social scientific theory of social change, which would eventually come to be known by the name *modernization theory*. Parsonian theory would provide a basis for uniting the particularistic studies being made in Area Studies programs into a single, coordinated research and policy agenda.

The DSR would shape modernization theory in four major ways. First, Parsons articulated more fully than any other contemporary American scholar a complex understanding of the concept of modernity that would provide a fundamental, if usually implicit, template for both intellectuals and policy makers in their understanding of the desirable direction and ultimate goal of change in the postcolonial world. Second, its members helped redirect postwar social theory away from social critique and toward the creation of a descriptive, omnidisciplinary theory of human action, elsewhere termed *human behavior*. (One should not mistake this omnidisciplinarity for multi- or interdisciplinarity, however, for by its nature it rejected the legitimacy of currently existing disciplinary boundaries.) This social theory would help justify the creation of technologies of social reform, mostly applied to non-Western countries. Third, the DSR was the institutional fountainhead for the promotion of Parsonian social theory, which provided the foundation for modernization theory. Even those modernization theorists (like Rostow) who did not draw directly on Parsons would make their theory compatible with his, particularly in aligning their pronouncements with the vision of modernity that Parsons painted. This is not so much a claim of influence but rather a claim that Parsons was articulating a view of modernity that was widely shared among the generation of scholars that was coming of age in the postwar years. Finally, the DSR provided an institutional presence for the employment and training of students of modernization. Most of the sociologists associated with modernization theory had some affiliation with the DSR as either professors or collaborators (including Talcott Parsons, David McClelland, Alex Inkeles, Edward Shils, and S. N. Eisenstadt) or as students (including Francis Sutton, Robert Bellah, Neil Smelser, Marion Levy, and Clifford Geertz). In addition to providing an intellectual history of the early years of the DSR, this chapter discusses why the social theory being developed at the DSR came to be embraced by American social scientists eager for a methodology that would allow them to understand the contemporary geopolitical situation of the newly identified "third" world. It is this embrace that provided the theoretical cornerstone of modernization theory.

Talcott Parsons

Son of a Methodist minister from Colorado and educated at Amherst and in Europe, Talcott Parsons had, from the 1930s, been developing one of the most elaborate and abstract sociological systems ever devised. In his first major publication, *The Structure of Social Action* (1937), Parsons claimed that late nineteenth-century and early twentieth-century European social theorists—in particular Vilfredo Pareto, Max Weber, Emile Durkheim, and Alfred Marshall—had converged on what Parsons called "the voluntaristic theory of action." (Convergence was a vital notion for Parsons, as it was for all modernization theorists: in convergence there was truth.) Parsons argued that the central intellectual struggle for all these thinkers had been over how to reconcile idealism with positivism. In the "action framework" upon which Parsons believed these thinkers had converged, the "means-ends" mode of analysis was retained but was modified with reference to cultural norms and beliefs—in other words, values. For Parsons, this scheme provided a synoptic framework within which the particular concerns of other social science disciplines could be placed. Economics was concerned with rationality in relation to limited material means and scarce, valued ends; political science dealt with Hobbesian power struggles; and sociology explained how social action could be integrated through shared values that defined overall priorities. (Parsons would soon weave post-Freudian psychology into this scheme to explain how individuals and personalities functioned within the social system.) The largest unit of analyses was the "social system," a biological metaphor that Parsons derived from Pareto.[1] This division of social scientific labor made the social action theorist preeminent—the adjudicator between the segmental concerns of the other disciplines.

The discussion of the intellectual origins of modernization theory in this chapter focuses on Parsons, not because every scholar who has been labeled a modernization theorist agreed with all of the particulars of Parsons's methodology, but rather because Parsons articulated the implicit understanding of modernity that undergirded the project of modernization theory better, earlier, and more thoroughly than anyone else. In this sense, Parsons was the first and most preeminent of modernization theorists. Understanding that the concept of modernization grounded Parsons's work makes it possible to gain a better understanding of some of the tensions within his oeuvre. (For example, an oft-noted tension exists between those who prefer Parsons's work in *Toward a General Theory of Action,* with its focus on how individuals generate meaning and thereby orient themselves toward activity in the world, and those who prefer *Economy and Society,* with its vision of an almost completely determining social structure.) My suggestion that Parsons's overall aim was to describe the process of modernization does not resolve or undo these tensions in his work; rather, it helps explain why Parsons pursued epistemologically and methodologically divergent projects, while insisting that his work should be read holistically. Modernity, Parsons believed at an implicit but fundamental level, formed a *coherent, unitary, uniform, and worthwhile* whole, and had to be apprehended by a social science that shared these qualities. While many weapons might be used in the chase, modernity was the singular quarry of sociological inquiry. As Stephen Savage has put it, Parsons sought to reproduce the ordering of reality in his theory's logical propositions.[2] Most early prewar American academics would share Parson's perspective that modernity was an essentially benign and comprehensible object, apotheosized in the contemporaneous United States.

When later theorists disagreed with Parsons, they rarely limited their attacks to pointing out tensions and even contradictions in his work. Parsons has been the object of intense and vitriolic attack, which is surprising, considering that Parsons himself never adopted a polemical tone. I believe that the vitriol directed against Parsons has to be explained in reference to a deeper hostility toward his construction of the object of sociological inquiry (a happy modernity). The demiurge behind the many and varied attacks on Parsons which began in the 1960s had less to do with objections to the particularities of his method or the niceties of his logic than it did with a radical rejection of Parsons's view of modernity as a coherent and desirable object. If Parsons's project seemed reasonable to scholars in the 1950s who shared his modernist premises about the fundamental nature of modernity, then as doubts emerged in the 1960s and 1970s about both the benignity and the coherence of modernity, Parsons's work began to look less like penetrating analysis and more like a mind-boggling theoretical turkey, trussed by turgid prose. In other words, for postmodernists as for modernists, Parsons's project seemed to reflect and embody modernity.

Parsons's various texts all assume that modernity constitutes a benign, coherent, and comprehensible whole. Though some of his followers may be uneasy with such a bald statement, I believe that all modernization theorists shared this view of modernity. They too regarded modernity as a coherent whole, and perhaps even more than Parsons they believed it to be benign, since without exception they believed that modernity should be promoted in societies emerging from colonialism. Although Parsons was generally unconcerned with the postcolonial regions and their problems, the basic question his project tried to answer was, "What made the West different?" Like Parsons, the postwar social scientists concentrating on postcolonial regions began and ended their discussions of change in these areas with this question in mind. Even if the particulars of his method were questioned, Parsons articulated an understanding of modernity that was widely shared among postwar American intellectuals, especially among those interested in the postcolonial regions. His influence, both direct and implicit, would be enormous during the first postwar decades, particularly in the field of development studies.

The Harvard Department of Social Relations

Parsons's action theory provided not just a novel reading of a particular set of European intellectuals but also a reconstruction of the social sciences as a whole. Audacious in his professional ambitions, Parsons proposed a reconfiguration of Harvard's social sciences to conform to his new intellectual synthesis. He found support in this endeavor from various colleagues. During the 1930s, Parsons had befriended several colleagues from other disciplines, including the social psychologists Gordon Allport and Henry Murray and social anthropologists Lloyd Warner and Clyde Kluckhohn. Despite their disciplinary and intellectual differences, all of these men shared Parsons's commitment to a new social scientific enterprise based on an appreciation of the individual's relation to the social collective. For reasons both intellectual and personal, moreover, all of these men were unhappy with their positions within the institutional structure of Harvard. In their effort to overcome their disciplinary dissatisfactions, they would use Parsons's rethinking of the social sciences as grounds for creating a new department, the Department of Social Relations. Parsons had hoped that the new department would be named the Department of "Human Relations," but this was rejected on dual grounds: first, the name had already been used (gasp!) by Yale, and second, it appeared to trespass on the interests of the business school. Hence "Social Relations" was settled on.[3]

These scholars argued that the Parsonian conception of social science required a new institutional framework. The subfields of social psychology and social anthropology were to be folded into the existing sociology department to create a kind of super-department of social science.[4] The proposal that Allport, Parsons, Kluckhohn, and Murray drafted to Paul Buck, the dean of the Harvard Faculty of Arts and Sciences, recommended the creation of a Department of "Basic Social Science." Although the draft claimed (disingenuously), that the word *basic* ought not to be taken to mean that they believed their work was more important than what was taking place in other departments, they nonetheless insisted that there existed "an independent field of human social development, interaction, and social transformation. The study of individuals and this adjustment to each other and to the impersonal environment may be said to be 'basic' to the more specialized studies of economics, government, and the like."[5] Using the category of human social behavior to unify the innovations in economics, sociology, psychology, and anthropology, the new department would provide a venue for the creation of a master social science, which would put the individual disciplines on a firmer theoretical footing. The faculty, sensing that perhaps the DSR could represent a path-breaking innovation that would elevate Harvard over social science faculties at other universities, enthusiastically approved the departmental reorganization.

The DSR was to serve as a launchpad for a radical leap in social science, one that would achieve the old Enlightenment dream of a science of man. The aim of the DSR, as for all of modernization theory, was to forge "a universal and general science of society and of human behavior."[6] Parsons's student Clifford Geertz may have been making a rhetorical exaggeration when he suggested that the aim was to produce "the sociological equivalent of the Newtonian system,"[7] but there is no doubt that, in the tradition of nineteenth-century social theory, Parsons believed that the ultimate goal of social science was to achieve a totalizing synthesis. He was driven, according to his student Robert Bellah, by "the ideal of an abstract content-free theoretical science from which one could deduce the laws of social life."[8] One recent Parsons scholar explained that the "central aim of Parsons' work was nothing less than the development of a conceptual scheme capable of subsuming all analytical knowledge of social conduct by breaking down the compartmentalization of the social sciences."[9] Parsons's acolyte Marion Levy declared that for social science to become a "systematic" and "cumulative" endeavor required the "erection of [comparable] frameworks of analysis."[10] In a programmatic essay on the aims of postwar social science, Parsons wrote, "All the major social science disciplines have fields of application in a total large-scale society. An integrated picture of the society must involve a synthesis of their applications. . . . Many larger projects require not only numbers of people, but the different types of knowledge and skill that derive from training and experience in different disciplines."[11] Parsons and his friends at the DSR shared a vision of armies of researchers working out the intricate details of particular social activities, resting their work on the theoretical foundation being built by the maestros.

The infectious sense of excitement, of being on the verge of unlocking the mysteries of human sociability, appears throughout the writings of modernization theorists (and indeed most social scientists of this period). "A very big scientific development has been rapidly gathering force," Parsons explained to Dean Buck. "I will stake my whole professional reputation on the statement that it is one of the really great movements of modern scientific thought."[12] Walt Whitman Rostow agreed that synthetic social science was nothing less than revolutionary: "The revolution may be defined as an effort to achieve a more unified application of the social sciences. . . . The revolution is apparent in the spate of cross-fertilized, interdisciplinary projects, usually of a team character."[13] He talked about his hopes of creating "a general biological theory of economic growth," a project that he believed would "get much assistance from the current generation of political scientists who are increasingly committed to the study of comparative politics in non-Western societies."[14] At the University of Chicago in the late 1950s, the Committee on the Comparative Study of New Nations, led by Lloyd Fallers, David Apter, Edward Shils, and Clifford Geertz, had similar omnidisciplinary ambitions: "Attempts were made to interpret the problems of the new states in broader categories and to bring together observations of anthropologists, economists, political scientists, and sociologists." The aim was to formulate "a comparative framework of some historical depth which would permit all the new states to be seen as variants of a single and complex class of phenomena."[15] DSR social psychologist David McClelland summed up the mood of the era by saying, "We had a wonderful time . . . dreaming dreams about how to foster basic science in a way that would also contribute to human progress."[16]

Even though Parsons and most of the members of the DSR were primarily interested in social scientific problems of the United States and Europe, their general social theorizing would be welcomed with especial warmth in development studies. The enormous problems facing the postcolonial countries made it appealing to "think big." The problems these countries faced seemed so monumental that an equally monumental theoretical apparatus seemed a necessity for understanding what was going on in these places. In this context, reconstructing the entire project of the social sciences seemed like the only way to confront the seismic shift in geopolitics and economics taking place in the postwar world. Not only was Parsons the sole American social theorist ambitious enough to propose reconfiguring the social sciences in toto, but as it turned out, the content of Parsonian theory—designed to comprehend the origins of the "modern" industrialized world—seemed most useful for overcoming the cognitive gap facing postwar American social scientists who were trying to understand the lands emerging from "tradition."

Challenging the Hegemony of Economics

If Parsons was to succeed in creating a new master social science, however, he would have to outdo the hegemonic pretensions of economics, which had in the 1920s already established itself as the most influential and prestigious of the social sciences. It was through a debate within the field of economics itself that Parsons would find the opening to make this attempt. During the 1930s, the economics discipline was divided between neoclassicists, who argued that economics ought to be defined by its commitment to model-based formalist rigor, and institutionalists, who argued that economics had to be prepared to confront a wider array of social issues than could be dealt with by modeling alone. Although at Amherst Parsons had been an undergraduate student of Clarence Ayres, a leading institutionalist, he realized that the mathematical rigor of neoclassical economic theory gave it enormous analytical power. For

Parsons, neoclassical economic theory epitomized the power—and the limits—of rationalism and positivism. To this tradition Parsons wanted to fuse idealism, both in the philosophical sense of German philosophy and in the political sense of English socialism. After spending time in Germany learning more social theory, Parsons received graduate training in neoclassical economics at the London School of Economics, which led to his appointment as an economics professor to the Harvard faculty, where neoclassicism reigned.

Despite his commitment to formalist rigor, Parsons continued to share an institutionalist discomfort with the exclusion of wider social issues from economic theorizing. In his own words, the moment had arrived "to search for an equivalent in sociology" to the formalist analytical power of neoclassical economics.[17] Parsons wanted to create a theoretical model that would answer the social questions of the institutionalists with the same degree of rigor as neoclassical economics answered its more restricted questions. It was in this context that Parsons shifted to the fledgling sociology department in 1931 and began to formulate the theory that he hoped would subordinate economics within a wider sociological system. The general theory of action that he would spend his life developing, in other words, emerged initially as a critique of economics. As he put it in 1956, "The general theory of action has been found to have large implications for economics, in that economic theory can be construed as a special case of a more general theory of social systems. Economic theory, in dealing with the functioning of the economy, treats a subsystem of society differentiated from others with reference to adaptive functions."[18] Parsons believed that his social theory trumped the hegemonic pretensions of economic theory, which he described as "a special case of the general theory of social systems."[19] For Parsons, the study of how values oriented action was the primary task of social theory; economics, on the other hand, dealt with only one set of values, namely how actors oriented their action toward the norm of material maximization.

In Parsons's view, the main contribution of economics to social science had been to sharpen the concept of rationality. Nevertheless, for him the central psychological postulate of economics, that "economic rationality" formed the essential core of human behavior, was inadequate as a means of sociological analysis because it relied on an outmoded utilitarian theory of value. With other subsystems, such as politics, norms and values other than utility maximization served to orient action. Economic rationality could only be understood in relation to the achievement and implementation of specific norms and values. "The problem of the limitations of technical economic analysis has long plagued economic theorists," Parsons claimed. "I believe that the only satisfactory solution to this problem lies in a positive theory of the factors which lie on the *other* side of the boundaries of economics. The sociological contribution to this problem area concerns a theoretical analysis of economic institutions."[20] Analysis of the economy alone was therefore not in itself sufficient for understanding social functioning, including the functioning of the economy.

So important did Parsons consider this subordination of economics to social theory that he dedicated an entire book to the subject, *Economy and Society* (1956), coauthored with Neil Smelser. Special attention was paid in this volume to the problem of economic development. While Parsons gave full credit to the innovative work done by economic theoreticians in the study of economic growth, he and Smelser emphasized that the "problem of structural change in the economy and every other subsystem of the society must . . . be treated as a sociological problem. Positive theoretical analysis in this area cannot be confined to economic theory, but must involve the specific interdependence of economic and sociological theory."[21] According to Parsons, one of the main flaws in economic theory was that it tended to assume that noneconomic variables were either constants or governed by a series of long-term "propensities," generally assumed to be linear. Citing Durkheim, Parsons and Smelser argued that the motive force behind the drive for development could not be the "inherent propensity" of humans to increase their standard of living or happiness. Rather, following Max Weber and Herbert Spencer, they suggested that the major dynamic force within social systems was the tendency toward "rationalization"—or what Parsons preferred to call "structural differentiation." In the subsystem of the economy, this tended to produce more efficient allocation of resources. In combination with constant technological improvement, the rationalization of the economic subsystem led to increased economic output—in other words, to growth.

To Parsons, the "nonrational" aspects of motivation were as important for understanding social action as were the "rational" ones. According to Parsons, nonrational action—that is, action not guided by means-ends logic—was the main mode of human action. For him the concept of the "unconscious" in psychology, "covert culture" in anthropology, and "latent function" in sociology all represented ways of attacking the problem of "nonrational" aspects of human motivation and behavior. Parsons claimed that these different approaches converged to help provide a singular analytical system for understanding the nonrational aspects of human behavior and society. In conjunction with the analysis of "rational" behavior being developed by economics, a total analytical system was on the verge of completion. "The concept of values provides the focal center for analyzing the *organization* of [social] systems, of societies and of personalities."[22] The aim of social action theory was to provide a framework for analyzing all of social behavior that mirrored the rigor of economic theory in its particular subdomain of economic behavior. "The essence of sociological development is, to my mind, in gradually coming to understand that there is a complex of phenomena in social systems which has a coherence comparable to that of the phenomena of exchange and price-determination in a differentiated economy [and] subject to study by the same general type of analytical theory which has proved its usefulness in economics."[23]

At this point, Parsons's theory began to appeal to the sociologists and political scientists trying to grasp what was going on in postcolonial regions. Even though economic improvement was the agreed sine qua non of development, social scientists in fields outside economics insisted that understanding the noneconomic implications and causes of economic growth was crucial for achieving that end. As we saw in chapter 2, the perceived success of the Marshall Plan had given economists the confidence that, between aid and their new Keynesian theory, they now had the tools to spur economic growth. As these ideas and policies began in the early 1950s to be exported to countries that had little prior experience with industry, however, it became apparent that economic theory and policy alone could not analyze or induce the changes associated with industrialization. The economies of these largely peasant societies were inseparable from local cultures, social structures, and political institutions. Changing the economy would require changing everything: industrialization entailed not just new technology but the creation of an industrial society. Staffing a new factory with former peasants turned out to be more difficult than rebuilding the old I. G. Farben factory and putting the Germans back to work. Although technological improvement and the prosperity it brought continued to define development, underdevelopment was soon understood to be a problem that extended far beyond the parochial disciplinary boundaries of economics.

For development specialists confronted by the failure of purely economic analyses to apprehend the complexity of "third world" economies, Parsonian theory stood ready with an explanation: economic models were inadequate because of their lack of attention to noneconomic factors. According to Parsons and Smelser, the subordination of economics within a wider sociological framework had especially important implications for the problem of economic development. In a prospectus to *Economy and Society,* they claimed that their aim was "*systematically* to outline the major *non-economic* relationships among the components of economic development."[24] Just as Parsons wanted to dethrone economics as the preeminent and most "scientific" of the social sciences, so, too, did modernization theory arise as a response to the perception that in the late 1940s, the process of development had been understood too exclusively in economic terms. Parsonian dualism seemed to dovetail nicely with the signature concept of early development economics, namely the notion of a "dual economy" split between a traditional and a modern sector.[25] The two-sector model that W. Arthur Lewis formulated in his celebrated "Economic Development with Unlimited Supplies of Labour" (1954) could be reinterpreted as yet another conceptual example of the utility of binary thinking within a Parsonian model.[26]

The success of development economics in winning the attention of U.S. policy makers convinced social scientists in other disciplines that they, too, could gain prestige and influence if they confronted the postcolonial problem in these terms. Modernization theory emerged out of the effort of sociologists and political scientists to emulate the institutional success of the economists by amending the findings and correcting the shortcomings of development economics. As Lucian Pye put it, "Economic criteria are not unimportant and certainly should not be casually disregarded, but they are not adequate for . . . our policy toward the underdeveloped areas."[27] Although noneconomists rarely admitted that their aim was to overcome the dominance of economics in development studies—instead couching their claims as complementary to economic analysis, as in the phrase the "noneconomic obstacles to growth"— the disciplinary rivalry between economics and other disciplines, especially sociology and political science, helped propel the growth of modernization theory. Even if technological improvement was the ultimate cause of development, modernization theory grew out of disillusionment with the results generated by exclusively economic or technical attacks on the problem of persistent poverty. It tried to understand how changes in other aspects of the human existence caused and were effected by economic growth and industrialization. But if the discourse on modernization to some extent resulted from the deflation of the exalted economic hopes of the immediate postwar years, it also signaled the American social scientists' commitment to reinforcing the foundations of development theory and policy. The text that would provide the most important elements of such a theory was the DSR's most important work, *Toward a General Theory of Action.*

Toward a General Theory of Modernization

Sponsored by the Carnegie Corporation, *Toward a General Theory of Action* resulted from a yearlong seminar of DSR professors, including Parsons, Kluckhohn, Allport, and Murray, as well as several well-known outsiders, most importantly sociologist Edward Shils of the University of Chicago. *Toward a General Theory of Action* consisted of a collectively signed introduction setting out the basic theoretical apparatus on which the authors had converged during the seminar, followed by individually signed essays on the application of this apparatus to methodological problems in psychology, sociology, and anthropology. In a way, *Toward a General Theory of Action* represented an institutional self-justification. According to its authors, it sought to provide "the theoretical foundations underlying the synthesis which had been worked out on the organizational level through the foundation of the Department of Social Relations." In their introduction, the collaborators hoped that this volume might prove useful not only to members of the department but "for the development of the social sciences in general." In short, this work was the foundational text of the social theory architecture that the DSR was setting out to design.

The aim of the volume, as stated in its first sentence, was "to contribute to the establishment of a general theory in the social sciences."[28] The use of the singular was telling: this was not an effort to create one more element in a plural theoretical field, but rather an attempt to establish a monolithic and exclusive theory. This general theory aimed to codify all existing knowledge systems, and thereby to be the point of departure for all further research. In short, it was a bid for theoretical hegemony. To achieve this, the collaborators had to create a "unified conceptual scheme." For these authors, the *action* of individuals and groups was to be the point of departure for theorizing in the social sciences. The authors asserted that people's actions are meaningful to them; in other words, actions are connected to physical or social objects or values. The purpose of social science was to uncover the objects that motivate people's actions. The attainment of scientific predictability in social affairs, and eventually the creation of technologies to influence these social affairs, was the overall aim of the project.

In large measure, this was a work of definitions and categories rather than theories per se. The structures that motivate people's actions, the authors agreed, could be classified into three basic categories: personality, cultural systems, and social systems. For our purposes, two important things should be noted about this scheme. First, the authors tended to subordinate personality to the cultural and social systems as an explanatory mechanism for any kind of multiple-actor activity. In other words, the authors consistently attenuated individual agency as an explanation for action or behavior. Second, the authors tended to regard both culture and society in *systemic* terms; that is, they tended to define these categories by their "consistency of pattern." The authors acknowledged that these consistencies were never complete, suggesting that the space for individual assertion emerged only from the aporias of the social system. Individuals fit into the social system through roles. Well-functioning social systems "institutionalized" these roles (creating "expectations of conformity"), meaning that they used the cultural system to provide individuals with justifications ("moral sanctions") for their roles. "Indeed, one of the most important functional imperatives of the maintenance of social systems is that the value-orientations of the different actors in the same social system must be integrated in some measure in a *common* system." A common set of values—what the authors referred to as a "moral consensus," in a foreshadowing of consensus historians—constituted the critical mechanism for securing the "pattern of commitment" from individuals. The inadequacies of these integrative mechanisms caused social pathologies. Individuality and unpredictability were thus linked, and since predictability was the principal goal of social science, the authors regarded "excessive" individualism as a form of social "malintegration." The more totalizing the social system, and the less personality intervened as an explanatory factor, the better. Hence the authors' conclusion: "A society is the type of social system which contains within itself all the essential prerequisites for its maintenance as a self-subsistent system." This assumption of a tendency toward equilibrium helped provide the justification for a static analysis similar to the equilibrium-oriented static analysis of neoclassical economics. It made equilibrium, homeostasis, and stability the norm for a "healthy" social body.[29] Tacit in these definitions were the notions that the highest social value was conformity and the highest political value, stability.

This theoretical structure provided the foundation for the individually signed essays that followed the general introduction to *Toward a General Theory of Action*. For the study of postcoloniality, one essay in particular would exercise enormous influence: Parsons and Shils's paper introducing their famous (or perhaps notorious) "pattern variables." The pattern variables were dichotomous pairings of value orientations that collectively constituted a system that allowed actors to determine the meaning of a situation. These pattern variables were as follows:

affectivity	affective neutrality
self-orientation	collectivity-orientation
particularism	universalism
ascription	achievement
diffuseness	specificity

The overall patterning value orientation provided the normative basis for any sort of action. According to Parsons and Shils, individuals and societies tended quite consistently to orient themselves to one side of each of these dichotomies. Moreover, these variables constituted an "exhaustive framework" for understanding the values to which individuals and societies subscribed.

Before I evaluate these dichotomies and what they say about midcentury American social science, let me review what these authors thought they meant. Whereas *affective neutrality* meant the ability to exercise self-discipline by renouncing immediate gratification in response to "evaluative considerations," *affectivity* meant that the actor did not feel any need to control his expression of emotion or desire for gratification. Whereas *collectivity-orientation* referred to a sense of "responsibility" to the group and a commitment to realizing the values of the group, *self-orientation* allowed the actor to pursue his own private interests without regard to the interests or values of the group. (The authors begged the question of how the group solidarity emerged or was defined.)[30] Whereas *universalism* required evaluating objects or people "in conformity with a general standard," *particularism* meant reacting "in light of their possession of properties which have a particular relation to the actor's own."[31] Whereas *achievement* meant responding to "specific performances," *ascription* meant responding "to specific given attributes of the social object." Finally, whereas *specificity* meant confining your "concern with an object to a given sphere," *diffuseness* meant accepting "any potential significance of a social object" that was compatible with the actor's other interests or obligations, and which might vary widely from one time or context to the next.[32]

Parsons and Shils suggested modestly that the pattern variables were merely a heuristic device for the phenomenological analysis of social situations. However, I would argue that the rapid embrace of these dualisms during the 1950s and 1960s among intellectuals interested in the process of social change resulted from an enthusiasm for the inexplicitly stated historical process that Parsons and Shils had embedded within these categories. The power of these seemingly ahistorical abstractions lay in an implied development narrative that helped fill the cognitive gap for social scientists struggling to understand what development might mean for countries utterly different from the United States or Europe. All of this was understated to the point of vanishing: Parsons and his colleagues would go no further than to say that the difference between "rationalism" and "traditionalism" was a matter of "patterned choices over a period of time."[33] Nevertheless, Walt Rostow was absolutely right when he observed in his review of the volume that "[t]o this observer, the most meaningful aspects of the general theory of action lie in some of the assumptions about relationship which are built into it, rather than in its particular categories."[34] The most basic of these assumptions was that the right-hand side of these value dichotomies was essentially "modern," while the left-hand, residual side was essentially "traditional," and the development meant moving from left to right.

The pattern variables amounted to an elaboration of Weber's rationalization hypothesis about the inner tendency of modernity. Parsons justified this division of values into the categories of "modern" and "traditional" by referring to the empirical record of Western European history. A triumphal story of progressive Enlightenment provided the master narrative for understanding modernity's emergence. The previous half-millennium of European history had been defined by the progressive displacement of particularism, ascription, and diffuseness by universalism, achievement, and specificity. For Parsons, universalism was the key value for promoting continual modernization because it engendered critical judgment by demanding that particular traits be judged according to broader and more general principles (i.e., rationalism), thus opening a gap between cultural norms and the object of judgment. Like Weber, Parsons believed that *the process* of applying universalistic value judgments *in itself* enacted the process of differentiation.[35] Parsons placed the emergence of modern society in the northwest corner of Europe in the seventeenth century, based on institutional innovations in the legal system, governmental organization, secular culture, and economic innovation. "The modern type of society has had a *single* evolutionary origin," Parsons argued. "This is a crucial fact parallel to that of the unitary origin of the human species, and with that, of culture, society and personality."[36] Elements of modernity included industrialization, rationalized banking, specialization of occupational roles, increased social mobility, urbanization, the "democratic revolution," ecumenism, and so on, all of which stemmed from alternations in values that could be subsumed under the sociological generalizations of the pattern variables.

Though the first emergence of modernity was a unique event of European history, Parsons argued that its "inner momentum" destined it to overcome all previously existing social systems. Moreover, this initial modernization provided social scientists with a blueprint against which all subsequent modernizations were to be evaluated. All societies would eventually attain this "modern" value pattern. Parsons claimed that "one cannot be a radical cultural relativist who regards the Arunta of Australia and such modern societies as the Soviet Union as equally authentic 'cultures,' to be judged as equals in *all basic* respects. Our perspective clearly involves evolutionary judgments—for example, that intermediate societies are more advanced than primitive ones . . . calling more 'advanced' the systems that display greater generalized adaptive capacity."[37] In keeping with a value-free analytical method, Parsons studiously avoided the suggestion that "advanced" might mean "superior" or "better." But in the United States of the 1950s, where progressive values were almost universal among intellectuals, the term *advanced* could not help but seem better than its antonym *backward*. Like the development economists mentioned in the last chapter, Parsons believed that modern societies provided backward ones with a road map for where they were going. He felt as if American society had reached the highest level of development and that therefore it blazed the path for other societies. Moreover, since historical change had to come from outside the system, Americans were obligated to go out and help other societies get moving toward greater differentiation.

As Parsons's student Jeffery Alexander recently observed, modernization theory "may be seen as a generalizing and abstracting effort to transform a historically specific categorical scheme [the pattern variables] into a scientific theory of development applicable to any culture around the world."[38] In the view of Parsons and other modernization theorists, modernity was a value orientation, best described as a progressive, tolerant, liberal rationalism, uncannily similar to Parsons's understanding of his own contemporary United States. If modernity meant attaining the value structure of the contemporary United States, then we can understand how the pattern variables, on the one hand, helped to sanction projects of social reform in the postcolonial regions, while on the other hand, dictated a policy of social conservatism at home. The right-side pairings were identified not only as the values of modernity in general but also as the extant dominant values of contemporaneous American society. On the one hand, social reform abroad would aim at moving the values of these foreign societies from the left-hand side to the right-hand side of these dichotomies. On the other hand, since the West, and more specifically the United States, was already "universalistic and achievement-oriented and specific,"[39] there would be no need for social reform there. Indeed, value change in the West could almost certainly only be for the worse. Such was the basis of "value neutral social science."

Parsons's work from the early 1950s exercised direct influence on modernization theory. Although his work after 1960 would exercise little direct influence on other modernization theorists, Parsons continued to develop his own version of modernization theory. With the publication of the essay "Evolutionary Universals in Society" in 1964, Parsons introduced a new element into his theory, attempting to answer critics who claimed that his theory provided an account only of static functioning of the social system, thus ignoring historical questions about the emergence of given systems. As Parsons's turn to evolutionary theory implicitly acknowledged, the difficulty with the pattern variables was that their synchronic descriptions of social patterning and functioning provided no account for how and why societies change, and no explanation for the direction of change. Even though the formulation of the pattern variables contained a normative preference for the "modern" half of each categorical distinction, as well as the scarcely veiled implication that this half of the typology had the force of history behind it, the categories did nothing in themselves to account for this change. Parsons believed that evolutionary theory could provide the theoretical justification for these assertions.

A classic of deductive reasoning, "Evolutionary Universals in Society" emerged out of a seminar Parsons co-taught with Robert Bellah and Schmul Eisenstadt in the spring of 1963 at Harvard. Parsons argued that there existed an essential pattern of organizational innovations that were likely to be "hit upon" by social systems with no knowledge of each other. According to Parsons, the basic elements of the action system—religion, language, family, and technology—all advanced in a definite sequence involving continually more complex differentiation within and between systemic subspheres, resulting finally and necessarily in a bureaucratically organized liberal democracy. Differentiation took place more or less mechanically, in a defined sequence. The emergence of *social stratification* was the first clear example of an evolutionary universal, according to Parsons. (In characteristic fashion, he did not probe the power relations behind stratification.) Because stratification led to a centralization of authority, it tended to "exert a pressure to generalized hierarchization, going beyond particular bases of prestige" and thus to incline systems toward universalistic norms. A second evolutionary universal was the rise of *cultural legitimation,* by which Parsons meant "the emergence of an institutionalized cultural definition of the 'we,'" distinguished from other groups by some historical factor. This collectivity-orientation helped "break through the ascriptive nexus of kinship . . . and of 'traditionalized' culture." Once legitimacy was established, the next stage of universal evolution was the emergence of *bureaucracy,* which to Parsons represented the further rationalization of the hierarchical structure. The next step was the appearance of money and the market, which was important not only because it lubricated all social relations (though he hastened to add that "one should not be able to purchase conjugal love or ultimate political loyalty"), but also because it taught men to think in "instrumental" terms. The next step in the process was the attainment of "generalized universalistic norms." As these examples show, Parsons was connecting his evolutionary theory to the pattern variable approach he had originally developed mainly for static analysis of social systems. The institutionalization of these norms within the legal system constituted the fundamental "hallmark of modern society," what set the German *Rechtsstaat* apart from the Byzantine Empire. Finally, and most significantly, Parsons concluded that the last evolutionary universal was "the democratic association with elective leadership and fully enfranchised membership."[40] Once respect for the rule of law, universal norms, and a good bureaucracy had been established, formal democracy was the necessary final step. Each subsequent innovation proceeded from and was predicated on earlier ones.

Though he did not specify the linkages, Parsons stated that advances in one sphere, like politics, took place in conjunction with advances in the others, such as social organization or the economy. Such innovations were universal because once hit upon, they so increase "the long-run adaptive capacity of living systems in a given class that only systems that develop the complex can attain the higher level of general adaptive capacity."[41] By mapping the synchronic value analysis of the pattern variables onto a diachronic account of human social evolution, Parsons made explicit that coming to terms with the "complex of modernization" was, in fact, his fundamental theoretical goal. Embedded in Parsons's system was a notion of historical convergence. Parsons tied the structural analysis of the pattern variables to the idea that institutions tended, through a dialectical of "differentiation" and "integration," to become ever more complex. Like Tönnies and Durkheim and Maine, Parsons viewed social evolution as generally a movement away from "traditional" communities and toward a more complex urban and industrial society. Integration was a more or less explicitly teleological concept, specifying that "the system" was tending toward ever-greater organizational complexity. Parsons took bureaucratic liberalism to be the final stage of social evolution, a perfectly adapted form of social organization, a perspective at one with the arguments that would soon be put forth in the end of ideology debate. Such a functionalist perspective lent "itself to problem solving—diagnosing technical obstacles and engineering appropriate adjustments—where the end goal is taken to be the system itself."[42]

Combining diffusionism with the convergence hypothesis led Parsons to embrace a teleological form of evolutionary theory that shared more with Lamarck than with Darwin. More complex, differentiated systems were, in Parsons's view, destined to outcompete simpler, less evolved social systems for much the same reason that humans had outcompeted other large predators: they were simply more flexible and better able to compete for resources. Those humans with the misfortunate to be born into such underevolved social systems were bound to undergo radical social change, and resistance was futile. But as with Lamarck, the question Parsons never managed to adequately address was, how had this modernist social system, this universal destiny, first come into existence? What was the basis for radical social change? The only answer Parsons could come up with to these fundamental questions was in the specific ideological origins of the system in seventeenth-century northwestern Europe. Since then, the future had been trending inexorably toward maximal productive efficiency and minimal social conflict in a society arranged according to the West. Parsons's sociology shared with the "obstacles to development" approach of development economics a teleological

vision of history that suggested that all the world was heading toward a pro-
ductivist industrial society similar to the one already visible in the United
States.

Using Weber to Trump Marx

A final point remains to be made about why Parsonian social theory would
prove so helpful for scholars wishing to challenge the dominance of economics in development studies. During the cold war, liberal American scholars
often associated economic theories of historical change with Marxism. Anti-
Communist social theorists wanted to find some way to combat what they
perceived to be the pernicious influence of Marxism on social theory.
Although Parsons himself was not particularly anti-Communist by the standards of the time (Shils was much more so), his theoretical subordination of
economics seemed to provide a tool for refuting Marxism. More strikingly,
Parsons's interpretation of Weber would provide American intellectuals with
a way of attacking Communism while accepting certain crucial elements of
Marx's own thought. In Parsons's interpretation of Weber (which even today
dominates American readings of Weber), Weber's main project had been to
attack Marx's analysis of capitalism by proposing that cultural factors rather
than economic ones determined the historical specificities of capitalism.
Rather than the unfolding of material contradictions within the "base,"
according to the Parsonian Weber it was the "spirit of capitalism" within the
hearts and minds of Calvinists that had been the driving force behind capitalism's emergence. Following this reading of Weber, modernization theorists as
various as Lucian Pye, Clifford Geertz, Robert Bellah, and David McClelland
would propose some variation of the notion that achieving "modernity"
required injecting the spirit of capitalism into the indigenous cultures of postcolonial peoples.

For those who wished to appropriate Weber this way, however, there
existed one main problem, namely that Weber himself had had an exceed-
ingly dour analysis of capitalist modernity ("specialization without spirit," he
called it, "sensualism without heart"). This negative view of capitalist modernity jarred with the optimistic temperament of postwar Americans. Despite
some misgivings that modernity might be a bit boring, liberal postwar
Americans generally rejected Weber's image of modernity as an "iron cage,"
perhaps cognizant of how this trope echoed the rhetoric of the "iron curtain."

Ironically, the optimistic, materialistic vision of modernity, common among postwar Americans as a system that relieved humans of the burden of scarcity in order to permit the full flowering of human individuality owed a great deal to the German romanticism of none other than the young Karl Marx. Although Marx's anticapitalism clearly would not do, his generally positive view of modernity was certainly much more congenial to postwar American intellectuals than the gloominess of Weber. The question was how to serve up a vision of modernity that combined Marxian optimism with Weberian antipopulism and inexorable rationalization.

It fell to Parsons to forge a Weber that would retain the critique of Marx while jettisoning the pessimistic understanding of modernity. Parsons did this by embracing Weber's description of structural differentiation (Weber's "rationalization"), but insisting that the progress of individual freedom depended on the continual furtherance of this differentiation.[43] By equating differentiation with emancipation through the increase of "choice," Parsons allowed Marx's historical happy ending to be located in the actually existing Western modernity whose features Weber had empirically described in useful positivist terms. Although similar to Marx in his confidence that history was a happy story of progressive enlightenment, Parsons disagreed sharply with Marx that the motor of history could be located in the material world. For Parsons, revolutions in consciousness, not the inexorable unfolding of technological power or the contradictions of class society, provided the critical turning points in history. Parsons claimed that what defined modernity was its embrace of science as its dominant cognitive modality. Following Weber, he traced the rise of this outlook to the Reformation and the Renaissance, which had unleashed the cognitive potential contained within Greek thought to produce universalizing ethical norms that drove the rest of the historical process. These ethical norms were the ultimate historical dynamo. For example, Parsons claimed that it was not the steam engine but the Common Law of England, with its privileging of procedural regularity and equality before the law, that provided "a fundamental prerequisite of the first occurrence of the Industrial Revolution."[44] Parsons's smiley-faced reading of Weber provided a remarkable updating of the Enlightenment view of progress, one perfectly suited not only for social scientists interested in attacking Communism, but also for development crusaders trying to sell the American version of modernity to postcolonial regions.

The question of idealism versus materialism represented a major fault line within modernization theory. Some modernization theorists, especially

Parsons's own students such as Clifford Geertz and Robert Bellah, as well as scholars like Lucian Pye, would concur with Parsons's relatively "culturalist" rather than "materialist" understanding of the development process. Other modernization theorists, like Walt Rostow or Bert Hoselitz, would embrace Parsons's optimistic reading of Weber, but claim that the allocation of material resources, rather than cultural disposition, was paramount for determining historical outcomes. These scholars continued an old Western habit of locating the progress of man in his technological achievement.[45] Whereas both Weber and Parsons had addressed the world-transformative qualities of the spiritual disposition known as rationality, in the hands of the more materialist modernization theorists, Weberian categories became tools for analyzing and promoting the social and spiritual changes being wrought by the more fundamental process of technological change. Just as Marx used the Hegelian dialectic to read the economic history of mid-nineteenth-century Britain, so the modernization theorists used Parsonian theory to understand the postwar changes in impoverished parts of the regions. By giving Marx a Weberian cleansing, these materialistic modernization theorists had created a Marx who stressed the universalizing qualities of science and technology, rather than a Marx who emphasized class struggle and political praxis in his explanation of modernization.[46] This version of modernization theory proffered a materialistic reading of Parsons and the Parsonian Weber to help explain how technology was changing "traditional societies." These modernization theorists, who rejected Parsons's cultural idealism and instead opted for a kind of post-Marxian materialism, in effect were returning to the "bourgeois materialism" that Marx himself had described in attacks on economists of the 1820s through 1840s.

Psychological Modernization

Although in general, social psychologists found Parsonian systems theory less compelling than sociologists or political scientists did, they would contribute to modernization theory by developing research methods to divine the psychological makeup of modern men. In contrast to political scientists (examined in the next chapter), who were interested in organizational and institutional definitions of modernity, the social psychologists wanted to focus on what modernity meant for the way people felt, valued, perceived, and expressed themselves. As Robert Bellah put it, modernity had to be understood "as a spiritual phenomenon or a kind of mentality."[47] Modernity, in other words, was a state of mind. As with Parsons's own project, the social psychologists were not merely interested in understanding the "modern mind." They were interested in developing techniques to allow them to influence men into the modern mind-set and, somewhat less often, to ease this often painful process. They wanted to discover the key tools for "making men modern."

In terms of its influence on other social scientific disciplines, psychology reached its apogee in the 1950s, and this influence extended to modernization theory. Modernization theory's ability to assimilate other social scientific methods into its basic framework meant that as psychological thinking became popular, modernization theorists adopted psychological discourse as one of the ways to buttress their own claims. Chapter 5 examines how Erik Erikson's developmental psychology, especially his notion of a late adolescent identity crisis, influenced Lucian Pye, one of the pioneers of "political development" theory. Scholars like Gabriel Almond and Walt Rostow also understood Communism as a form of psychopathology. But before examining how psychology inflected modernization theory in political science, let us consider the work of two actual social psychologists from the DSR, Alex Inkeles and David McClelland, who themselves have often been identified as modernization theorists.

Alex Inkeles and Making Men Modern

Alex Inkeles began his career at Harvard studying social change in the Soviet Union at the Russian Research Center. Although Inkeles considered the Soviet state a totalitarian monstrosity, his study of the Soviet people gradually convinced him that Russia had overcome its "backwardness" and had at last achieved a kind of psychosocial parallelism with the West.[48] The tests he created in the 1960s to measure "Overall Modernity," what he called the "OM scale," were derived with reference to the ideals the Soviets were trying to inculcate in their citizens, namely eschewing the "traditional Russian fatalism" in favor of rationality, consciousness, and purposiveness. While he did not claim that there was no difference in psychology between "socialist man" and "capitalist man," he argued that both these "modern" types had more in common than either did with "traditional man." From the late 1950s onward, Inkeles widened his attention from an exclusive focus on the Soviet Union to consider what made people living in modern society different from those living in what he termed "traditional society."

Becoming Modern was Alex Inkeles's magnum opus. Although published in 1974 (by which time Inkeles had departed the DSR for Stanford), Inkeles had completed the basic theoretical work fifteen years earlier.[49] Inkeles conceived of his work as a quantitative testing of the hypotheses of modernization theory. It represented the fruit of a decade and a half of detailed empirical investigation in six countries—East Pakistan (Bangladesh), Nigeria, Chile, India, Argentina, and Israel—all of which were undergoing industrialization. Based on interviews with 5,600 young men (like McClelland, he interviewed only men), Inkeles believed he had evidence that the process of industrialization resulted in broadly similar psychosocial transformations in each country. Indeed, a striking feature of the book is that there is no discussion of any differences between the experiences of the men in these disparate countries. As far as Inkeles was concerned, "what defines man as modern in one country also defines him as modern in another."[50] The experience of modernity, in other words, was a universal one.

Inkeles asserted that since modern economies and polities required a modern citizenry, the most important question for social psychology was what made people modern. Inkeles began with a definition of what he called the "syndrome" of modernity. The modern attitude included the following traits, all of which tended to correlate with one another:

1. An openness to new experience
2. The assertion of increasing independence from "traditional" authority figures
3. A belief in the efficacy of science and medicine; an abandonment of "passivity"
4. High occupational and professional ambition
5. A preference for people to be on time
6. Strong interest and active participation in civic and community affairs and politics
7. Striving to "keep up with the news," especially international news[51]

"Which end of the continuum was considered modern and which was considered traditional," Inkeles remarked rather cryptically, "was determined theoretically."[52] This theory, in its essentials, was that of Talcott Parsons.

Modernity was neither an inbred characteristic nor a national trait. Instead it was something learned through "particular life experiences." Certain critical institutions provided the crucial "experiences of modernity." The factory was

the most important institution. Although "there was more to national development than a high GNP," Inkeles said that he derived "his conception of the
modern man in part from the forms of conduct [he] saw as likely to be inculcated by work in the factory, which [he] took to be the epitome of the institutional pattern of modern civilization."[53] His slogan was, "The factory can be a
school—a school for modernization."[54] Schools were themselves crucial institutions for remaking traditional men into modern men. According to Inkeles, the
mass media, schooling, and experience working in a factory accounted for 90
percent of the variance in determining whether men had a "modern" mentality. Inkeles's definition of "modern man" as a product of the factory recalls
Adorno's dry remark that Marx wanted to turn the world into a factory. Indeed,
Inkeles defended Marx explicitly, noting that "Marx the social psychologist
stands up better than Marx the economist. Marx enunciated the principle that
man's relation to the means of production determines his consciousness. . . .
Marx clearly took a broader view of consciousness, using the term to stand for
basic social values, attitudes, needs, and dispositions, much as a contemporary
social psychologist would speak of personality."[55] In other words, according to
Inkeles, Marx had gotten the psychology of modernization just about right.

David McClelland's Need for Achievement

Trained as a social psychologist at Missouri and Yale universities, David
McClelland began his work on achievement motivation in 1947 when he was
teaching at Wesleyan University, working on research funded by the Office of
Naval Research.[56] The 1949-50 academic year he spent as a fellow at the DSR
encouraged him to locate his work within a larger body of social theory. His
1953 book, *The Achievement Motive,* studied how to measure and arouse in
human subjects the need for achievement—a category that McClelland never
defined but which seems to have amounted, more or less, to materialist ambition.[57] The research began by assuming that the need for achievement was like
the need for food: the longer one went without it, the more one wanted it. To
the contrary, McClelland and his collaborators discovered that some individuals seemed to have a greater intrinsic need to achieve than others.
McClelland later referred to this need as "*n* Ach." He measured *n* Ach in his
subjects—all high school or college-aged males—by showing them a set of
slides and then asking them to write a narrative recounting what they had
seen. He then counted how frequently they stated achievement goals within
these narratives. Based on a model that took individual *n* Ach levels as the

dependent variable and "the family dynamic" as the independent variable,[58] the research revealed that "unaccepting" and highly authoritarian parents (especially authoritarian mothers) produced sons with relatively high n Ach. Indulgent mothers, on the other hand, produced the worst results.

In 1956 McClelland left Wesleyan to join the permanent staff of the DSR, where he soon set about to apply his work on human motivation to the problem of development. The result became his most celebrated work, *The Achieving Society* (1961). While he did mildly criticize Parsons's use of the pattern variables (for neglecting the matter of achievement motivation), his basic approach operated within Parsons's framework of assumptions about modernization. For example, McClelland assumed that modernization was an inevitable and beneficial process that proceeded more or less evenly in all spheres. He asserted that "traditional norms *must* give way to new ones."[59] He assumed, moreover, that the psychological causes and effects of modernization were the same everywhere. The aim of McClelland's book was to determine "the factors underlying [the English Industrial] Revolution which were common to other such waves of rapid economic development." Like the others at the DSR, McClelland had read the economists and found their work to be inadequate for explaining development. Economics went astray by assuming that utility maximization and the profit motive existed in everyone in equal measure. More specifically, he took issue with Walt Rostow and Max Millikan's argument that the best way to spur economic growth was to pour capital into postcolonial countries in the form of foreign aid (on Rostow and Millikan, see chapter 5). Noting that Rostow and Millikan had "neglected the human factor, namely motivation," McClelland argued that entrepreneurship could serve as a substitute for capital in poor countries, and indeed, that without the presence of high levels of entrepreneurialism, foreign aid might simply go to waste. After cheerfully admitting in the preface that he knew practically nothing about history, McClelland examined the historical record and found that empirically, the existence of entrepreneurship correlated closely with the existence of high levels of n Ach in the society. McClelland "proved" this hypothesis by testing the contemporary n Ach levels in several countries, notably Japan, Germany, the United States, and Brazil. It turned out that the n Ach levels for each of these countries corresponded quite closely to their current growth rates. Moreover, both growth rate and n Ach correlated with the existence of high levels of entrepreneurship. There seemed to be good evidence, then, that these elements might all be linked.[60]

McClelland proposed, therefore, that a "social experiment"[61] might be run in which policies to increase *n* Ach would be introduced into one country while another country was "held constant" as a control group. He suggested that the most effective way to achieve this augmentation of *n* Ach would be "to try to change the parental habits of child-rearing," though he conceded that this scientific ideal might encounter resistance from "backward" and "tradition-minded" peoples.[62] The important thing to note is how casually McClelland could propose radical interventions into the family (presumably to make fathers less "dominating" and more "unaccepting" and mothers more "authoritarian"—since this elevated *n* Ach) that would have caused conservatives and liberals alike to scream, had these interventions been foisted upon Americans. Alas, McClelland was never able to implement such an experiment. Instead, he settled for a more modest anthropological comparison of two Mexican villages in Chiapas, one of which had recently been converted to Protestantism while the other remained Catholic.

Citing Max Weber's thesis on the Protestant work ethic, McClelland hypothesized that Protestantism produced higher *n* Ach levels. McClelland took the Calvinist striving for this-worldly evidence of salvation as equivalent to the need for achievement. Having substituted *n* Ach for the this-worldly drive of the Calvinists, McClelland followed Weber in arguing that this psychological quality often manifested itself in entrepreneurialism. Comparison of the two villages revealed that in the decade since the conversion, the Protestant village had outperformed its neighboring Catholic village economically, a result judged mainly from the cleaner appearance of the village. McClelland took this as evidence that Protestantism led to higher *n* Ach, and that this in turn had led to entrepreneurialism. McClelland assumed that the Protestantism was the only thing that had changed in the two villages. He failed to consider that the missionaries who had performed the conversion might also have led a cleanup campaign and that in any event, cleanliness alone scarcely indicated increased *n* Ach, much less entrepreneurialism. On a theoretical level, moreover, the analysis inserted not one but three assumed causal links between the conversion and the cleanliness—namely, that the conversion increased *n* Ach, which then contributed to increased entrepreneurialism, which contributed to prosperity, which ultimately manifested itself in increased cleanliness. Even assuming that these linkages in fact existed, it would seem odd that a mere ten years of Protestantism would have significantly raised entrepreneurialism, since *n* Ach levels were supposed to result from child-rearing practices. In other words, it ought to take at least a generation for Protestant conversion to increase *n* Ach scores, and hence at least a generation for it to contribute to entrepreneurialism. The case of McClelland can be read most charitably as a cautionary tale about the dangers of mapping a solid research project onto the latest trendy "theory." What is truly amazing is that no one called McClelland to task either for his pernicious research proposals or for his shoddy analysis. No doubt this is because in 1961, most in the American academy agreed with his basic assumptions.

Modernization as Convergence

The most important of those assumptions was that development entailed a universal convergence on a monolithic "modernity." While debates flourished about its normative and positive features, its necessary and sufficient conditions, or how to achieve it, most postwar American social scientists agreed that development meant achieving a unique goal: modernity. From time immemorial, "traditional" people had been mired in a myriad of varied and discrete traditional practices, the description and cataloguing of which has been the primary responsibility of anthropologists and archaeologists. And yet, beneath that apparent diversity there existed a fundamental unity. All of these times and places shared low productivity, superstition, and technological stagnation, to mention only a few features. In this sense, "tradition," for all the diversity encompassed by that term, was itself a unity. The first transition away from tradition had taken place in northwest Europe, and this process had eventually been exported to the rest of the world. Shils stated this point emphatically: "Historically, the modern type of society has originated only once, in the Western world, and hence its transformative effect on the rest of human society and culture must be understood from that base line, a fact which is at least implicit in the extremely wide contemporary concern with the problems of 'modernization.'"[63] All modernization theorists agreed that this "transformative effect" resulted in great turbulence for the countries concerned. This turbulence made it crucial for the postcolonial countries to think about the lessons that might be learned from the history of the "first movers." Whether it was Parsons arguing that specific, universalistic, achievement-oriented values were the hallmark of modernity; or it was McClelland declaring that a population with high *n* Ach would create modernity; or it was Inkeles claiming that the factory experience created "modern" notions about family, life, and politics, modernization theorists agreed that modernization was a consubstantial phenomenon which again and again, regardless of time and place, worked the same basic results for the same basic reasons. The world was homogenizing: all countries, insofar as they were "modern," would eventually look more or less alike, and modern people would all think, act, feel, and behave more or less alike. The notion that the world was converging from a panoply of traditional lifeways onto a single and universal modernity was the central leitmotif of modernization theory.

Two factors accounted for the convergent tendencies of contemporary global civilization. First was the role of elites. All modernizing societies were led by "modernizing elites," who by definition possessed "modern" psychocultural traits. These elites would bend (possibly recalcitrant) populations to their modernizing will. The tautological nature of this argument did not seem to jar its proponents, such as Shils or David Apter. The second reason for convergence lay in technological diffusion. As William Form put it, "Stripped of its ideological baggage, the convergence hypothesis is a version of technological determinism."[64] Having denied class struggle a causal role in history, Rostow suggested that "[i]n Britain and the well-endowed parts of the world populated substantially from Britain the proximate stimulus for take-off was mainly, but not wholly, technological."[65] Even someone as averse to technological determinism as Parsons agreed that factories, the media, and bureaucracies were destined to crowd out older ways of producing, communicating, and organizing. Parsons's student Marion Levy used a linear scale based on the use of inanimate power sources and tools to measure the "degree" of modernization.[66] Complex machinery, McClelland claimed, "represents symbolically the new age, introduces a new kind of social mobility and ultimately should spread attitudes typical of the modern era."[67] According to the modernization theorists, there was only one form of technological modernity (albeit an everevolving one).

The second crucial assumption of modernization theory was that the United States (and perhaps Europe) had already all but "completed" modernity. As possessors of both unimpeachably "modern" elites and the highest technology available, "the West" was essentially synonymous with modernity. Modernization was understood as an asymptotic approach toward an ideal-typical baseline; the United States was so close to that baseline that for analytical purposes, it had achieved modernity. In effect, that meant that the present of the United States and Europe represented the future of the "underdeveloped" lands. As the MIT Center for International Studies admitted in 1961, "Implicit . . . in the use of such words as 'transitional' and 'modernizing' are some basic assumptions which we have asserted rather than proved—that is, that these societies are indeed going through a process which will produce in them social and economic changes parallel to those which have occurred in modern Western states."[68] Those scholars studying postcolonial politics made the same assumption of convergence; as Robert Ward put it, "The concept of 'political modernization' rests upon the hope that it validly and objectively defines the essential features of the political developments which have occurred in all so-called advanced societies and that it also represents the pattern toward which politically underdeveloped societies are now evolving."[69] Likewise, Cyril Black observed that his fellow modernization theorists tended "to assume that the Western pattern will be reproduced all over the world in all its aspects. Indeed, modernization is frequently thought of as a process by which non-Western societies are transformed along Western lines."[70]

At the same time, during the period of transition, there were better and worse paths to the convergence. Although materially the transformation was similar everywhere, there existed sharply divergent cultural and especially different political ways of attaining modernity. According to Walt Rostow, for example, from a material perspective, modernization always entailed the identical replication of five stages of economic growth. Technological improvement, capital accumulation, and growing GNP proceeded in a strictly evolutionary manner. Rostow would have been the first to point out, however, that from a political or cultural perspective, the transition was hardly unilinear. In Rostow's view, there were in fact two political paths to modernity: the democratic-capitalist method of the "free world" and the totalitarian method that the Soviet Union employed. (Repressed in this model were fascist paths to modernity, which were perhaps still relevant in certain postcolonial contexts.) But regardless of the political-cultural trajectory employed, all countries were destined to wend their way toward a uniform industrial modernity. What is crucial to note is that *Communism represented a morbid path to modernity, not a deviation from it.* As Shils put it, darkly, "There is no straight and easy road to the city of modernity. Whatever the main road chosen, there will be many tempting and ruinous side roads; there will be many marshes and wastes on either side, and many wrecked aspirations will lie there, rusting and gathering dust. . . . Yet, some roads are better than others; some destinations are better than others."[71] Belying their strictly anti-Communist image, modernization theorists tended to see the Soviet Union being increasingly similar to the United States, in that both were manifestations of modernity.[72] In Talcott Parsons's words, "underneath the ideological conflicts [between capitalism and Communism] that have been so prominent, there has been emerging an important element of wide consensus at the level of values, centering in the complex we often refer to as 'modernization.'"[73] Although there might be several cultural-political paths to a completed modernity, at the end of the day, that modernity was bound to look pretty similar everywhere—not just on a material level but also from a cultural and political point view.

Several policy implications follow from this philosophy of history. First, because capitalist modernity has been "completed" there, the United States and Western Europe were no longer susceptible to the Communist disease—technocratic tinkering would solve all problems in these societies. (The modernization theorists were elitist but liberal anti-Communists, not populist right-wing McCarthyites.) Conservatism was the order of the day at home. Second, there was no point in confronting the Soviets directly, since they were already embarked on their pathological path to modernity. Once the choice has been made, intervention would do little good (although undermining ongoing Communist modernization projects could help provide evidence that Communism was a poor means of modernization). Thus, the goal of American policy ought to be to coop the Soviets up and wait patiently for them to "converge" with the United States. The convergence hypothesis thus provided theoretical justification for the containment policy that formed the basis for postwar American policy toward the Soviet Union. Third, the real point of conflict—the point where intervention was necessary—was in countries beginning to undergo the transition process. Military attention should be directed toward these areas in order to "inoculate" them from the Communist "contagion." As the next two chapters show, these were precisely the conclusions of the political scientists who would map the political realities of the postwar years onto the assumption that the historical tendency was toward convergence on a universal modernity. It was also as a formalization of the convergence hypothesis that modernization theory would exercise its widest intellectual influence.

The Lonely Crowd and Demographic Transition

The convergence hypothesis found many subscribers outside the fold of the DSR and development studies. Consider David Riesman's work of 1951, *The*

Lonely Crowd, not a work usually associated with modernization theory.[74] In this book, Riesman argued that Americans were undergoing an epochal transformation of their consciousness and character. Specifically, American men (like much of modernization theory later, Riesman's argument applied much more to men than to women) were in the process of transition from what Riesman called "inner-direction" to "other-direction." Paralleling Rostow's early three-stage theory of tradition → takeoff → maturity, Riesman elaborated a three-stage theory in which "tradition-directed" social characters gave way to "inner-directed" characters before finally yielding to "other-directed" character types. Although conceived, researched, and written in the late 1940s, a decade before modernization theory would come into its own, the intellectual architecture of *The Lonely Crowd* shows how modernization theory's normative framework first issued as a way to understand the United States.

The point of departure for Riesman's scheme was the notion of "the demographic transition," a newfangled theory being promoted by Frank Notestein and his colleagues at the Office of Population Research at Princeton University.[75] The theory itself was simple enough: in "traditional" societies, population was fairly stable, with high birthrates balanced by high death rates. During the transition, high birthrates and death rates were replaced by lower ones; a lag invariably took place between the drop in death rates and the drop in fertility, creating a population "explosion." Eventually, a new population "equilibrium" would emerge, characterized by relatively low fertility and mortality rates. Though such typologies of European demographic patterning had appeared as early as 1929,[76] these descriptions would be elevated in the postwar period to a universal diachronic "theory" that claimed that all countries of the world would eventually replicate the demographic experiences of Western Europe.[77] Notestein and his brilliant protégée Irene Taeuber claimed that the "transitional" process that had already taken place in Western Europe and the United States would soon be reiterated throughout the world. Postwar American social scientists would embrace the notion of a demographic transition in part because of the rise of modernization theory, which would place demographic transition theory within a more encompassing metahistorical narrative. Modernization theory and demographic transition theory, in short, were mutually reinforcing analytical frameworks.

Although in the 1940s Taeuber and Notestein did not concern themselves very much with the sociological causes of changing fertility patterns, insofar as they did so, they foreshadowed the arguments of the modernization theorists: "As industrialization extends over time and expands over wider segments of a nation," Taeuber explained in 1950, "the demographic transition of declining mortality and declining fertility becomes a necessary consequence of the accompanying economic pressures and cultural stimuli."[78] Although demographic transition theory countered the old racist claim that the Asian masses were essentially and almost limitlessly fertile, it also justified the continuation of prewar antifertility programs in Asia and Latin America by deracinating the programs of eugenicists and translating them into the idiom of modernization.[79] Taeuber and Notestein noted that with the experience of "industrialization, urbanization, and technological modernization,"[80] Japan had undergone the same demographic shift as the West. Typifying a modernist universalism, Taeuber and Notestein argued that cultural differences made almost no difference in this process and that other Asian countries would soon copy Japan's experience. In a process of circularly reinforcing argumentation, the theory of the demographic transition would also become conventional wisdom for modernization theorists. Rostow, for example, would observe that "[i]t is clear that the rapid growth in population makes difficult a rapid increase in human welfare in Asia," but cheered himself, with reference to the theory of the demographic transition, by noting that "such population increases are normal at this stage of Asian history."[81]

Taking the proto-modernization theory of the demographic transition as his point of theoretical departure, Riesman proceeded to elaborate a schema for explaining how these changes in macrodemographics produced different sorts of dynamics within individual family units and hence changes in the "social character" of different societies. In good Durkheimian manner, Riesman argued that the primary goal of every society was to secure social solidarity. "Malthusian" demographic regimes of high fertility and high mortality produced societies in which the "culture, in addition to its economic tasks, or as part of them, provides ritual, routine, and religion to occupy and to orient everyone. Little energy is directed toward finding new solutions of the age-old problems, let us say, of agricultural technique or medicine." In the West, "the Middle Ages" had been the period of tradition-direction, and in this milieu of closed and unchanging communities, *shame* had functioned as the primary psychological mechanism for securing conformity. During the "early industrial period" in the West, as mortality declined and family sizes "exploded," the outward forms of shaming had given way to feelings "implanted early in life by the elders and directed toward generalized but nonetheless inescapably destined goals." As a result, *guilt* became the primary mode of securing obedience and commitment to social norms. Finally, in the "advanced industrial" period, "other-directed" men emerged whose social conformity was secured through *anxiety* about the judgments of peers (rather than the judgments of elders).[82]

Though Riesman intended this final point as a critique of contemporary American culture (and indeed, he spent the bulk of the book showing how "other-direction" contributed to various unfortunate features of postwar American life), modernization theorists would instead read it as a useful prototype for putting together the different elements of the modernization process. Riesman insisted throughout his volume that he was not describing reality so much as constructing ideal types—just as many of the modernization theorists did. But he gave himself away by claiming that these "ideal types" mapped onto actual, concrete places like China, Russia, or the United States. Since the demographic transition was a fact of developmental life, other countries were bound to undergo a similar transition, which logically meant that China would eventually become more like the Soviet Union, and both of these would become more like the United States. If Riesman remained vague about the ultimate causal element in his schema, there was no question that it all fit together neatly, as shown in table 1.

Table 1. *Structure and Function in David Riesman's* The Lonely Crowd *(1951)*

"Direction"	Demographic Pattern	Dominant Economic Sphere	World	Conformity Mechanism	Coeval Example
Traditional	High fertility/ High mortality	Primary (extraction)	Third ("Others")	Shame	China
Inner	High fertility/ Low mortality	Secondary (industry)	Second ("them")	Guilt	Russia
Other	Low fertility/ Low mortality	Tertiary (services)	First ("the West")	Anxiety	United States

Scholars with a greater appreciation for the irreducible messiness of authentic reality might have remarked that it all fit together a little *too neatly*. Even though the *normative* dimension of Riesman's argument constituted a critique of the conformism and anxieties of postwar American life, later modernization theorists would take from it only its *positive* analytical structure. And rather than use it to criticize the United States, they would use it to celebrate the contemporary United States as a representation of the foreordained future of the postcolonial world.

In his discussions of tradition-, inner-, and other-directed character types, Riesman crafted broad generalizations that the literature on modernization would echo for the next two decades. Just as Riesman claimed that changes in family structure resulting from the demographic transition had proven decisive in creating the character transformations that accompanied development, so, too, would McClelland argue that family structure was crucial for creating the psychological circumstances necessary for "achievement orientation." Riesman suggested that the tradition-direction of members of Malthusian societies had a "stagnatory" life attitude; that the inner-direction of transitional societies created the iron will that was both appropriate and necessary for countries undergoing industrialization; and that other-direction was the natural result of a society in which the main point of consumption was not subsistence but "keeping up with the Joneses." Contemporary American men no longer secured their identity by mastering and leading the process of production, as had inner-directed men; instead, their identity emerged from the process of learning how to negotiate the complicated symbolic world of consumer goods available in what Rostow would celebrate a decade later as "the Age of High Mass Consumption." *The Lonely Crowd* was a prototypical work of modernization theory in its unargued assumptions about the interconnected and convergent patterns of demographic, psychological, social, and even political change.

Clark Kerr, the Industrial Man

If *The Lonely Crowd* represented a nascent effort to understand the manifold changes that accompanied, caused, and were created by "the transition," then a much more explicit attempt would be made over the next decade by another group of American social scientists, led by industrial sociologist and later University of California president Clark Kerr, to theorize more precisely the process of convergent modernization. Kerr made his first statement of the problem in November 1953 at a conference at Cornell University entitled "Human Resources and Labor Relations in Underdeveloped Countries." The research following this conference, performed in the same collaborative manner that the DSR had championed in producing *Toward a General Theory of Action*, would culminate in a volume entitled *Industrialism and Industrial Man* (1960). Because the project had been completed before Shils's June 1959 espousal and celebration of the term *modernization,* Kerr used the term *industrialization* instead. Kerr employed this term, however, to mean the same thing his contemporaries would mean when they used the term *modernization:* industrialization, Kerr explained (tautologically), was the "transition from the traditional society toward industrialism."[83]

Kerr's contributions are emblematic of the technocratic moment in modernization theory. Kerr had inherited the term *industrialism* from the godfather of technocratic thought, Claude Henri de Rouvroy, Lecomte de Saint-Simon, who used it to designate an economy in which wealth derived from production and machinery rather than through seizure and war. In Kerr's usage, *industrialism* was a synonym for the labor-related dimensions of modernity. *Industrialism and Industrial Man* provided both a description of labor relations at the terminus of the industrialization process (something that Kerr believed had already been more or less achieved in the United States) and an analysis of how industrialism could be achieved in postcolonial countries. In attempting to theorize these two problems simultaneously, Kerr and his collaborators based their reflections on labor problems in the postcolonial world on their understanding of what was going on at home. The understanding of how to implement industrialization in the postcolonial world developed dialectically out of reflections about labor relations at home. The ideal of technocracy bound together the organizational questions that Kerr believed faced all three worlds of development.

Kerr argued that industrialization was a convergent process in which the lifeways of rich countries inexorably displaced anciens régimes in postcolonial settings. "Industrialization came into a most varied world," Kerr explained, "a world with many cultures, at many stages of development from the primitiveness of quasi-animal life to high levels of civilization, under the rules of many different elites and beliefs. . . . Into the midst of this disparity of systems there intruded a new and vastly superior technique of production; a technique which by its very nature always pushed for identity since the modern was always the more superior. This technique knew no geographical limits; recognized no elites or ideologies. Once unleashed upon the world, the new technique kept spreading and kept advancing." The result of this convergence would be a homogenized world in which "the differences will be between and among individuals and groups rather than between and among the major geographical areas of the world." Like Parsons, Kerr believed he had grasped the essence of modernity. His breathtaking historical vision pictured an immense technological force, driven by its own internal and irresistible logic, sweeping away all hitherto existing societies. But unlike Parsons, Kerr believed that the new culture would utterly erase the old forms as a "new culture based on mass tastes and mass consumption . . . gradually overwhelms the many and varied preexisting cultures. It is the great transformation—successful, all-embracing, irreversible." The essential unifying force was technology: "The same technology calls for the same occupational structure around the world. . . . Social arrangements will be most uniform from one society to another when they are most closely tied to technology." As in the case of the early development economics, any "traditional" cultural differences that slowed the process of industrialization were dismissed as mere "obstacles," destined to be socially engineered into the dustbin of history.[84]

Kerr asserted that mankind's destiny lay in "pluralist industrialism"—a technologically advanced society composed of decentralized but collaborative groups of managers. Like Shils or Parsons, Kerr shared with Weber (and Soviet apparatchiks) a vision of industrialism as a society administered by those who had received scientific training at what Kerr elsewhere referred to as "the multiversity."[85] Like Saint-Simon (and fellow modernization theorists Alex Inkeles and Daniel Lerner), Kerr believed that industrialism called for "new men"— engineers, builders, planners—who would lead the new society.[86] "Industrial society must be administered," Kerr explained, adding that as industrialism takes hold, "the administrators become increasingly benevolent and increasingly skilled. They learn to respond where response is required; to anticipate the inevitable. The benevolent political bureaucracy and the benevolent economic oligarchy are matched with the tolerant mass."[87] This sense of the inexorable effectiveness of bureaucracies was inherited from Weber but unencumbered by any of Weber's misgivings about the suffocation—"sensualists without spirit, specialists without heart"[88]—that accompanied a bureaucratized modernity. Not once did Kerr express doubt that the lives of modern men and women were, in all relevant ways, superior to those of premodern humans. And neither Weber nor Kerr nor any of the modernization theorists anticipated how often postcolonial bureaucracies would descend into self-serving incompetence or worse.

Having established that convergence was both inevitable and salutary, Kerr next asked what institutional arrangements would best maintain the stability and continuity of the work process. Kerr claimed that this technical question transcended the usual left versus right ideological debates, or at any rate, the

Soviet-American struggle. For both systems, heightened control over workers was the means of creating stability. "The structuring of this web of rule," Kerr argued in 1955, "must be undertaken regardless of the form of industrialization, in Russia and the United States alike."[89] Industrialization required the same "new rules and relationships" regardless of the social, political, or institutional milieu within which they took place.[90] Kerr echoed modernization theory's tenet that the Soviet and American industrial systems were "converging." Although Kerr made sure to add that "pluralistic industrialism will never reach a final equilibrium," he, like other modernization theorists, believed in some sort of asymptotic convergence on an arrangement very close to the system the United States had already achieved.

As the "superstructural" counterpart to the "materialism" of the convergence hypothesis, the end of ideology debate was very much in Kerr's mind during the writing of *Industrialism and Industrial Man*. Raymond Aron had been among the first to suggest that the Soviet Union was coming around to a pragmatic rather than ideological attitude toward social and economic organization. Aron concluded that "by various paths, spontaneously or with the help of the police, the two great societies [the United States and the Soviet Union] have suppressed the conditions of ideological debate, integrated the workers, and imposed consensus."[91] Echoing Aron, Clark Kerr stated that the point of departure for *Industrialism and Industrial Man* had been the "sense of the decline of the importance of competing ideologies. More and more, the questions are technical as well as philosophical. . . . Rather than two fixed points, there are several changing ones; technicians are taking their place along with the social theorists."[92] At the end of the industrialization process, Kerr explained, "the age of ideology fades," replaced by an age of "realism." Kerr would have found little to disagree with in Daniel Bell's 1973 account of why ideology was ending: "While the phrase 'technological imperative' is too rigid and deterministic, in all industrial societies there are certain common constraints which tend to shape similar actions and force the use of common techniques. . . . From this point of view there are some common characteristics for all industrial societies: the technology is everywhere the same. . . . Ideology, to this extent, becomes irrelevant and is replaced by 'economics' in the guise of production functions, capital output rations, marginal efficiency of capital, linear programming and the like."[93] Unlike Kerr, however, Bell had the wisdom to foresee that politics would never be abolished, that it would always exist "prior to" the rationally administered world, and that it was always liable to upset that world.[94]

Like other modernization theorists, Kerr believed that American society by 1960 had transcended the class struggle and happily given itself over to technocrats. In other words, if the Soviet Union was verging on what Kerr referred to as "industrial pluralism," then the United States was already there. "History has seldom if ever proved a theorist to be so incorrect and at the same time so influential as Marx," Kerr explained. "The wave of the future may more nearly be middle-class democracy . . . than the 'dictatorship of the proletariat' (which, in fact, is the dictatorship of a single party)."[95] Making the same assumption of an unlimited horizon of endless growth and political stability, the MIT Center for International Studies would echo Kerr by asserting that "[a]s economic growth becomes a permanent condition in capitalist, democratic societies, it has proved possible to distribute the fruits of modernization so as to avoid the bloody class conflicts on which Marx counted and to avert the progressively more acute crises of unemployment which he believed would inevitably lead advanced societies into Communism."[96] The end of ideology argument assumed that growing the economic pie could help resolve the distributional issues that were, postwar liberals believed, the fundamental cause of political conflict.

Having established a technocratic world as the pot of gold and the end of the rainbow of industrialization, the major concern of the volume was how the "underdeveloped" countries could best achieve industrialism. Kerr differentiated himself from more Marx-influenced modernization theorists like Rostow by stressing the multiplicity of paths to industrialism. Kerr argued that where "Marx had seen a unilinear course to history; we see a multilinear one. There are several roads, *each of which leads to industrialism*."[97] Although Kerr suggested that the force of technology would relentlessly lead to a globalization of "pluralist industrialism," some room did remain for human agency to advance or impede this outcome. Invoking Weber, Kerr claimed that any one of several groups of "industrializing elites"—including political leaders, industrial organization builders, top military officers, associated intellectuals, and sometimes leaders of labor organizations—could take charge of the development process, each with their own "style and emphasis." In strongly led feudal or quasi-feudal regimes, the dynastic elites could themselves lead the process; in commercial societies, the middle classes would lead; in weakly led feudal or colonial regimes, "nationalists" would lead, or if they failed, "revolutionary intellectuals" would take over; while in "primitive" systems, colonial administrators would lead (at least until they had created a "colonial" society, at which point, presumably, nationalist leaders would take over).

Interestingly, this typology of appropriate developmental regimes accurately described the *actually existing leadership of virtually every poor country in 1958*. Every regime on earth, in other words, was a developmental regime being led by the appropriate elite (as indeed they all claimed). The good was also the true, and all was for the best in the world's current political arrangements: the Africans had their colonial leaders, the South Asians had their U Nu and their Nehru, the Europeans had their middle classes, the Eastern bloc their revolutionary intellectuals, and in due course they would all end up more or less resembling the United States. The only wiggle room in the model was that if nationalists did not make adequate alliances with the indigenous middle class, revolutionary intellectuals threatened to displace them. Though this outcome ought to be avoided if possible, it would not be disastrous in any event, since the force of technology meant that sooner or later, everyone would end up governed by a "managerial elite" resembling no one so much as . . . well, to tell the truth, no one so much as Clark Kerr and his collaborators.

CHAPTER 4

The Rise of Modernization Theory in Political Science

The SSRC's Committee on Comparative Politics

A new science of politics is needed for a new world.
—ALEXIS DE TOCQUEVILLE, *Democracy in America*, 1845

As the example of the Department of Social Relations (DSR) in the last chapter began to show, the promulgation of modernization theory flowed through specific institutional channels. These institutions constituted networks in which the lines between personal friendship, intellectual accord, and the emergence of social scientific consensus were often hard to determine. Relying on an archive containing, among other things, private correspondence between various political scientists, this chapter will examine in detail the way one of these institutional networks, the Committee on Comparative Politics (CCP) of the Social Science Research Council (SSRC), helped to fashion the emergent scholarly consensus on modernization theory. These scholars would take an existing field of scholarship, the comparative study of political institutions in traditional great powers, and transform it into a field dedicated to understanding how the politics of the postcolonial world differed from that of the industrialized world. To do this, they would develop a new theoretical foundation for comparative politics, drawing on the theorizing being done at the DSR about the nature of modernity and the process through which nations achieved modernity, and especially on Edward Shils's translation of the Parsonian project into political terms. If they adopted the work of the DSR, however, the view of modernization that the political scientists would propose would be significantly darker than that of the sociologists. More anti-Communist than Parsons and more focused on the application of modernity to the postcolonial world than on its domestic manifestations, these scholars did not believe that modernization was going to be an easy process or that modernity would replace tradition wholesale. Rather, they would critically adopt Parsonian modernization theory to ground their own efforts to make political science more "scientific" and to provide (1) an overall narrative of the process of development; (2) an ideal-type or, more basically, a comprehensive vision of the ideal end point of development; and (3) a discursive lodestone to unify a series of inquiries into postcolonial politics which otherwise threatened to veer off in unpredictable, uncontrolled directions.

Looking back on the eventual influence the CCP would wield, Hans Daadler commented, "Under the leadership of Gabriel Almond [the CCP] became so influential that for the academic community the short term 'the Committee' usually suffices."[1] By examining how this group of young Turks transformed the field of comparative politics, we can observe how a social scientific paradigm emerges from a set of disparate ideas to become an actionable research agenda. The early history of the CCP exemplifies many of Thomas Kuhn's theories about the sociological basis for scientific consensus. The case of the CCP will show, most notably, how consensus about development and "modernization" as the keys to understanding postcolonial politics was reached not so much through active persuasion of doubters as through the exclusion of rival viewpoints.

Rethinking Comparative Politics

Formed in the 1920s using Rockefeller monies, the SSRC was from the beginning organized around topical committees. These committees performed two functions. First, they provided a forum where social scientists from different universities and departments interested in similar problems could debate issues of mutual concern. Second, by channeling funds from places like Ford, Rockefeller, and Carnegie, SSRC committees supplied crucial funding for work in these same areas, with the ultimate aim of providing the social sciences with the same pride of place that the natural sciences had enjoyed since the late nineteenth century. By providing a locus for training, organization, communications, and funding, SSRC committees throughout the twentieth century have been highly influential in their given areas of interest. Some of the best-known committees of the early postwar period were interdisciplinary. For example, the Committee on Economic Growth included political scientists, sociologists, and anthropologists in addition to economists, and the Committee on Political Behavior included both sociologists and political scientists.

The CCP was unusual in that it was composed only of political scientists, but the interdisciplinary interests of its leading members vitiated this monodisciplinary background of the committee's personnel.

In addition to these general functions, during the 1940s and 1950s the SSRC took an active role in promoting the pan-disciplinary revolution of behavioralism, a program that aimed to raise the social sciences to the same level of rigor and respect that the natural sciences enjoyed. Behavioralism was the revolutionary methodology of one of the SSRC's founders, Charles Merriam of the University of Chicago.[2] In 1921 had Merriam published his behavioralist manifesto, *The Present State of the Study of Politics*, which proposed that to become more "scientific," the study of politics ought to first, focus on the sociological and psychological bases of political behavior, and second, test these ideas using quantitative methods. Most of the names associated with the postwar behavioralist revolution, such as V. O. Key, David Truman, Herbert Simon, Harold Lasswell, and Gabriel Almond, were students of Merriam. After Merriam's retirement in 1940 and the academic shuffling that resulted from the war, Yale became the center of behavioralism, with such figures as Harold Lasswell, Gabriel Almond, Karl Deutsch, Robert Dahl, and Robert Ward all on the Yale staff during the 1950s. All of these figures would also be linked to modernization theory.

Even its advocates admit that behavioralism is difficult to define. Robert Dahl claimed that behavioralism was, as much as anything else, a mood, including a skepticism about the current intellectual scene, a sympathy with "science," and an optimism about the prospects for improving the practice of political science.[3] Karl Deutsch had a more cynical but suggestive view: "The word 'behavioral' had nothing to do with the old notion of 'behaviorism' in psychology. It was introduced in its new context by Harold Lasswell and his associates because some members of high-level foundation boards objected to the word 'social' science, which seemed to remind them too much of socialism. The term behavioral was politically neutral."[4] Whatever its impetus, behavioralism contained three key components: (1) a focus on observable individual behavior as the locus of social scientific inquiry; (2) an emphasis on empirical and "value-free" methods, aimed at discovering formal laws of social and political processes, to be tested by applying the quantitative sample-and-survey methods being pioneered by Paul Lazarsfeld and others; and (3) an orientation of systematic research to the grand theory of the classic European tradition. Inspired by the epistemological and methodological assumptions of the natural sciences, behavioralism defined itself against "a tradition of ideographic, descriptive, noncumulative, and institutional case studies that had dominated much of the discipline . . . for several decades."[5] Behavioralism has been criticized for its "naïve scientism," but at the moment it arose, it represented a step forward from the "naïve empiricism" that had hitherto dominated political science.[6]

After Merriam retired, the SSRC would become the champion of behavioralism, setting up a special committee to study political behavior. In setting out its reasons for establishing the Committee on Political Behavior (CPB), the SSRC annual report for 1944-45 stated that the council had decided to develop a new interdisciplinary approach to studying political behavior that would be defined by a methodological focus on "the behavior of individuals in political situations" and on "formulating and testing hypotheses concerning uniformities of behavior in different institutional settings."[7] The success of the committee and its members was almost instantaneous. In 1951 CPB member David Truman, with his behavioralist classic *The Governmental Process* hot off the press, wrote, "Political behavior is not and should not be a specialty, for it represents rather an orientation or a point of view which aims at stating all phenomena of government in terms of the observed and observable behavior of men."[8] The CPB made no bones about its revolutionary ambitions: "[P]olitical behavior," it claimed, "is not properly a subfield within political science, but an approach that is relevant to most if not all of the problems within the conventional scope of the discipline."[9] By the early 1950s, what had been a controversial critique of mainstream political science twenty years earlier had emerged to become the dominant center of the profession.

Behavioralism's fascination with the classic nineteenth-century European sociological theory is of critical significance to its relationship to modernization. Discussions of behavioralism often underemphasize this link, but this shared interest is what connected it to the Parsonian theory examined in the last chapter. The founders of the CCP, Pendleton Herring and Gabriel Almond, conceived of the CCP as a vehicle for promoting behavioralism. Even though Parsons was only briefly mentioned in the CCP's initial statement of purpose, the committee would turn to Parsonian theory as its efforts to build a theory of "political development" began in earnest. For the members of the CCP, Parsonian theory complemented behavioralism by providing the "grand theory" foundation for the more microcosmic approach of behavioralist studies. As CCP member Joseph LaPalombara would put it, Parsons's "claims for the scientific objectivity of his emerging general theory [underpinned] the claims of other social scientists who extol the 'scientific' qualities of their disciplines."[10] The systems approach helped behavioralism explain how individuals aggregated into collectivities. The political scientists on the CCP saw themselves as creating intermediate special theories useful for systematic empirical research, but to a large extent they would base these intermediate theories on the systematic theoretical orientation that Parsonian theory provided.

The man responsible for establishing new committees at the SSRC was its president, Edward Pendleton Herring. The sort of figure often ignored in many intellectual histories, Herring exercised his influence more through his organizational abilities than through his own scholarship. A professor of government at Harvard, Herring's own intellectual career had been as a pioneer in the study of "pressure groups"—the various forms of influence peddlers in a democracy who serve as intermediaries between legislators and the interested citizenry. Instead of dismissing these groups as parasites who debilitated the democratic process, as most previous political scientists had done, Herring treated them as legitimate and useful political participants.[11] Just as Herring affirmed the role of institutionalized pressure groups in politics, he saw such pressure groups as having a place within the academic world as well. Indeed, as president of the SSRC, he positioned himself as kingmaker for postwar social science, a sort of one-man pressure group for promoting his ideas about how social science should be conducted.

One of Herring's ideas was to challenge the legal-institutional methodology of his rival at the Harvard Department of Government, Carl Joachim Friedrich. Author of a canonical textbook in comparative politics, *Constitutional Government and Politics* (1937), Friedrich was the dominant figure in American comparative politics during the 1940s.[12] Though he contributed to all areas of political science in his lifetime, Friedrich's work dealt mainly with the interactions and formal political processes within and between political parties and democratic institutions in the Great European Powers, as well as with how social, cultural, and historical forces informed the operation of these institutions. Friedrich's "anti-method," as he called it, was largely descriptive and historical.

In December 1951, Herring penned a brief memorandum describing the need for a more systematic approach to comparative politics, the construction of which he viewed as a good task for a new SSRC committee.[13] Without naming Friedrich specifically, Herring criticized existing comparative politics on two grounds: first, it tended to be descriptive rather than analytical; second, it tended to focus too exclusively on Western Europe. Herring suggested that a good starting point for a more rigorous approach to comparative politics would be an examination of "the history of governance in the non-industrialized areas of the world." In addition to encouraging social scientific rigor, such an approach was motivated by a specific policy question: "What can the study of comparative government offer concerning the viability of democratic institutions in countries lacking the cultural tradition and economic development that have accompanied the growth of representative institutions in Europe and the USA?" Herring circulated this document to comparativists all over the United States as a way of stirring up thought about this matter. The enthusiastic responses Herring received to this memorandum led to a research seminar in the summer of 1952 on the topic of comparative politics, planned with the aid of the CPB.

Consisting of scholars under the age of forty, the 1952 SSRC summer seminar was held at Northwestern University and included Samuel Beer, George Blankstein, Richard Cox, Karl Deutsch, Harry Eckstein, Kenneth Thompson, and Robert Ward. Directing the seminar was a young comparativist at Northwestern named Roy Macridis. An ethnic Greek, Macridis was born Christmas Day 1918 in Istanbul and became a naturalized U.S. citizen in 1944. He attended Athens College in Greece and law school at the Sorbonne before receiving an M.A. and Ph.D. in political science from Harvard, where he was a favorite student of Merle Fainsod, the chair of the government department and an expert in Soviet politics. A few months before the seminar was to begin, Macridis announced that its aim was to produce "comprehensive concepts that transcend individual governmental structures." The result would be a small volume that would outline a new methodology for comparative politics.[14]

In their report on the results of the seminar, the participants began by lamenting the "parochial" (i.e., European) focus of comparative politics. These comparativists hoped to overcome the Eurocentrism of the previous generation of comparativists, as typified by Friedrich. Following the work of various SSRC fellows,[15] the seminar agreed that an "Area Studies approach" would helpfully widen the topical scope of the discipline. The postwar comparativists were the first group of American political scientists to consider non-Western countries worthy of systematic empirical inquiry. However, just as Parsons was proposing at the DSR, this Area Studies approach was not an end in itself but rather the starting point for further theorizing. On a method-ological level, the first proposal was to reorient the field of comparative poli-tics toward a "problem approach." Different problems suggested different theoretical orientations, of the sort cataloged by Robert Merton.[16] There were problems such as the power of dissolution and ministerial stability in parlia-mentary systems that provoked narrow-range theory; there were problems such as the "political consequences of industrialization on underdeveloped areas of the world" that demanded middle-range theory; and there were pol-icy problems, such as how to discourage colonial nationalism from Soviet-style Communism.[17] The second proposal was to formulate a "precise conceptual scheme" that would allow political data to be compared in a sys-tematic way. Although a rhetorical gesture was made toward the need for "a general theory of politics as well as a general theory of political change,"[18] no guidelines were set out for how to approach this ideal. In general, the empha-sis on the need for "pluralist" rather than "unitary" theoretical approaches ran counter to the search for a general scheme.[19]

Macridis presented these two methodological proposals as complementary critiques of the current state of comparative politics. He believed that the problem approach represented a first step toward the creation of a wider con-ceptual scheme. But in fact, as other scholars would soon point out, the prob-lem approach, by suggesting a permanent deferral of theory building, was at odds with the attempt to develop a "precise conceptual scheme." Seen retro-spectively, the most telling moment in the conference report appeared on the ultimate page, in Dwight Waldo's comment on the overall report. Observing that the conferees had urged that politics be understood in terms of economy, social structure, and culture, Waldo asked, "How do the various 'social sci-ences' fit together in a pattern that gives meaning to each and unity to the whole? Should we all become students of sociology (or whatever the most general term is) first, and students of politics second? What, for example, of the place assigned politics in the schemata of Talcott Parsons in *The Social System?*"[20] Waldo had put his finger on the basic problem with the proposals being made by the seminarians: the failure to assimilate the latest and most comprehensive social theory.

The participants in the 1952 summer seminar nonetheless considered it a great success. They concurred with Herring that a new committee on compar-ative politics would be a useful addition to the SSRC's stable of committees.[21] But Herring himself was dissatisfied with the discordant note that the seminar had struck. This disappointment led him to seek out the advice of the maverick senior comparativist Rupert Emerson. Author of a successful book on contemporary Germany, *State and Sovereignty in Modern Germany* (1928), Emerson had turned his attention in the 1930s to the study of Malaysia, the Dutch East Indies, and the American colonial presence in the Pacific.[22] Emerson was thus both an established Europeanist of the institutionalist school and one of the first American comparativists to focus his attention on the world outside the North Atlantic. In response to Herring's enquiry, Emerson wrote a sharp five-page memorandum, which would turn out to be one of the most significant unpublished writings of postwar American political science.[23]

Emerson argued that understanding the relationship between "tradition" and "modernity" was the central problem for contemporary comparative politics. "In the underdeveloped areas," he proposed, "the most significant form of tension at the present time is between the forces which are pressing for development on modern Western lines and those which want to cling to traditional patterns, blocking change either through inertia or through active resistance." Although this tension was close to universal, there were a few areas outside the European diaspora that had managed to carry though "the process of adaption"—Emerson used a key word from Parsonian theory—"to the modern world." In other words, a few places had "completed" modernity. Emerson argued that of all the non-European countries, "only Japan has so far made a reasonably sustained and consistent advance into the modern world." For other areas with developmental aspirations, such as Ceylon, Turkey, or India, it was "an essential and characteristic feature of the social structure that there is a relatively tiny Westernized elite at the top and a large tradition-bound mass at the bottom." More than half of mankind was in "transition between old forms and ways and some still undetermined new configuration."

Domestic and international events convinced Emerson that future research would have to be organized around the modernity-tradition polarity. On the one hand, the United States was now and forever coupled to the rest of the world. The rise of the United States to "leadership of the free world" and the "shrinkage of distance under modern technological conditions" had added urgency to the quest for an improved understanding of what was happening in the rest of the world. On the other hand, the situation in the rest of the world was changing rapidly. First, the "Asian-Arab-African bloc" was beginning to demand economic, political, and social development. Second, the cold war was forcing all countries to choose between the two "variant forms of modernization or Westernization," Communism and non-Communism. Third, the incipient end of colonialism was about to unleash "hundreds of millions of people to independent statehood." For Emerson, an anticolonialist since the 1930s, the crucial issue was the last. Like it or not, new countries were about to emerge into independence, and hard political choices would have to be made about the directions these countries would take. As the preeminent international leader, the United States had a duty to guide these choices. Comparative political research, Emerson believed, was capable of contributing to good decision making on this issue. Although he adopted neither the behavioralist nor the structural-functional method, Emerson defined the geopolitical problem and established the vocabulary that modernization theorists in political science would address over the next two decades. Emerson's memorandum set the table for the grand feast of theory which Almond and the CCP were about to serve up.

The Creation of the CCP

If Herring was dissatisfied with the results of the 1952 summer seminar, then he was no happier with Emerson's report. Emerson's sweeping analysis of the geopolitical situation had still led to what Herring called "conventional questions." Herring failed to appreciate the novelty of Emerson's suggestion that comparative politics be grounded in a comparison of "underdeveloped areas" with the "modern world."[24] Still, with only the summer seminar and Emerson's memo to work with, Herring used these two reports as the starting point in his search for a scholar who could lead the team research project that the summer seminar had concluded was necessary for promoting the subfield. He wrote three letters, one to Henry Hart at the Department of Political Science in Madison; another to John Gange, the director of the Woodrow Wilson School of Foreign Affairs at the University of Virginia; and the last to Lucian Pye, a newly minted Ph.D. from Yale. Pye was working at Princeton on a book concerning Communist guerrillas in Malaya, and CPB member Gabriel Almond had recommended him to Herring as one of his prize students. Pye expressed interest in working with such a group. Herring made it clear to Pye that what he wanted was "a conceptual scheme which would lead to higher comparability of data," which should be "devised in terms of its practical utility to guiding field work."[25]

If Herring did not fully appreciate the value of Emerson's geopolitical vision, Lucian Pye did. His enthusiastic response to Herring's letter led to his appointment, along with Almond, to lead a CPB-sponsored conference, called "The Comparative Study of Political Processes in 'Underdeveloped' Areas," being held at Princeton on December 11-12, 1953. Present at the meeting were Marion Levy, Lucian Pye, and Gabriel Almond, who constituted the intellectual heart of the group; Lloyd Fallers and Levy's student David Apter; Roy Macridis, Guy Pauker, Ralph Braibanti, and Joseph LaPalombara; and finally, most of the members of CPB, including David Truman, Conrad Arensberg, Alfred de Grazia, Oliver Garceau, and V. O. Key Jr.

An outraged letter by Roy Macridis to Kenneth Thompson, an officer at the Rockefeller Foundation, provides an illuminating account of what took place at Princeton during those two days.[26] Macridis had apparently expected that his own ideas about the future of the discipline would be the main focus of the conference. After all, he had chaired the summer conference at Northwestern eighteen months earlier, and the ideas generated there had received prominent coverage just weeks earlier in the fall issue of the biggest academic journal in political science, the *American Political Science Review*. It was not until the second day of the conference, Macridis reported, that he realized "that the people from Princeton who participated . . . were so much of a team." (The "people from Princeton" included Almond, Pye, Levy, Apter, and Fallers.) It had dawned on "the outsiders" that the Princeton gang were operating as a unified cohort on the basis of "a broad conceptual scheme consisting of the trinity developed by [Marion] Levy in his book: role allocation, recruitment, and political process, which claims to open the door to any and all societies and all cultures, and which involves an exhaustive typology and implies a systematic theory of social action." Macridis objected to the "Procrustean" nature of Levy's scheme, its subordination of "research and intellectual curiosity to the total scheme," and most of all to its emphasis on sociological jargon. Macridis further derided Pye's declaration that comparative politics would benefit from a focus on the "underdeveloped" countries because it would be "unencumbered by the weight of academic tradition" (Macridis quoted Pye). Horrified by the iconoclastic attitude, Macridis realized that "the Princeton gang" had in mind nothing less than a methodological and institutional revolution in the field of comparative politics.

Although Macridis emphasized that he had "no objection to a group of students or scholars using such a scheme of inquiry," he also noted that he "would certainly hate to see it spread beyond the walls of Princeton." After deriding the Princeton group for being in thrall to "this new religion of scientism,"

Macridis ended his gripes by noting that "twenty years from now the Rockefeller [Foundation] and Carnegie [Corporation] may have to spend millions to liberate us from the conceptual straight-jacket that the sociologists are wrapping around us." Though Thompson forwarded this letter to Herring, Macridis's warnings would go unheeded. The Princeton gang's "total scheme" was just what Herring had been looking for when he proposed that the SSRC take an interest in comparative politics.

As Macridis had sensed, Marion Levy was a crucial figure. A student of Talcott Parsons, Levy pioneered the application of Parsonian theory to problems of development. In 1952, Levy had published *The Structure of Society,* an abstruse work that in many ways mirrored Parsons's *The Social System* (1951). Levy had derived his basic scheme from the theoretical work done by Parsons in the early 1940s. Like Parsons, Levy aimed to construct "a general conceptual scheme and theoretical system for beginning the comparative analysis of societies."[27] The book had begun as notes taken during a private seminar held at Harvard in the summer of 1947, which included David Aberle, Albert Cohen, Francis Sutton, and Arthur Davis, all students of Parsons. By reading Parsons and the sociologists who had been the basis for Parsons's synthesis, that seminar had produced the definition of society and its functional prerequisites that formed the basis for Levy's monograph.[28] Levy spent over five hundred pages defining the various "functions" that permit a society to continue to exist and the "structures" of society—in other words, the institutions and activities through which these functions were carried out. Levy's aim was to fashion Parsonian theory into a tool for rigorous empirical cross-societal studies. Levy wanted ultimately to construct a theoretical scheme that would allow the comparative analysis of the United States, Republican China, Russia, Japan, modern France, modern England, modern Germany, and at least one nonliterate society. (Levy chose these particular societies, first, because they represented radically different types of industrialization, and hence their analysis would, he hoped, shed light on contemporary social problems, and second, because knowledge of these societies was of "strategic" interest.) To promote this plan, Levy put together an interdisciplinary committee that included Johns Hopkins anthropologist David Aberle, Harvard sociologist Alex Inkeles, Harvard historian David Landes, Harvard anthropologist John Pelzel, Harvard economic historian John Sawyer, and Harvard sociologist Francis Sutton. By gathering a group of young social scientists interested in creating tools for comparative analysis,

Levy was extending the "Social Relations" methodology, just as Parsons had hoped would happen.

In *The Structure of Society,* whenever he paused from his theoretical disquisitions to provide concrete examples, Levy used the contrast of the United States and China to show how his analysis applied to both "advanced" and "traditional" societies. Levy's interest in Asia had begun during World War II, when he had worked as a Japanese language officer for the navy, then for the Office of Strategic Services (OSS) in China, and finally for the Foreign Morale Analysis Division of the Office of War Information. According to the Princeton *Alumni Weekly,* Levy believed that the most immediate application of *The Structure of Society* would be in the study of the "modernization of under-developed areas." Levy's work revealed "the requisites for 'modernization,' and what sorts of changes are likely to take place if 'modernization' is attempted."[29] Levy's first publication upon completion of *The Structure of Society,* "Contrasting Factors in the Modernization of China and Japan," used his structural-functional scheme to interpret why Japan had industrialized while China had stagnated economically during the nineteenth century. Levy argued that two distinguishing traits, one sociopsychological, the other sociopolitical, had contributed to Japan's relative "success" in comparison with China. On a sociopsychological level, the process of industrialization (Levy asserted) led to the decay of older familial forms of social ordering. In China this meant that the achievement-oriented values of industrialism undermined the father's traditional right to determine the profession of his sons, hence disrupting the family and, with it, the system of social control over deviance, resulting in the social disorders China had experienced in the first half of the century. In Japan, by contrast, norms of social veneration for the nobility combined with the family to maintain social control. As the "ascriptive" and "particularistic criteria" of the family gave way to the "achievement-oriented" and "universal" norms, the Japanese state (as a proxy for the nobility) stepped up its role in controlling social deviance. Hence industrialization had not led to social disorder in Japan. In essence, an authoritarian state ensured a peaceful transition to modernity.

Levy's argument also had a more sociopolitical side. Although the industrialization of the United States and England had required "relatively little centralized planning," China and Japan, as "later-comers" to the process of industrialization, needed a great deal of "coordination" to accomplish the task. According to Levy, the state was the only institution strong enough to accomplish this "coordination." "The problem of coordination involves a problem of control," Levy argued, "by force if necessary, in cases in which deviance develops or threatens. More importantly, it requires that there be patterns in operation that tend to minimize the development of deviance." Since the state was, by Weberian definition, the only institution capable of applying legitimate force, the state had to lead the development process. Here again, the Japanese had had an advantage, because prior to 1868 Japan had already had "one of the most tightly and effectively controlled feudal systems the world had ever seen," as well as a leadership more than willing to "manipulate the social structure for purposes of control." Prefiguring Walt Rostow's argument that "reactive nationalism" provided the basic impetus for modernization, Levy concluded that "the Japanese who seized control from the Tokugawa were determined to prevent the domination by Japan of outside forces." The Japanese state had thus ruthlessly imposed modernization from above. By contrast, the Chinese had succumbed to the colonial invasion, leading to the political disintegration of the centralized state institutions that would have been necessary to lead the industrialization process.[30]

Sometimes Levy used the term *modernization* to denote the transformation of the entire social system, in the Parsonian sense, but at other times, he used the term as a synonym for "industrialization," which in turn he equated with the factory system. Like Alex Inkeles later, Levy argued that industrialism imposed "engineering criteria of efficiency" that brooked no political debate. The basic problem of modernization was the maintenance of political order and social control during "the transition." The institution that had to be responsible for the maintenance of that order and control, according to Levy, was the state. According to Levy, modernization in effect required "social engineering." Levy noted that only Japan, Germany, and Russia—all countries whose recent political history in 1953 left a bit to be desired—had been "conspicuously successful at industrialization." Levy believed that the modernization process had a singular outcome, but that multiple politically distinct paths to modernity were possible. But Levy went one step further in asserting that late modernizers were *obliged* to blaze new political paths to modernity, since "the stage of industrialization reached elsewhere may already preclude that route for others." According to Levy, the "structures of modernization . . . constitute a sort of universal social solvent," which undermined old modes of "social coordination and control." To prevent derailing itself through political and social instability, a modernizing society had to achieve some new form and measure of social control. "Ideological wishful thinking is not helpful in these matters," Levy concluded. "I happen to like the implications of the clichés of democracy," but the later a society started in on modernization, "the greater the degree of centralization that must be achieved if stability is to exist."[31] Levy's authoritarian views on the modernization process would prefigure the prevailing attitudes on the CCP.

Struggles to Define the CCP's Agenda

Kenneth Thompson forwarded Macridis's outraged letter to Herring at the SSRC. Despite Macridis's objections, Herring decided on the strength of the conference to set up a new SSRC committee to address the issue of comparative politics, based on a $10,000 grant from the Carnegie Corporation. On January 21, 1954, Herring wrote to Almond that he had been selected as the first chairman of the Committee on Comparative Politics. The other inaugural members were Pye, Macridis, George Kahin, Guy Pauker, and Taylor Cole.[32] In other words, Macridis found himself from the beginning outnumbered by the very group whose theoretical machinations he had decried only a month earlier. Herring should have expected that conflict would be the inevitable result.

Almond, at the age of forty-three in 1954, had already established himself as an important figure in American political science. Four years earlier he had published the acclaimed *The American People and Foreign Policy* (see chapter 2), and his study, *The Appeals of Communism,* was on its way to press.[33] A student of Charles Merriam and Harold Lasswell's at Chicago, and a junior member of the CPB, Almond was in the vanguard of the behavioralist revolution. Like virtually everyone in his generation at the University of Chicago, Almond had been trained as an Americanist, but his interest in European theory and politics had been stimulated by sharing an office in graduate school with Edward Shils, and furthered by his marriage to a German and his wartime service for the Bureau of Intelligence of the Office of Facts and Figures as well as the United States Strategic Bombing Service.[34] Almond would soon use his new committee chair to propel himself into one of the leading figures of postwar American social science.

Though he had yet to settle on a theoretical language with which to express his insights, Almond's projects had rarely addressed the formal apparatus of the state. Instead, they addressed more diffuse dimensions of "the political system." These interests positioned him well for understanding the shape of politics in those parts of the world that did not have as elaborated a formal state apparatus as the North Atlantic powers. Like the members of the 1952 summer seminar, Almond agreed that the new committee "would have as its focus the nonformal institutions and processes of politics" and would include "persons familiar . . . with the problems of political development in the non-Western areas."[35] Perhaps referring to Macridis, Almond wrote of the first meeting of the committee that "[i]t was suggested that a 'forced draft' approach to theory construction often produces harmful results." In language reminiscent of the warnings given to drug users, Almond noted that the afore-mentioned critic had stated, "When used by inexperienced persons 'system-atic theory' often inhibits imagination and hinders effective assimilation of the data to which the scholar is exposed."[36] Right from the beginning, in other words, the CCP was struggling over theory.

If Roy Macridis expressed indignation at what he perceived to be the prospective annexation of comparative politics by sociological theory, it was in part because he had a counterproposal for how comparative politics ought to be redirected, which he expressed in his programmatic pamphlet, *The Study of Comparative Government* (1955).[37] Following the insights generated out of the 1952 summer seminar, Macridis aimed to reformulate comparative politics around a fourfold focus on decision making, power, ideology, and institutions. The basic aim was to describe the various "political groups" in a given society in terms of this quartet. Macridis selected these particular categories because he assumed that "the essence of politics is to be found in the deliberative or decision-making processes through which power aspirations and conflicts . . . are reconciled."[38] This approach emphasized process, power relations, and con-sequences rather than concepts, structures, and causes. Compared with older comparative methodologies, Macridis's extended the definition of political institutions beyond "government" and other formal political institutions such as parties. (Ironically, Pendleton Herring had been a main pioneer of the "group" approach in political science, but this approach would find little favor on the CCP, despite Herring's sponsorship.) Macridis advocated studying non-governmental institutions with political clout, such as unions, tribes, educa-tional institutions, and the media. Conspicuously absent from Macridis's work was any discussion of "behavior" or "system" or "function," all of which lay at the heart of Almond's approach.

Although Macridis's approach had nothing wrong with it per se, it did not represent a serious rethinking of either the mission or the essential

categories of political analysis in light of the incipient postcolonial geopolitics that Emerson had spelled out in his memorandum. Nevertheless,
Macridis identified the same problems for study as the other members of the
CCP. "For instance," he noted, "careful comparative study of underdeveloped areas receiving economic aid might well indicate that a rapid rate of
technological aid may bring about political instability that could be chan-
neled into revolutionary political movements. It may indicate that rapid
economic growth in a number of areas is incompatible with democratic
forms." Although attuned to the same geopolitical questions as the rest of
the CCP, Macridis did not see a need for a new political theory to answer
these questions. Macridis agreed with Almond and Pye that the old way of
doing comparative politics was static and limited to the description of government structures. But he disagreed about what ought to be done about it.
Like Parsons in sociology, Almond believed that the goal of political science
was the construction of the master system or theory. For Macridis, theory
was an instrumental tool for getting a handle on concrete, empirical political situations. Although Macridis criticized the mere descriptiveness of traditional attempts at comparison, his approach was itself descriptive (as
opposed to policy- or theory-oriented) when compared with the more radical theoretical reformulations that Almond and Pye would propose.
Although he acknowledged that theory building was an appropriate and
important task for comparative politics, he ended his pamphlet by noting
that "it is too premature to attempt even to suggest a general theory for the
study of comparative political systems."[39]

Macridis's refusal to formulate a general theory of political change appropriate to the geopolitical situation on the early postwar years would soon lead
to his marginalization on the CCP. For Macridis, it was "irrelevant, indeed,
whether we study an African community, a recently liberated colonial country, or a Western system of political institutions."[40] For Almond, by contrast,
the focus on non-European countries necessitated an increase in theoretical
sophistication as great as its widened geographical scope. Almond's approach
not only redefined the institutional role of political theory in the context of
the cold war, but also contained, embedded in its reformulated categories, a
programmatic policy agenda for use by the American government in postcolonial regions during the cold war. Macridis's more plodding institutional
approach was less suited than Almond and Pye's to the political needs of the
early cold war years. Macridis's tepid approach would never have appealed to

either American or postcolonial intellectuals hankering for an overarching theory of political change to rival Marxism.

How Macridis was excluded from the inner workings of the CCP provides evidence supporting Thomas Kuhn's hypothesis that paradigms consolidate themselves as much by excluding and ignoring dissenting voices as through rational persuasion.[41] From the beginning, the deck was stacked against Macridis and in favor of Almond, who held not only the committee chair but also the ear of the SSRC's president, Pendleton Herring. Moreover, working at Northwestern, Macridis was physically isolated from the CCP (which met in New York, halfway between Pye's Princeton and Almond's Yale). As a result, he found himself increasingly out of tune with the ideas of the rest of the group. As the details of the story show, the success of behavioralism in comparative politics was not without its collateral damage in the form of devalued careers and personal embarrassments.

On February 19, 1954, the CCP had its first meeting.[42] Almond and Pye used the occasion to declare that the purpose of the CCP was, first, to expand the subject of comparative politics beyond the North Atlantic nation-states to include the "underdeveloped" world, and second, to rethink the methodology of comparative politics using social theory, including the concepts of process, system, role, role structure, and orientation. It was suggested that "some uniformities of political behavior" would provide the basic units of political comparison. Behavioralism was the primary agenda. The structural functionalism of Levy and Parsons lurked in the background. Despite this nascent synthesis, no consensus existed within the CCP about the purpose or place of theory in comparative politics. Probably citing Macridis, the minutes stated that the committee should "avoid a 'master plan' for study of comparative politics," but still noted that "it might be possible at a later time to explain and relate these concepts to each other within a theoretical framework."[43] Someone (we may again assume Macridis) pointed out that "the adoption of a theoretical framework for research might result in limiting a scholar's perceptiveness and causing serious mistakes in interpretation which would have been avoided in a search for understanding exempt from categories and 'theoretical binds.'" Nevertheless, someone else made sure to emphasize the importance of searching for a new understanding of "the total political process."[44] Despite Macridis's reservations, the CCP leadership's commitment to behavioralism was already apparent, and the resulting tensions on the committee are evident even in the passive voice of the meeting minutes.

At first Macridis may have felt he was prevailing in the battle over how comparative politics ought to be practiced. At the second meeting, each member of the CCP presented a paper on trade unions in their country of expertise. This first project chosen by the CCP corresponded at least as closely to Macridis's vision of "the new comparative politics" as it did to any behavioralist vision. Reviewing this meeting, Macridis wrote, "In our first meeting we agreed to undertake the 'study of organized labor in politics.' The selection of this topic signifies, at least to me, that we were committing ourselves to the 'group-theory' of analysis according to which the political process is viewed in terms of group activity and group conflict."[45] Macridis's tentative tone ("at least to me") resulted from a fundamental difference with other members of the CCP: whereas Macridis wanted to talk about political groups, the others wanted to focus on how the differences between trade union functions in different countries were a dependent variable, where the independent variable was the "inherent differences" between political systems. "The question was raised," the minutes of the board meeting noted in a telling use of the passive voice, "whether these considerations did not suggest that it was possible to distinguish a process of phasing in the analysis of political institutions, perhaps even a 'natural history' of political development."[46] This usage marked the first appearance of the theoretical obsession with "political development" that would mark the rest of the CCP's activities. Someone else (Macridis?) replied that trying to build a model of non-Western political systems before sufficient data had been gathered would lead to "sterile and melancholy logic-chopping."[47] Macridis may have felt that this was a victory in his efforts to stay the assault of the theory builders on the CCP.

If he believed this, he was mistaken. Macridis's stubborn reiteration of his antibehavioralist line led to a rather unusual move on the part of Gabriel Almond. Five weeks after the final meeting of the CCP in the spring of 1954, Almond sent a memo to all members of the CCP, *except Macridis,* suggesting that the "purpose of research on the non-Western areas is to develop a body of knowledge on the basis of which predictions can be made as to how these mixed traditional and rational systems will develop. What are the major factors which will affect the pattern of this development? What kinds of traditional systems and institutions are most likely to assimilate to the Western rational pattern with the least dislocation and instability? What kind of impact of Western rational institutions is most likely to produce a stable adaptation?"[48] Although this did not directly contravene the agreement made a month earlier to focus on policy-oriented problems and to stay away from theory, Almond was smuggling in the theoretical agenda by referring to an assumed "pattern of development." Already a basic dichotomy of "traditional systems" and "Western rational systems" was being assumed rather than explicitly argued. After just two meetings, it seems that Almond had decided that if Macridis was not going to submit to the theoretical agenda, then he was simply going to be excluded from the conversation.

The main result of this first year of work from the CCP was Kahin, Pauker, and Pye's essay, "Comparative Politics in Non-Western Countries." Following the Macridis injunction to theoretical modesty, the Pye-Kahin-Pauker approach was oriented toward comparing "political groups." Comparing how different groups in different societies performed a uniform and universal set of "functional requisites" provided a means for interpolity comparisons. Although Pye, Kahin, and Pauker emphasized that it was "an open question whether the future will bring [the non-Western countries] a liberal democratic form of politics or some type of authoritarian rule such as communism," they also claimed that these countries were moving to an "idealized future" based on "some variant of the Western model of government and politics."[49] In other words, the CCP chose "the Western model" as normative because these countries (or rather, their elites) desired this outcome.

The committee concluded its essay by making a tentative attempt to rehabilitate "the comparative method of the nineteenth century." Although the committee acknowledged that the "broad evolutionary schemes" of the nineteenth century had collapsed under the "overwhelming evidence proving that unilinear evolutionism was not defensible," it nevertheless hoped to discern "the patterns of political development in societies that have set as their goal the liberal democratic model of politics." The committee concluded that success in developing such a "systematic comparative politics" would constitute "both a scientific and a moral-political" triumph.[50] When the committee began to meet again in the fall of 1954, it was suggested that the term "political process" was not clearly defined but that "if one model were clearly presented, students would then be aided in discovering deviations from the model in the areas they studied. One model, for example, might be given of a democratic political process in the West." In other words, the "democratic political process in the West" was being defined as the norm against which Others would be judged.[51]

While Macridis deemed this cross-national survey quite an achievement in itself, it instead became a point of departure for deeper theorizing by Almond and his allies on the CCP. For Almond, the institutional-empiricist approach, with its meager methodological or theoretical component, tended to "miss the point, particularly when they are used in the strikingly different political systems of pre-industrial areas."[52] As Almond put it in a letter to Macridis a couple of years later, this approach did not "satisfy the needs of effective comparison" that most members of the committee wanted.[53] So there would be no misunderstanding about what he was doing, Almond explained that the committee "is not a representative committee and does not view itself as a spokesman in any sense of the field. It is intended to be a catalytic committee, a committee willing to take risks and encourage others to do so." In a sign of growing impatience in the late winter of 1955, Almond noted that the committee had "decided to postpone theory and methodology in heavy doses until the Committee had developed a certain knowledge of and tolerance of one another's peculiarities." "Nothing," he continued, "seems to divide people so quickly and integrally as does discussions of theory." However, enough was enough. "Having worked together effectively for over a period of a year, we are now ready to turn some of our energy to methodological and theoretical problems." To that end, a conference was being arranged at Princeton "to explore the applications to comparative politics of social theory." The committee, he concluded, had finally achieved an identity, consisting of four elements. It would: (1) provide a balanced focus on theoretical and policy interests; (2) offer a forum for presenting research on the non-Western areas; (3) "assimilate and cumulate" research results "for the instrumental purpose of orderly and sound comparison and cumulation"; and (4) provide a staging area for greater national and international scholarly collaboration.[54]

Three months later, in June 1955, the CCP held its first conference. Two crucial papers were presented at this conference: Francis Sutton's "Social Theory and Comparative Politics" and Gabriel Almond's "Comparative Political Systems." Although Sutton's paper was not published until 1963, everyone at the conference agreed that it exercised an important immediate influence on their thinking. Sutton had begun his academic career with several well-regarded essays, including coauthorship of a widely cited monograph on the ideology of the American business class.[55] After participating in Marion Levy's 1949 Cambridge seminar and subsequent committee on comparative research, Sutton in 1954 became an officer at the Ford Foundation, where he would eventually rise to the position of vice president for economic development. Sutton's position at the Ford Foundation guaranteed that as

Ford began to devote its enormous resources to development, those with an inclination to social theory would find themselves favored. If behavioralism had been the initial impetus behind the formation of the CCP, this conference consolidated the Parsonian method as the preferred way of realizing the behavioralist agenda.

Sutton took as the starting point for his essay Durkheim's suggestion that science should deal with the general rather than the unique. Comparative sociology, Sutton quoted Durkheim as saying, was not just a subfield of sociology, it was the essence of sociological theory itself.[56] For Sutton, this Durkheimian proposition constituted a challenge to comparative politics as well. Sutton proposed that "two broad types of societies" could be distinguished: the "agricultural" and the "modern industrial." "Agricultural society" involved a "predominance of ascriptive, particularistic, diffuse patterns; stable local groups and limited spatial mobility; relatively simple and stable 'occupational' differentiation; [and] a 'deferential' stratification system of diffuse impact." By contrast, "modern industrial society" contained the following sociological features: "predominance of universalistic, specific, and achievement norms; high degree of social mobility; well-developed occupational system, insulated from other social structures; 'egalitarian' class system based on generalized patterns of occupational achievement; [and] prevalence of 'associations,' i.e., functionally specific, non-ascriptive structures."[57] Sutton noted that "modern industrial society" had long been accepted "as a type," but that it was only since Robert Redfield's proposals about "the folk society" that "the predecessors of modern industrial society" had become perceived as having much in common.[58]

Sutton ended by suggesting that this synchronic typology contained an implicit developmental trajectory. "The major societies of the modern world," Sutton concluded, "show varying combinations of the patterns sketched in the ideal types of society I have sketched out. Some stand close to the model of industrial society; others are in various transitional states that hopefully may be understood better by conceptions of where they have been and where they may be going."[59] The idea of a "transitional" society played a crucial role in this passage. It implied that for traditional societies, there could no longer be any "standing still": these societies were destined to leave the "agricultural" world behind. More important, despite Sutton's hedging use of the conditional tense in the last phrase, there was a sense that the ideal-type of "modern industrial society" was in fact the destination of this "transitional" movement. As C. S. Whitaker remarked a decade later, "Use of the very term 'transitional' as a general category connotes unilinear direction, i.e., from one known type or class of society to another already defined one."[60] The passage also suggested that some societies had already "arrived" at modernity: such societies were no longer in motion (as Sutton put it, they "stand close" to the ideal-type). These societies thus outlined the future for the transitional societies. In a word, the concept of the "transitional" society linked the two ideal-types in a developmental narrative.

The essential role of political systems, according to Sutton (echoing Levy), was to aid in integrating social systems. The difficulty was that this "transition" (Sutton did not yet call it "modernization") radically transformed the social integration role of the political spectrum, causing stress and possible rupture. In general, political systems were responsible for, first, "controlling individual deviance," and second, "coordinating" imperfectly integrated groups. The difficulty for transitional systems was that the definitions of deviance were undergoing rapid change. This made norms of political action difficult to define. Moreover, the rapidity of change increased social disorganization, complicating the coordination of groups. Precisely because of all this complexity, the political scientist had a special claim for understanding how integration functioned in total societies. According to participants at the June 1955 conference, Sutton's paper had an enormous impact on the way members of the CCP regarded the contemporary world.[61] Reporting on the results of the conference, Almond said that "Francis X. Sutton on applications of social theory to the study of political systems . . . proved suggestive for the committee's program. . . . Talcott Parsons' concept of 'pattern variables' . . . appeared to be applicable in distinguishing cultures and ideologies of different political systems."[62] Years later, Almond would acknowledge the importance of Talcott Parsons and Marion Levy in the formulation of the CCP's approach to comparative politics. "What we are doing here," he wrote in a 1964 memo, "is simply an elaboration and adaptation of their work."[63]

The other important paper to be presented at the June 1955 conference was Almond's "Comparative Political Systems," which he published a year later in the *Journal of Politics*.[64] In this paper Almond made the first sustained application by a CCP member of Parsonian social theory, claiming that the "political system" was the proper unit of analysis for comparative politics. Almond argued that a political system was "oriented toward political action" by its "political culture," a term that Almond coined and applied for the first time in this essay. The political culture of a country was in effect the political dimension of its national character, though Almond emphasized that political culture was not reducible to national character. Not only could political culture transcend national boundaries, but also individual national territories could contain several discrete political cultures, often in competition with one another. For example, whereas Almond noted that while "Anglo-American political systems are characterized by a *homogeneous, secular* political culture," many "preindustrial" political systems contained "mixed political cultures" in which a "Western system" with its various imported structural elements coexisted uneasily with the "pre-Western" or "traditional" elements. In addition to the Anglo-American and preindustrial political systems, Almond identified the "totalitarian" and the "continental" political systems as relatively common. That the totalitarian system was abhorrent went without saying. Almond also worried that the continental system was susceptible to "Caeseristic" political movements in which charismatic political leaders could seize the reins of politics as a way of breaking through the political "immobilism" that Almond identified as a primary characteristic of these systems. In other words, the only good political system was the Anglo-American one.[65]

A rapid transition began to take place following the June 1955 conference. Although the committee's work continued to focus on political parties, as Macridis wanted, the grounds for studying parties was defined in a Parsonian theoretical language. Parsonian theory provided the "grand theoretical" foundation for realizing the behavioralist ambitions of Almond and Pye. Political parties were of particular relevance, Almond felt, because of their "function" of transmitting "impulses which originate in the society" to the instrumentalities of the state. Studying this intermediary network therefore suggested particular "diagnoses of the condition of the society."[66] The functionalist view of society as an organism was now the guiding theoretical assumption behind the committee's agenda. The political system was a subsystem of the social system, and the state was in effect an epiphenomenon of the political system. As Almond remarked around this time, "My own conception of the distinguishing properties of the political system proceeds from Weber's definition—the legitimate monopoly of physical coercion over a given territory and population. The political system with which most political scientists concern themselves all are characterized by a specialized apparatus which possesses this legitimate monopoly, and the political system consists of those interacting roles which affect its employment."[67] If modernization theorists like

Almond understood the "autonomy" of the state at all, they underestimated how completely states might act with disregard to the interests, desires, or needs of its citizens. By accepting at face value not just the development rhetoric of the first generation of (Western-educated) postcolonial leaders but also Parsonian privileging of the social sphere, modernization theorists in the 1950s failed to foresee the emergence of states uninterested in promoting social welfare. During the 1950s, American political scientists feared populism and Communism, not self-interested states. Even where such a possibility was contemplated, most considered it the aberrant result of individual political monsters, rather than a potential embedded within the bureaucratic state as such. Almost no one foresaw the rise of states engaged in the plunder or murder of its own people in the name of "revolutionary democracy."

By the end of 1955, with the committee just about two years old, Macridis was so marginalized that he provoked an embarrassing incident with the Ford Foundation. Under Almond's leadership, the committee had proposed to the Ford Foundation that it fund both field research and a series of seminars to be run each summer for the rest of the decade to build on the insights that had emerged from the June conference. In the meantime, Macridis had written independently to the Ford Foundation to propose a *different* summer seminar series, to be held at Northwestern, predicated on the notion of breaking down the "country-by-country" approach. He suggested making the cross-national comparisons that everyone at the CCP agreed should be done, but he excluded the Parsonian theory from his proposal.[68] Assuming that Macridis did not make this additional grant proposal merely to make trouble for the committee, this incident at least indicates how completely Macridis had been excluded from the workings of the CCP. His objections to Almond's agenda meant that he had been frozen out of the workings of the committee, to the point where he was unaware even of the proposals the committee was making.

Although he did not explicitly describe his proposal as being on behalf of the CCP, the arrival of Macridis's proposal at the Ford Foundation elicited confused inquiries by the foundation as to what was going on at the CCP. Almond quickly wrote to explain that Macridis's proposal did not conflict in either substance or timing with the official proposal of the CCP.[69] (Almond was vague about whether Macridis's proposal had received the official imprimatur of the committee.) Although Almond's hedging was correct regarding the specific issue of the *timing* of the summer seminar, it misrepresented the real theoretical differences between his and Macridis's proposals. Macridis's suggestion to do away with the country-by-country approach contradicted the macrosocietal analytical approach favored by Almond's functionalism. Putting this discrepancy aside, the Ford Foundation awarded to the CCP the funds Almond had requested and declined those Macridis had requested. This money provided the basis for five years of field research on the study of political groups in various types of political systems.

This event effectively finished Macridis's role on the committee. Although he would remain an official member of the CCP for two more years, he no longer attended the committee's meetings and did not take part in any further conferences. The committee's commitment to the functionalist approach was now uncontested. As with most disciplinary victories, however, it was a triumph that was soon assimilated by the victor as the inevitable result of the march of scientific progress. A little over a year later, Almond seemed to have forgotten the conflicts with Macridis when he wrote to Herring that "from the beginning of its program the Committee on Comparative Politics has had as one of its major aims the development of more adequate theories of political groups, institutions, and processes."[70] When the CCP met in April 1957 at Stanford University, Almond declared that the ultimate purpose of the committee was to promote "advances in the general theory of politics."[71] A month later, the CCP was even more specific about the nature of this general theory when it declared that "the main concern of the Committee [is] to move toward a theory of political development."[72] This general project was to "encourage political scientists, sociologists, and anthropologists to utilize existing bodies of knowledge for the purposes of developing generalizations about political processes viewed comparatively."[73] To operationalize the CCP's turn from empirical data gathering toward a process of "synthesis, analysis, and development of theory,"[74] Almond recommended that the committee add Myron Weiner, Joseph LaPalombara, Robert Ward, and Herbert Hyman to replace Macridis, who was stepping down. The immediate task of this reconstituted committee was to plan a conference on "political development" for the following June, a conference that would turn out to be a crucial synthetic moment in the formation of modernization theory.

The case of Roy Macridis thus exemplifies the Kuhnian hypothesis about how paradigms establish themselves as much through exclusion as through rational persuasion of doubters. The ultimate irony of this whole story is that eventually, despite all this resistance, Macridis would embrace modernization theory and go on to edit two important volumes of collected essays on the subject.[75] By that time, rather pathetically, modernization theory had long since ceased to be a cutting-edge methodology and was on its way out as a formal social scientific paradigm.

"Political Development" as Political Modernization

From the beginning, there had always been scholars who objected to the contrast of "Western" and "traditional." At one CCP meeting, shortly before he was invited to join the committee, Myron Weiner declared that he considered it impossible to distinguish between Westernized and traditional groups in non-Western societies. Politically sophisticated and university-trained people, the very groups usually referred to as "Westernized," he pointed out, led the so-called traditional groups. Only the composition of the political groups was unusual by Western standards.[76] In addition, decolonization meant that "traditional groups" could no longer act as they had during colonial times—which called into question the very meaning of the term "traditional." Throughout the first five years of the CCP's existence, there was a constant search for a language in which to describe its activities, reflecting a restless dissatisfaction with the discursive status quo. Although the consensus seemed to be that the terms "Western" and "traditional" had an invidious ring, replacing these terms was a tricky matter, since the distinction (however phrased) was fundamental to the enterprise of the CCP. Communications specialist Daniel Lerner was only slightly cruder than the modernization theorists on the CCP when he argued, "What the West is, the Middle East seeks to become."[77]

In this search for a proper discursive framework, "modern" and "modernization" would emerge as strategic terms. The occasion for this terminological shift was the CCP's "Conference on Political Modernization," organized by Lucian Pye and held from June 8 to 11, 1959, at Dobbs Ferry, New York. The participants at this meeting included all of the important members of the CCP—including Gabriel Almond, Lucian Pye, Taylor Cole, Robert Ward, and Joseph LaPalombara—as well as many other figures whose names are associated with modernization theory, such as David Apter, Cyril Black, Karl Deutsch, Rupert Emerson, Everett Hagen, Bert Hoselitz, Alex Inkeles, Daniel Lerner, Francis Sutton, and future CCP members James Coleman, Myron Weiner, and Sydney Verba. The aim of the conference was to define the differences and relationship between the former colonial states and "the West," and more specifically, the contemporary United States. At one of the planning meetings, the CCP stated that the aim of the conference was "the elaboration of a 'creative theory' which would 'liberate' research. . . . Central to the Committee's curiosity was the question of the existence of a 'sequential' process in political development."[78] The keynote speaker at this conference was sociologist Edward Shils, who had been invited by Almond, his old University of Chicago officemate, to give the agenda paper.

Edward Shils, born in 1910 in New England, was the child of agnostic Eastern European Jewish immigrants and was raised in Philadelphia. As an undergraduate he attended the University of Pennsylvania, where he majored in French literature. (S. N. Eisenstadt remarked that Shils "came to social science through literature,"[79] a fact that would inform Shils's understanding of modernity and modernism.) After graduating from college, he worked as a social worker in Chicago's Black Belt during the Depression. Invited to join the University of Chicago in 1933 as a research assistant to Louis Wirth, he attended the last few Robert Park and Frank Knight seminars on Max Weber, which introduced him to continental social theory. One of his earliest publications was a translation of Karl Mannheim's *Ideology and Utopia*. Throughout his career Shils kept up a steady flow of politically engaged scholarship on topics as various as McCarthyism, the history and sociology of science, the social basis of troop morale in the Wehrmacht, the role of art and literature in a civilized society, and the significance of gender and Jewishness in scholarly production. Endowed with both a nose for an important subject and an engaging prose style, Shils invariably found himself at the center of sociological innovations and controversies.

In addition to his scholarship, Shils played a central role in a remarkably diverse set of midcentury American institutions. Like Almond, Shils spent World War II in the army's Psychological Warfare Division working on the bases of German civilian and military morale. After the war he launched the *Bulletin of the Atomic Scientists,* which lobbied for civilian control over nuclear energy, and in 1962 he founded the journal *Minerva,* devoted to addressing the various contexts of scientific scholarship.[80] Together with Allan Bloom, John Nef, and Saul Bellow, he founded the University of Chicago's celebrated Committee on Social Thought, participated in the planning committee for the MIT Center for International Studies, and later joined David Apter and Clifford Geertz to found the Committee on the Comparative Study of New

Nations at the University of Chicago. He was also one of the leading organizers of the Congress for Cultural Freedom, the main engine of early cold war liberal anti-Communist propaganda.[81] As noted in the last chapter, he collaborated with Talcott Parsons to formulate the pattern variables.

Despite this remarkable résumé, Shils remains a neglected figure in American intellectual history, in large measure, one suspects, because of a caustic personality that limited the number of his followers. In their eulogies to him at the time of his death in 1995, even Shils's friends describe him as "cantankerous,"[82] "abrasive and unhelpful,"[83] "very confrontational,"[84] even "vituperative."[85] A telling characteristic of Shils's personality is that he went out of his way to dismiss not just the work of someone like Camille Paglia, but also that of Christopher Lasch, David Halberstam, Hannah Arendt, Allan Bloom, Susan Sontag, Isaiah Berlin, Michael Harrington, the Frankfurt School, the New York intellectuals, and Michel Foucault, to name but a few.[86] It is a testament to his energy and brilliance, however, that despite his character, he exercised such a tremendous influence on postwar social science. With the possible exception of Talcott Parsons—whom Shils called "one of the most important sociologists in the entire history of the subject"[87]—Shils was probably the most original scholar associated with modernization theory. Shils, more than anyone, promoted the idea that modernity should be taken as the normative end point of development theory's historical metanarrative.

Shils became interested in the fate of the nations undergoing decolonization in the early 1950s. In 1958 he published a study of the culture of Indian intellectuals in the new Indian state. Countering the cliché of the "schizophrenic" or "rootless" postcolonial intellectual, Shils described how *little* the Indian intellectual had escaped the "traditional" beliefs and habits of Indian society, making the paradoxical observation that the "alienation of the intellectual from Indian society is probably less pronounced than is the alienation of most other Indians from Indian society."[88] In contrast to the analysis of Lucian Pye (see chapter 5), Shils argued that the psychological problem of the postcolonial intellectual stemmed not from being *too* modern, and therefore alienated from the masses, but rather from being *insufficiently* modern. "They are ashamed," Shils claimed, "that their country is not a 'modern country,' that its institutions are not abreast of the institutions of Great Britain and 'the modern world.' "[89] This shame explained the essential "xenotropism" of the postcolonial intellectual—his attraction to things foreign. In the final analysis, however, Shils noted that the solutions to the problems of Indian intellectual life would emerge from some synthesis of "traditional culture" and the "universal culture" of modernity.

Shils's usage of the term "modern" in his agenda paper for the 1959 CCP conference represents a crucial moment in the genesis of modernization theory. The article thematized not only the dichotomy of tradition versus modernity, but also the sense that contemporary history should be conceived as a transition from the former to the latter. Shils argued that the term "modernization" avoided the unpleasant colonial memories awakened by the constant references to "the West" as the counterconcept to backwardness or tradition. Although Shils's paper continued older ways of constructing the relationship between "the West" and "the Rest," his emphatic rephrasing of this distinction seemed to provide a way out of the linguistic straitjacket that had bound the discourse of comparative politics up to this point.

The goal of Shils's paper, published with slight revisions a year later, was to give a sense for what the postcolonial peoples—or, more accurately, postcolonial elites—expected from the development process. According to Shils, what they wanted was to be included "within the circle of modernity." The paper sought to map the meaning and content of that modernity, not only for metropolitan elites but also for postcolonial elites. (Shils felt no bashfulness about speaking on behalf of the indigenes.) "Among the elites of the new states," Shils began, "'modern' means dynamic, concerned with the people, democratic and equalitarian, scientific, economically advanced, sovereign, and influential." It meant "dethronement of the rich and traditionally privileged [and also] playing a part in the larger arena of world politics."[90] Modernity meant having a profound sense of individuality, an acceptance of "economic development" as the responsibility of the state, and a belief that religion had no place in political discussions. A given society's success in achieving modernity, Shils believed, depended on a "widely dispersed sense of civility."[91] The components of this civility were a strong sense of national identity, but without excessive commitment to national symbols; a widespread interest in public affairs; a general sense of the legitimacy of the existing political order; a sense of "rights" and the sanctity of the private; and a "sufficient degree" of overall value consensus.

Despite the epigrammatic style in which the paper was written, there were unresolved tensions in Shils's thoughts. For example, he argued that the modern intellectuals in the new states not only "overlapped" with the political elite and insisted on "large scale political action," but also tended to be rather "anti-political," by which Shils meant that they were inclined toward an oppositionist attitude and a "disproportionately high readiness to associate themselves with alienated movements aspiring to extremist solutions of the problems with their society."[92] Another tension concerned the dubious modernity of Communists. On the one hand, he identified the Soviet Union as a modern state. On the other hand, he denied the modernity not only of revolutionaries, since by definition they rejected the legitimacy of the contemporary political order, but also of totalitarian regimes, because of their "overcommitment" to nationalism and its symbols, as well as their disrespect for individuality and privacy.

The central and unstated assumption of the paper was that modernity was a monolith and that its basic contours were the same for both the postcolonial areas and the old metropoles. The states of Western Europe and North America "need not *aspire* to modernity. They *are* modern. Modernity is part of their very nature." Modern meant, in fact, being Western without the albatross of dependency. In a rich phrase, one that he would repeat again and again, Shils stated, "The model of modernity is a picture of the West detached in some way from its geographical origins and locus."[93] He continued: "The elites of the new states have lying before them not the image of a future in which no one has as yet lived or of fragments of a still living and accepted past, but rather an image of their own future profoundly different from their own past, to be lived along the lines of the already existent modern states, which are their contemporaries."[94] Although Shils emphasized in the last paragraph of the paper that "there is no straight and easy road to the city of modernity," the destination of the road was clear: this modernity represented an idealized version of the contemporary United States.

Shils had sent a draft of "Political Development of the New States" to the CCP in October 1958. It was meant to provide the theoretical point of departure for the June 1959 conference. Although some members of the CCP had felt that Shils's paper paid scant, surely insufficient attention to the processes of political transformation (i.e., development), they agreed that it identified "significant research areas relating to the process of 'modernization,' in its economic and social, as well as its more specifically political aspects."[95] But if there was general agreement that "modernization" was what everyone wanted to explain, the scholars participating in the conference nonetheless contested almost every element of the definition of modernization that Shils had put forth.

At the first general discussion session, on the afternoon of June 8, Shils took the floor to elaborate on some of the ideas he had presented in his paper. From the outset, Shils cast doubt on his own distinction between tradition and modernity, arguing that these two categories were empirically very difficult to distinguish from each other, and that in any event, no one should simplify matters into thinking that all things traditional were without value. Despite his various claims about modern society, he admitted that he "did not feel that we ourselves knew what constitutes a 'modern society'; if we looked at *our* modern societies, they were, in a way, all a bloody mess—in an unsatisfactory condition from the point of view of meeting the requirements for making democracy work. In our demands for the new states, we assume a condition of affairs in modern society which is more ideal than any state has achieved in the present century."[96] Nor was the other half of the dichotomy any clearer; on the second day of the conference, Shils confessed that "the word 'traditional' is much used, but we do not have a definition for it. The essential feature of a traditional society is not structural; the essential things are certain beliefs and rules and practices that are observed simply because they have some quality of 'pastness' about them."[97] Epistemologically, it was unclear whether Shils's "model of modernity" was (1) an ideal type in the Weberian sense, or (2) a normative account of the way modern societies *ought* to organize themselves, or (3) a positive, empirical description of what modernity meant to the intellectuals in the new states. What was clear, however, was that the West possessed modernity and "the non-West" did not. Shils underlined this point by telling the assembled scholars that they had to commit themselves "to a Western conception of modernity—if it were not Western no one would recognize it. If 'modern' means 'Western' then this is a misfortune of world history. Most of the new states have formed themselves on that image. We should, however, avoid the term 'Westernization' because it suggests something attached to the West—'modernization' would be a preferable term."[98] The one thing Shils was sure of, in other words, was that modernization meant to become "like the West" but (in principle) without the subordination that this implied.

Definitional issues loomed large in the discussions that followed. Some scholars thought modernization ought to be defined economically, because a materialist definition of modernity was more recognizably universal. Russian historian Adam Ulam of Harvard, for example, recommended that "a more relativistic scale of values, without using this horrible term 'West,' should be developed in talking about research priorities. You start with the assumption that there is something non-West about the non-West, but you use terms like interest articulation that have meaning only in the West; these terms have a fragile meaning in [a place like] Nigeria. Would a simpler scheme of socio-economic relationships not be more meaningful in dealing with industrialization and the development of centralized states? These are 'Western' but only because certain processes took place first in what is called the West."[99] Joseph LaPalombara asked whether "modernization" was not synonymous with "industrialization," and if not, what the relationship between the two was. Harvard political scientist Karl Deutsch suggested that "modernization" was a better term than "industrialization," since it included the impact of "modern practices such as commercialization."[100] Modernization, he argued, was a more inclusive term than industrialization. This comment raised the issue of what constituted the "leading" or independent variable in the process of social change. To this, David Apter replied that there was "a convergence in the comparative field. . . . The modernization focus was a good one as a special aspect of industrialization—those considerations that produced modern man. On industrialization, there is a feeling that there was something irrevocable about it and that it is produced by similar institutions wherever it occurs. Modernization does not make the same assumptions; we can divorce the notion of modernization from that of industrialization. Modernization involves the development of new forms of handling contemporary problems of an industrial and change sort."[101] LaPalombara summarized the discussion by concluding that political scientists ought to think of development as a dependent variable and then look at "instrumentalities both technical and intellectual. . . . We are interested in socialization only so far as we can discover what patterns of socialization are getting to the point of giving off people who are not well-related to a given set of goals."[102] In other words, development resulted from the creation of people somehow or other not well suited to the old "traditional" environment, and who would (therefore?) either create modernity or else surrender to chaos.

Another possibility, if modernization was defined politically, was that it meant democratization. Soviet historian Cyril Black of Princeton, who after this conference would begin work on his highly regarded *Dynamics of Modernization* (1966), suggested that modernity "could be defined as democracy," in which case, "'modernization' would be movement toward democracy." On the other hand, "[m]odernization could be defined as the impact of modern institutions on ideas, and such impact might be assessed in the year 2000." He also proposed that modernization was the social result of the continuous "expansion of knowledge." Black challenged others to come up with a definition of "modernization" or "modern society." Robert Ward, however, advocated Shils's own pattern variables as a means for defining modernity. "Mechanical things can change easily," he noted, "but political attitudes are about the last things to change. In Asia there are few societies that have achieved modernity, [except] Japan." Daniel Lerner proposed that a country be considered modern when its literacy rate reached 60 percent. But Karl Deutsch disagreed, arguing that the critical issue was social mobilization—by which he had meant a "levee en masse" in the Napoleonic sense—"the readiness to change values or goals according to state directive." All in all, there seemed to be no accord about the basic criteria for defining modernity.[103]

Nevertheless, the participants did agree with Shils that the cause of modernization was the combination of the intrusion of the West with nationalist reactions of local elites. Joseph Spengler of Duke University said that "we must always search for the novelty factor—the destabilizer." There was universal accord that the "destabilizer" of the traditional system was the intrusion of the West. Everett Hagen of the MIT Center for International Studies suggested that "the tendency toward modernization occurs when some important group in society feels its status has either been violated or threatened and in reaction it asks how it can move to restore itself to the place it wants to have." Rupert Emerson noted that the nationalist leaders of the newly independent states were generally Western trained. According to Emerson, this meant that they would "make bows in the direction of the traditions of the past, but they are prepared to sacrifice the traditions wherever that gets in the way of political modernization." He suggested that "where you have in nationalist movements a swing toward modernization, and a desire to adopt strictly Western-style institutions, it is all right to speak of the 'West.' These leaders do not turn to their own traditions, but to Western style institutions adopted intact from the West." For Shils as well as for Emerson, modernization meant Westernization.[104] Cause and effect were thus conflated: contact with the West led willy-nilly to Westernization.

Most of the gathered social scientists agreed with Shils's assessment that modernization meant undergoing experiences similar to those that Western nations had experienced a century and more ago. Throughout the conference, however, scholars continually expressed doubts about whether the distinction between modernity and tradition had ontological validity. Almond, for example, proposed that "to try to use social theories to distinguish traditional and modern political systems may be dangerous if it suggested the difference were a polarity not found in fact. . . . The modern system is really a particular kind of fusion of traditional and modern elements. . . . In social theory or in anthropology, ways of handling different combinations of modern and traditional components are lacking, and we now feel the need for them when we seek different developmental models of change." In a rather tautological comment, he suggested that the "more modern the traditional system is the more able it is to become modern." And if modern and traditional were in fact completely interpenetrated, then Everett Hagen drew the logical conclusion that "the difficulty of defining modernization was that there is no one such type of animal to find in actual life." This observation was quite threatening to some. James Coleman agonized that if "'modernization' did apply to the non-West," then was there "a focus that will allow us to be universal again"? He worried that if the assembled scholars failed to come up with such a universal focus, then "we are in danger of becoming non-West"! Coleman apparently believed that to be modern, social science required an Archimedean point from which a universal claim could be made. In creating modernization theory, in other words, the modernization theorists had to enact and embody modernity themselves.[105] Despite these initial misgivings, Almond and Coleman would rapidly embrace the concepts of modernity and modernization.

Then there was the case of the Soviet Union, which not only raised troublesome questions about the content of modernity, but paradoxically also made the term necessary. Even before the conference, Daniel Lerner had encouraged the use of the term "modernization" because, as he put it, "[a]ny label which describes the West as the fount of innovation is bound to seem parochial at a time when similar westernizing influences also come from the U.S.S.R. Accordingly, nowadays, we speak simply of 'modernization.'"[106] Likewise, Lucian Pye noted that in Burma, "the West was seen in the image of the administrator. . . . People are asking why, when acculturation is toward the 'Western' model of an independent state, they should not acculturate toward the Russian, rather than the United States model." Even though he had suggested defining political modernization as democratization, Cyril Black admitted that he had little faith that democracy represented the unique political form of modernity. "It was dangerous to regard democracy as *the* modern form," Black said. He "doubted the wisdom of assuming that societies would move in the direction of a certain goal. Mr. Khrushchev, for example, says the world would move toward a socialist society in due course." Alex Inkeles "stressed the need for caution in talking about what is 'modern.' In many cases 'modernization' was made possible because of the existence of all-encompassing autocratic rules. This was important in Russia. . . . The spirit of modernity is not a sure road to success." Again and again, Russia appeared as the bogey of modernity, an example of a malignant version of modernization—but never as anything other than modern.[107]

Finally, there were those who suggested that the whole distinction between tradition and modernity was little more than a projection of these social sci- entists' own ideals about their own society. Most pointed was Rowland Egger of the University of Virginia, who suggested that "we were drawing most of our inspiration for research by looking into a contemporary mirror. Most of the things we want to research re: economic development assume the exportation of the Sherman anti-trust act and the Federal Reserve System. Much of the difficulty comes from defects in our own educational system. We are really versed in the institutional development of our own country and we have not thought enough about the U.S. as an underdeveloped country. We should be humble about this whole area. Our economists do not know much about markets other than that of the U.S." Wendell Bell of the University of California also expressed doubts about whether "the modernization going on in the new states is a political, social, and economic set of changes moving in the direction of what large scale industrial societies were some time ago." He suggested, instead, that "the emergent patterns of values [in the new states] are things that would not be modern by some definitions offered at this conference. He was disturbed by the concept of modernization because it assumed an endpoint." Similarly, William Fox of Columbia asked whether modernization was "a real term." He asked, "What is it that the West is doing while the non-West modernizes? Modernization may contain the notion that when you reach a threshold you are modernized, but we ourselves are not at a fixed point in a continuum." The suggestion—made in various ways by Parsons, Levy, Sutton, and Shils, among others—that modernity was somehow "upon us," seemed to him misguided. The West, too, was undergoing its own historic transformations.[108] But Bell, Fox, and Eggers were lonely voices in this group; for the most part, there was an implied consensus that the West had "reached" modernity once and for all. Was it a coincidence that neither Bell nor Fox nor Eggers ever participated in another CCP-sponsored conference?

One would think, upon reading this debate, that the CCP would have concluded that Shils's terminology was more confusing than clarifying. Yet after the Dobbs Ferry conference, those associated with the CCP began to use "development" and "modernization" as virtual synonyms. Shils's basic effort had been successful: the sociologists and political scientists may not have agreed about what constituted modernity, but at least they agreed that modernity was the desirable and necessary outcome of development. As Cyril Black observed, the conferees had made "an assumption of movement toward some kind of homogenization."[109] Despite disagreement about how to define "modern," "modernity," and "modernization," Shils had convinced the gallery that political science needed some metatheoretical concept denoting the difference between the West and non-West, of the sort betokened by "modernization." The minutes of the October 30-31, 1959, meeting of the CCP indicate the basic synthesis that had been reached at the conference. The CCP now felt confident that it could define "a process of political modernization, analogous to the process of economic growth." Although the CCP did not feel capable of producing a definition of "the concept of political modernization," it did seem convinced that it knew "about the 'terminal' characteristics of models of performance of the political functions in modern societies."[110] Following this meeting, Robert Ward penned a memo defining political modernization as "a process of political change wherein the political attitudes, behavior, and institutions of a group gradually lose their 'traditional' attributes and acquire 'modern' ones." Although he claimed that the concept of modernity was "open-ended and continually evolving," he gave it a definite and static definition:

A politically "modern" group or society is characterized by: a) the allocation of political roles by achievement rather than ascription; b) rational, scientific and secular techniques of decision-making; c) widespread popular interest and involvement in the political system, though not necessarily in the decision-making aspects thereof; d) the predominance of functionally specific rather than generalized political roles; e) broad and increasing ambit of explicit government involvement in, responsibility for, and regulation of the economic and social aspects of individual and group life; f) increasing centralization of [political] responsibility; g) impersonal system of law; f) a population which is in major part literate, urban, educated, socially mobile, and favorably oriented at least toward the concept of social change. . . . *This may suffice as a working definition of . . . the*

modernizing process, regardless of whether particular forms of political organization are
democratic or totalitarian in nature.[111]

Defining modernity in Parsonian terms, the CCP had concluded that the political dimensions of modernity involved a centralized, interventionist state governed by scientifically inclined elites. By this standard, the Soviet Union was as modern as the United States.

Gabriel Almond's Synthesis: The Politics of Developing Areas

In addition to Shils's paper, the Dobbs Ferry conference also witnessed, on the morning of June 9, 1959, Gabriel Almond's first unveiling of his functional model of comparative politics. In building this model, Almond credited long discussions with anthropologist John Roberts at the Center for Advanced and Behavioral Studies in Palo Alto during 1958 on "how primitive [political systems] were like, rather than unlike modern ones" with encouraging him to construct a comprehensive analytical scheme that could encompass all political systems, Western and non-Western alike. In introducing this model Almond explained that "the idea of assimilating non-Western systems into the discipline of comparative government was the first job of the Committee [on Comparative Politics]. We wanted to say something theoretically valid about how these systems worked, and not just make remarks about their stability in non-systematic terms. We distrusted structuralism and institutionalism."[112] Even though Almond had formulated this model before the Dobbs Ferry conference, when he published it as the introductory chapter to *The Politics of Developing Areas,* a collection of essays he edited along with James Coleman, under the title "A Functional Approach to Comparative Politics," he made sure to present his model in terms of the modernity-tradition dichotomy that Shils had promoted at the conference: "The political scientist who wishes to study political modernization in the non-Western areas," Almond wrote in 1960, "will have to master the model of the modern, which in turn can only be derived from the most careful empirical and formal analysis of the functions of modern Western polities."[113]

According to Almond, all political systems "from the Bergdama to Britain" had these things in common:

1. There are political structures. Comparisons could be made according to the degree and form of structural specialization. Almond rejected the state/nonstate distinction: political functions take place in all societies, though they might be discharged by very different structures.

2. They have the same political functions. Comparisons could be made based on what structures perform these functions and how regularly they do so. A main task of political theory is to identify these functions. Almond followed David Easton in dividing the functional elements of political systems into "inputs" and "outputs."[114] The political inputs were (a) political socialization and recruitment; (b) interest articulation; (c) interest aggregation; and (d) political communication. The outputs were (a) rule making; (b) rule application; and (c) rule adjudication.

3. All political structures are multifunctional. The "degree of specificity" may be compared. The degree of "political modernity" or "political development" was essentially to be determined by this degree of specificity.

It is not hard to see how Almond drew his categories from the experience of the "advanced" countries. For example, it was evident that the categories of rule making, rule adjudication, and rule application mapped almost identically onto the Western legislative, executive, and judicial branches of government (even if, as Almond pointed out, the American judiciary sometimes made rules and the Congress sometimes adjudicated them). Though Almond made sure to qualify that "[n]o political system, however modern, ever fully eliminates intermittency and traditionality," his collaborator James Coleman added that "it is clear . . . that the Anglo-American polities most closely approximate the model of a modern political system described [by Almond]." As Almond admitted, "We derived our functional categories from the political systems in which specialization and functional differentiation have taken place to the greatest extent."[115]

The utility of *The Politics of Developing Areas* as a model for comparative politics was based in part on its reception within the context of the overarching framework of modernization that Shils proposed. Just as there was an implied developmental narrative in the systemic analysis of Parsonian theory, so, too, was there an implied developmental narrative in Almond's functional analysis of political systems. As Almond himself pointed out, what made a country more or less politically developed was its degree of differentiation, or in other words, the degree to which its different structures carried out the functional tasks his theory laid out. This meant that the United States, with its constitutionally codified separation of functions, was the most political modernized society on earth. Because it promoted the greatest possible degree of functional differentiation, the American Constitution represented the apex of modernity. To become modern politically meant to adopt American political forms. Taking the basic functional categories from the contemporary United States conformed with Almond's implicit acceptance of the convergence hypothesis fundamental to Parsonian theory. The implicit developmental narrative of modernization made Almond's static model seem comprehensive and compelling.

Almond did make one important amendment to the use of the pattern variables. As he had pointed out at the conference, *dualism* was the salient reality of all societies, by which he meant the coexistence of both "modern" and "traditional" elements within one system. Not only was the modernity of a particular place shot through with traditional elements, but there always remained unmodernized pockets within even the most modernized polity. "All political systems are 'mixed' systems in the cultural sense. There are no 'all-modern' cultures and structures, in the sense of rationality, and no all-primitive ones, in the sense of traditionality." Thus political systems as a whole existed on "a continuum," and tradition and modernity did not represent "a dichotomous distinction." In other words, the pattern variables were excessively polarizing. Since dualism existed in all societies, what differentiated "Western" from "traditional" systems is that Western systems had far more differentiated "secondary structures" rather than the wholesale elimination of tendencies toward particularism, diffuseness, affectivity, and ascription.[116]

Although Almond's was not the only formulation of political modernization, with the publication of *The Politics of Developing Areas,* the paradigm of modernization theory reached fruition in political science. The two most basic elements were there: the structural-functional approach to politics based on the Parsonian notion of system, and the idea that the transition from tradition to modernity was the basic problem to be explained in postcolonial development studies. A template for understanding the process had been found, and for the next decade or so, the work of the CCP would mostly take place within these paradigmatic assumptions.

On the basis of the Dobbs Ferry breakthrough, the CCP submitted a major grant proposal to the Ford Foundation on January 19, 1960. The sense of excitement about having finally achieved a paradigm was palpable in the CCP's proposal. The proposal began by citing what was by now a mantra among sociologists and political scientists, namely that development economics was not enough for understanding the non-Western world: "Scholarly interest in the 'revolution of rising expectations' had earlier been shown on the part of economists, but it soon became evident that the problems of economic growth were accompanied by problems of political development, and about the latter little was known either empirically or theoretically."[117] The committee declared that its purpose was "to prepare by the end of 1963 a manuscript that would constitute an introduction to a theory of modernization."[118] The grant proposal asked Ford for money to operationalize the theoretical program that had been worked out at Dobbs Ferry. A series of weeklong conferences would bring together members of the CCP with area specialists and government officials, and would culminate with the publication of a series of books on political modernization.

In April, the Ford Foundation notified the CCP that it had been awarded $273,000 to support a program of "interdisciplinary seminars and training institutes on political development."[119] With that grant, the committee was set to run a series of semiannual conferences on a variety of topics intersecting with the concept of modernization. Once this money was secured, Almond decided to step back from his central role at the CCP. In formulating this effective theory of political modernization and securing a grant that would permit its theoretical and empirical elaboration, Almond felt that his task as chair had been accomplished. In 1963 he stepped aside to allow Lucian Pye to assume the chair of the CCP. It was under Pye's leadership that the Princeton series on "political development" would be produced. In the winter of 1961-62, the committee negotiated with Princeton University Press to publish a multivolume series entitled Studies in Political Development. The success of the political development series was such that by 1969, Bernard Brown would write that although few theorists were willing to admit a belief in progress, "virtually all political scientists now believe in the concept of 'modernization. . . .' All of the problems and subjects of political science are now being reexamined in terms of some concept of modernization."[120] In the end, seven volumes would be published in the Princeton series, and countless spin-offs in the main journals addressing comparative politics: *World Politics, Comparative Politics,* and of course, the *American Political Science Review.* The American study of postcolonial politics in the 1960s is essentially made up of these works. Scholars associated with the CCP achieved professional success, while those operating outside its orbit were, for the most part, marginalized.

In sum, the political development school of the 1960s, rooted in modernization theory, was the dominant social science paradigm of its day, pumping out prodigious amounts of work as it elaborated on the model that had been established in the 1950s. Indeed, the early history of the CCP provides a blueprint for how to establish a dominant social scientific paradigm. First, begin by finding a perceived global social crisis for which no social scientific answers currently exist. Second, find a sponsor with deep pockets—ideally the government or a private foundation—and a vested interest in finding answers to the topic at hand. Third, having secured funding, set up committees and think tanks and professional organizations that will act as institutional beachheads from which to attack the stolid mainstream of the profession. Fourth, identify potential allies in other disciplines and eliminate rivals within one's own. Fifth, issue programmatic manifestos that claim that the new method is both supple and powerful enough to solve all unanswered problems in not only your own discipline but also possibly several others. Finally, organize high-profile conferences to enlist new devotees. The way in which Herring and Almond used the CCP to promote modernization theory thus provides a textbook example for how to promote a methodological revolution in social science.

The success of the CCP in establishing modernization theory as a social scientific paradigm led to the highest disciplinary honors for its members, most notably the presidency of the American Political Science Association for Gabriel Almond in 1966. Almond dedicated his presidential address that year to describing the way in which political science was undergoing a "scientific revolution" (Almond explicitly invoked Thomas Kuhn) and finally, after millennia of effort, moving from theory to true scientific status.[121] Almond began by comparing himself to the biblical Rachel. His quest had been to bear a Joseph, "the instrument of Israel's salvation," in the form of a science of politics. Almond claimed that the key innovation that had succeeded in turning the study of politics into a scientific discipline was the conceptual structure he had introduced into the discipline, namely that of a "system" defined by its "structure" and "functions." In contrast to the political sociology or psychology of "pre-scientific" theorists like Plato and Aristotle, Almond's own methodological innovations "represented a genuinely important step in the direction of science . . . comparable in significance to the ones taken in Enlightenment political theory over the earlier classical formulations." Combined with the differentiation of variables and the use of statistics, the system concept represented "a significant step into the modern world of science." Led by the theoretical innovators in comparative politics, political science was finally leaving behind "the pressures of ethnocentrism and the distortions of the Cold War" to help provide "part of the solution of the ultimate problem of man's enlightenment." In Almond's own view, modernization theory represented the acme of the Enlightenment project—the end of a barren, prescientific study of politics—and augured the secular deliverance not just of the discipline but of mankind itself.

CHAPTER 5

Modernization Theory as a Foreign Policy Doctrine

The MIT Center for International Studies

> If I wanted to punish a province, I would give it an intellectual as a ruler.
> —attributed to FREDERICK THE GREAT

> We're all great experts on the nature and problems of the Vietnamese War
> . . . namely, in order to win the guerilla war, one must create at forced-draft
> the bone structure of a modern nation.
>
> —WALT ROSTOW,
> "The New Nations and Their Internal Defense," 1963

Many critics of modernization theory have placed its anti-Communist politics at the center of their analysis of its meaning. They suggest that modernization theory was little more than an ideological reflex of the cold war: an outgrowth of the anti-Communist foreign policy of the United States in the chilly geopolitics of the early postwar years. One reason for this historiographic phenomenon is that many modernization theorists eagerly advertised their anti-Communist credentials, proclaiming that their theories would help comprehend the Communist phenomenon in the postcolonial world. According to modernization theory, the non-Western world was where the battle between a monolithic "Communism" and a pluralist "free world" would be fought. Specialists in the politics of postcolonial regions thus considered themselves to have a privileged understanding of the dynamics of contemporary Communism. Modernization theory and the cold war seem inseparable. Nowhere was this more true than in the work done at the MIT Center for International Studies (CIS), the early history of which is the subject of this chapter. CIS scholars such as Lucian Pye grounded their analyses of Communism in a psychological interpretation of the appeal of Communist movements, focusing on the special susceptibility of individuals in countries undergoing modernization to the wiles of Communist political organizations. Taking a more socio-structural than psychological approach, Walt Rostow attempted to understand why some countries were especially susceptible to Communism and, in particular, at what moment in the development process a country was vulnerable to what Rostow called "the Communist disease."

By placing Parsonian theory within a context of cold war geopolitical imperatives, the CIS would forge a politically palatable rationale for U.S. interest in promoting development, presenting modernization theory as a capitalist alternative to the Leninist developmental model. At the same time, the CIS's anti-Communism was complicated by its recognition of the definite modernity of the Soviet Union. Unlike totalitarian theory, modernization theory considered Communism a *politically* pathological but *organizationally* effective means of promoting development and achieving modernity. Even in the work of Rostow, usually considered the most hawkish anti-Communist of the modernization theorists, the relationship between his own thought and that of Marx was more complicated than simple rejection. At the same time, in discussing how the CIS applied modernization theory to the concrete problems of development in the 1950s, I hope to make clear just how crucial anti-Communism was to its policy agenda. In fact, the very creation of the CIS was the result of a top secret anti-Communist propaganda project conducted at the Massachusetts Institute of Technology in the fall of 1950.

The Creation of the CIS

In the spring of 1950, the State Department faced a problem: the Soviet Union had discovered a way to jam the Voice of America (VOA), a main channel of the United States' international propaganda apparatus. Before the war, solving this problem would probably have involved only engineers. During the late 1940s and early 1950s, however, the U.S. government was recasting the concept of propaganda (which had an unsavory ring to it in a post-Nazi world) as "psychological warfare," understood as a science requiring both technical proficiency and an understanding of the psychology of its subjects. Given this technical-cum-social understanding of the propaganda problem, the State Department decided that the research on how to overcome the jamming of VOA could best be carried out by a team of academics. Accordingly, it approached MIT president James Killian to propose that the institute produce a study on how best to "get information into Russia." Accepting the offer, MIT spent the summer of 1950 assembling an interdisciplinary team of scholars from around the country to participate in the top secret project, which would be named Troy, in reference to the classical tale of covert infiltration behind enemy lines on the basis of false gifts.

In November 1950, with the Korean War raging, Project Troy began its study sessions at MIT's Lexington Field Station outside Boston. It adopted a pathbreaking methodological approach. Interdisciplinary panels began by surveying various approaches to specific propaganda problems. These surveys were discussed and critiqued by the whole group, and then handed off to working groups composed primarily of technical specialists. These specialists produced reports, which were again reviewed by the entire group. After this appraisal, the reports were turned over to an editorial committee, which prepared a penultimate draft, subject to a final total group review. Modeled after the Manhattan Project, Project Troy undertook an unprecedented interdisciplinary and collaborative approach to work between natural scientists, engineers, and social scientists, and the final report was about as close to an expression of the "group mind" of the participants as it is possible for a social scientific document to be. Submitted to the State Department on February 15, 1951, the report considered numerous propaganda alternatives or supplements to the VOA, including movies, intelligent travelers, library services, student exchanges, direct mail, professional journals, commercial publications, and even banal commodities such as flashlights and fountain pens.

The Project Troy report exceeded the technical particularities of how to overcome the jamming of the VOA. Adopting the phrase "political warfare," the report argued that successful defense against Communist expansionism depended on providing social and economic carrots as much as on propagandistic and military sticks. In examining the various target populations for the "political warfare" campaign, the report stated that "careful planning of basic research requirements carried out jointly by policy makers, government research officers, and university scholars implemented by a flexible policy of contractual grants to university centers can be of vital help in assuring a backlog of vital research."[1] Even before the report was filed, Killian began to organize a "second phase" of Project Troy, which included the production of a scholarly study of contemporary Soviet society, and the establishment at MIT of a permanent research facility aimed at continuing and extending the interdisciplinary collaborative research exemplified and advocated by the

Project Troy report. In the fall of 1951, working out of a warehouse in East Cambridge, a project on "Soviet vulnerability" had begun under Rostow's direction, which would result in the August 1952 publication of Rostow's *The Dynamics of Soviet Society.*[2] In the meantime, Killian's call for a permanent research center would result in the creation of the CIS in January 1952. The man charged with running the CIS was a leading participant in Project Troy, MIT economist Max Millikan.[3]

Max Millikan had spent the year between the end of Project Troy and the foundation of the CIS working as an assistant director of the Central Intelligence Agency. Millikan was an archetypal member of his generation's social and intellectual elite. The son of Nobel laureate physicist Robert Millikan, Max attended Phillips Academy and received both undergraduate and Ph.D. degrees in economics from Yale University, where he specialized in national income estimates with particular reference to the Soviet Union. It was as an undergraduate at Yale that Millikan had first met Rostow, in a 1934 seminar on black market economics directed by Richard Bissell, who would go on to mastermind the Bay of Pigs operation. Between his undergraduate and graduate degrees, Millikan studied with J. N. Hicks at Cambridge University, thereby coming into early contact with those intellectuals whose theoretical work would provide the foundation for postwar development economics. As director of the CIS, Millikan would help broker the reception of these economic ideas in the United States.

Like Pendleton Herring of the SSRC, Millikan exercised his intellectual influence more through his organizational skills than through his scholarship. Millikan's broad-minded vision of the CIS's purpose gave the center its sense of mission. Gathering top specialists in a variety of different fields, Millikan recruited to the CIS communications specialists Ithiel de Sola Pool and Daniel Lerner, political scientist Lucian Pye, and economists Walt Rostow and Everett Hagen. He also brought in economist Paul Rosenstein-Rodan, whom he had met at Cambridge University, to anchor the theoretical economics of the development proposals the CIS would make. All of these scholars would participate in formulating modernization theory. The initial seed money for the CIS came from the CIA, which at the time was well funded and whose finances were unknown to the public.[4] Targeting an extended communications research program, the Ford Foundation would provide the CIS with $875,000 of initial monies, distributed by a planning committee made up of Project Troy alumni Hans Speier (chair), Jerome Bruner, Wallace Carroll, Harold Lasswell, Paul Lazarsfeld, Ithiel de Sola Pool, and the ubiquitous Edward Shils.[5] The Rockefeller Foundation and Carnegie Foundation would also contribute funds over the next decade.

Millikan stated that the CIS's aim was to "apply social science to problems bearing on the peace and development of the world community."[6] The purpose was to throw light on the American role in promoting economic, social, and political change abroad. In addition to the direct study of change in the postcolonial regions, there were two parallel tracks of inquiry. The first track of inquiry was the study of Communism. From its inception, the CIS would study Communism, with Rostow leading the way by writing two general studies of contemporary Russia and China, as well as a policy appraisal of the American role in Asia.[7] The second track was an examination of American society. (Chapter 6 will examine these latter findings in detail.) Through the 1950s the CIS would function just as Project Troy had recommended, by bringing together academic specialists from numerous disciplines to participate in research and discussions on matters of "political warfare," broadly defined. Like the Harvard Department of Social Relations (DSR), the CIS emphasized the importance of interdisciplinary research.

Unlike the DSR, however, building a grand social theory was not the ultimate purpose of the institution. The CIS declared itself to be "problem-oriented"; that is, its research agenda would be set by practical policy concerns. The CIS encouraged its staff to devote substantial time not only to problems germane to their individual disciplines but also to "practical and applied issues, the solution of which requires, as a matter of common sense, attention to a variety of factors outside his normal disciplinary competence."[8] The aim was to build a community of specialists aware of the limits of their disciplines and willing to reach out to include other perspectives. To generate its policy proposals, the CIS adopted Project Troy's pioneering approach to social science: sociologists and anthropologists would examine the changing lifeways of the targets, economists would promote economic growth, political scientists would discuss the dangers and opportunities associated with such change, and communications specialists would develop the propaganda program. By applying this research technique to international problems, social scientists could make major contributions to the international development mission. As Walt Rostow said in June 1962, "Out of the counterpoint between intellectual life and the working experience of governments we can hope to develop . . . a much firmer grasp on the total process of development and modernization than we now have."[9] Both truth and justice would be served.

The CIS saw its mission as cognate to the government- and military-oriented work being done in the natural sciences. According to Rostow, "In developing an effective American policy in underdeveloped areas the social scientists have a role equivalent to that of the physical scientists in the arms race." American "national interest" could not "operate simply by instinct or with analogies drawn from the peculiar circumstances of our own national experience." Instead, American policy makers had to achieve a "scientific perspective" on how to "influence the evolution of the underdeveloped areas."[10] As the CIS put it in its 1955 annual report, "The Center's research is planned from the standpoints both of scholarly value and of relevance to public policy. It is intended to contribute both to our understanding of human behavior and to the solution of some of the long-term problems of international policy which confront the decision makers in government and private life."[11] The aim of attaining social scientific truth was not seen as incompatible or even as being in tension with, for example, the aim of "encouraging the sound growth of . . . vigorous agencies of popular control."[12] Thinking of its own work as comparable to natural science may have prevented the CIS from acknowledging that pursuing social scientific truth while advancing its particular sociopolitical goals represented a conflict of interest. The belief that American social science had attained a value-free method allowed its practitioners to avoid asking themselves tough ethical questions about the ends and uses of their research.

The Intellectual Foundations of the CIS

This section considers the main texts that laid the intellectual groundwork for the CIS's policy proposals. First, a theory of economic development, advanced by Walt Rostow and Paul Rosenstein-Rodan, would provide the base on which the CIS would build its superstructure of political and sociological claims. Second, Harold Lasswell would supply a political psychology and conception of the social function of the intellectual. Third, Lucian Pye, whose connection to modernization theory had begun when he helped found the CCP, would pioneer the application of Lasswell's political psychology to the "underdeveloped" countries. And finally, Daniel Lerner, with the publication of *The Passing of Traditional Society* (1958), would use a study of political and social change in the Middle East to produce the first fully elaborated example of modernization theory.

Walt Rostow, born in New York in 1916, was the child of Russian Jewish immigrants. His parents' assimilationist zeal and democratic-socialist politics can be judged by the names they chose for their three sons: Walt Whitman, Ralph Waldo, and Eugene Victor. Walt was a prodigy. Admitted to Yale at sixteen, he decided as a freshman that his life purpose was to construct a theory of economics and history capable of countering Marx's. After completing Yale in three years, he attended Oxford on a Rhodes scholarship, and a year later, in 1940, earned his Ph.D. in economics from Yale. During the war he first worked for the Office of Strategic Services in its research and analysis branch on studies of the Soviet economy, where he argued that the Russians had the ability to stand up to the German invasion. He then went to the air force, where he studied the effectiveness of bombing raids in Germany. Foreshadowing his Vietnam policies, he concluded that bombing was most effective when aimed at oil stocks and refineries rather than transport infrastructure and industry. After the war he lectured at Oxford on American diplomacy before taking a position as an assistant to Gunnar Myrdal at the Economic Commission for Europe. In 1950 he accepted a position as professor of economics at MIT. Although he had been a founding member, Rostow formally joined the CIS on his return from Europe in 1952.

That year Rostow published a monograph entitled *The Process of Economic Growth*. Formally, this work was an intervention into the post-Keynesian theoretical debate about economic growth. But Rostow's work was, in three senses, also an early example of development economics. First, it used a definition of development that would become orthodox for development economics during the next two decades. Second, its focus on extra-economic factors to explain the sources of the developmental impulse would set it off from the neoclassical economic theories of growth being proposed by, among others, Nicholas Kaldor, J. R. Hicks, and Evsey Domar. Third, *The Process* would frame economic growth within a wider picture of social evolution. It sought to understand the factors that had spurred growth in the industrial countries in order to use this knowledge to help solve the problems of endemic poverty in the so-called underdeveloped countries. Basing his analysis on a critique of R. F. Harrod's cutting-edge theory of economic growth in industrial economies, Rostow defined *economic growth* as increased aggregate national income growth and capital accumulation. This definition accorded with politically popular postwar definitions of growth. As chapter 2 pointed out, postwar leaders of both postcolonial and metropolitan countries agreed that augmenting prosperity was the foundation of any effective development. In the early 1950s, economists and politicians alike equated aggregate national income growth with increased prosperity. Increased output of goods and services became a proxy for improvement in human capacities and conditions. Accepting this geopolitically correct understanding of development, Rostow's work helped define the classical paradigm of development economics by suggesting that national income growth and capital accumulation were the sine qua non of development.

In addition to this definition of development as aggregate growth, Rostow's theory emphasized the importance of extra-economic factors for explaining economic growth. Rostow proposed that human beings were imbued with varying degrees of certain "propensities," in addition to profit maximization, that governed their responses to varying socioeconomic conditions. These propensities were as follows:

1.   the propensity to develop fundamental science
2.   the propensity to apply science to economic ends
3.   the propensity to accept innovations
4.   the propensity to seek material advance
5.   the propensity to consume
6.   the propensity to have children

As analytical tools, the propensities would "permit the general analyst of societies to bring his methods to bear on the determinates of economic growth."[13] Dynamically related in a self-reinforcing pattern of growth, these variables linked economic theory to sociology, anthropology, psychology, and history in a Lamarckian scheme in which societal evolution depended on the exertions of the societies in question. Not only was the language of "propensities" drawn directly from Lamarck, but the notion that Western intrusion was the spur to modernization in non-Western countries mirrored Lamarck's notion that organisms develop new traits because of a need created by the environment, which is then transmitted to offspring.

The propensities were Rostow's way of describing the economically relevant aspects of a culture, but the mere enumeration of these propensities did not provide any account of what caused societal propensities to change. While much of Rostow's book analyzed the impact of these propensities on economic performance, he happily admitted that he did not know what shaped these propensities in different populations. Rostow's position synthesized cultural and technological determinism: technology was the ultimate driver and definer of modernization, but it was culture that determined how a society took up that technology. And yet, peculiarly, he felt no need to explain why a culture or its ideas would shift, spurring the move from one stage to another. Rostow entrusted noneconomists with disentangling "the motives and societal processes which might determine the effective strength and course of change of these variables."[14] In other words, Rostow's stages of growth, while appearing to be a theory of historical evolution, in fact had no account for the root causes of historical change.[15] It was a problem with his theory that he would bump up against throughout his career but never manage to resolve.

Though he did not yet use the term *modernization*, Rostow attempted to solve this problem by contextualizing economic growth within a more general process of social evolution—one adopted implicitly from Talcott Parsons, whose *Toward a General Theory of Action* he had eagerly read the year before. While he did not believe that understanding the economies of poor countries required an entirely different economic theory,[16] his emphasis on extra-economic factors bridged the gap between the formalist orthodoxies of neoclassical theory and the institutionalist ideas that had been steadily losing ground within the economics profession since the turn of the century. Institutional economists had long recognized that economic growth could not be understood without reference to extra-economic factors. In this respect, Rostow's theory proceeded from the same insights as the work of Talcott Parsons, who, as chapter 3 explained, developed his social theory out of a critique of the autonomy and supposed explanatory power of neoclassical economics. While Rostow did not endorse Parsons's aim of subordinating economics within a wider social theory, Rostow, too, wanted to produce "a kind of biological theory [of growth], of process and pattern."[17]

Introducing his most famous metaphor, Rostow explained that economic growth, if sustained, resulted in "take-off," by which he meant the transition of a society from a mostly agricultural to a mostly industrial basis. If this take-off were successful, it would yield a "self-sustaining growth pattern."[18] Making clear the ultimate technological determinism of his model, Rostow noted that in the case of England, it had been the application of Arkwright's mule that had provided the initial basis for take-off, which had then been reinforced by shifts in the propensities. In late-industrializing Japan, by contrast, a state-directed shift in the propensities had been the determining variable. "The systematic analysis . . . of the take-off process," Rostow concluded, would "constitute an exercise in the art of relating economic, social, and political factors over time."[19] In practice, the CIS would advocate large amounts of state-provided economic aid as a way to promote development.

Beyond Rostow's work, economist Paul Rosenstein-Rodan would lead the CIS's efforts to analyze the economics of foreign aid. An important prewar contributor to equilibrium theory, Rosenstein-Rodan had written what is often cited as the first article of development economics, "Problems of Industrialization of Eastern and South-Eastern Europe" (1943).[20] For Rosenstein-Rodan and other interwar continental liberals, the largely agricultural Eastern European economy was the model "backward economy" from which a great deal of the early theorizing of development economics began. These economists assumed that people on the land were mired in tradition, and that this traditionalism meant a lack of political sophistication and hence susceptibility to political demagoguery. These liberals' politically motivated antiruralism and antipopulism encouraged them to support top-down, elite-led industrialization projects that would turn peasants into industrial workers, which, the liberals hoped, would neutralize their political fecklessness.[21] Noting that Eastern European economies contained large amounts of surplus labor, Rosenstein-Rodan argued that overcoming endemic national poverty required a massive (and therefore state-planned) "Big Push" in several economic sectors simultaneously, creating a virtuous circle of economic growth.[22] Although Rosenstein-Rodan's proposals differed from Soviet proposals by favoring labor-intensive rather than capital-intensive models of economic growth, both theories shared biases against agriculture and in favor of state-led development.

With a cutting-edge economic theory rooted in a congenial political theory, Rosenstein-Rodan was an obvious fit for the CIS, and Max Millikan made it one of his first acts in 1952 to invite Rosenstein-Rodan to join the operation. At the CIS, Rosenstein-Rodan wrote an article entitled "International Aid for Undeveloped Countries" (1961), which would provide the most elaborate justification for the specific aid levels proposed by the CIS. Using Rostow's vocabulary, this article argued that the main point of the aid program was to spur the process of "take-off" until growth became "self-sustaining." (Rosenstein-Rodan made a careful distinction between *sustained* growth, which might require indefinite aid inputs, and *self*-sustained growth. The aim, contrary to the opinions of some critics, was not to create a situation of permanent dependency but rather to get countries over the hump of backwardness.) Appropriate aid levels depended not on short-term political or military goals but on the "absorptive capacity" of the particular postcolonial countries, defined rather vaguely as the "ability to use capital productively."[23] The aim was not to increase income in the short run, or to equalize incomes in different countries, but rather to spur the locals to "increased effort."

In addition to these economic theories, the CIS would also draw on a psychological theory of politics influenced by Harold Lasswell.[24] Born in 1902 in Illinois, son of a Presbyterian minister, he did his graduate work at the University of Chicago under the direction of Charles Merriam, who retained him as a professor after he had completed his doctorate. Though Lasswell's only formal affiliation with the institutions of modernization theory was as a member of the CIS planning board, he was a shadowy presence in the work of many modernization theorists. While a professor at Chicago, he taught both Edward Shils and Gabriel Almond. He collaborated with Daniel Lerner and, upon moving to Yale after the war, instructed Lucian Pye. Although he did not share the compulsive concern with "modernity" that was the hallmark of modernization theory, both his psychological conception of the political and his ideas about the social and political role of social scientists would mark modernization theory.

Lasswell's 1930 text *Psychopathology and Politics* was among the first systematic empirical studies of political behavior to employ ideas drawn from clinical psychology.[25] Deriving his ideas from the Freudian psychoanalytical movement that was only just beginning to make serious inroads in the United States, he reduced political behavior, roles, and ideologies to cathexes of private libidinal urges. This application of psychoanalytical methods to the study of political behavior precipitated tremendous growth in the study of activities previously considered "nonpolitical" by the reigning institutional-legal methodologists in political science. Following Lasswell's lead, a variety of scholars in the 1950s, including the modernization theorists, began to ask questions about the relationship between ego functioning, personality development, and political behavior. Methodologically, the interpretation of politics as a way of releasing nervous tension would become an important, if usually unstated, presupposition of modernization theory's construction of politics.

Equally important for modernization theory was Lasswell's focus on psychopathology. According to Lasswell, the political arena served as a site for the displacement of private psychic disturbances. The malleability of political symbols, Lasswell suggested, made them well suited for the introjection of individual "issues." In other words, individuals could invest political symbols with all sorts of personal meanings that would allow them to work through their own psychological processes. He reasoned that if political activity in general represented the playing out of individual psychodynamics, then the discontent that generated the "extreme" response of political radicalism had to result from some equally extreme psychological disturbance. In a series of subtle rhetorical moves, *Psychopathology and Politics* reduced political dissent to an expression of psychological deviance. Indeed, Lasswell's analysis implied that the truly well-adjusted person would have no reason to enter politics at all. Lasswell's position anticipated modernization theory's views on political radicalism in the postcolonial world. The apparent madness of Hitler and Stalin and their strange popular appeal during the 1930s and World War II would make many American social scientists receptive to the idea that the political behavior of the masses had to be (or at least could be) explained by their psychopathologies.

Lasswell also influenced modernization theory through his conception of the social function of the social scientist. Already in 1930 *Psychopathology and Politics* had celebrated the figure of "an omnicompetent, interdisciplinary social scientist–policy advisor."[26] With the rise of Nazism and his experience working on American counterpropaganda during World War II, Lasswell became even more skeptical of the political capacities of the masses. Echoing Lester Frank Ward's calls for "sociocracy" (but discarding Ward's populist sympathies), Lasswell proposed that an intelligentsia assume the leadership of society. He believed that social scientists ought to have the same relationship with society that psychotherapists had with their patients: helping their patients to achieve self-fulfillment on their own terms. In practice, this meant adopting a managerial attitude toward society, creating what Lasswell called a "technology of politics" in which both elites and citizens would conform to the imperatives of scientific knowledge.[27] If in 1927 he had criticized Woodrow Wilson's manipulation of public opinion during World War I, by the 1940s he had become an ardent advocate of propaganda and psychological warfare both at home and abroad.

Typical of late Progressive thought, the search for order became the main purpose of Lasswell's theory. Historian Christopher Simpson argues that Lasswell advocated "not just order in the abstract sense, but rather a particular social order in the United States and the world in which forceful elites ruled in the interests of their vision of the greater good. U.S.-style consumer democracy was simply a relatively benign system for engineering mass consent for the elites' authority; it could be dispensed with when ordinary people reached the 'wrong conclusions.' "[28] According to Lasswell, the role of the social scientists was both to describe the functioning of society and to design a system for controlling and manipulating that would achieve a eurythmic social order.[29] Because Lasswell conceived of the political impulse in individuals as a manifestation of psychopathology, his "idea of a democracy found expression in terms of elite scientific social planning and mass manipulation. . . . His early work might even be construed as devoted more to the elimination of politics than its management."[30] In this sense, Lasswell epitomized the antipolitical attitude that James Scott has identified as a trademark of authoritarian high modernism.[31]

The psychopathological conception of politics and the elitist theory of democracy would come together in Lasswell's idea of "policy science." In 1951, in a book he co-edited with Daniel Lerner, Lasswell published a programmatic essay to promote what he called the "policy sciences."[32] As Lasswell conceived them, the policy sciences would bring together the abstract insights that earlier generations of social scientists had generated to help inform better policy making on the part of policy elites. Acting as "guardians of democracy," the policy scientists would find a solution to the "major problem of our epoch," namely "the completion of the revolutionary processes of our historical period with the smallest human cost."[33] In other words, Lasswell in 1951 looked forward to a postrevolutionary world society in which the policy sciences would stand alone in guiding political activity. Lasswell's ambitions for the policy sciences set the agenda for the CIS's attempt to understand and promote a single, interlocking, global modernity. Two scholars who would help advance this agenda were Lasswell's protégés Lucian Pye and Daniel Lerner.

Lucian Pye joined the CIS in 1956, on the strength of his newly published book, *Guerrilla Communism in Malaya*. Born in 1921 in Fenchow, Shansi Province, China, Pye—like so many of the other figures who contributed to the modernization discourse—was the child of clerics, in his case Congregationalist educational missionaries. Pye attended the North China American School in Beijing, as well as Carleton College, and spent the war in Asia as an intelligence officer for the Marine Corps. After the war, Pye enrolled in graduate school in political science at Yale University, which was becoming the postwar center of the behavioralist revolution. While at Yale, Pye studied with Harold Lasswell, Nathan Leites, and Gabriel Almond, all of them students of Charles Merriam.[34]

One of Pye's main contributions to modernization theory was to unite the study of political psychopathology with the study of postcolonial countries. *Guerrilla Communism in Malaya* reflected not only the indirect influence of Pye's professor Harold Lasswell, but, even more strongly, the direct influence of Pye's other professor (and fellow student of Lasswell's), Gabriel Almond. In 1954, just as he accepted the chair of the CCP, Almond had published his own application of Lasswellian theory, a study entitled *The Appeals of Communism*. Basing its claims on the psychoanalytical and quantitative methodologies that Lasswell had been advocating for twenty years, Almond's *Appeals* sought to understand what sort of men joined Western Communist parties. On the one hand, Almond argued, Italian and French Communists tended to be workers joining what was often the only party in their country to advocate their "immediate interests." On the other hand, in the United States and Britain, where class divisions were allegedly not so severe as on the Continent, Almond concluded that Communists were "alienated," "psychologically maladjusted," or "deviational" men, who felt cut off from other sorts of familial or social institutions, and who sought out the discipline of the party in order to feel whole again.[35] By linking a celebration of the American social structure with the denigration of Communism, Almond's psychological approach to understanding social conflict mirrored the approaches that contemporary American historians were taking to understanding conflict at home in the United States. As John Higham commented of these historians, "A psychological approach to conflict enables historians to substitute a schism in the soul for a schism in society."[36] The same was true for many postwar American social scientists.

Pye's innovation was to place Almond's ideas within a developmental framework. *Guerrilla Communism* argued that Malaya was a society in "transition." Based on intensive interviews with sixty ethnic Chinese who had joined and then left the Communist movement in Malaya, Pye concluded that the real basis of the Communist appeal in underdeveloped countries was the sense of rootlessness felt by people separated from their "traditional ways" and unable to realize their ambitions according to new ones. The loss of the "traditional way of life" and the attempt to attain a "modern" one had created great psychological stresses. According to Pye, the party structure helped his respondents to find grounding for themselves in their rapidly changing world. Like Almond regarding the French and Italian Communists, Pye expressed a limited empathy for why Malayans felt disaffected by their circumstances and why Communism could seem an appealing option under those circumstances; but at the same time, he also claimed that the desire to join the

Communist Party was at bottom a response to the psychological disturbance of "transition" and thus a manifestation of psychopathology.[37] The discourse of psychopathology positioned the social scientist as a dispassionate physician, lording his wisdom over a postcolonial country bereft of legitimate subjectivity, thus making the postcolonial "transition" a matter to be handled by "experts" rather than by politicians or (heaven forbid) the demos.

After he joined the CIS in 1956, Pye broadened his ideas about the psychopathology of modernization. Crucial in his evolving understanding of this dynamic was his reading of Erik Erikson's celebrated psychobiography, *Young Man Luther* (1958). In *Young Man Luther*, Erikson sought to explain how and why Martin Luther became a world-historical figure. Erikson located the crucial moment in Luther's personality formation in what he called an "identity crisis," which Erikson believed was a near-universal phenomenon, most commonly afflicting adolescents struggling to define themselves as adults. The young person, having processed the experiences and reactions of earlier stages of childhood, had to commit him- or herself to a self-definition sufficient for both individual stability and social recognition. The individual had to arrive at a "central perspective and direction" that would allow for a "meaningful resemblance between what he has come to see in himself and what his sharpened awareness tells him others judge him and expect him to be."[38] In the case of Luther, various psychological experiences of late adolescence led to the formation of the combination of faith and wrath that was the psychological foundation of his political ideology. Erikson considered Luther a marvelous example of the successful condensation of a teenage identity crisis into a whole and principled adult personality. However, it was also clear that during the period of crisis, extreme emotional volatility was the norm rather than the exception. In addition, Erikson argued that the process of identity crisis and identity formation could also go awry and result in permanent personality disfiguration or dysfunction.

Although Erikson's volume is a rich work in its own right, in this context what is important is how Erikson's description of personality development informed Lucian Pye's work on political development. Pye mobilized Erikson's theory to help understand two distinct phenomena of postcolonial politics. First, he used it to analyze the personalities of individual postcolonial political leaders. Working on the Burmese case, Pye argued that the leaders in many postcolonial countries did not possess a "coherent" personal identity. What explained the volatility (and volubility) of these leaders was that they were still in the experimental phase of their identity formation, which meant that they were "anxious to try out . . . all manner of ideological forms." This lack of stable leaders was unfortunate, however, because "before a nation can develop, leaders must emerge who have found integrity in their own quests for identity."[39] Combining the Eriksonian method with an elitist theory of politics thus led to a rather grim diagnosis of the political prospects for post-colonial countries.[40]

The second and even more important way in which Pye applied Erikson's theory to the postcolonial situation was to understand the process of *collective identity* formation in these countries. This application of Erikson's individual identity theory to help understand group identity went beyond anything that Erikson had himself proposed. For Pye, an essential part of the transitional process involved "the creation of an inner coherence of values, theories, and actions for the entire polity." In other words, "nation-building" involved forging a national identity or national character. "Those who hope that national identity can come from modernization cannot escape the depressing psychological fact that modernity, in the mind of these people, has always been the monopoly of those who were their former masters."[41] Adopting a literally paternalistic stance, Pye argued that postcolonial nations faced difficulties in their efforts to form coherent identities because they had not resolved their conflicts with their (post)colonial "fathers." This way of conceiving postcolonial psychology turned political radicalism into an expression of Oedipal insecurity or neurosis in the postcolonial leader or nation, rather than a legitimate protest against ongoing economic exploitation and political and military domination. Pye thought of the postcolonial nations as essentially rebellious adolescents, potentially susceptible to Communist delinquency, which in turn might lead to a life of international crime.

The metaphor of the postcolonial nations as "young" or "immature" appears throughout the literature on modernization.[42] In 1963, for example, Seymour Martin Lipset claimed that "[c]ountries, like people, are not handed identities at birth, but acquire them through the arduous process of 'growing up,' a process which is a notoriously painful affair."[43] This way of conceiving and talking about the non-Western world had a distinguished pedigree in American colonial thought, most infamously expressed in William Howard Taft's comments about "our little brown brothers" in the Philippines. More proximate in the postwar context were General Douglas MacArthur's comments about occupied Japan to the Senate in 1951: "If the Anglo-Saxon is, say, forty-five years of age in his development in the sciences, the arts, divinity, and culture . . . the Japanese . . . measured by the standards of modern civilization . . . would be like a boy of twelve as compared with our development of forty-five years."[44] Considering non-Western peoples and leaders as psychologically akin to teenagers could license various attitudes. It might justify forbearance with regard to the "youthful" folly of posturing political radicals. It might be invoked as part of a call for greater instruction and assistance. Or it might, especially in the 1950s, be raised to conjure the specter of delinquent youth in need of discipline. The metaphor of non-Western nations as younger and possibly wayward siblings was never invoked, however, along with the injunction not to be one's brother's keeper.

Harold Lasswell's psychologistic approach to politics would also inform the work of Daniel Lerner, his collaborator on the *Policy Sciences* volume. Trained as a sociologist, Lerner had spent World War II as a member of the army's Psychological Warfare Division, and his career typified the trajectory of many postwar scholars from wartime propaganda work into cold war "communications" scholarship.[45] Though Lerner was a wide-ranging specialist in communications studies, he is best remembered for his classic work of 1958, *The Passing of Traditional Society*.[46] Produced as a joint venture between the CIS and the Bureau of Applied Social Research at Columbia University, this work provided the first explicit theorization by a postwar American social scientist of a process called "modernization." Though crude in its formulations, *The Passing* embodied the spirit of modernization theory as completely as any other work.

On an overt level, *The Passing* was a study of the modern media's impact on the people of the Middle East. Its theoretical ambitions made all this work much more than just another Area Study. Lerner claimed that the media, by informing readers, viewers, and listeners of the experiences of other people, heightened "empathy," which he defined as "the capacity to see oneself in the other fellow's situation."[47] Lerner's notion of empathy echoed the concept of "other-directedness" that David Riesman had developed in *The Lonely Crowd* (1950). In that work, as we saw in chapter 3, Riesman had argued that modern American man now derived his identity not from his internal discipline and ability to live up to social norms but rather from his relations with others.[48] Lerner's twist on this theme was to abstract the psychological quality of other-directedness away from the American historical context and to elevate its derivative—the notion of empathy—to the central psychological feature of "modernity." In so doing, moreover, he excised the tone of lament that had accompanied Riesman's analysis of contemporary America (in much the same way that Parsons had excised the pessimism from Max Weber's writings). The emergence of empathy (or other-directedness) became the key to modernization.

Lerner saw the progress of empathy as driven by technology. According to Lerner, mass communication technologies were the essential vehicle of modernization, creating similar cultural traits everywhere they penetrated. Using the latest quantitative methods, Lerner measured the "degree of modernization" within a population by the degree of penetration of the mass media and by the internalization of the messages of the mass media. He asked his subjects, for example, how many newspapers did they read? How often did they listen to the radio? Did they have opinions about the things they read and heard therein? Lerner assumed that to listen was to hear, and to read was to absorb, and that these experiences influenced almost all individuals in the same way. For him, literacy was the best "index and agent" of modernization.[49] (The main flaw of the book, as other modernization theorists would later see it, was that it attributed excessive causal weight in the process of modernization to the single "independent variable" it examined, namely the media. Alex Inkeles would refine Lerner's work by deeming the media to be but one causal factor, subordinate to education and above all the factory system, in the "modernization of men.") In its rigorous quantitative approach and value-free posturing, *The Passing* was a classic of behavioralist analysis.

What made this work the first full expression of modernization theory was that Lerner grounded his analysis of the psychological impact of media exposure in a model of unilinear development from tradition to modernity. Although Lucian Pye's *Guerrilla Communism in Malaya* had also used a developmental hermeneutic, Lerner's book represented the first attempt to state a theory of modernization in a systematic manner. Lerner explained that the process of modernization was an abstracted model of what had happened in "the West."[50] Generalizing from the Western experience, one could observe that modernization was a "phased" process. According to Lerner, the four phases of modernization were urbanization, increased literacy, media participation, and finally political participation. Urbanization allowed for more effective schooling techniques, which in turn promoted increases in literacy. Greater literacy meant more access to the news media. These media increased awareness of the world, including the world of commodities. Indirectly, the media presented hitherto unimagined images of the lifeways of others, a process that Lerner claimed generated greater empathy, thus creating the fundamental psychological aspect of modernity.

Lerner was unflinching in his modernist universalism: in his view, there was nothing alienating about being told that one's own private experience was but a repetitive moment of a larger human phenomenon. "To see the common human situation of diverse people," Lerner explained, "can be humanizing in the measure that enlightenment leads to betterment. The perception of regularities may, in this sense, be the main gift of social research to social policy."[51] Lerner was adamant in his faith in the uplifting and universalizing quality of modernization. Increased communications technology would lead to more transparent, rational, noise-free forms of political discourse and social organization. Traditional practices were regarded as noise to be eliminated by the clarity of modern forms of communications. True, modernization involved the dislocation of individuals from their old lifeways, but overall the benefits were unquestionable. As Lerner asserted, "In every country, the rural villagers declare themselves the most unhappy fellows. In every country, the modernizing individuals are considerably less unhappy—and the more rapidly the society around them is modernized the happier they are."[52] Unsympathetic toward the local, the particular, and the unique, Lerner did not doubt that reaching modernity along the path blazed by the West was something that every country should desire. Resolute in its convergent universalism and scornful of all that stood in the way of its realization, Lerner's modernization theory expressed no romantic nostalgia for the destruction of premodern heterogeneity.

While not lamentable in itself, this destruction of the premodern world did create certain dangers. The problem with the Middle East was that it was "a deviation, in some measure a deliberate deformation, of the Western model."[53] Modernization was a "systemic" process, and the various "sectors" of a modernizing society had to be "balanced."[54] If a country's social change went "out of phase" or if there was an "over-production of Transitionals"—Lerner used this uppercase word as a noun to indicate men en route between tradition and modernity—then a baleful political radicalism was a likely result. Lerner argued that the intrusion of mass media technologies had created such a situation by implicitly encouraging political participation (what Karl Deutsch later called "mobilization"[55]) by the socially and economically disenfranchised masses. Lerner acknowledged that the lingering resentments of colonialism made many countries want "modern institutions but not modern ideologies, modern power but not modern purposes, modern wealth but not modern wisdom, modern commodities but not modern cant. It is not clear, however, that modern ways and words can be so easily and totally sundered. Underlying the variant ideological forms which modernization took in Europe, America, and Russia, there have been certain behavioral and institutional compulsions common to all."[56] The critical policy issue was how to manage postcolonial anti-Western resentment, on the one hand, and the anxieties attendant upon the dislocation of the modernization process, on the other, in such a way that the masses did not turn to a "radical" solution. Though Lerner did not propose specific mechanisms, his analysis provided a framework for developing such policies.

Lerner's main policy concern was with how to prevent "radical" solutions to the stresses of the modernization process. His analysis recognized that modernization destroyed the integrating function of "traditional" political symbols. "The symbols of race and ritual" were "fading into irrelevance" and had to be replaced.[57] With the loss of the old legitimizing symbols, vitriolic nationalism and class-based radicalism became significant dangers. Showing the influence of his mentor Harold Lasswell, Lerner declared that the goal was to create "a functional new elite"[58] capable of mobilizing new symbols that would "otherwise provide guidance" to the masses.[59] While Lerner was pessimistic about the prospects for the creation of such elites, he and his cronies would eventually realize that there did in fact exist one group in postcolonial societies that was particularly suited for this role: the military.

Modernization Theory as a Policy Proposal

Beyond these intellectual antecedents, there were prosaic political considerations that led to modernization theory's entry into the political public sphere. Prime among these contexts was the ascendant power of conservatives in Washington. With the election of Dwight Eisenhower to the presidency in 1952, and the concomitant Republican majorities in Congress, resistance to foreign economic aid strengthened. Perceiving that the foreign aid program was a global extension of the New Deal program they loathed, Republicans had already blocked funding for the Point Four program during President Harry Truman's administration. They associated foreign aid with Truman's secretary of state, Dean Acheson, the object of unexcelled hate among conservatives. The isolationist wing of the Republican Party, while not as powerful as between the wars, was still noisy enough to raise doubts about the utility of devoting large amounts of resources to foreign aid.[60] With the hardening of cold war battle lines by the mid-1950s, conservatives increasingly tried to link economic aid to specific demands about the political and military behavior of the recipients. For conservatives, the Korean War underlined the need to link economic aid to military aims. Liberal internationalism found itself on the defensive.

It was within this context of skepticism about economic aid that the CIS fashioned its policy proposals between 1954 and 1961. The CIS had planned on devoting its first five years to theoretical expositions of the sort I outlined in the preceding pages. However, the political situation both globally and in Washington made it evident that the liberal internationalists needed to set out their policy position as quickly as possible. For the CIS, foreign economic aid was an integral part of the anti-Communist containment policy that had begun with the Truman Doctrine in 1947. By the mid-1950s, in the wake of Korea, most American leaders "worried mainly about the psychological appeal of Communism to frightened citizens of unstable countries. Hence the need for 'patient' containment, mainly via the means of economic aid."[61] Over the course of the late 1950s, the CIS would make a series of increasingly elaborate arguments for why the United States had to continue—and indeed augment—its foreign economic (as opposed to merely military) assistance. The CIS also proposed that economic aid be "unlinked"—in other words, that the aid be given without attaching political strings. It was out of this process of justifying the economic aid programs that modernization theory would enter the public political domain in the late 1950s and early 1960s.

The CIS's first extended intervention into the debates about foreign aid policy began in connection with a meeting organized in May 1954 in Princeton, New Jersey, by Time/Life correspondent and vice president C. D. Jackson, a former member of the army's Psychological Warfare staff and former special assistant for international affairs to President Eisenhower. In a typical Establishment event, Jackson brought together businessmen, labor leaders, government officials, and academics for two weeks of informal discussions about how the United States could better promote its interest in free trade while maintaining both its own security and geopolitical stability. Particular attention was given to the "underdeveloped" countries. Max Millikan and Walt Rostow were among those invited. As Rostow recollected, "At the Princeton Inn a rough-and-ready consensus did emerge that an enlarged global initiative by the United States in support of development was required."[62]

Jackson invited Millikan and Rostow to write a report on how the aid program for the "underdeveloped" countries could help promote economic growth and political stability. Millikan and Rostow produced a first draft in late May 1954. Two months later, a revised manuscript began to circulate among academics and policy makers, including members of Congress considering the 1956 foreign aid bill. Described as a product of the entire CIS staff, it would be entered into the *Congressional Record* at the beginning of 1957 under the title "Objectives of the United States Economic Assistance Programs."

The "Objectives" began by reviewing the history of American foreign aid, noting that the postwar aid programs were the heirs of the wartime Lend Lease Program, which had been continued in the relief and rehabilitation efforts of 1944-46, in the reconstruction and Marshall Plan contributions of 1947-50, and in the continuing military support for Europe.[63] The report explained that the goal of American foreign policy since the war had been to create a prosperous, expanding world economy in which trade would become increasingly free and currencies increasingly convertible. The aim was to create a world in which "the productive possibilities of exchange among nations" could be exploited without reference to national security problems.[64] Though few politicians in the immediate wake of the Korean War doubted the necessity of continued multifocal military aid for the "underdeveloped" areas, the CIS noted, many had begun to question the necessity of economic aid. Though lamentable, this questioning was understandable, because the United States still lacked for the "underdeveloped" areas "an equivalent to the balanced economic-military approach represented in Europe by the Marshall Plan and NATO. In a basic sense we have not yet clarified our national interest in the underdeveloped areas."[65] The goal of the CIS report was to outline the theoretical basis for a unified policy approach for the postcolonial regions.

The basic proposal was for the United States to provide great amounts of unlinked economic aid to help spur worldwide economic growth. Rapid change was inevitable for the "underdeveloped" world, the CIS argued. The only question was what role the United States would play in that process. Though the United States could not *create* change, American technical and social scientific knowledge could help poor countries to realize the changes they desired. Aiming to defuse conservative criticism, the CIS claimed that economic growth, of a rather unspecified sort, would fulfill the "basic desires" of the peoples of underdeveloped countries, thus lessening the appeal of Communism. As Rostow put it in 1955, "Success in resisting the combination of subversion and guerrilla operations depends directly on the political, economic, and social health of the area attacked. A substantial part of American and Free World policy must be devoted to eliminating or preventing those circumstances under which subversion can succeed."[66] Promoting "take-off into sustained economic growth" would bolster "military strength and the will to resist Communist aggression, particularly in the nations bordering on the Soviet bloc."[67] "The Objectives" foresaw no political dangers to America in promoting economic growth abroad, in contrast to the CIS's later arguments, which would note the politically destabilizing effects of economic growth.

The 1954 report was an aid proposal but not yet a "modernization" proposal. Although the CIS advocated sustained growth and industrialization, it did not yet have a convergent conceptualization of that process. Nor did a world-historical narrative underpin the "Objectives." It was merely a call for unlinked economic aid, social scientific expertise, and a plea to avoid a strictly military approach to foreign policy. The modernist ambitions were growing quickly within the CIS, however, as we can see by reading the refined version of "The Objectives," which the CIS published in 1957 under the title *A Proposal: Key to an Effective Foreign Policy.*[68] The argument of the *Proposal* proceeded along three axes. The first was a historical argument. The CIS claimed that the bulk of the world's population was caught up in a cataclysmic, world-historical revolutionary transformation away from an inwardly oriented "apathy" toward a "receptivity to change." The second element of the argument was economic. The CIS argued that aid should be linked neither to political conditions nor to military purposes, but rather should be granted to all non-Communist states on the basis of their ability to use the funds efficiently (the assumption was that if the funds *could* be used efficiently, then these states *would* use them efficiently). Third, there was the political agenda of the aid program, which would speak in interesting ways to modernization theory's anti-Communism. Although the *Proposal's* policy recommendations repeated those of the "Objectives," the way in which the CIS made these arguments reflected the growing influence of modernist ideas.

This growing influence was reflected, above all, in the historical narrative on which the *Proposal* rested its case. As Rostow would later explain, the problem with the Eisenhower administration's approach to foreign aid was that its "stance toward the developing world had been shaped by military and budgetary tactics rather than a theory of history."[69] By contrast, the CIS believed that the aim of the foreign aid program was to promote "the evolution of stable, effective, democratic societies abroad which can be relied on not to generate conflict because their own national interests parallel ours and because they are politically healthy and mature."[70] Their interests would be "parallel" to those of the United States because these countries' social, economic, and political structures would become akin to those of the United States. The *Proposal* closed with a quotation from Rostow's namesake, Walt Whitman, suggesting that development meant convergent historical evolution:

> One thought ever at the fore—
> That in the Divine Ship, the World, breasting Time and Space,
> All peoples of the globe together sail, sail the same voyage
> Are bound to the same destination.[71]

That destination was a world filled with factories, inhabited by politically attentive but docile subjects, in a society based on nontraditional social relationships (e.g., equality for women, end of caste and feudal relations, and so on). Although the terms "modernity" and "modernization" did not yet appear, the *Proposal* envisioned development as a universal, unilinear process of the sort described at the end of chapter 3. This unilinear vision of development had not appeared in the "Objectives."

Second, the *Proposal* systematized the economic arguments first stated in the "Objectives." Although it rejected linking aid to specific political demands, the CIS did stipulate economic criteria for determining the appropriate level of aid for a given country. First, the country had to be evaluated for its technical and administrative (or "absorptive") capacity to use the aid effectively. Technical assistance in the manner of Point Four would help establish the "preconditions for take-off." Aid would unblock bottlenecks, especially in infrastructure, during the "transitional" or "take-off" period—an idea described as similar to Ragnar Nurkse's notion of "the Big Push."[72] Second, the project had to be conceived within "an overall national development program designed to make the most effective use of its resources." Finally, the recipient country's overall national development program had to be "consistent with the requirements of expanding world commerce and the international division of labor."[73] (The contradictions between these criteria did not daunt the authors.) The ultimate aim of the aid program, the CIS explained, was to "lubricate" world trade and to prevent countries from striving for autarchy.[74] In an appeal to conservatives, the CIS argued that American economic assistance would "hasten the day when currency and trade restrictions growing out of the postwar dollar shortage can be done away with."[75] The *Proposal* envisioned a post–cold war, American-led world economy, integrated on the basis of American economic aid.

Third, there was the political argument of *A Proposal.* Although aid was not to be tied to any specific political arrangement (other than non-Communism), the political objective of the aid program was to create "stable, effective societies moving in a democratic direction." External economic assistance would be successful if it promoted "the evolution of . . . politically healthy and mature" societies—in other words, "societies that are stable in the sense that they are capable of rapid change without violence." Backing away from its 1954 position that economic growth was itself a *solution* to the problem of political instability, the CIS argued that the instability associated with development transcended the particular conflict of the cold war. "The dangers of instability inherent in the awakening of formerly static peoples," the CIS observed, "would be present even in the absence of the Communist apparatus." The CIS still did not consider that democracy and economic growth could end up at loggerheads.[76]

As appealing to policy makers as to academics, the *Proposal* had an important impact in Washington. As Arthur Schlesinger Jr. put it, "It represented an immense improvement over the philosophy of the country store. It gave our economic policy toward the third world a rational design and a coherent purpose. It sought to remove our assistance from the framework of the cold war and relate it to the needs of nations struggling for their own political and economic fulfillment."[77] By grounding its claims on a seemingly unassailable "scientific" analysis of the development problem, it spoke across the partisan divide about foreign economic aid. Certainly it helped that by 1957 the Democrats had regained control of both congressional chambers, but as Russell Edgerton noted, "Nothing else on the scene in Washington rivaled the grand scale of the Millikan-Rostow proposal [for] the sophistication of its presentation. . . . As different parts of the Executive and Congress launched reappraisals of aid in different directions with different motives, Millikan and Rostow supplied them all with a common theme."[78] That theme, of course, would soon come to be called "modernization."

But was *A Proposal* already a work of modernization theory? The answer is, not quite. True, the convergent, evolutionary universalism was there, as when the CIS claimed that "the intensive work of social scientists" had come to recognize the "common elements in the patterns of development." And yes, the

CIS was already drawing on the sociological theory of modernization, echoing Marion Levy by suggesting that modernization was a "social solvent." And no doubt its optimism about "building a better world" signaled its allegiance to a constructive, progressive, pro-Enlightenment conception of modernity. But it was not yet an explicit theory of modernization. It was not until around 1960—specifically until after the 1959 Dobbs Ferry meeting of the SSRC Committee on Comparative Politics (see chapter 4)—that the CIS would fully embrace the idiom and theory of modernism to describe its goals. Attending that 1959 conference had been members of the CIS, including Everett Hagen, Lucian Pye, and Daniel Lerner. While it might be a mistake to ascribe excessive causal influence to a single conference, it is clear that many of the theoretical elements that had earlier appeared in the interrogative voice would show up in the declarative (or imperative) voice in CIS's 1960 Senate study entitled "Economic, Social, and Political Change in the Underdeveloped Countries."[79] The modernizing perspective that had been implicit in 1957 was now made explicit.

The policy recommendations of the 1960 study did not differ significantly from those proposed four years earlier, though they were more fleshed out. The aims included the following:

- to put foreign economic aid on an unlinked, long-term basis
- to set unambiguous and firm (economic) standards for receiving aid
- to continue to provide technical assistance, especially in agriculture
- to increase the amount of capital aid and distribute it over many projects so as to sustain a "big push"
- to coordinate aid with other developed countries
- to promote land reform
- to build a career corps of "development workers"

Only the last two elements were new, and they were motivated by specific recent events. As far as land reform was concerned, the Cuban Revolution had made it clear that supporting *latifundistas* would undermine the status of the United States in the eyes of locals. Furthermore, as part of the various postwar reconstruction efforts, the United States had been implementing land reforms in Japan, Formosa, and South Korea, all of which were widely considered successful. The proposal to professionalize the development industry also responded to a recent event, the publication of *The Ugly American* (1958), Eugene Burdick and William Lederer's novelistic critique of American policy in Asia.[80] *The Ugly American* had claimed that the American foreign service and development programs were filled with naïfs and dilettantes, whose lack of professionalism constituted a liability in the ongoing struggle with Communism for the hearts and minds of the third world. Although Burdick and Lederer's anti-intellectualism did not resonate with the attitudes of the CIS, their critique of the foreign policy status quo provided a background to the CIS's proposal to professionalize foreign policy through the application of social science. Other than these two additions, however, the CIS was making the same pitch in 1960 as it had in 1956.[81]

Though the CIS's 1960 policy suggestions reiterated those of 1954-56, the language of the 1960 Senate study shows the evolution of the CIS's ideas from an under-articulated modernism into full-blown modernization theory. In its opening, the report stated that its brief was "to outline the complex process of change shaping the lives of millions of people in the underdeveloped countries of the world as their nations seek the way toward modernity. In a real sense our subject is revolution for the entire fabric of these societies with which we are concerned is being torn apart, the old and time-honored being replaced by totally new economic, political, and social forms." The study argued not only that social science could discover generalizations about development that transcended the circumstances or histories of individual countries, but also that these generalizations could help policy makers. Although lip service was given to the complexity and uniqueness of every country, the study emphasized that "[g]eneralization is essential if we wish to understand and to cope with the problems which the revolution of modernization presents." Events could not be understood one at a time, but had to be cast within "a general framework of analysis which makes it possible to relate each separate decision to others and to an overall set of objectives." Though the "overall set of objectives" had not changed since 1956, the CIS explained, the "general framework of analysis" had been greatly elaborated. That general framework was modernization theory.[82]

The study's dynamic derived from its distinction between tradition and modernity. In broad brushstrokes, the CIS explained to the Senate the key features of traditional society: limited technology; the preponderance of agricultural employment; the lack of a middle class to challenge agrarian elites; the "lack of adaptability" of the workforce; the importance of "face-to-face relationships"; the "fatalism" of the population; and the lack of human bonds based on "specific functional" relationships. The object of the study was the "transitional process" whereby traditional societies were "super-seded" by modern ones. Traditional societies were being "swept aside" in a complex process in which the old ways of doing things were undergoing "drastic alteration." While the CIS acknowledged that the old culture always left its mark on the emergent modern one, it was nevertheless true that mod-ernization was forcing "men" to renovate their cultures, to accept "new forms for the organization of political power," and to transform their savings and investment habits until "continuing economic growth becomes the nor-mal condition of the society." Significantly, the CIS revealed the same urban-ist bias that plagued Marxism by celebrating cities as the spatial vanguard of the modernization process: "Cities often develop a quite modern way of life, standing as advanced enclaves in a society still predominantly rural and primitive."[83]

Although the CIS defined the "traditional" half of the tradition-modernity dichotomy explicitly, it was much sketchier about characterizing the "mod-ern." The CIS avoided making its definitions of the modern too explicit, for fear of offending conservative senators. Whatever the content of modernity, however, it undoubtedly meant "like us." Where the *Proposal*'s invocation of convergence had been limited to its closing quotation of messianic verse, the CIS now explained that, although it would take many years, "the transition to modernity is inevitable in some form" and would result in "a considerable degree of uniformity" throughout the world.[84] As long as the content of the modern was left vague, it offended no one in the Senate to suggest that the United States could be a model for the world.

The CIS was much more explicit than it had been about what had kick-started modernization in the "underdeveloped" lands: colonialism. Despite a disapproval of European-style colonialism that was typical of postwar Americans, the CIS (like Marx) credited colonialism with having "set the sta-tic traditional societies in motion, so to speak, moving them into transitional status." Unfortunately, colonialism had merely "destroyed the cohesion and integrity of the traditional system," without helping the colonial societies to "attain the full status of modern societies." Even worse, the arrogance of the colonialists had besmirched modernity's good name. "Colonialism often cre-ated in the indigenous population an ambivalent attitude toward the West— the symbol of modernization," lamented the CIS. "They respected the power of the westerner and imitated his manner of living, but at the same time they resented his presence, hated his behavior, and determined to eject him and what he stood for, including his business enterprises." The CIS proposed that the arrogance of the European imperialist be replaced by the supposed modesty of the American modernizer. Whereas the European imperialist had sought to keep the colonials as his subjects, the American modernizer sought to include the postcolonial masses in modernity. Whereas the Europeans believed that the colonial peoples would never be able to emulate their superior example, the Americans felt sure that the postcolonial peoples would both be able and want to emulate theirs.[85]

Reflecting the influence of Daniel Lerner and Lucian Pye (and, more indirectly, of David McClelland and Alex Inkeles), the new Senate study contained a greatly increased emphasis on the psychological dimensions of modernization. "In one sense," the CIS noted, "the most basic economic change required is psychological. Men must cease to regard the physical world as fixed. They must learn that it is capable of being understood and manipulated in terms of stable and logical rules which men can master."[86] Becoming modern meant adopting an instrumental view of nature; it meant learning to see nature as a standing reserve of resources, waiting to be exploited by resourceful men. Despite the careful protestations about respecting the local traditions of the countries undergoing modernization, the study subscribed to the modernist notion that numerous "traditional" habits represented "obstacles" to modernization. For example:

1. Scorn for industrial pursuits
2. Respect for traditional learning, since it siphoned off talented individuals into economically useless activities
3. Tendency to inhibit individual initiative
4. Requirements of sharing income with the family

Overcoming this last "obstacle" was particularly important, since familial income sharing was seen as preventing the accumulation of saving and investment necessary for growth. (Letting the extended family go hungry was apparently one of the prices of modernization.) Economic growth, as we observed in discussing Rostow earlier, remained the *ne plus ultra* of development. Without economic growth, modernization was impossible. Even if the roots of economic growth were psychological, economic growth was still the first condition of development.

The 1960 Senate study also reflected the maturation of the modernization paradigm in its wholesale adoption of the term "political development."

Using the categories proposed by Edward Shils in his 1959 Dobbs Ferry address, the CIS told the senators that "transitional" states fell into three categories: potentially democratic societies, modernizing oligarchies, and traditionalist oligarchies. The *potentially democratic societies* included Turkey, Brazil, Mexico, Malaya, India, the Philippines, and Colombia. According to the CIS, these countries were "on the right track" and just needed to be encouraged to keep doing the same thing. The *modernizing oligarchies* included most of the former colonial countries: "These countries share a common goal—in a sense, a common mood. The leadership in each one of them seeks to develop a strong, prosperous state along modern lines and at the same time to preserve the unique qualities of the traditional society." The continued desire "for the fruits of modern life," combined with the drift toward increased authoritarianism, "have caused political life in most of these countries to become increasingly characterized by frustration, disillusionment, impatience, fear of failure, and uncertainty."[87] Economic aid, however, could help these countries overcome these difficulties.

Most dangerous were the *traditionalist oligarchies,* which included countries like Ethiopia, Saudi Arabia, Yemen, Cambodia, and Laos. These countries had not had the privilege of experiencing thoroughgoing colonial penetration and, as a result, languished in utter backwardness. According to the CIS, "The traditional oligarchy tends to suppress the forces of change, knowing that it is unlikely to be able to survive their onslaught." These were countries whose leaders rejected modernity even in principle. Their unwillingness to embrace the modernizing wisdom of the Americans meant that "the gap between the old ways and the new demands grows steadily greater and more dangerous. The threat of explosive and undemocratic development is heightened today by the presence of Communists, waiting in the wings to encourage and exploit any drift toward mob rule." Since modernization was inevitable on either Communist or "free world" terms, these countries represented the gravest threat to American interests because their procrastination about the inevitable meant that pressure was rising, and the inevitable uncorking of the modernization process was liable to be all the more explosive.[88] In contrast to its views a few years earlier when it had published the *Proposal,* the CIS no longer believed that political radicalism was the result of mere poverty or stagnation. It was a product of repressed or partial modernization. As Lerner and Pye had suggested, radicalism was a condition of a society in transition or, more specifically, a society in which the transition was "out of phase." Ideological restiveness afflicted societies only during a certain stage of development. If that stage could be overcome without a Communist takeover, then the potential for political or military unrest would be done away with as well.

If it adopted the categories of the CCP, however, the CIS toned down the democratic rhetoric of Shils's earlier views of political development. Reflecting the evolution toward a more authoritarian form of modernism, the CIS proposed that dictatorships be considered as acceptable developmental regimes. Whereas in 1956-57 democracy had been the explicit goal of political development, now the aim was to "progressively meet the aspirations of a majority of their people without resort to totalitarian controls" and to "move toward increasingly wide and responsible participation by all groups in political, social, and economic processes under stable rules of law, that is, toward their own version of working democracy."[89] Given the lack of media penetration, the CIS suggested that it was hopeless to expect "genuine popular participation in the political process."[90] Although it did not represent a "permanent solution," authoritarian leadership of either a charismatic or military sort was often the best the United States could hope for.[91] Democracy was important, but it could be justifiably deferred. Whereas colonialists had argued that the "backwardness" of these countries required authoritarianism, American social scientists now suggested that "Weber may have been right when he suggested that modern democracy in its clearest form can occur only under capitalist industrialization."[92] And if capitalist industrialization was a precondition for democracy, the question then became how to achieve capitalist industrialization, deferring the question of democracy.

By the late 1950s, it was becoming clear that the mere departure of colonial authorities would not automatically generate democratic societies and practices in the postcolonial regions. On the one hand, military dictatorships were sprouting up all over, notably in both Pakistan and Burma in 1958. (Burma's coup made an especially large impression because many Americans had been buoyant about Burma's prospects for modernization.) On the other hand, the Cuban Revolution (not to mention guerrilla insurgency in Laos, the Congo, and Vietnam) generated fear of Communist seizures of power in postcolonial countries. Since it was unacceptable to permit other countries to make their own political choices if that meant letting them choose to turn left, it began to seem as if advocating military dictatorships was the only option for American policy makers. Daniel Lerner's rehabilitation of the Turkish autocrat Kemal Ataturk (1880-1938) from a bloody butcher of

Greeks, Armenians, and Kurds to a forward-looking "modernizer" inaugurated modernization theory's reconsideration of the role of the military in the modernization process.[93] Considering the modernizing capacities of the military represented the social scientists' attempt to find (and then emphasize) a silver lining the black cloud of American support for growing numbers of military dictatorships. The turn toward explicit advocacy of military dictatorship did not represent a radical break with the core sentiments of modernization theory. Rather, it mobilized an always latent possibility within the modernist social and political program.

In August 1959, just two months after the CCP's Dobbs Ferry conference, the RAND Corporation in Santa Monica, a think tank devoted to strategic and military matters, sponsored a conference on the role of the military in the "underdeveloped" countries. With key papers delivered by Edward Shils and Lucian Pye, this conference became an important moment in the application of modernization theory to military questions. In his preface to the volume published out of the conference proceedings, Hans Speier (chair of the RAND Research Council, former director of Project Troy, and chair of the advisory committee to the CIS communications program) pointed out that the military had played three salutary roles in postcolonial countries: "As a revolutionary force [the military] have contributed to the disintegration of traditional political order; as a stabilizing force they have kept some countries from falling prey to Communist rule; and as a modernizing force they have been champions of middle-class aspirations or of popular demands for social change and have provided administrative and technological skills to the civilian sectors of countries in which such skills are scarce." Given the commodious effects that military dictatorships could have, Speier lamented that sociology suffered from a "time-honored intellectual bias" against the participation of the military in civilian life. Modernization theory would be used to reverse this "bias" and to rationalize the backing of military regimes.[94]

The scholar who did more than anyone else to elaborate the modernizing potential of the military in the "underdeveloped" countries was Lucian Pye. Though Pye was not particularly happy about posing this question, since his personal predilection was to consider democratic practices and representative institutions archetypal of political modernity, the evolving empirical situation in postcolonial regions led him to ask whether the military could serve as a *means* of achieving that modernity. Speaking in terms that the CIS would also enunciate to Congress, Pye claimed that the military could play a positive role in the process of modernization in three basic ways. First, it could help to overcome the psychological problems that he considered an unavoidable, if unfortunate, by-product of decolonization and modernization. Second, the military was in many—if not most—instances the force most likely to be able to provide "stability" during the modernization process. Third, the military could provide practical training in the instrumentalism that was the functional face of modernity.

According to Pye, the military establishment was capable of bringing "people out of a tradition-oriented world and into the modern secular world under conditions that tend to reduce personal anxiety."[95] Pye claimed that postcolonial nations suffered from two sorts of psychological problems. On the one hand, there were the psychological problems of postcolonial leaders. "One of the basic obstacles to development in most former colonial territories," Pye explained, "is the existence, particularly among the national leadership, of a constellation of psychological insecurities and inhibitions,"[96] which specifically manifested itself as anti-Westernism. Rather than deeming anti-Westernism a reasonable reaction to decades or centuries of colonial oppression, or considering that anti-Americanism might have something to do with contemporary American policy toward postcolonial regions, Pye psychopathologized those reactions. Military leaders, however, did not seem to suffer from this problem. "The intimate way in which our military leaders have been able to work with soldiers of the so-called neutralist countries" showed that postcolonial military leaders were relatively psychologically well adjusted.[97] In other words, to collaborate with the American military indicated good mental health; any disinclination to do so was suspect.

On the other hand, postcolonial nations supposedly suffered from macrosocietal psychological problems associated with the lack of a coherent national identity. Here again the military could prove useful because it could provide people with "a sense of identity and national pride . . . and national consensus." As Pye explained, "People need more than improvement in their economic life to find their basic sense of identity. The need to achieve a sense of adequacy in the military realm seems to be an essential prerequisite for national development." Armies made soldiers identify with a group larger than tribe or caste and taught them the attitudes required to deal with complex, impersonal, and standardized patterns of behavior. Echoing the rationale of Prussian reformers in the 1810s, Pye argued that by educating recruits about their membership in a national community, thus eroding allegiances to caste, tribe, ethnicity, or region, armies provided "a natural focus for citizenship training." Armies provided a means of upward mobility, in contrast to the "static" conditions of traditional society. "It is possible to conceive of a military establishment in an underdeveloped country as providing a unique, and in some respects unequalled, setting for rapidly preparing tradition-oriented and village bound people for participation in a modern society." One sign of the influence of consensus discourse on modernization theory was that Lucian Pye even tried to justify military dictatorship by its capacity as a form of "consensus building," arguing in 1961 that "armies may be a fundamental institution in providing national pride and a national political consensus."[98] Just as Raymond Aron had suggested, without apparent irony, that the Soviet Union and the United States had "imposed" political consensus, so, too, would Pye suggest that the institution defined by its monopoly on coercive force could be a vehicle of consensus building in the postcolonial world. Nor was Pye simply referring to the totemic quality of the military as a symbol of national pride and unity. Rather, it was the army's instrumental capacity that made a useful vehicle for imposing consensus on a fractured and potentially fractious polity that made it so valuable. In the postcolonial world, consensus apparently did not require discursive rationality, but could also be achieved at gunpoint. Pye claimed that being a modern citizen and being a modern soldier amounted to more or less the same thing: both soldiers and citizens had to adapt themselves to allegedly rational authoritarian hierarchies.[99]

The second way the military could promote modernization was by providing stability or orderliness, code words for preventing left-wing regimes (often tagged with the monolithic label "Communist") from coming to power. Lucian Pye observed that military leaders often played a "dynamic and self-sacrificing" role by furthering the modernization process.[100] (Pye downplayed the fact that the military was, at least in terms of numbers of regimes toppled, by far the most prevalent *destabilizing* force in most postcolonial countries: Latin American military officers, for example, would replace thirteen governments during the 1960s.) Earlier in the decade, improving living standards had been the primary purpose of the modernization process, a purpose that, if achieved, would perforce do away with the temptations of Communism. By the late 1950s, post–New Deal liberals increasingly conceptualized modernization as a tool for preventing "political instability." "In those parts of the world where political stability is threatened by mounting discontent with low living standards," the CIS noted in 1955, "the ideals of freedom and political responsibility can have little appeal without a progressive improvement in the standard of living."[101] By 1961, however, the CIS had made a subtle but crucial shift in emphasis. Backing away from the idea that economic improvement and political stability went hand in hand, the calls for economic growth were now modified by the phrase "while maintaining political stability." To achieve this stability, the Communists had party discipline; the West had to counter with military discipline. Japan and Turkey both modernized under military dictators, Pye noted, echoing Rostow's observation in *The Process of Economic Growth* that "reactive nationalism" against foreign intrusion was in most instances the main spur to modernization.[102]

A final reason why Pye and the other modernization theorists felt that armies could be effective agents of modernization was that their actual operations were of necessity oriented toward the modern. As the CIS told the Senate in 1960, military forces inculcated "essentials of modern life . . . such as respect for authority and organization. . . . The army can be a highly significant training ground for large numbers of men, preparing them for new roles in society."[103] Although economists tended to think of armies as inherently wasteful institutions, at best necessary evils, "armies in underdeveloped countries can perform many essentially civilian functions more effectively than the existing civilian institutions in these countries." On a functional level, Pye explained, "armies in underdeveloped countries are likely to behave more like civilian institutions than military establishments."[104] The army performed modernizing functions in two basic ways: first through their positive orientation toward technological change, and second through their supposedly achievement-oriented pattern of promotion, which tended to undermine older social hierarchies, based on ascription.

Because armies were competitive institutions in the sense that they had to (at least in theory) match themselves against other foreign armies, they had much more reason to be aware of the "shortcomings" of their societies in relation to other countries. The logistical aspects of running a modern army strengthened "the technological basis of the society."[105] Its relatively high degree of exposure to advanced technology gave military men "a rational outlook." Because modern warfare was an industrial enterprise, contemporary armies had to become "industrial-type entities."[106] "Military organization represents one model of an industrial-type organization that is relatively easily created in an underdeveloped country. Once established, it is possible to utilize the military establishment for instruction in the skills and techniques basic to the machine age and a modern society."[107] Armies provided recruits with technical training useful in the civilian industrial world—chemical warfare, explosives, machinery, and so on. In this argument we again see an implicit technological determinism.

To be sure, Pye and the others at the CIS qualified every essay concerning the salutary role of the army in modernization by saying that military dictatorships had to be regarded as interim solutions, and that any analysis of the role of the military in national development had to "include some considerations of how the tutelage functions might best be terminated."[108] Nevertheless, Pye's discussions implicitly sanctioned the indefinite deferral of democracy in the name of stability. By the early 1960s, "stability" was displacing development as the fundamental goal of American policy toward the underdeveloped world. CIS communications specialist Ithiel de Sola Pool explained the reason for this shift by saying, "To the extent that a society is backward its potential contribution to support of America is small and its susceptibility to Communism large. Thus, the less developed a society, the more important for America is the goal of stability relative to the goal of winning support."[109] When one reads these justifications of military dictatorships of postcolonial nations, it is difficult not to sympathize with Irene Gendzier's view that the discourse about the modernizing capabilities of military dictatorships represented an elaborate scientistic casuistry on behalf of gruesome regimes whose only real virtue was their anti-Communism. It is difficult to escape the conclusion that American postwar apologists for military dictatorship occupy a moral position akin to Martin Heidegger's in his celebration of early Nazism.

Walt Rostow: Standard Bearer for Modernization Theory?

One of the oddities of the literature on modernization theory is that the name most commonly associated with modernization theory, Walt Rostow, is that of an economist. Although in many ways Rostow deserves his status as the emblematic modernization theorist, his elevation to the symbolic head of the movement has resulted in two historiographic misconceptions. First, although formulated primarily by sociologists and political scientists who considered strictly economic interpretations of development inadequate, modernization theory is often misapprehended as primarily a theory of *economic* development. Second, because of a tendency to judge books by their covers (or in this case, by their subtitles), Communist containment has been seen as the single-minded and overriding concern of the modernization theorists. As its resurgent post–cold war popularity indicates (see chapter 7), however, the theory of modernization was driven by more than *merely* an anti-Communist agenda. It is better viewed as the initial social scientific rationalization of the post–World War II American drive to achieve global free trade and American geopolitical hegemony.

Rostow agreed with other modernization theorists about the fundamental nature of modernity and the American obligation to propagate modernity. Rostow not only wrote the most widely cited work of modernization theory, *The Stages of Economic Growth: A Non-Communist Manifesto* (1960), but also, as national security advisor to President Lyndon Johnson, achieved the highest political position of any modernization theorist, which gave him a chance to implement many of his ideas. As much as any other figure in this narrative, Rostow held a modernist conviction about the conjoined moral and scientific rightness of his theories. Heeding the example of the natural sciences, Rostow thought that by applying high standards of academic professionalism and integrity, work on practical policy problems could also contribute to scientific knowledge. Bereft of self-skepticism, Rostow (like his rival Marx) believed he had discovered *the* pattern of historical development—and (like Marx) he meant to use this insight to formulate better policy. "It was this which made him intellectually interesting and challenging," David Halberstam noted in his magisterial survey of Vietnam-era intellectuals, but it was this "which made him dangerous as well because, some felt, he did not know when he had gone too far, when to stop, when the pattern was flimsier than he thought."[110] Halberstam's description of Rostow is a caricature of the archetypal modernist I have been attempting to describe in this narrative. Like any good caricature, the very extremity of its features reveals essential truths about the whole.

The Stages of Economic Growth is the great synthetic text of modernization theory. Written at Cambridge University during the 1958-59 academic year, *Stages* was Rostow's *summum*. It brought together not only his own work of the previous decade but also the insights of other modernization theorists including, crucially, those generated in June 1959 at the CCP's Dobbs Ferry conference. Its importance lay not so much in its originality as in its self-confident presentation of recondite academic ideas in a language accessible to nonprofessionals. According to Rostow, economic growth had five stages:

1. the traditional society
2. the preconditions for take-off
3. the take-off
4. the drive to maturity
5. the age of high mass consumption

Rostow's stages formed not so much logical categories of the forms of economic organization as schematic descriptions of the episodes in the economic development of a society. What emerged from Rostow's analysis in
The Stages of Economic Growth, M. M. Postan remarked, "was not so much a
historical account . . . but an evolutionary model. In this respect, a comparison with Marx's *Capital* . . . was quite justifiable. Rostow in his book, like
Marx in his, transformed a mere chronological sequence of past experiences
into an evolutionary progression of related social institutions."[111] Rostow's
categories drew directly on the discourse of modernization that had crystal-
lized during the previous two years. Relying on a functionalist input-output
model compatible with Parsonian theory, these stages specified the phases of
the "transition" process.

Rostow was unabashed about listing all countries on this single scale of
modernity and about (retrospectively) dating the exact moments at which
they had made their transitions from one stage to the next.[112] Even though
some modernization theorists disavowed the rigidity of Rostow's scheme, a
staged conception of development was essential to the intellectual project.
The 1957 *Annual Report* of the CIS, for example, stated that "[t]o the extent
that we can assume that there are patterns of evolution common to a number
of societies which find themselves at different historical stages, we can try to
learn something about contemporary situations which are representative of
these various stages."[113] To be sure, Rostow did not believe that poor nations
would exactly duplicate the path of Western nations. In the first place, there
was the matter of cultural differences: a country's specific profile of "propensities" would determine its fashion of modernization. Second, partially accepting the insight of economist Alexander Gerschenkron, Rostow noted that the
underdeveloped countries would be able to take advantage of the latest technology and science to accelerate the modernization process. There is no deny-
ing, however, the essential unilinearity of Rostow's model; at the very least,
Stages implied that modernization meant convergence toward "the" (singular)
Age of High Mass Consumption.

The first and last stages in Rostow's scheme corresponded to the categories of "tradition" and "modernity" that during the previous two years had become the central sociological and political science concepts for understanding development. Echoing what the CIS had told the Senate in 1960, Rostow said that traditional societies were based on "pre-Newtonian science and technology," were rooted in agriculture and "a hierarchical social structure . . . of family and clan connection," and were pervaded by "what might be called a long-run fatalism." Likewise drawing on already-existing definitions of "modernity," Rostow specified two crucial components to the Age of High Mass Consumption (a phase he claimed the United States had entered during the 1920s). The first element was a shift of manufacturing toward consumer durables and services. The cheap mass-produced automobile was modernity's "decisive element," a technology that by itself "altered the whole style of a continent's life, down to its courting habits." (Other countries were following the United States down this path. Rostow noted that after World War II, "Western Europe and Japan . . . in their own ways . . . entered whole-heartedly into the American 1920s.") The second element of the Age of High Mass Consumption was the emergence of the welfare state, including, specifically, the redistribution of income through progressive taxation. This second element allowed Rostow to interpret even the Depression years of 1930s as an era of progress: "When the engine of growth based on the automobile, suburbia, and durable consumers' goods broke down, the United States threw its weight hard towards a post-maturity alternative, that is, to increased allocations for social welfare purposes."[114]

Rostow had conceived of the "take-off" metaphor almost a decade earlier. He now made this image central to his entire book and used the noun "modernization" to describe the process sparked by take-off. Rostow argued that late eighteenth-century England had witnessed a fundamental historical break that had made technological invention and innovation endemic. Subsequently, other countries had emulated the English example and also taken off, their economies driven by specialization in some particular industry. Sharply discontinuous with older forms of economic organization, take-off required a massive effort. As the CIS explained to the Senate in 1956, "Launching a country into self-sustained growth is a little like getting an airplane off the ground. There is a critical ground speed which must be passed before the craft can become airborne; to taxi up and down the runway at lower speeds is a waste of gasoline."[115] Take-off instigated a "revolutionary" process that generated "deep changes to ways of life." Rostow noted that "take-off usually witnesses a definitive social, political, and cultural victory of those who would modernize the economy over those who would either cling to the traditional society or seek other goals." As much as anything, it was the rhetorical power of this image of take-off that would establish (for better and worse) the reputation of *Stages*.[116]

The new elements in Rostow's scheme were the second and fourth stages, "the preconditions to growth" and "the drive to maturity." Building on his analysis of the "propensities" in *The Process of Economic Growth*, Rostow claimed that the "preconditions" stage witnessed inter alia a decline in birthrate, a shift of consumer power toward those interested in productive investment, the emergence of a centralized state, and the spread of the notion that the physical environment could be "rationally understood" and "manipulated."[117] The fourth stage, the "drive to maturity," experienced differentiation of the industrial process. Depending on the timing of this period, different societies proceeded along different paths to maturity. Britain, for example, had taken off with textiles and matured with railroads. Sweden, by contrast, had taken off with railroads and timber exports, and driven to maturity with hydroelectric power and electrical engineering. The critical point to note about this stage is its discursive formulation in terms of "maturity" and "backwardness," based on essentially technological criteria. If Rostow explicitly defined these two stages by technical and socioeconomic criteria, however, it was politics more than economics that motivated their inclusion in his scheme.

Even though Rostow couched his *Stages* in primarily economic terms, the primary spur to modernization, according to Rostow, was "reactive nationalism—reacting against intrusion from more advanced nations."[118] It was not the profit motive that directed men to destroy their own traditional societies in the name of progress, but rather that those traditional societies had failed to protect against "humiliation from foreigners."[119] Citing the examples of Germany, Japan, Russia, and China, Rostow argued that modernizing impulses had resulted either from (usually military) degradation at the hands of "more advanced" foreigners or from the threat of such degradation. More recently, these humiliations had taken the form of colonialism. The aim of American policy was "to see emerge a new relation of cooperation among self-respecting sovereign nations to supplant the old colonial ties."[120] Modernization was the only sure way to maintain or achieve national liberation.

The difficulty with postcolonial reactive nationalism as a spur to modernization had to do with the way it manifested itself in the context of the cold war. According to Rostow, the Soviet Union was exploiting the "xenophobic nationalism" of the postcolonials by presenting Communism as an anti-Western way to modernize.[121] Already in 1957 Rostow had worried that "the danger is that the underdeveloped countries will develop along lines hostile to the West and Western tradition."[122] Channeling anticolonial feelings into a wider anti-Westernism, Communism also presented itself as a viable means of achieving modernization, and hence national liberation. But Communist modernization was a false liberation, merely replacing backwardness and colonial forms of oppression with newer "totalitarian" ones.[123] Rostow in no way acknowledged that American neocolonial exploitation or American alliances with former colonial powers could have something to do with the anti-Western sentiments of many postcolonials. Nor did Rostow express any sense that violence constituted an intrinsic part of the development process; true to the Lamarckian (rather than Darwinian) model of development that he had first proposed in *The Process of Economic Growth,* Rostow consistently downplayed the significance of violent struggle and emphasized the importance of will in achieving each successive "stage of growth."

For Rostow, Communism was an opportunistic virus that took out infant nations not yet blessed with a constitutional "maturity." Though he did not make the citation, Rostow may well have been remembering Robert Langbaum's 1955 article in *Commentary,* entitled "Totalitarianism: A Disease of Modernism," in which Langbaum concluded:

Communism makes headway in those backward areas of the world where people want the fruits of democracy and technology without understanding the cultural ground from which they spring. In its practice at least, present-day Communism is the penalty for human failure. It is what happens to those backward peoples who try for a short-cut to technological modernity by avoiding a slower but surer way of total evolution—an evolution of political restraint, social conscience, and individual self-realization, all of which should accompany a technological culture. Communism is China's totalitarian short-cut to modernity as compared to, say, India's democratic but roundabout way. In the sense that totalitarianism accompanies the movement for modernization and exploits the technology and democratic idealism to exercise control, it is the specifically modern political disease. Yet the most modern of Western nations seem to have acquired, through long exposure to the specifically modern dangers, sufficient antibodies to protect themselves against the totalitarian disease. It is the nations new to modernism who are most susceptible.[124]

Although Rostow was more optimistic than Langbaum about the possibility of finding nontotalitarian "short-cuts" to modernity, he followed Langbaum in labeling Communism "an international disease."[125] "Communism is not the wave of the future," Rostow claimed, "it is a disease of the transitional process which well-trained, well-organized cadres seek to impose on societies at the early stages of modernization."[126] In spelling out this view of Communism's relationship to modernity, Rostow was making explicit what had been implicit or latent in modernization theory. As we saw in chapter 3, Parsons and the sociologists of modernization had constructed a model of "healthy" societies that implicitly pathologized difference and dissent. Likewise, Rostow's CIS colleague Lucian Pye regarded Communism as an ideology that appealed to "disturbed" individuals, adrift amid the changes of modernization.[127] Rostow agreed with Gabriel Almond that a society's susceptibility to Communism depended on its ability to handle the "social disorganization"[128] that was a requisite part of the modernization process. Though Rostow avoided the psychologizing of his political science colleagues, he subscribed to the same basic views of Communism's appeal.

According to Rostow, the most politically dangerous period in a nation's development was the "preconditions" stage. During this stage, the social dislocation of traditional society and attendant psychological insecurities would be accelerating, but few of the concrete material benefits of modernization would yet be manifesting themselves. Communism's authoritarian methods could help overcome these difficulties. "Communism is not a form of social organization which emerges naturally from the imperatives of modern industrialization," Rostow argued. "It is a pathological form of modern state organization capable of being imposed by a determined minority on a transitional society frustrated and disheartened in its effort to complete the movement to modernization by less autocratic means."[129] This argument corresponded to the metaphor of take-off: as with real airplanes, disaster was most likely to strike during the rush down the runway. In other words, political explosions were most threatening during the period of most rapid economic acceleration. Rostow explained in a speech to the graduating class at the U.S. Army Special Warfare School in Fort Bragg, North Carolina, on June 28, 1961, that the Communists had only a "limited time" in which to seize power in the underdeveloped areas. Communists, Rostow claimed, knew that "as momentum takes hold in an underdeveloped area—and the fundamental social problems inherited from traditional society are solved—their chances of coming to

power decline. It is on the weakest nations, facing their most difficult transitional moments, that the Communists concentrate their attention." In a characteristic rhetorical flourish, Rostow concluded that Communists were "the
scavengers of the modernization process."[130]

The corollary to Rostow's argument that take-off presented a limited win-
dow of opportunity for Communism to subvert the modernization process
was that if a society could get past the take-off, it was destined for an easy jour-
ney to a salubrious modernity. The Democratic administrations of the 1960s
took Rostow's theory to mean that if the United States could shepherd underdeveloped countries safely through the take-off stage, then the Communist
contagion could be arrested. By providing a theoretical articulation of how the
containment doctrine applied to the underdeveloped areas, *Stages* thus justified both the optimistic and extensive economic aid programs of the early
1960s, and the idea that the United States had a responsibility to counter mil-
itarily the Communist onslaught in the underdeveloped lands until take-off
could be achieved.

The Communist virus's main mode of transmission, according to Rostow,
was guerrilla warfare. Guerrilla warfare was "a systematic attempt to impose a
serious disease on those societies attempting the transition to modernization."[131] As far as Rostow was concerned guerrilla war was "a crude act of international vandalism."[132] It was from these insights that Rostow developed
what came to be known as the "Rostow thesis," which recommended destroying the "external supports" to guerrilla insurgents. A combined physical and
psychological assault on these "external supports" would demonstrate the
painful consequences of supporting the guerrillas. To deal with the social and
political disarticulations associated with modernization, the military would
not only hold the line against insurgents but also direct the modernization
process itself. As the epigraph to this chapter suggested, Walt Rostow believed
that "in order to win the guerrilla war, one must create at forced-draft the bone
structure of a modern nation." Already in 1964, Rostow advocated the use of
American ground troops along the Ho Chi Minh Trail in order to block North
Vietnamese support for the Vietcong. He also advocated bombing North
Vietnam as early as the summer of 1966 and called for the invasion of Laos in
1967.[133] Though the path to modernity was fraught with roadblocks, Rostow
felt confident about the inevitability of the victory of the good guys in the
cold war. Despite what Rostow and the other modernization theorists would
like to claim today, modernization theory and practice contributed directly to

justifying the militaristic approach to third world politics, above all in Vietnam.

In 1961 President John F. Kennedy appointed Rostow to serve as the chair of the State Department's long-range strategy department, the Policy Planning Staff (PPS). The post was a reward for Rostow's service as a policy advisor to Kennedy during the previous two years and during the 1960 presidential campaign. Rostow had first met Kennedy at a garden party thrown by Arthur Schlesinger Jr. in Cambridge in 1956, though they did not have a serious talk until after Rostow had testified on February 27, 1958, before the U.S. Senate Foreign Relations Committee, during hearings in response to the CIS reports. Kennedy, the junior member of that prestigious committee (which also included Huey Long Jr., William Fulbright, and Al Gore Sr.), immediately liked Rostow, who seemed like one of the few intellectuals who understood how politics really worked. Rostow soon became an advisor to Kennedy. In addition to his formal responsibility for developing Kennedy's military policy, Rostow coined several of Kennedy's best-known slogans from the 1960 presidential campaign, including "Let's get this country moving again" and the "New Frontier."[134] It was at Rostow's behest that Kennedy declared the 1960s the "Development Decade."

As David Halberstam noted, the chair of PPS was "a job which seemed ideal for [Rostow], a good place for an idea man and not too close to the center of action."[135] The State Department had created the PPS in 1947 to help coordinate a global approach to the proliferating area and topical desks that were swamping the department after the war. In other words, it played the same role within the institutional structure of the State Department that modernization theory did on a theoretical level with regard to the burgeoning Area Studies programs at American universities—the vehicle through which the insights of geographically or disciplinary-specific insights would be brought together into an overarching, comprehensive whole. With his grand theoretical comprehension of the world scene, Rostow seemed an appropriate successor to the position previously held by such worthies as George Kennan and Charles Bohlen.

Some fellow modernization theorists were less than pleased with Rostow's professional success. The day Rostow's appointment was announced, his CIS colleague Lucian Pye walked into a seminar at MIT and after a long pause, looked at his class and said, "You know, you don't sleep quite so well any more when you know some of the people going to Washington."[136] But Rostow would go on to become the highest-ranking official to serve throughout the Kennedy and Johnson administrations. On April 1, 1966, ignoring the objections of John Kenneth Galbraith, President Lyndon Johnson promoted Rostow to national security advisor.[137] Rostow would serve as the most ardent of Vietnam hawks, and his visionary rhetoric would end up justifying the bombing of several countries back through several "stages of growth." Already his *Stages of Economic Growth* was the most widely read work of modernization theory, and with these important policy posts within the Democratic regimes of the 1960s, Rostow would become the public face of modernization theory.

While a full discussion of Rostow's activities in Washington exceeds the scope of this narrative, what must be underlined is the fact that Rostow's policies harmonized with the theory that had been synthesized at the CIS over the previous three years.[138] Despite the reservations of some modernization theorists about the choice of Rostow to be their public representative, his policy positions followed logically from the positions that all of the modernization theorists had been developing. As long as modernization was conceived as a unitary and unidirectional process of economic expansion amid political consensus—a position that the modernization theorists had collectively developed—backwardness and insurgency would be explicable only in terms of deviance and pathology. Indeed, the language of convergence and pathology would provide the foundation for the next thirty years of American counterinsurgency strategy in Southeast Asia, Latin America, and Africa. Other modernization theorists may have been somewhat more theoretically nuanced than Rostow, but nothing that Rostow did in Washington would ever have been discredited *on theoretical grounds* by any of the work produced by any of the modernization theorists. Even if becoming a Vietnam hawk was not the *only* possible policy reading of modernization theory, there was also nothing in the theory that would have given a hawk pause.

The topic of Vietnam returns us to the topic with which this chapter started: anti-Communism. Although the example of Rostow makes it clear that modernization theory's association with liberal anti-Communism is to some extent deserved, the remainder of this chapter will show how Rostow's engagement with Marxism was more complicated than the anti-Communist label would seem to allow. For, strange as it may seem, Rostow was in fundamental agreement with Marx about the basic enterprise of social science. When he said in the preface to the first edition of *Stages* that he was attempting to find an "alternative [to] Marx's solution to the problem of linking economic and noneconomic behavior," he was tacitly admitting that the essential *problematic* of modernization theory was the one that Marx had set out a century earlier.[139] Rostow inherited from Marx the ambition to construct an overarching theory capable of relating economic change to other social and political variables. Although Rostow did not like what he perceived to be Marx's economic determinism, he agreed that Marx had asked the right questions: What was the interrelationship between economic theory and economic history? How did economics, politics, and society interact? What were the universal structure and direction of History? As Rostow explained in 1961, "I decided as an undergraduate I would work on two problems. One was economic history and the other was Karl Marx. Marx raised some interesting questions but gave some bloody bad answers. I would do an answer one day to Marx's theory of history."[140]

Unlike Pye or Almond, but just like Marx, Rostow had little time for psychological interpretations of the modernization process, preferring to concentrate on the material determinants of social and political change. Rostow may well have been thinking of himself when he noted that "Marx's framework for relating economic, social, and political factors has found its way much more deeply into Western academic thought than most practitioners are aware."[141] Fellow modernization theorist Seymour Martin Lipset suggested that the association between economic development and democracy had led many Western statesmen and political commentators to conclude that the pressure for rapid industrialization formed "the basic political problem of our day." According to Lipset, commentators like Rostow assumed that if only the underdeveloped nations could be launched on the road to high productivity, "we can defeat the major threat to newly established democracies, their domestic Communists. In a curious way, this view marks the victory of economic determinism or vulgar Marxism within democratic political thought."[142] Lipset's friend Daniel Bell could just as well have been speaking of Rostow as of Marx when he wrote, "The metaphor is biological, the process is immanent, the trajectory of development unilateral."[143] Rostow's intellectual enterprise, in short, took place on a Marxian theoretical horizon.

Rostow had two main quarrels with Marx. First, Rostow claimed that humans were driven by more than economic motives, which he believed meant that people were more likely to seek political compromise than chiliastic final solutions. Second, the progressive immiseration of the working classes that Marx had predicted had not taken place, which meant that the working classes were rather satisfied with their lot. For example, in a speech entitled

"Some Lessons of History for Africa," given in June 1960, Rostow declared that "while conflicts of economic and group interest are part of the modernization process, in its largest sense it is a communal and a human task. It calls, essentially, not for class conflict but for a sense of brotherhood within nations and cultures and between nations and cultures."[144] What are we to make of these two criticisms of Marx? We can only conclude that the first criticism resulted from a rather impoverished reading of Marx. Marx undoubtedly believed that individual humans were motivated by more than simple economic self-interest, as even Rostow himself acknowledged elsewhere.[145] (In fact, Rostow's first criticism applies better to neoclassical economics than to Marxian theory.) The second criticism was more acute: an extra hundred years of historical evidence did provide compelling evidence that progressive immiseration was not the inevitable fate of the working class under capitalism. In essence, what separated Rostow from Marx was his appreciation of capitalist modernity as essentially fulfilling rather than alienating. In other words, not Communism but the Age of High Mass Consumption represented the happy outcome of history.

If we read Rostow carefully, what we discover is not an anti-Marxism but an attempt to reclaim Marx from the Communism of the Soviet Union. Even as he subtitled *The Stages of Economic Growth* "A Non-Communist Manifesto," he made sure to point out "the anti-Marxist character of Communism."[146] Rostow's attempt to disengage Marxism from "actually existing" Communism was even more explicit in his earlier work. In *The Dynamics of Soviet Society,* Rostow claimed that what was wrong with the Soviet Union was not its Marxism but its "Russianness." According to Rostow, Lenin's "mutilation" of Marxism "had its roots not only in pre-1914 Russian conspiratorial practice but also in the contours of Russian political thought and experience over the previous century."[147] Rostow denied that what was happening in the Soviet Union was the necessary outcome of Marx's theoretical propositions. "If, in fact, present Soviet practice were to be given a full theoretical foundation, freed of the necessity of maintaining a strain of continuity with Marx, such a theory of society would approximate a conception of political (rather than economic) determinism. In effect Lenin and Stalin have reversed Marx's effort and set Hegel right side up again."[148] Rostow claimed that the Soviet regime had "turned Marx on his head by seeking (without complete success) to make political power exercised by a single dominant figure the basis for economic, social, and cultural change."[149] By refuting the Soviets, Rostow hoped to put Marx back on his feet.

Should modernization theory therefore be considered a form of contrapuntal Marxism? Like Communism, modernization theory had an ambivalent position on whether modernization was a metahistorical process or a project to be directed by those who understood it. This tension between modernization as a planned process and modernization as a metahistorical process infected both the official discourses of politicians and the bureaucrats under its influence. In addition to the tension between prescription and description, both Marxism and modernization theory glorified the social scientist. If modernity was seen as a directed process, then the social scientist, by virtue of his superior understanding of how modernization works, was given the authority to draw up the plans. If, by contrast, modernization was seen as a metahistorical process, then the social scientist achieved the seat of honor as the person endowed with the best understanding of this process.

Perhaps Rostow hoped to develop an alternative version of the Marxian tradition, a version that he felt had been cut off by the orthodoxies of the Third International and, even more, by the chilling post-1917 Soviet effect. Interestingly, his attempt to retrieve this lost Marxism began with a rehabilitation of Engels, usually the villain in most Western Marxist attempts to recuperate Marx from the Soviets. "There are a few passages in Marx—and more in Engels," Rostow explained, "which reveal a perception that human behavior is affected by motives and objectives that need not be related to or converge with economic self-interest. This perception, if systematically elaborated, would have altered radically the whole flow of the Marxist argument and its conclusions. It is from this perception that my analysis begins."[150] Rostow hoped to construct a theory of historical change that encompassed all social scientific factors and which culminated in a postideological society all but free from material want. He even argued in favor of revolution—the revolution of modernization. Whereas Marx believed that that revolution would constitute some sort of millennial upheaval that, at a stroke, would do away with the contradictions of contemporary society, Rostow believed that there was no need for such a cataclysmic event, because that utopia already existed just outside his front door in Cambridge, Massachusetts. Rostow hoped to make the social democratic welfare state the final outcome of world history, and he had the courage to recommend that the necessary sins be committed in order to bring it about.

CHAPTER 6

The Collapse of Modernization Theory

> History warns us that it is the customary fate of new truths to begin as heresies and to end as superstitions.
>
> —THOMAS HENRY HUXLEY,
> *The Coming of Age of the Origin of Species*

In the summer of 1960, a group of scholars gathered in Athens to discuss nothing less than the future of the earth. Led by polymathic urban planner Constantinos Doxiadis (1913-75), the Athens Center for Ekistics decided that the time had come for a comprehensive social scientific study to predict how the Industrial Revolution would inform the destiny of humanity. More than one hundred scholars would collaborate for more than fifteen years to produce a series of studies, culminating in Doxiadis's own master synthesis, entitled *Ecumenopolis: The Inevitable City of the Future* (1974), a book exemplifying social scientific modernism in full cry.

"Ecumenopolis" was Doxiadis's designation for the climax community of humanity ("Anthropos"). Around the year 2100, Doxiadis and his collaborators predicted, Anthropos would stabilize at a population of around twenty billion, having subjugated Earth ("the Container") into a single, interlaced system of cities, farms, and parks controlled by a utilitarian, rationalizing technocracy. Replete with maps depicting population distribution, land use patterns and climate change, as well as detailed predictions about the future evolution of command and control systems, Doxiadis's book projected that by the year 2000, national boundaries would give way to a federated world government "making use of such sophisticated techniques of planning and management as systems theory, cybernetics, and control and decision theory."[1] Cultural divisions in Ecumenopolis scarcely warranted discussion, and ideological distinctions were pointedly ignored.

Ecumenopolis typified social scientific modernism in two crucial respects. First, its methodology, *ekistics,* embodied the modernist ambition to unify the entire system of knowledge. Invented by Doxiadis in 1946, ekistics represented "the science of human settlements," a new master discipline combining anthropology, systems theory, ecology, architecture, and regional planning with the aim of forecasting the future of Anthropos and its relationship to the Container. In its methodological ambitions, *Ecumenopolis* was cut from the same cloth as Walt Rostow's Center for International Studies (CIS), Gabriel Almond's Social Science Research Council's (SSRC) Committee on Comparative Politics (CCP), and Talcott Parsons's Harvard Department of Social Relations (DSR). In each instance, the idea was that social scientists from diverse disciplines would generate data that a single, towering genius would synthesize into a formal, rigorous, and syncretic master theory. Second, in its substance, *Ecumenopolis* expressed virtually every trait of social modernism. Relentlessly optimistic, *Ecumenopolis* characterized mistakes as learning opportunities and assumed that human societies had a "natural inclination" to assume harmonious and balanced forms. Its expectations about how human population would stabilize stemmed from the theory of the demographic transition, a key tributary to modernization theory. Like Edward Shils's vision of modernity, Doxiadis's vision of Ecumenopolis drew on welfare state norms: he assumed that Ecumenopolis would witness the reduction of income inequalities and experience social harmony under the guidance of postideological technocrats. Moreover, *Ecumenopolis* was unabashed in its anthropocentrism, conceiving of nature as a standing reserve of resources to be marshaled for human purposes. Doxiadis expressed no regrets over—indeed barely recognized—the cultural or ecological losses that "ecumenization" would create. And finally, he assumed that Ecumenopolis would be politically and economically homogeneous, with spatial distinctions resulting from geographical rather than historical, political, or economic differentiation.

Ecumenopolis was a visionary work, a serious attempt to think on the largest scale about the global implications of modernization. Nonetheless, today it is all but forgotten, long out of print, and only rarely cited even in texts on urban theory and regional planning. The reason for this neglect is that it was published too late: by the mid-1970s the social modernism it was a part of was in collapse, and no one was in the mood to listen to such pie-in-the-sky dreams of the future. For reasons to be examined in the next chapter, the early 1970s witnessed a loss of faith in the social modernist idea that a meliorist, rationalizing, benevolent, technocratic state had the capacity and duty to solve social and economic ills. As social modernism went into crisis, what emerged was a reinvigorated antistatist movement led by the likes of Margaret Thatcher and Ronald Reagan.[2] This pro-market, anticollectivist movement would promote the rollback of welfare states in the first world and question the rationale behind the developmental state in the third world. By the mid-1990s, even the World Bank would be arguing that a major obstacle to growth was "the expectation that the government should provide all services."[3] The collapse of modernization theory, that apotheosis of social modernism, should be interpreted against the background of this wider crisis.

How did all this come to pass? How could a project that was everywhere in 1965 have become almost irrelevant by 1975? We have observed throughout this book how deeply embedded modernization theory was in the social scientific dogmas of its day. This very embeddedness made the theory vulnerable to changes in the intellectual environment, much as an apparently hardy riparian plant can be swept away by a savage flash flood. Drinking from the well of dominant liberal ideas about the American national identity would initially reinforce the popularity of modernization theory, but it would also make the theory susceptible when those ideas about the national identity began to change in the late 1960s. As New Deal liberalism's dominance began to slip amid the crises of the late 1960s—notably the catastrophe in Vietnam and the failure of the War on Poverty at home—anyone motivated by a hatred of modernization theory's liberal vision of world transformation would soon be taking on the theory. As a result, by the early 1970s, it seemed as if attacks were coming from virtually every direction. Having stood at the helm of postwar liberalism's thrust into internationalism, modernization theory was about to go down with the sinking liberal ship. If modernization theory was perceived to be wrong about how to transform the world, it was because it was wrong, in the first place, about how it understood its model for development, the contemporary United States.

The America Project

In everything they did, modernization theorists were seemingly always also engaged in sub rosa dialog about the nature of American history and national identity during the 1950s. Understanding modernization meant understanding modernity. And the most modern place on earth, postwar

American intellectuals agreed, was the United States itself. Even if they could agree on nothing else, everyone seemed to agree that at minimum, modern was what "we" were. If the United States was to be the model for development, if the United States was the "first new nation," it was then necessary to study the United States. And in fact, the modernization theorists were studying the United States. In 1955 the CIS had established the "America Project," a Rostow-led and Carnegie Corporation–funded attempt to theorize the meaning and nature of the United States. The two major fruits of the America Project were, first, a conference held at Endicott House in Dedham, Massachusetts, May 23-27, 1957, and second, the CIS's participation in the creation of the American Pavilion to the 1958 World Exposition in Brussels. Both of these interventions would not only reveal the liberalism subtending modernization theory, but also, by exposing this liberalism explicitly, open modernization theory up to a deep political backlash—a backlash that would adumbrate the kinds of attacks that would destroy modernization theory a decade later.

According to the CIS program statement, the aim of the America Project was elemental and explicit: to understand the third world, American scholars had to understand their own nation, and these two projects were best performed simultaneously. As Max Millikan said in his introduction to the volume that emerged from the Dedham conference, *The American Style: Essays in Value and Performance,* the "implicit premise" of all the work being done at the CIS during the 1950s was that "the characteristics of our own society are as important as developments abroad in determining the shape of our foreign relations." The gathering in Dedham, therefore, sought "new approaches to the analysis of contemporary America."[4] Participants and planners of the conference included Clyde Kluckhohn and Henry Murray of the DSR; Walt Rostow, Max Millikan, and Elting Morison of the CIS; as well as David Riesman, Richard Bissell, J. Robert Oppenheimer, Richard Hofstadter, George Kennan, David Potter, and McGeorge Bundy. In short, it was a roll call not only of intellectuals associated with modernization theory but also of figures who would play crucial roles in implementing modernist ideas in the Kennedy administration. While all the contributions to this conference could be discussed at length, I will limit myself to discussing Rostow's paper on "The National Style" and Riesman's commentary on Rostow's paper. "These two essays," conference organizer Elting Morison commented, "if put together are a remarkable single document."[5]

Rostow's essay sought to understand the "national style" of the contemporary United States, by which he meant an effort to determine how "the national character . . . reacts to and acts upon its environment." Cast as a loose narrative of American history since the Revolution, the essay claimed that most of American history had been taken up with "building a rich modern society out of an empty continent." Regional and group conflict had been sharply reduced, "by the sustained growth and high output per head which has marked the history of the modern American economy. This not only gave reality to the concept of progress but also permitted men to achieve compromises in which they shared the increments to communal wealth without the bitter, corrosive conflicts which came about when men feel they can only rise at the expense of someone else's decline." Echoing Potter and the other consensus historians, Rostow argued that the United States had attained its status in the world "by cumulative experiment" rather than "radicalism," a process that had "been progressively strengthened by the gathering success of the American adventure." (Rostow used the word "success" no less than ten times to describe the United States.) Long quotes from Tocqueville studded the essay, and Rostow specifically referred to Hartz's interpretation of Tocqueville that Americans had been "born free." "Compromise," "equilibrium," "consensus," and "balance" were the themes that Rostow repeated like a mantra. Experiment and practical problem solving had prevailed over principle or radical innovation; episodes like McCarthyism or the Civil War were "exceptions."[6]

An individualist-utilitarian commitment to social welfare—what Rostow called "the values of the Enlightenment"—had been the "paradoxical" goal of American history from day one. By the 1950s, "we had reached a stage of economic, social, and political development where a uniquely comfortable life under conditions of relatively low political and social tension was probably possible." Segregation was the only serious blemish on the nation's domestic report card. The only thing preventing the United States from solving its remaining problems, Rostow claimed, was the danger of Russian and Chinese Communism, which was forcing the United States to pipe some of its energies away from the building of a "welfare state" and toward the building of a "garrison state." Even worse, the United States' happy history had left it ill prepared to understand how postcolonial countries' ambitions exceeded mere material success. Even Rostow admitted that the world crisis was forcing "us to look at ourselves and the world in terms of a set of abstractions new to

American thought and history. The automatic transfer of concepts from our own round of life no longer suffices."[7]

Riesman's commentary to Rostow's paper provides an intriguing weather-vane for the mental climate of American intellectuals in the late 1950s. Riesman began by dissociating himself from some of his own earlier positions. Although he identified with Rostow's politics, he no longer shared Rostow's fundamental optimism about American life, nor his sense that modern politics had no place for radicalism. "When I got through his paper," Riesman explained,

> I ask myself what kind of America [Rostow] would fashion were he suddenly made dictator with the power to alter men, events, and institutions? From what he says, he would do many necessary things, civilized things and intelligent things. Many negative perils would be removed or ameliorated: rivalry in the armed services, segregation in the South, the blight of our cities, the stifling of individual initiative in large organizations, and so on. There would be more vigor in America, and less decay. Yet, I had no sense that the America he wants is radically, unmanageably, explosively different from present-day America; and I cannot believe that without a larger dream of America people would willingly make the sacrifices necessary to achieve even the minimum-decency-America that Mr. Rostow sees as viable.

Riesman explained that he found Rostow to be fundamentally "complacent" in his vision of what the United States could be. According to Riesman, Rostow acknowledged the disorderliness of modern American, but ended up with a vision of "chromium-plated harmony." Rostow's work was "culture bound," Riesman claimed. "Mr. Rostow has admirably freed himself from the parochialism of academia . . . only to succumb to the very much larger parish of the United States of America itself. . . . I get the sense that Mr. Rostow hasn't asked himself what would seem at least a threshold question, namely whether the American style is really worth it even with all the modifications he proposes." Who exactly was this "we" that Rostow kept referring to, Riesman wondered. Because he failed to acknowledge any of the idealistic or transcendental aspects of American life, Rostow had no sense that the American people were "ill at ease in Zion." Most of all, Riesman condemned Rostow's overconfidence about "the rationalistic elements in America." The notion that he might have too sanguine a view of American life—not to mention of the desire or ability of other countries to achieve such "modernity" themselves—simply never dawned on Rostow, as the other major episode in the American Project reveals.[8]

That episode was the CIS's contribution to the formulation of the American Pavilion to the 1958 Brussels World Exposition. The State Department, which was charged with organizing the American Pavilion, hoped to come up with a more sophisticated presentation of the United States than the boosterish one being proposed by the American business community. One business group that actively sought to define the American "way of life" for foreign audiences during the 1950s was the Advertising Council, an advertising industry public relations association formed during World War II. The Advertising Council sponsored a series of gatherings for academics, business executives, and media leaders "to attempt to distill the American way of life into a formula" capable of competing with the Soviet Union's propagandistic images of Communist utopia. Ted Repplier, head of the American Advertising Council, believed that American propaganda had focused too much on the negative aspects of the Soviet Union, rather than emphasizing what was positive about the United States. Repplier suggested that American propaganda efforts promote the idea that the United States had already achieved what Communism only promised. Interestingly, there was little disagreement between the Advertising Council and the Soviet Union about what constituted the good life: both subscribed to the modernist vision of a classless society of economic abundance. Promoting a publicity campaign named the People's Capitalism, the Advertising Council created an exhibit (first put on at Washington D.C.'s Union Station in February 1956) that displayed what it envisioned as the essence of the American way of life: the origin of American life in the pioneer's log cabin, the enormous productivity of the American industrial economy, scenes of domestic bliss (reflecting stereotypical gender roles), and above all, the joys of a consumer economy. Employing historian David Potter as its front man, the Advertising Council would in 1956 and 1957 convince the United States Information Agency (USIA) to disseminate the People's Capitalism campaign throughout the USIA's global archipelago of libraries and cultural centers.

Ever since the Crystal Palace exhibit in London in 1851, countries had used world's fairs and expositions to showcase the best they had to offer: technological innovations, cultural achievements, natural beauties, and so on. In conjunction with the USIA, the State Department organized a roundtable discussion at MIT in April 1957 called the Cambridge Study Group (CSG), the purpose of which was to help clarify the image of the United States that would be presented at the Brussels World Exposition the following summer. Included in the CSG were the most prominent members of the CIS staff, including, among others, Walt Rostow, Max Millikan, and Ithiel de Sola Pool. When approached by the State Department, however, the CSG proposed a radical departure from this approach. Based on their findings in the America Project, the CIS believed that the United States in the mid-1950s faced an unusual international public relations problem. No one needed to be convinced, the CIS felt, of America's material achievements. Indeed, a common charge of many foreigners (especially in Europe) was that Americans were a soulless folk, bent on the relentless and mindless pursuit of material achievement, at the expense of social reform. Moreover, international opinion over the previous year had fixed its gaze on the ugly scene in Little Rock, where Arkansas governor Orval Faubus had used the National Guard to block the Supreme Court mandate that schools be desegregated. Simply displaying commodities or business practices would not suffice for sprucing up the American national image. Instead Rostow suggested that the exhibit show "the evolution of America on the world scene" in order "to project the manner in which Americans have become convinced that their destiny lies with the world."[9]

Rostow proposed, therefore, that the American Pavilion directly confront the problems facing the United States, such as education, urban reconstruction, and most controversially, racial integration. Instead of sweeping unpleasant details about the contemporary United States under the iconographic rug, which he thought would only aggravate distrust among foreign audiences, Rostow wanted to represent these issues as "a natural part of America's sprawl and energy. . . . The presentation of American shortcomings, such as the history of race relations, would lend credibility to the exhibits, so long as they were contained within a progressive narrative, ending with new technological trends such as automated factories." Labor leader Victor Reuther and *Time* vice president C. D. Jackson (who earlier had organized the May 1954 meeting in Princeton that had led to the CIS's "Objectives of U.S. Economic Assistance Programs"—see chapter 5) agreed with Rostow that "the overall theme of the exhibits should be 'America's Unfinished Business,' because this presented social shortcomings in progressive terms, as works in progress, instead of as final achievements." The American Pavilion as a whole was soon named "Unfinished Work." Rostow wanted "Unfinished Work" to showcase the "ideals of the CIS, especially regarding the role of the United States in developing nations." His own ideals and the supposed ideals of the

United States had become identical in Rostow's mind. While innocuous enough on the face of it, the difficulties that "Unfinished Work" would encounter would illuminate the limits of American postwar liberalism.[10]

"Unfinished Work" was divided into five categories: Land and People, Life and Work, Science and Technology, Culture, and American Idealism in Action. Rostow decided to work on the American Idealism in Action portion of the exhibit, and when the *New York Times* first reported on the ideas for the Idealism in Action portion of the show in a front-page article on March 11, 1958, it credited Walt Rostow with having created an exhibit that would counteract "the self-righteousness and boastfulness often associated with the United States." In addition to representing diverse American activities in the "underdeveloped" areas, Rostow recommended that the exhibit contain the following elements:

a. Some statistics and perhaps a racial chart showing how the Melting Pot has evolved over recent years.

b. A brief, compact exhibit on the progress made by Negroes in the past fifty years in terms of income and education levels, etc.

c. A desegregation exhibit focused on three cases, each told pictorially, LIFE-style: Clinton, where the facts of rioting and violence at one stage should not be shirked; Louisville; and St. Louis.

Rostow's proposal reflected the influence of his old boss from the Economic Commission for Europe, Gunnar Myrdal, who in *An American Dilemma: The Negro Problem and Modern Democracy* (1944) had argued that the new universalism and internationalism generated by the war demanded that the United States demonstrate to the (soon-to-be post-) colonial peoples that it was committed to social and political equality for blacks. Myrdal had predicted that American race relations would soon come under international scrutiny. Rostow liked Myrdal's representation of race relations in this country because, in his view, Myrdal was "optimistic." In a memorandum entitled "Some Unfinished Business of the American Community," Rostow argued that the "desegregation problem cannot be evaded. It will be underlined rather than evaded by omission. The correct setting for it is within the framework of the American commitment to struggle towards its peculiar version of common Western aspiration." He proposed that "the message to be projected" was that "it is the wisdom and responsibility of citizens and their voluntary associations, rather than the Supreme Court decision itself, which is now bringing slowly into effect the desegregation decision, not by ukase, but by living social process at the local level."[11]

The planning for "Unfinished Work" went ahead over the winter of 1957–58. The aim was to show the United States' historical success in confronting the problems of segregation and urban decay. The troubles of poor American communities were to be metaphorically connected to problems in the developing world, with presentations of the United States' own urban poverty appearing next to information about American foreign aid programs for postcolonial nations. In suggesting an identity of all underprivileged peoples, the exhibit would show that the United States was trying to raise the standard of living everywhere by extending the middle-class ideals of 1950s America to a global level. "America," read a caption to a picture of a middle-class white family walking into the glow of a rising sun, is determined "to solve her problems." Taken as a whole, the exhibit endorsed the notion that divisions of class, race, and gender were being overcome by technologies that would promote upward mobility, creativity, and equal opportunity.

The trickiest issue, inevitably, turned out to be how to deal with the United States' nasty race situation. In general, the exhibit planned to juxtapose racial strife and disparities to exhibits of the improving condition of blacks since the Civil War. However, in what would prove to be a momentous decision, Rostow decided to go further, tackling the segregation issue head-on by suggesting that white resistance in the South would soon be overcome. In "The National Style," Rostow had noted that the main exception in the trend toward national uniformity was "the problem of the social status of the Negro" which he regarded as a "residue" of slavery.[12] Using Rostow's liberal-progressive vision of a deracinated, universalist modernism, the exhibit would show how the United States was "in the process of building up its own underdeveloped area," the South.[13] Following the line that American problems were to be presented within a progressive narrative that indicated their incipient resolution, Rostow proposed that the exhibit portray segregation as a soon-to-disappear remnant of America's benighted past. Moreover, the solutions to social problems in the United States would soon be available for export to other countries facing similar problems.

Rostow foresaw the possibility of a backlash "by deep South Senators against the segregation exhibit. It was decided that this was one of the issues on which the Committee would just have to stand firm."[14] After the 1954 *Brown v. Board of Education* Supreme Court decision, Rostow had been convinced that the "real America" was a liberal and progressively desegregating one.[15] Despite being willing to represent the presence of such attitudes, Rostow was excluding self-righteous, illiberal bigots from the definition of what America was all about—democracy might be about equality, but liberal social scientists were certainly more equal than Southern racists. Invoking the same metaphors of social health and pathology that Rostow had elsewhere found so useful, the exhibit featured a newspaper clipping explaining that "Fellow Governors Treat Faubus Like Flu Carrier."[16] Rostow's vision for the exhibit thus linked the struggle for civil rights at home with the process of modernization abroad. In other words, the representation of domestic racial strife in "Unfinished Work" operated as a covert challenge to the passivity of the Eisenhower administration regarding the foreign aid program.

Not surprisingly, southern conservatives were furious at the suggestion in "Unfinished Work" that southern "customs" were anything akin to the backwardness of other countries. On June 23, 1958, the *New York Times* reported on page 1 that representatives Prince Preston of Georgia and L. Mendel Rivers of South Carolina "made no secret of their outrage that the pavilion should be telling the world that segregation was a problem the United States must solve." They denounced the pavilion's representation as "one-sided" and argued that it should considered the "problem" of "the influx of Puerto Ricans." One journalist suggested that the exhibit was "the weird spawn of Rostow's brainstorm. . . . It's a sure bet Soviet Russia will not have any exhibits at Brussels showing the slave workers in the mines at Vorkuta, or the miserable peasants on their cooperative farms."[17] Georgia senator and arch-segregationist Herman Talmadge wrote to Secretary of State John Foster Dulles, "It is incomprehensible to me that the United States Government should be a party, either directly or indirectly, to a fawning display of its internal problems before the rest of the world. Regardless of whether one favors or opposes segregation, the question is one which, by its very nature, directs itself solely to the people of the States and regions directly affected and cannot by any stretch of the imagination be said to be one of the legitimate concerns to the citizens of other countries."[18] Southern congressmen had no intention of letting some secularizing Yankee Jew tell them that they were "backward" or "underdeveloped." Proposing such a view of Africans, Asians, or Latin Americans might be acceptable, but to say this about upstanding white Americans was infamous.

Eventually, conservative political pressure forced the withdrawal of the American Idealism in Action portion of "Unfinished Work." It was replaced halfway through the summer with an exhibit on public health. The message was clear enough: conservatives would only tolerate the social reformist dreams of Rostow and the other liberals at CIS if they were applied to other countries and not at home. By objecting to the notion that the United States would advertise its domestic social problems, they were also taking aim at Rostow's liberal vision of cosmopolitan modernism. But Rostow's vision of social modernism and modernization were inseparable. Indeed, the entire project of modernization theory was constructed on the basis of a solidly liberal, technocratic, and elitist vision of modernity that most American intellectuals took for granted as a vision of the good life. It was a vision of the good life as an America purged of its last few remaining problems, as seen from the point of view of privileged white male intellectuals. Although Riesman's comments in 1957 and the scandal of the 1958 World Exposition should have given them pause, Rostow and the other modernization theorists were so confident that their vision of modern America represented a secular utopia that it would take much greater catastrophes for them to begin to appreciate how insular their vision of the modern really was.

The Collapse of the Institutions of Modernization Theory

Quite aside from the ambient ideological environment in which they operate, social scientific paradigms like modernization theory characteristically tend to generate their own oppositions. First, just as modernization theorists climbed into their positions of authority over the backs of their elders, so, too, would the modernization theorists discover younger scholars seeking to establish their own reputations by attacking them. Second, if contemporaneous discourses such as the end of ideology, consensus history, and the elite theory of democracy had tended to support and confirm modernization theory during the 1950s, the declining purchase of these ideas would cause modernization theory to be found guilty by association. Finally, the very success of the modernization paradigm rendered its advocates insensate to intellectual currents that were flowing against the paradigm—a problem compounded by the tendency to dismiss counterconcepts being nurtured in other institutional spaces. What at first was a revolutionary theory, aiming to overturn disciplinary sacred cows, upon success became a vested interest of its own.

Consider the CCP, whose members by 1960 dominated the field of comparative politics. During the 1960s, the CCP was sponsoring most of the major conferences in the field. These were invitation-only, all-expenses-paid affairs, and the CCP, of course, extended invitations only to those engaged in "relevant" research. The leaders of the CCP defended their turf by systematically excluding countervailing voices, in much the same way that they excluded Roy Macridis (see chapter 4). To circumvent this blockade to their professional recognition and advancement, young scholars from outside the modernization inner circle would sometimes attempt a flanking maneuver. For example, in early June 1965, Princeton political scientists Klaus Knorr, James Rosenau, and Harold Sprout—none of them members of the CCP—wrote to Pendleton Herring, president of the SSRC, to suggest that a new SSRC committee be set up to examine the "complex linkages between national and international systems." This new committee, they suggested, would address a critical gap in modernization theory's conceptualization of political development, namely the notion that the main unit of analysis ought to be the nation-state, assumed to be an autonomous, sovereign entity. Knorr, Sprout, and Rosenau argued that this new committee was needed because works like Almond's *The Politics of Developing Areas* devoted "no consideration to the impact of external variables [on nation-states]," and singled out the work of CCP members Myron Weiner on India and Leonard Binder on Iran as examples of works that focused too exclusively on internal political factors to explain political development. Knorr, Sprout, and Rosenau concluded their proposal with a list of topics that the new committee might cover. Here, already in 1965, was a proposal raising an issue that would soon become a key point in the criticism of modernization theory. Moreover, this intellectual challenge was being framed as a challenge to the institutional hegemony of the CCP within the field of comparative politics.

The way the CCP responded typifies how some dominant paradigms defend their preeminence through a combination of personal and intellectual appeal. On June 17, 1965, Herring sent the Knorr-Sprout-Rosenau proposal to Gabriel Almond and Lucian Pye, asking for their feedback and noting that he had scheduled a meeting on June 23 with Knorr, Sprout, and Rosenau. Almond and Pye each responded the next day. Pye acknowledged that Rosenau's recent work made a good effort to link comparative politics and international relations, but he suggested that "it might be premature to set up a committee." Almond was blunter. He suggested that although Rosenau's proposal "makes great sense," it was not true that the CCP had ignored this subject in the past, though perhaps this theme could receive more attention, as "Lucian Pye, Sid Verba, Lenny Binder, and I have proposed." In any event, Almond continued, it was not "timely to establish a special committee," since the special committee "would have to draw heavily on the Committee on Comparative Politics." Instead, Almond suggested that a conference be held on the topic, under the auspices of the CCP. Just in case he might be misunderstood, Almond concluded that "I know Jim Rosenau very well and would be a little worried about an enterprise which he would carry through by himself. It might end up like his proposal for the meeting of the American Political Science Association in 1966 in which he confuses a check list with a program."[19]

Herring got the message. On June 24, the day after having a "very good talk with Knorr, Sprout, and Rosenau," Herring wrote to Almond that he had proposed to the Princeton troika that they further develop their "substantive suggestions" but eliminate "the organizational suggestions." Instead of providing grounds for a rival organization to develop an alternative methodology, the interdependencies of national and international development became the subject of a CCP-sponsored conference in March 1966. In fact, it turned out not to be even a formal conference, but rather "an exchange of ideas." Rosenau and Sprout were given the privilege of reading their papers ("Toward the Study of National-International Linkages"[20] and "National Political Systems and International Politics"[21]) to the assembled members of the CCP—who duly proceeded to ignore everything that these young scholars had to say. Had the perspective of these scholars begun to appear in the work of the CCP, then we might conclude that the leaders of the modernization project were indeed sensitive to sensible challenges to their ideas and willing to expand their operation to take these ideas into account to make room for the people with the new, good ideas. Instead, the multilateral dimension of modernization was reduced to a mere anomaly in the dominant model of national modernization, and the challenge to the unique authority of the CCP within the comparative politics intellectual establishment was turned back. We can only imagine the disappointment and perhaps resentment of Rosenau, Sprout, and Knorr.

Predictably, this and similar successes in closing off challenges to modernization theory's intellectual and institutional authority only tended to convince the leaders of the paradigm that these challenges were neither legitimate nor serious, confirming in the minds of paradigmatic advocates that their ideas represented scientific truth. The suppression of dissent thus became a confirmation of the "scientificity" of the modernization paradigm.

Daniel Lerner, for example, explained that "[e]ach researcher obviously will decide for himself [what direction his research should take]—since the SSRC flow of funds will not be sufficient to induce bright boys to follow this committee's star rather than their own."[22] True, funding alone might not force "bright boys" to research subjects they found unimportant, but a lack of funding might well prevent them from researching the things they *did* find important. Through the 1960s, the CCP, the DSR, and the CIS would stave off all similar attacks to their authority and the authority of modernization theory.

By the early 1970s, however, these tactics to defend the paradigm were no longer working. Attacks based on the same kind of criticism that had been defeated in the 1960s would hit home with devastating force in the 1970s. In 1973, the CCP would disband, its Princeton University Press series on political development a volume short of the ten originally envisaged, with the last volumes presenting not the anticipated metahistorical crescendo of theory, but rather a dirge to the intellectual cadaver of modernization theory. Likewise, in 1974, the DSR would dissolve, and while the CIS would continue to operate into the early twenty-first century, after 1970 it would abandon the study of development, Communism, and their interlinkages and redirect its energies to strategic issues like nuclear proliferation. After decades of strenuous self-promotion and turf defense, the leaders of the institutions all chose to walk away from their charges. Why did all these organizations, which had been going concerns for two or more decades, choose to retire at virtually the same time? On this critical question, oddly enough, the historical record is quiet. Neither an examination of the copious records of the three organizations nor my interviews with many of the principals yielded much on this phase of the history of modernization theory and its institutional matrix. Despite generating helpful and detailed information on a host of questions, the leaders of these movements tended to react with a shrug when asked about the waning of the movement.

After nearly three decades of institutional longevity, the scholars in the DSR in 1974 chose to return to their original departments of sociology, psychology, and anthropology. Parsons had retired, and with him went the vision of a unified supra-theoretical department of social science. According to those who participated, no single reason accounted for the breakup. According to their own testimony, its members had "gotten tired" of working in the same department with scholars "from other fields" and felt that the sort of work they wanted to do could best be done in separate disciplinary formats.

Some participants cited personal animosity as a factor. Yet, such animosity besets many—if not most—academic departments but only rarely results in departmental dissolution, so this is not a sufficient explanation. The reality is that the reasons for the DSR to stay together that had been articulated in the 1940s and 1950s no longer made much sense. The idea of a single, grand, metanarrating social science was simply no longer compelling. The fact that the participants felt as if they were in a department filled with scholars "from other fields" suggests very precisely the shift in mood.

Similarly, in trying to explain why the CCP didn't even bother to seek new funding after 1973, Gabriel Almond claimed that the CCP had "achieved its mission" of making politics comparative and that it "no longer seemed necessary" to promote this agenda. Finally, scholars at the CIS have explained the timing of its institutional redirection away from development by noting that Max Millikan, the director who had guided the CIS's attentions to development and Communism, died in 1970. But this does not explain why Millikan's friend Walt Rostow, whose ideas were so central to modernization theory, was not invited back to MIT in 1969, at the end of his service as national security advisor to Johnson. (Rostow instead moved to the University of Texas, Austin, to continue his work there, while the CIS pursued other topics in international relations.) There is no doubt that the modernization theorists did achieve the victory to which Almond lays claim: they made the study of politics more comparative. But the institutional matrix of modernization theory dissolved in a mood of mildly concealed defeat, not in a spirit of victory. They quit not because they had won but because they came to realize that—in their capacity as defenders of the modernization paradigm—they were losing. The specific theories that made comparison work for Almond, Pye, Binder, and their colleagues were no longer working. What had died was the notion that there existed a singular and knowable path to a kind of materialist redemption or salvation in the form of modernity. Seen in this light, the collapse of modernization theory constitutes an important episode in the demise of reformist, technocratic liberalism.

Modernization Theory's Attempt at Self-Criticism

Even though Almond and Pye managed to beat back attacks to the authority of the CCP throughout the 1960s, they could not stop the rising criticisms of the modernization paradigm that accompanied the crisis in social modernism.

This section examines the crescendo of critiques of modernization theory that arose during the late 1960s and 1970s, resulting in the abandonment of the paradigm. The section begins with some of the more sympathetic criticisms that sociologists and political scientists leveled at modernization, and then goes on to some deeper ideological and epistemological criticisms. Just as the success of modernization theory was related to its deep enmeshment with parallel discourses from the 1970s, the criticisms of modernization theory would emerge from and gain their strength from a far wider ideological and epistemological shift in postwar American intellectual culture during the 1970s. In this section, discussion of the critiques of modernization theory is divided into three categories: internal critiques, conservative critiques, and left-modernist critiques.

The best place to begin a discussion of the criticisms of modernization theory is with a now-forgotten essay by Mancur Olson, a young economist whose epochal *Logic of Collective Action* (1965) would soon spawn a sub-genre of game-theoretical analysis of mass political behavior.[23] Olson's interest in using economic models to understand political behavior began with "Rapid Growth as a Destabilizing Force," an essay published in 1963, at the apex of modernization theory's influence. Modernization theorists like Seymour Martin Lipset were at this time claiming a direct correlation between political stability and increased GNP, while Walt Rostow was winning friends and influencing people with the argument that to usurp the threat of Communist takeover, the "take-off" stage ought to be accelerated. Against such arguments, Olson assembled an impressive array of empirical data to show that while absolute income *level* was correlated to political stability, income *growth rates*—especially in poor countries—were correlated to instability.[24] Despite contradicting a key element of modernization theory, Olson went out of his way to affirm the social welfare ethos that underpinned modernization theory by suggesting that Americans ought to support poor nations' efforts to provide a minimal level of social welfare, even when it slowed the overall growth rate. In Kuhnian terms, Olson was operating as a "normal scientist" within the confines of the modernization paradigm, observing anomalies and tinkering with the model rather than rethinking the paradigm more broadly. Only the general historical experience of the 1960s would finally get liberals to admit that one might have to choose between economic growth and political stability.

Two more searching internal criticisms of the modernity/tradition dichotomy appeared in 1967: Reinhard Bendix's "Tradition and Modernity

Reconsidered" and Joseph Gusfield's "Tradition and Modernity: Misplaced Polarities in the Study of Social Change." Sketching a history of the tradition-modernity distinction back to Enlightenment figures such as Adam Ferguson, Bendix tried to present a complex view of modernization's intellectual lineage that included not just celebrators of modernization but also intellectuals who had been quite critical of modernization, like Goethe, de Bonald, Marx, and Tönnies. In looking to this more critical intellectual tradition, Bendix sought to salvage modernization by purging it of the unilinearity that a Walt Rostow, a Daniel Lerner, or a Clark Kerr had ascribed to it. Without getting into specifics, Bendix noted that multiple forms of tradition existed and that the patterns of modernization depended on the anterior traditional forms. To avoid "forcing all types of change into the Procrustes bed of the European experience,"[25] Bendix proposed a distinction between modernization—a process of change rationalization and differentiation in a particular "sphere"—and modernity, a concept Bendix did not define. In the end, Bendix defended the concept of modernization as embodying the ideals of egalitarianism, democratization, and what he called "the welfare state," which he felt could serve as a useful model for the postcolonial world's own development. Writing his essay amid the turbulence of Berkeley in the mid-1960s, Bendix was suggesting that a more modest social scientific concept of modernization would make its ethical core more defensible.

Gusfield was more skeptical. Using the case of India—modernization theory's quintessential example of a "traditional" country—he observed that developing societies had never been static societies and that the impact of colonialism had indeed been a huge factor in determining contemporary conditions in a place like India. He argued that traditional culture had neither a consistent body of norms and values nor a homogeneous social structure, as modernization theory assumed. Questioning whether modern and traditional social and political forms necessarily conflicted, Gusfield asserted that there was no empirical reason to believe that the advent of modernity would displace tradition, or that modernity and tradition were mutually exclusive. Like fellow Indologists Lloyd Rudolph and Susanne Rudolph in their work *The Modernity of Tradition,* also published in 1967,[26] Gusfield suggested that certain traditional beliefs or social structures, far from disappearing in the face of modernization, might instead serve as a foundation for modernization. Finally, he observed that rather than weakening tradition, such "modernizing" practices as mass education might renew interest in local linguistic and artistic traditions. Despite all these helpful criticisms, however, Gusfield refused to abandon the notion of an entity called "modernity," defined by "high standards of living and egalitarian societies," toward which all societies ought ideally to strive.[27]

Another sign of the waning of the modernization paradigm was the increasing tendency of scholars to contextualize and historicize its rise. One of the first to do so was the brilliant young sociologist Ian Weinberg, who would commit suicide in 1970. In papers delivered to the American Sociological Association meetings in 1967 and 1968, Weinberg argued that the rise of social scientific interest in development was connected to the self-confidence of the United States in the late 1940s in relation to decolonization and the cold war. The interest in "modernization," however, was a response of the late 1950s to the disappointment with the early, purely economic version of the developmental model. Weinberg observed that the concept of modernization, with its all-encompassing and flexible definition, signaled "an unwillingness, in the present state of knowledge, either to assign priority to one or other factor, whether it be, for example, economic or political, or to estimate the relative weight of these factors in a situation where prediction was demanded." Weinberg suggested that modernization served as a "rain check term," allowing the social scientists to put off making definite conclusions that might compromise their aura of scientific legitimacy.[28]

Weinberg was also the first to identify the convergence hypothesis as the central leitmotif of all modernization theory. Weinberg argued that the structural-functional models of Talcott Parsons, Wilbert Moore, Marion Levy, Neil Smelser, and S. N. Eisenstadt all assumed the inevitable convergence of industrial societies, a belief Weinberg considered unwarranted. Connecting the convergence hypothesis to an elitism that attributed social change to the activities of scientific and political elites, Weinberg argued that the "inherent notions in much of modernization theory of a monolithic and dominant scientific elite, of the inevitable and expanded role of the state, its benevolence for the process of economic growth, and the dichotomy between desirable modernity and the static barbarity of traditional society, repeat the non-empirical and ideologically motivated errors of the [Enlightenment] *philosophes*."[29] In the same article, Weinberg noted that the implicit technological determinism of modernization theory helped explain why scholars believed in what he called the "recapitulation hypothesis" of historical change. Weinberg's criticism echoed the argument posed in 1966 by CCP member Joseph LaPalombara, who claimed that the central proposition of the end of ideology hypothesis was "that ideology tends to wane as societies reach levels of social and economic modernization typified by Western countries."[30] LaPalombara observed that this "more modernization-less ideology formulation" rested on "the assumption (or hope) that socio-economic-cultural development is moving in a deterministic, unilinear, culture-specific direction, whereby the future will consist of national histories that are monotonous repetitions of the 'Anglo-American' story. In short, the decline-of-ideology writers seem to believe that 'they' are becoming more and more like 'us.'"[31] Despite these cogent criticisms, however, Weinberg and LaPalombara, like Gusfield and Olson, remained unwilling to reject the concept of modernity altogether, and groped for a nonteleological notion of modernization.

This sort of criticism of modernization theory would reach its apogee in a 1973 essay by sociologist Dean Tipps that is often cited as the tombstone of modernization theory. In explaining the declining appeal of the modernization concept, Tipps contrasted Bendix's suggestion that it was "useful despite its vagueness" with more contemporary views that depicted it as hopelessly confused. Tipps would provide a lasting and much-quoted criticism of modernization when he wrote that the "attempt by modernization theorists to universalize historically specific values and institutions from western societies may be understood in part at least as a means by which fledgling students of the 'underdeveloped areas' could resolve the cognitive crisis they confronted as they turned their attention during the 1950s and 1960s to the task of attempting to comprehend the course of events in societies whose history, culture, and social organization appeared alien and unfamiliar." Tipps also argued that the consensual, complacent view of American society during those years had informed the theory.[32] Though many texts informed by modernization theory contained excellent insights, Tipps argued, these occurred outside the theory itself and indeed were more often obscured than illuminated by the theory. Tipps's argument generalized British economist A. K. Cairncross's observation of Rostow's *Stages of Economic Growth* that "[t]he reader may admire [Rostow's] insight without feeling that it derives from the stages-of-growth analysis. . . . A great deal of what Rostow says is undoubtedly helpful. But it is so, in my view, in spite of, rather than because of, the stage approach which he adopts."[33]

Tipps classified modernization theory into two approaches. The first was the "critical variable" approach, which equated modernization with some other singular factor, such as industrialization, rationalization, or differentiation.

Advocates of this approach included Marion Levy, who *equated* modernization with industrialization, and Wilbert Moore, who used "modernization" to indicate the social and political *consequences* of industrialization. Since this substitution of terminology spawned needless confusion, Tipps suggested that it would make more sense to drop the word "modernization" and instead use the more specific term. The second, more common variety of modernization theory was the "dichotomous" approach. Dichotomizing theories of modernization posited an evolutionary relationship between the ideal-types of "tradition" and "modernity." Tipps suggested that this approach included the work of Neil Smelser, Daniel Lerner, Schmul Eisenstadt, Cyril Black, and (somewhat misleadingly) Samuel Huntington. Tipps criticized these dichotomous approaches for considering the United States as the fulfillment of some inexorable geohistorical evolution, a belief that Tipps (like many others by 1973) linked to the "American expansionism" of the 1950s. Empirical events in the third world had revealed the inadequacy of the concept of "tradition" for describing what was going on in those places. In Tipps's view, nothing could overcome the fundamental methodological problems associated with trying to use a single scientific concept to chart such vast and variegated historical changes.

By the 1970s, even its proponents knew that modernization theory had lost its way. Instead of proposing a grand theoretical synthesis, as Almond had hoped, the final volumes of Princeton University Press's Studies in Political Development series presented ruminations on the limits and failures of the modernization paradigm. The seventh volume in the series, *Crises and Sequences in Political Development* (1971),[34] was as close as the CCP would come to achieving a synthesis. Even this volume reflected the changed mood about modernization. Instead of a happy story of ascent toward the Age of High Mass Consumption, the process of political modernization was now depicted as a precarious passage through a common set of crises. The contributors each detailed an emblematic crisis of modernization—identity crises, legitimacy crises, crises of governmental capacity and resource distribution, and so on—but as a whole, the volume was unable to reach any definitive conclusions about the "sequences" (the word "stages" having been quietly set aside) in which these crises took place, or even whether each crisis was a necessary part of modernization. In fact, in the closing chapter, Sydney Verba backed away from the word "theory," preferring to describe the volume as providing a "framework," and even admitting that there was "some ambiguity as to what exactly the crises or problems are." Matching these epistemological doubts were growing qualms about the normativity of the West as a model for a completed and stable modernity. "To the extent that a more developed society is less plagued with instability and conflict than a developing country," explained Lucian Pye in the foreword to the book, "it is only because more effort and resources can be mobilized for coping with the inherent tensions in the development syndrome."[35] Growing skepticism about domestic modernity reinforced uncertainty about the modernization process as a whole.

Things would only get worse in the next two volumes. According to Charles Tilly, an outsider invited to edit *The Formation of National States in Western Europe* (1975), the CCP had sponsored the volume in the hope "that a careful look at European history would help edit the scheme." The volume included ten essays on various classic themes of modernization theory, such as the role of the military or the building of bureaucracies in the process of modernization. Even though modernization theory had by the mid-1970s been exposed as inadequate for understanding what was happening in the postcolonial world, the CCP still hoped it could be helpful for understanding Europe. Instead of supplying a corrective, however, European history seemed to suggest that modernization theory should be discarded altogether. "Most of these [political development] writings remain vague about just what is to be *explained*," Tilly groused. "This vagueness of the *explicandum* pervades the field. In fact, the same difficulties beset a whole family of related concepts: modernization, mobilization, not to mention the now abandoned word progress. With all of them, we attempt to explain so much that we end up explaining nothing." As far as Tilly was concerned, the main problem with political modernization theory was that its unit of analysis, the state, was both underdefined (he noted that David Apter's *Politics of Modernization* did not contain any discussion of the organizational apparatus of the state) and at the same time intrinsically limiting for understanding historical change in most places. Tilly concluded, "In my review of recent writings, I have encountered impressively little discussion of the way the structure of world markets, the operation of economic imperialism, and the characteristics of the international state system affect the patterns of political change within counties in different parts of the world. . . . Something specific about the analysis of political development appears to have blocked the effective introduction of the proper international variables into existing developmental models." In other words, Tilly was flogging modernization theory for ignoring the very sorts of issues that a decade earlier Klaus Knorr, Harold Sprout, and James Rosenau had proposed that the CCP examine. In 1965 Almond and Pye had parried this attack. A decade later, an editor of one of their own volumes would criticize them for their failure to heed that advice.[36]

The final insult would come in the ninth volume, *Crises of Political Development in Europe and the United States,* edited by Raymond Grew.[37] For this volume, the CCP invited a group of eminent historians to use the "framework" developed in *Crises and Sequences* to write histories of ten North Atlantic nations. Even the title of this work reflected the shift in intellectual mood about the domestic state of affairs. Instead of presenting a template of success, European and American history now appeared as a painful, tortured process that few would want to emulate, even if they could. Even worse, the authors of this volume did not content themselves with merely rejecting modernization theory's helpfulness for understanding particular national histories, but went out of their way to interrogate the ideological motives underpinning the theory. Keith Thomas, in his discussion of the United Kingdom, was downright nasty: "Beneath the talk of 'modernization,' 'politically mature societies,' 'balanced growth,' and 'the successful resolution of crises,' one can discern the assumption that the contemporary institutions of North America and parts of Western Europe represent a universal culmination of the political process, and that 'stability' and 'performance' are the ideal political goals for all societies. The political process, it appears, is to be studied from the point of view of the ruling group or 'elite'; and the investigator's main problem is to classify the methods by which that elite manages to fend off or satisfy demands from below without involving 'societal dissolution.'"[38] Given the direction things were going for the Studies in Political Development series, it was just as well that the planned tenth volume was never published.

The Conservative Critique

As the end of the last chapter began to discuss, modernization theory was linked to a liberal ideal of an egalitarian, secular, progressive welfare state. Although the New Deal consensus dominated the political landscape of the 1950s, conservative leeriness of state-led social change would appear, for example, in the congressional backlash against the CIS's depiction of Jim Crow segregation in the American South as a premodern atavism. Although on the defensive in the 1950s, conservatives kept up a steady drumbeat of criticism about foreign aid programs. Understanding the political and ideological

identity of modernization theory demands that we recognize that these intellectuals were, within the politics of the time, considered men of the left. The
idea of spending lots of money to aid poor countries was the twin of social welfare programs at home: both were the children of the social modernist faith in
that a benign technocratic state could help overcome social ills. Nor did conservatives fail to remark on these connections when the Kennedy White House
decided to launch the "Development Decade" in 1961. If the expansion of welfare contributed to social harmony, it certainly was not obvious during the
1960s. The expansion of the welfare state under Lyndon Johnson's Great
Society program had been accompanied by increased class and racial conflict
on the domestic front. All of this emboldened right-wing critics of the social
modernism of which modernization theory and the foreign aid regime were
central components. Sociologist Robert Nisbet would fix the blame for the perceived failure of the Great Society on social scientists who had "oversold" both
their theories and their ability to execute a plan based on those theories.[39]

One volume dedicated to debating the modernization theory–inspired liberal orthodoxy was the influential *Why Foreign Aid?* (1962). CIS director Max
Millikan would write a stirring defense of the foreign aid program as a necessity forced on Americans by the inevitability of modernization and the need
to help guide this process to bring the underdeveloped countries' "evolution
into greater consonance with United States interests over the next couple of
decades." The aim of the foreign aid programs, Millikan explained, was a "fundamental transformation of social structure, of loyalties and values . . . to
reduce the explosiveness of the modernization process."[40] This desire to
change foreign countries' societies and cultures would be anathema to conservatives, represented in this volume by Edward Banfield. Singling out
Millikan, Rostow, Hoselitz, Weiner, Shils, Lilienthal, and John Galbraith,
Banfield labeled these writers "moralizers" for the naïve belief (he quoted the
CIS's *Emerging Nations*) that "our political and moral interests coincide." On
the contrary, argued Banfield, "[d]emocracy and freedom are too foreign to
the experience of backward people to make sense to them." Though Banfield
questioned neither the definitions of tradition and modernity nor the superiority of the United States, he was dubious about whether aid could contribute
to social or psychological modernity. "Some societies may never fully enter
into modern ways," Banfield asserted. "The American Indian, for example, has
had extensive aid for decades, but he is in most cases far from belonging to the
modern world."[41] Sounding the "culture of poverty" note that would make

him famous, Banfield claimed that some people's cultures disinclined them to create "self-sustaining growth," a point similar to the one that Harvard psychologist David McClelland had made in discussing the variable distribution of "the need for achievement." But what made McClelland a liberal and Banfield a conservative is that McClelland believed that state policies could raise the need for achievement, while Banfield believed that little could overcome a culture of poverty. As Hans Morgenthau concluded in his own contribution, the foreign aid program was a "gigantic boondoggle."[42]

If Morgenthau and Banfield represented the policy end of the conservative critique of modernization, then the intellectual critique came from Robert Nisbet, whose 1969 volume, *Social Change and History*, surveyed the post-Aristotelian use of the biological metaphor of development to describe sociological processes. The payoff of this analysis for Nisbet was the chance to savage the functionalism of Talcott Parsons, Marion Levy, Neil Smelser, and their followers. For Nisbet, the methodological weakness of functionalism was that it made all change a result of immanent social dynamics, thereby obscuring the historical importance of such "external" phenomena as imperialism and colonialism. Instead of making it easier to understand what was going on in the postcolonial world, the metaphor obscured the phenomenon by naturalizing it. Modernization theory, according to Nisbet, tried to build a theory of historical change out of a set of abstract, static categories unsuited for explaining empirical events. Modernization theorists attempted "to make concepts regarding change seem analytically useful within finite, concrete, and historical circumstances when these concepts are the products of developmental ways of thinking that were meticulously defined by their principal makers and users as non-finite, non-concrete, and above all, non-historical." Referring to Neil Smelser's work on British industrialization, Nisbet noted that while no one would deny that increasing complexity and structural differentiation constituted the general historical trend of the last few hundred years, this trend explained nothing about the dynamics of one particular industry (cotton spinning) in one particular country (England) during one particular period (1770-1840)—the subject of Smelser's work. Nisbet's main point was that modernization theorists engaged in an impossible concretization of inductive arguments: Rostow, for example, stood accused of "endowing England with the same kind of self-containment, the same conceptual autonomy, the same mechanisms of dynamism with which Marx had endowed not any historical nation but capitalism."[43]

Morgenthau, Banfield, and Nisbet's critiques of modernization theory form the background for the more radical and fundamental criticisms of political scientist Samuel Huntington. One of the peculiarities of the literature on modernization theory is that Huntington is routinely misclassified as a modernization theorist. This misconception is ironic not only because modernization theory was the most consistent counterpoint to Huntington's own theoretical impulses throughout his career, but also because Huntington penned some of the most trenchant historicizations and contextualizations of the origins of the theory. Like Walt Rostow, Huntington was a brilliant scholar from a young age, earning a B.A. from Yale in 1946, an M.A. from the University of Chicago in 1948, and a Ph.D. from Harvard in 1951 at the age of twenty-four. In 1957 Huntington published two landmark texts: "Conservatism as an Ideology," and *The Soldier and the State: The Theory and Politics of Civil-Military Relations,* a work that remained a best-seller among American soldiers into the twenty-first century.[44] In both the structure and substance of its argument, "Conservatism as an Ideology" foreshadowed the work Huntington would soon be doing on political development. According to Huntington, conservatism could be understood neither as a narrow ideology justifying aristocratic resistance to the French Revolution, nor as a universal and timeless set of ideas about the family, private property, and the state. Rather, it was an ideology that arose from time to time in response to "excessive" attempts to change the status quo. "When the foundations of society are threatened," Huntington explained, "the conservative ideology reminds men of the necessity of some institutions and the desirability of the existing ones." Huntington made sure to point out that conservatism was a pragmatic ideology: in order to safeguard social and political fundamentals, change on secondary issues might sometimes be accepted. Once a social system had been decisively overthrown, conservatives (in contrast to reactionaries) would accept and even defend the new regime. Huntington's redefinition of conservatism eviscerated it of any specific ethical content and made it simply a defense of the status quo. Thus, being a real conservative in 1950s America meant, in Huntington's view, defending the New Deal (but only at home). Not only did this text foreshadow the substance of Huntington's future political opinions in its principled defense of the status quo, but it also exemplified the characteristic Huntingtonian move of declaring allegiance to an idea, but only after redefining it practically beyond recognition.[45]

In *The Soldier and the State,* Huntington built on this definition of conservatism to argue that the military was the most consistently conservative force in the United States. Taking the insights from this work and turning his attention to the postcolonial world, Huntington began in the early 1960s to suggest that in many of these lands, the military, as patriotic conservatives, could be a great force for stability and in many cases were well suited for keeping a lid on "the impatience of the masses." We can see, then, the basis for the confusion about Huntington's relationship to modernization theory, for on the face of it, it would seem that Huntington was a member of the team. Like Louis Hartz, Huntington accepted the view that American society was an essentially and monolithically liberal one. Like Edward Shils or Gabriel Almond, Huntington distrusted the masses. Like Lucian Pye, he advocated the military as a positive force in modernization. Like Walt Rostow, he would become a hawk on the Vietnam War. Furthermore, at Pye's invitation, Huntington enlisted in 1965 in the CCP, the very wellspring of political modernization theory.

However, despite these commonalities, Huntington was at odds with modernization theory on two fundamental points: first, he rejected the modernization theorists' desire to impose technocratic change on the postcolonial world; second, he rejected the notion that modernization was a progressive, convergent, or inevitable force. Impatient with prophetic utopianism, Huntington throughout his career was a maverick critic of all forms of liberal progressivism, including modernization theory. If Ithiel de Sola Pool or Walt Rostow, like other liberal internationalists suffused with the New Deal ethos (such as TVA chief David Lilienthal), believed that the social engineering of progress could be reconciled with democracy, Huntington adopted the much tougher perspective that progress could only be imposed on the masses—and that even then, it might not be desirable. If Huntington shared Shils and Almond's antipopulism, what was embarrassing about Huntington, as Donal Cruise O'Brien noted, was not the content of his hostility toward political expressiveness on the part of the masses, but his strident and unambiguous expression of this hostility.[46] Whereas Lucian Pye felt squeamish making the observation that military dictatorships could sometimes serve as a modernizing force, Huntington lobbied actively to promote military dictatorships in the third world. Huntington would draw the logical conclusion that the liberal Mancur Olson had refused to: if rapid growth was the cause of political instability and political stability was considered a paramount foreign policy objective, then slowing growth rates in the postcolonial world ought to be a foreign policy objective. Rejecting the notion that the United States had a moral obligation to help poor countries to modernize, and instead proposing that "stability" was the main thing the United States ought to promote, Huntington argued that the United States ought to be trying to *prevent* development in the third world.

Huntington's assault on modernization theory would begin with the 1965 article "Political Development and Political Decay."[47] Just as he had redefined the definition of conservatism in order to subscribe to the category, so, too, would Huntington use this essay to redefine the concept of "political development," and then declare himself a proponent. Whereas liberal modernization theorists like Seymour Martin Lipset had used the phrase "political development" to denote the progressive development of political institutions in the direction of parliamentary democracy, for Huntington "political development" referred to the capacity of the state to impose order and stability on the lawless, formless, confused, and violent hoi polloi. Eschewing modernization theory's assumption that modernization entailed a unidirectional and progressive path, Huntington pointed out that the arrival of modernity in non-Western lands could just as well result in "political decay" (i.e., excessively rapid change in which state control diminished). Whereas scholars like Rostow and Almond had argued that the threat to modernization lay only during a certain transitional stage—and at that, the threat was not that modernization would stop, but rather that it would be canalized into a Communist version of modernization—Huntington argued that modernity was never secure and that "demodernization" was always possible. Huntington cited numerous instances in which seemingly stable regimes had descended into revolutionary chaos. Although he did not question the inexorability of technical advance, economic growth, changing birthrates, or other elements of "modernization," his questioning of modernity's political telos would set the stage for more wide-ranging questioning.

Huntington developed these themes in his 1968 classic, *Political Order in Changing Societies*, the very title of which signaled Huntington's definitive break with the language of "development" and "modernization." For Huntington, "the most important political distinction among countries concerns not their form of government but their degree of government." Modernity was no longer to be measured by how close a society came to replicating liberal-democratic political institutions but by how effective it was at imposing order. Huntington claimed that the higher the degree of government—the greater its ability to impose its will on the population—the more developed the government.

"Development" did not mean overcoming poverty, ignorance, or disease but rather entailed helping postcolonial countries increase their degree of government (i.e., their ability to impose order on their populations). "Economic development and political stability," Huntington claimed, "are two independent goals and progress toward one has no necessary connection with progress toward the other." In Huntington's opinion, any radical attempt to try to cure social or economic ills was likely to increase social mobilization and thus further erode the degree of government. Huntington argued that if the goal was to achieve political development, then democratic institutions in the underdeveloped world were downright counterproductive.[48]

Even though he rejected the convergence hypothesis, Huntington agreed that the United States and the Soviet Union, because of their shared ability to impose order on their populations, had more in common with each other than either did with underdeveloped countries. According to Huntington, the contemporary United States—with its race riots, feminists, antiwar protests, and student radicals—far from being the exemplar of modernity, was experiencing political decay. By contrast, the Soviet Union (then at the height of its power) was just as modern as, if not more modern than, the United States. Indeed, Communism was probably a more effective vehicle for modernization than capitalism: "The real challenge which communists pose to modernizing countries is not that they are so good at overthrowing governments (which is easy), but that they are so good at making governments (which is a far more difficult task). They may not provide liberty, but they do provide authority; they do create governments than can govern. While Americans laboriously strive to narrow the economic gap, communists offer modernizing countries a tested and proven method of bridging the political gap."[49] Concluded Colin Leys, "Huntington carried his anti-revolutionary outlook to its logical conclusion by separating it from anticommunism. For him, it was the ideal of a fundamental reconstruction of society that was pernicious, because utopian and destructive of order."[50] In sum, what separated Huntington from Almond or Rostow was his rejection of the liberal hope that gradual change would lead postcolonial countries toward the American model of modernity.

Another way to clarify Huntington's differences from modernization theory is to consider his own self-description as a "Leninist Burkean."[51] While the Burkean half of that couplet referred plainly to Huntington's conservative hero, the Leninist half referred to his more unusual appreciation of Lenin's qualities as a forceful leader and theorist of leadership. As Colin Leys observed, "Far from being anticommunist, Huntington expressed almost unqualified admiration for the political regimes of Stalin and Mao, criticizing Stalin only for his weakening of the party from 1936 onward and Mao for launching the Cultural Revolution."[52] Huntington admired Lenin not as a revolutionary but as the leader who had halted the political collapse of the Russian state and indeed succeeded in making that state stronger than it had ever been under the tsars. He admired Leninism's focus on centralized control through a political vanguard, and no doubt would have agreed with Paul Averich's aperçu: "The great achievement of the Bolsheviks was not in making the revolution, but in slowing it down and diverting it into Communist channels. . . . The astonishing feat of the Bolsheviks was their success in checking the elemental drive of the Russian masses toward a chaotic utopia."[53] Huntington rejected as naïve the hopes of liberal modernization theorists like Ithiel de Sola Pool that this political vanguard could be replaced by a technocratic analog, a vanguard of social planners.

These theoretical disquisitions underpinned Huntington's emergence as one of the most ardent intellectual champions of the Vietnam War. Huntington correctly perceived that the aims of the Vietnam War had to be defined in political as much as military terms. Many modernization theorists hoped that progressive social reform could overcome political strife.[54] By contrast, Huntington believed that the only solution to political problems underlying the war lay within the realm of the political. Following the logic set out in *Political Order*, Huntington argued that the problem in South Vietnam was a lack of central political authority. The real requirement for winning the war, therefore, lay in strengthening the effective authority of Saigon over the Vietnamese people. In "The Bases of Accommodation," published in *Foreign Affairs* in 1968 in the immediate wake of the Tet Offensive, Huntington argued that the strength of the Vietcong lay in their organizational abilities among peasants in the countryside. Recasting an argument that Gabriel Almond and Walt Rostow had promoted since the 1950s, Huntington said that "[s]ocieties are susceptible to revolution only at particular stages in their development. At the moment the rates of urbanization and of modernization in the secure rural areas exceed the rate of increase in Vietcong strength. . . . In this sense, history—drastically and brutally speeded up by the American impact—may pass the Vietcong by."[55] Huntington therefore proposed that military planners ought to try to undercut the political power of the

Communists by engaging in what he called a "steady population drain" of the countryside, where the authority of the Saigon government was weak. "So long as the overwhelming mass of the people lived in the countryside," Huntington told the *Boston Globe* on February 17, 1968, "the VC could win the war by winning control of those people—and they came very close to doing so in both 1961 and 1964. But the American sponsored urban revolution undercut the VC rural revolution." Huntington seemed to be arguing along the old modernization theory lines that the "good" American revolution could thus defeat the "bad" Maoist revolution. But if the liberal Arthur Schlesinger Jr. argued that the United States should try to "persuade the developing countries to base their revolutions on Locke rather than Marx,"[56] the conservative Samuel Huntington was calling for them to base their revolution on Hobbes. Putting an even finer point on it, one of his colleagues commented, "Sam simply lost the ability to distinguish between urbanization and genocide."[57]

Huntington did not stop his revision of modernization theory with his redefinition of one of its most important categories. In 1971 he published "The Change to Change: Modernization, Development and Politics," a sagacious application of the dialectical method to both summarize and dismantle modernization theory. Already in *Political Order* Huntington had rejected the assumptions of irreversibility and progressiveness contained in the word "development." In this article he began to question the epistemological roots of the concept of modernization. He argued that the dichotomy of traditional and modern was "asymmetrical": theorists had defined "modernity" abstractly and then created the category of "tradition" out of the historical leftovers. He wondered whether the historical phases described by modernization theory were actual stages in historical evolution or abstract Weberian ideal-types. Like Robert Nisbet, Huntington claimed that modernization theory had never provided a rigorous account of the causes of political change, nor proven the existence of supposed systemic connections between various aspects of modernization, nor provided accurate or exclusive definitions of the putative stages of modernization. The principal function of the modernization concept, Huntington concluded, was "neither to aggregate nor to distinguish, but rather to legitimate"—though Huntington coyly refused to name exactly who or what it was that modernization theory had been attempting to legitimate.[58] Huntington claimed that modernization theory had subscribed to an "optimism of retroactive progress," an intellectual phenomenon whereby "[s]atisfaction about the present leads to an optimism about the past and about its relevance to other societies."[59] In other words, because modernization theorists in the 1950s saw the United States as a unique success, they believed that its history could be mined for useful lessons. With the withering of confidence about the contemporary United States, optimism about the utility of using American history as a template for modernizing others also declined. In the end, Huntington proposed to do away with the term "modernization" and to replace it with the (more) neutral word "change."

Just as the modernization theorists had based their faith in social modernism on their sanguine reading of the state of the United States in the 1950s and 1960s as a success, Huntington's condemnation of modernization theory stemmed from his perception in the late 1960s and 1970s of the antinomies if not failures of social modernism. Under the aegis of the influential Trilateral Commission, Huntington published in 1975 *The Crisis of Democracy*, which claimed that too much responsiveness to the public—what Huntington called "an excess of democracy"—was leading the rich nation-states toward a crisis of "ungovernability."[60] Surveying the American political scene around 1970, Huntington did not conclude that the United States was an illiberal place (or that liberalism was itself a sham), but rather that it was an excessively liberal place, in which the government had lost the capacity to impose its will on the populace. In Huntington's morbid view, political decay, or "demodernization," was setting in almost everywhere. Huntington believed that only (re)imposition of state authority both at home and abroad could halt this decay.

The Left-Modernist Critique of Modernization Theory

If Robert Nisbet, Hans Morgenthau, and Samuel Huntington took issue with the liberalism of modernization theory by proposing a conservative alternative, an even more vocal and oft-cited set of criticisms would come from the left in an intellectual movement known as *dependency theory*. Associated in the United States with the New Left, the dependency theorists defined themselves in one polemic after another in specific contradistinction to the modernization theorists. According to dependency theorists, what distinguished these left modernists most sharply from the modernization theorists was their radical break with the convergence hypothesis, which formed the historiological kernel of modernization theory. Development could not be understood in terms of a series of self-contained nation-states, all destined to become increasingly alike. Instead, all countries were part of a single economic system designed to yield different outcomes for different countries. Instead of considering the United States a normative model for a completed modernity, dependency theorists tended either to look to Communist models or to claim that no contemporary regime exemplified a rational, benign modernity.

Like modernization theory, dependency theory emerged as a critique of existing mainstream theories of economic development. In the late 1940s, Argentinean banker Raúl Prebisch and his colleagues at the United Nations' Economic Commission for Latin America (ECLA) began to question the standard neoclassical economic idea that trade provided mutual benefit to all parties. Leading what would become known as the structuralist school of development economics, Prebisch compiled evidence that in the long run, the terms of trade always moved against the primary producing countries. Neoclassical economics predicted that the application of comparative advantage on a regional basis would result in different specializations. The composition of the mid-twentieth-century global economy meant some countries would end up specializing in industry, while poor nations specialized in agriculture and extractive industries. Prebisch's insight was that because technological efficiencies were harder to wring out of primary production than industry, over time the terms of trade would decline for these countries. Since the incomes of primary producing countries were destined to fall further and further behind the industrialized countries, the only solution to this problem was to encourage the burgeoning of industry in those lands. As it happened, the policy implications were not necessarily at odds with modernization theory, which also advocated the industrialization in the South so as to achieve convergence.

If the ECLA was one tributary to dependency theory, the other was the journal *Monthly Review,* founded in 1947 by Paul Sweezy, a student of Joseph Schumpeter's. Sweezy's Marxist inclinations and independent means encouraged him to set up a journal outside the academy to keep up a steady, if largely ignored, drumbeat of opposition to the mainstream liberal orthodoxy of the 1950s. Unafraid to use words like "imperialism" and "exploitation," the scholars associated with the *Review* depicted the Western industrial democracies as predatory and parasitical on the colonies and ex-colonies of the

European empires. Updating the theses of Lenin and Rosa Luxemburg about the economic role of imperialism, Sweezy argued in *The Theory of Capitalist Development* (1942) that only a revolutionary break from the empire could liberate postcolonial countries from the yoke of "dependency." This analysis would be taken up in the 1950s by economist Paul Baran, who suggested that the differential outcomes that Prebisch described were not just an unhappy by-product of differing rates of technological change in different industrial sectors, but in fact were the very point of international capitalism. The capitalist economic bloc constituted "one system," Baran asserted, and since the terms of trade were always cast against the poor countries, the only way to achieve growth was to exit the system. Far from representing the point of departure for development, as Rostow would claim in *The Stages of Economic Growth,* colonialism had been the occasion for deindustrialization. Baran contrasted the British empire's deindustrialization of Bengal with Japan's initial isolation and subsequent incorporation on its own terms into the world economy, which, according to Baran, was the decisive factor that had allowed it to ascend into the first ranks of industrial nations.[61]

The basis of dependency theory would come from the catenation and conflation of this neo-Marxist perspective with the left-liberal arguments being made by ECLA in Latin America. Mexican sociologist Rodolfo Stavenhagen, for example, argued that Latin American societies were not characterized by a duality of tradition and modernity, but rather were part of a singular historical process that created both the current forms of tradition and the modern economic sector. He argued that, contrary to the liberal U.S. understanding of Latin American, there was no essential conflict between a local "feudal aristocracy" or landlord class and a "progressive" group of industrialists, but rather that these two groups worked together to keep the masses oppressed. This implied that "progress" would not result from the spread of industrialization into the so-called traditional and Native American parts of the country. Such spread would only destroy local industry and therefore further limit local autonomy. Chilean economist Osvaldo Sunkel extended Stavenhagen's critique of modernization theory by noting that underdevelopment did not result from an absence of historical development, but rather resulted from being part of the low-income, slow growth, marginalized fringe of the developed capitalist economy. Like Gusfield, Sunkel argued that tradition and modernity often existed check-in-jowl, and modernity was not necessarily displacing tradition. Inequality and chronic unemployment were to be expected in countries whose geoeconomic role was that of providing a single mineral or crop to the international market. Although scholars like Enzo Falleto, Henrique Cardoso, Celso Furtado, Samir Amin, and Orlando Fals Borda would debate these issues throughout the early 1960s, these discussions were largely ignored in the United States.

The synthesis and reception of these ideas in the United States would be led by Andre Gunder Frank, a former student of Bert Hoselitz and Kenneth Boulding, who for a time also worked at the CIS and in the 1960s was living in Chile, participating in these local debates. Frank would detonate these ideas on the American intellectual scene with the incendiary "The Development of Underdevelopment," an essay he wrote in 1963 but could not find a publisher for until 1967, when the *Monthly Review* picked it up. The basic argument was simple: underdevelopment did not result from a *lack* of capitalism, nor did it indicate "stagnation," as modernization theory claimed, but rather it was the necessary counterpart to capitalist development in the first world.[62] Like Baran, Frank pointed to the British deindustrialization of India, the destructive effects of the slave trade on Africa, and the razing of the Aztec and Inca civilizations as examples of how the incursion of capitalism, far from improving the economic situation of indigenous peoples, had degraded their internal economic capacities. Frank also argued that because of the historical unity of development and underdevelopment, the experiences of the first movers were irrelevant to the predicament of currently underdeveloped countries. England and the United States had at one time been "undeveloped," but they had never been "underdeveloped." Further, those countries that had developed at a relatively late date, like Switzerland or Japan, had in no way replicated the protean English development experience. Although England might have undergone one particular path of development, this path was very different from the one adopted, say, by Japan. If Huntington and Olson criticized Lipset's claim that there was a positive relationship between socioeconomic modernization and democratic stability and had suggested that the relationship might be curvilinear, Frank went one step further and argued that there was a negative relationship. Having thus disposed of mainstream development economics and political modernization theory, Frank turned his attention to the sociological theory of modernization in "The Sociology of Underdevelopment and the Underdevelopment of Sociology."[63] In this article, he argued (as Huntington and Nisbet had) that Parsons's structural functionalism did nothing to distinguish rich countries from poor ones empirically. For example, cultural traits like particularism and ascribed status, which Parsons had indicated were signs of backwardness, clearly persisted in the United States. Frank wondered whether the fact that brothers Walt and Eugene Rostow both had important posts in the Johnson administration was the result of the "achievement orientation" of American society. Frank suggested that modernization theory, by ignoring the destructive effects of development on the former colonies themselves, was little more than a self-serving mythology.

In the end, however, Frank's influence was more significant as an angry pamphleteer than as a profound critic of modernization theory. His scheme of Western pauperization of the colonial world did nothing to explain the poverty of peoples like the Tibetans or the Yanamamo, who were virtually untouched by either colonialism or capitalism. The scholar who would give Frank's ideologically driven criticism the requisite intellectual ballast was sociologist Immanuel Wallerstein. An Africanist by training, Wallerstein would develop a more sophisticated and theoretically sound version of dependency theory, which he would call *world-systems theory*. Like Frank, Wallerstein's project was to extricate contemporary sociology from what he termed "the cul-de-sac known as modernization theory." Wallerstein wrote, "We do not live in a modernizing world but in a capitalist world. What makes this world tick is not the need for achievement but the need for profit. The problem for oppressed strata is not how to communicate within this world but how to overthrow it. Neither Great Britain nor the United States nor the Soviet Union is a model for anyone's future. They are state-structures of the present, partial (not total) institutions operating within a singular world-system, which however is and always has been an evolving one."[64] For Wallerstein, the globe since the fifteenth century had been enmeshed in a single economic system that had to be analyzed as such. Adopting his key categories from the work of none other than Edward Shils,[65] Wallerstein explained that under the "modern world-system," the world was divided into three essential geographic categories. The "core," which consisted of the primary sites of capital accumulations, was characterized by urbanization, rapid technological advancement, a skilled and relatively well-paid labor force, and most important, political power. The "periphery," by contrast, consisted of politically enfeebled places whose role in the world economy was to provide primary goods and foodstuffs at a cheap price to the core. On the periphery, technological growth tended to be slow, urbanization minimal, capital accumulation close to nil, and remuneration much lower than in the core. The linchpin of Wallerstein's analysis was the semiperiphery, those liminal states on the rise (or sometimes fall) from the periphery to the core. Semiperipheries were crucial not only because their mobility deflected anger and revolutionary activity by providing hope for promotion within the world economy, but also because they, as Daniel Chirot and Thomas Hall wrote, "served as good places for capitalist investment when well-organized labor forces in core economies cause wages to rise too fast."[66]

Wallerstein would deploy the metanarrative of the evolution of the modern world system to demolish modernization theory, beginning with his multivolume work of the 1970s, *The Modern World System,* and then onward with many more monographs and essays in the 1980s and 1990s.[67] Modernization theory and world-systems theory differed in three essential ways. First, the primary unit of social scientific analysis for world-systems theory was the world system as a whole, while for modernization theory it was either the nation-state or the individual. Second, whereas world-systems theory asserted that differential outcomes were intrinsic to the system (at least until the arrival of the final revolutionary break), modernization theory argued that nation-states would converge on the model of "American-style" consumer-oriented industrialism, with individual psychology converging on high achievement orientation, universalism, collectivity orientation, specificity, and affective neutrality. The third and most important difference between modernization theory and world-systems theory lay in their political sympathies. Modernization theory was procapitalist and anti-Communist, favorable to American geopolitical hegemony, and skeptical of working-class radicalism, and tended to regard political radicalism as a form of psychopathology. World-systems theory, by contrast, was resolutely anti-imperialist and sympathetic in principle to the anger and concerns of those whom Franz Fanon, who greatly influenced Wallerstein, referred to as "the wretched of the earth."

Despite these differences, however, world-systems theory and modernization theory had a good deal in common. Both agreed that social science and history were not opposed categories and together could provide the keys to unlocking contemporary political dynamics as well likely future results. Both believed that the primary goal of the state ought to be the provision of popular welfare. Both placed the Soviet Union and the United States in the same category, as opposed to the lands of the South—modern versus traditional in the case of modernization theory; core versus periphery in the case of world-systems theory. Both were unconcerned with gender or environmental issues; both were reflexively secular, cosmopolitan, and relativist in their cultural outlook; both had a faith in rationalism and celebrated scientific progress. But perhaps the most important shared trait of the two schools was their shared embrace of metanarrative. Both modernization theory and world-systems theory constituted metanarratives that claimed not only to explain how everyone had gotten to where they were, but also to provide a framework for predicting the future. However, as we shall now see, at the same time as Wallerstein was developing his own countermetanarrative to modernization theory, others inside and outside the academy were developing an incredulity toward metanarrative of any sort.

CHAPTER 7

The Postmodern Turn and the Aftermath of Modernization Theory

Visions of the future help determine the future.
—CLARK KERR, *Industrialism and Industrial Man,* 1960

In addition to the critiques from left and right, the years around 1970 also witnessed the emergence of a critique of modernization theory that I shall with some trepidation label *postmodern*. To understand this label, it is important to recall the ideological underpinnings of modernization theory, for these postmodern critiques were not so much directed at modernization theory per se as they were at the modernist mind-view underlying modernization theory. Modernization theory was implicated in a whole series of contemporaneous discourses during the 1950s, including the elite theory of democracy, the theory of the demographic transition, the theory of industrial society, the argument about the end of ideology, and so-called consensus historiography. These liberal modernist discourses shared a rarely stated but widely held belief that a technocratic, welfare-delivering, development-promoting state—which I described in chapter 1 as the "social modernist" state—was both the natural telos and the primary source of historical progress. As Jean-François Lyotard would observe, Talcott Parsons's work typified this "optimistic" discourse in that it aimed at "the stabilization of the growth economies and societies of abundance under the aegis of the modern welfare state."[1] These discourses shared a hidden faith that rationalism, social scientific universalism, and cultural relativism represented the convergent tendency of all states and societies in the modern world. Built on a foundation of American national self-confidence, these various social modernist discourses were mutually reinforcing during the 1950s, and modernization theory stood at the center of this discourse.

In the late 1950s and early 1960s, current events both at home and abroad seemed to corroborate and reinforce the optimistic assumptions of the social modernist mind-view underpinning modernization theory. By the late 1960s there had been twenty years of nearly unbroken economic increase throughout the industrialized world, which seemed to confirm that Keynesian economic science had mastered the old problems of capitalist economic cycles. In his influential *The New Industrial State* (1967), John Kenneth Galbraith painted a compelling portrait of social modernism at the apex of its influence and confidence: the government would provide capital for investment in large infrastructure projects and a social safety net of welfare benefits, while an oligopoly of civic-minded large corporations would pump out consumer goods for what Rostow had labeled "high mass consumption," guaranteeing lifetime employment for their workers and maintaining good relations with their employees through their union representatives.[2] In terms of social reform, New Deal and Fair Deal programs had achieved such perceived successes that they provided the political capital for President Johnson to launch his Great Society programs to increase federal commitment to education, to fund disease research and health care for the poor and elderly, to sponsor public housing, to stimulate depressed regions, to eradicate poverty, and to remove obstacles to the right to vote. Moreover, by the late 1960s, the United States population had reached its historically lowest percentage of foreign-born residents, an underestimated factor in the achievement of the 1950s national consensus. While domestic racial injustice was still a fact of life, prior to 1965 the general tendency (for white liberals, at any rate) was to see improvement in the works. The assimilation to "whiteness" of "European ethnics" like Jews, Eastern Europeans, and Southern Europeans appeared to be a model for the assimilation of African-Americans to a wider American society.

American liberals in the late 1960s believed that these achievements had become a permanent state of affairs in the United States. For modernization theorists, moreover, these achievements would be transposed into a model for the future of the postcolonial world. American liberals of the mid-1960s surveyed the world with cautious optimism. Nearly the entire colonial world had achieved independence, and while the 1950s and early 1960s witnessed nasty postcolonial conflicts, things at first had not gone as badly as the more wild-eyed pessimists had predicted (with notable exceptions, like the Congo). A similar optimistic vein can be seen in the self-confidence with which the United States tackled the "conquest" or "taming" of nature by science. The first two postwar decades experienced the beginnings of the so-called green revolution—the introduction of high-yield new varieties of genetically engineered wheat and rice seeds that would double or even triple agricultural output in many regions. Major progress appeared to be made in the suppression of infectious diseases like smallpox, polio, malaria, and yellow fever. Dam building—the ultimate symbol in the ideological struggle over man's domination of nature—was at its all-time height and rarely questioned as being anything other than an unadulterated good that would prevent floods and increase agricultural yields. Justified or not, in the eyes of mid-1960s American liberals, history seemed to be on their side.

Over the next fifteen years, however, things would fall apart, and what had seemed like an inexorable trend would begin to be perceived by American liberals as a high point followed by declension. If in the 1950s a faith in social modernist ideals grounded modernization theory, then as these grounds eroded, modernization theory would become a lightning rod for attacks from anyone skeptical of any element of the social modernist mind-view. As Immanuel Wallerstein suggested, "What had seemed in the 1960s to be the successful navigation of Third World decolonization by the United States—minimizing disruption and maximizing the smooth transfer of power to regimes that were developmentalist but scarcely revolutionary—gave way to disintegrating order, simmering discontents, and unchanneled radical sentiments."[3] Attacks on core social modernist beliefs such as rationalism, secularism, and scientism did not target modernization theory directly, but nonetheless sapped the ideological foundations of modernization theory. Like tethered-together mountain climbers, social modernist discourses were interconnected so that if one went down, it was likely to be saved by its linkage to others. Then again, if enough of these ideas slipped at the same time, the entire crew risked going down together. Just this sort of catastrophe befell social modernist ideas from the late 1960s on, with modernization theory at the center of this star-crossed constellation of ideas. The crisis of modernization theory was thus but a moment in a much wider world historical crisis—a crisis which in the first world would lead to the steady erosion of the welfare state, in the third world would mean the gradual loss of legitimacy for the ideal of state-led development, and in the second world would precipitate the full-scale collapse of the Soviet system. In the context of this fundamental shift, modernization theory did not need to be argued against—it just no longer made sense. The generalized nature of this crisis goes a long way toward explaining why its exponents slunk away to pursue other projects, rather than engaging in a vigorous but losing defense of their beliefs.

A whole series of phenomena would cause a shift in "the structure of feeling" (to use Raymond Williams's term) in the United States. Consider the many different registers in which the shift away from social modernist confidence took place:

- Domestic political crises: From the time of President John F. Kennedy's assassination in 1963 (the symbolic beginning of the end of postwar American self-confidence), American liberals began to doubt their political superiority over other nations. If Kennedy's assassination suggested to some that the United States might be less different from a banana republic than Americans liked to imagine, then later events like the Watergate debacle (1972-74) and the hostage crisis in Iran (1979-81) would further undermine American geopolitical self-confidence. The assassination of Malcolm X and Martin Luther King and race riots in places like Detroit and Los Angeles in the mid- and late 1960s would set the stage for conflicts over school bussing in Boston and elsewhere in the 1970s. The apparent intractability of interracial animosity dashed liberal hopes that African-Americans would be assimilated into the dominant cultural bloc as easily as Eastern and Southern Europeans had been after 1923.
- International political crises: In the late 1960s, terrible internecine conflicts in postcolonial regions like Indonesia (1965) and Biafra (1967-68) undermined hopes that postcolonial political life would be better for many indigenes than the colonial ancien régime. Military coups toppled elected governments in nearly every Latin American country during the 1960s, undermining the notion that alliance with the United States would lead to progress.[4] The breakdown of order in many postcolonial countries—whether in the direction of Communism as in Vietnam or toward mere military dictatorship as in Zaire—led to a disillusionment with the honestly held liberal optimism of the immediate postcolonial years.
- Student radicalism: Beginning with the 1964 Free Speech Movement (FSM) at the University of California, Berkeley, student protests would indicate not only the decline of deference to authority but also a refusal to be happy operating what FSM leader Mario Savio referred to as "the machine." In the spring of 1964, just months before the FSM

would commence, Frederick Frey of the CIS would claim, "Modern nations are presumed to differ from traditional societies in their ability to command the loyalty and enthusiasm of their citizens."[5] If this were true, then student protests and a refusal to defer to elders and elites constituted a performative disproval of the United States' modernity. University of California president Clark Kerr, a conspicuous fellow traveler of modernization theory, would become the living symbol of the out-of-touch, arrogant technocrat. Student radicalism was itself part of a wider suspicion of professionalized rationality—typified by the rise of "alternative" medicine, which exalted herbs and homeopathy as superior to "Western" medicine.

- Radical environmentalism and "deep ecology": Starting with the reception of Rachel Carsons's antipesticide manifesto *Silent Spring* (1962) and accelerating in the 1970s,[6] a radicalized environmentalist movement emerged that envisioned nature as an end in itself rather than as a standing reserve of resources to be tamed and harnessed to human ends. The first Earth Day in 1970 represented the coming of age of a movement that perceived harmonious coexistence with nature's flows as the desirable human relationship toward nature.[7] In contrast to the modernist ethos of "conservation" with the aim of rationalizing the exploitation of nature by man, the new ethos entailed "preservation" of nature as a value apart from mankind. The Endangered Species Act (1973) codified the right of animal species to exist, regardless of their human use value. Dam builders found themselves demonized; whereas the 1960s were the all-time high point of global dam building, by the 1980s more dams were pulled down than built in the United States.[8] The new environmental movement would find its philosophical voice in the "deep ecology" movement, which French philosopher Luc Ferry described as "the first major counter to the Cartesian, democratic, individualistic, human-oriented civilization that has been characteristic of the West for the past three centuries."[9]

- Shifting patterns of disease and health care: In the arena of infectious disease, the change in mood was largely attributable to the growing realization that the dream of eliminating infectious diseases had been too sanguine. If the modernist moment in the fight against infectious diseases lasted from 1948, when Secretary of State George Marshall publicly predicted the elimination of infectious diseases, through

1969, when the U.S. surgeon general declared that the time had come to "close the book on infectious disease,"[10] to the 1977 global triumph over smallpox, then the reemergence of drug-resistant infectious diseases (notably AIDS) in the 1980s suggested that these modernist hopes had been overweening. On an institutional level, the fight against infectious disease shifted away from the collective action of mass campaigns on behalf of public health and eliminating "diseases of the poor," to be replaced by research on "diseases of the rich" conducted in laboratories of for-profit pharmaceutical companies. A similar retreat from campaigns for egalitarian delivery and distribution of medical benefits appeared in the decline of public health care systems and their replacement by privatized and unequal health care delivery mechanisms.

- The attack on modernist architecture: If Robert Moses with his Faustian remaking of the urban infrastructure of New York represented the apotheosis of modernist urban planning,[11] then starting with Jane Jacobs's *Death and Life of Great American Cities* (1961), many urban and architectural critics began to criticize the "cold" rationalism of the postwar high modernist or "International" style of architecture and urban planning. Jacobs criticized this style of rigid straight lines, highrises, and starkly open and transparent urban settings as being indifferent to neighborhood and unconscious of the texture, depth, and "palimpsest"-like qualities of smaller, more intimate communities.[12] While Jacobs celebrated the social spontaneity of the street, other critics of the International style in the early 1970s thematized the "aesthetic populism" of more commercial places like Disneyland or Las Vegas.[13] In the view of these newer critics, the city ought not be conceived of and designed merely as a place of production, consumption, and the making of "modern" citizens through education and political participation; instead, it was and ought to be a place of play and "excessive signification." The ideal for the new city was a multicultural "magical urbanism."[14]

- The transformation of gender: The modernist moment in American feminism stretched from the rise of the Woman Movement in the late nineteenth century to the establishment of the National Organization for Women (NOW) by Betty Friedan in 1966, which declared as its aim the "full equality for women in America in an equal partnership with men"—with universalism and egalitarianism as the key terms. A radical feminist critique of NOW's rationalism and equalitarianism began to appear in the 1970s. These feminists emphasized and celebrated the *differences* between men and women, some advocating, for example, separation of women from men through lesbianism. Modernization theory would be criticized for having failed to acknowledge gender[15]— a category that modernization theorists believed stood for one type of particularism they wanted to overcome. In a related movement, the late 1960s and 1970s witnessed the rise of a cross-class, cross-race "gay rights" movement that sought not just toleration but legitimacy and legal recognition of homosexuality.

- The "crisis" of the nuclear family: Modernization theory hailed the nuclear family as "modern" because it freed people (i.e., men) from the "traditional" filial constraints imposed by extended families, allowing them to pursue personal goals (i.e., material gain). The baldest early statement of this view was Edward Shils's suggestion that "[t]he more widespread the establishment of nuclear or immediate families outside the range of the extended family, the more likely we are to encounter economizing behavior."[16] But as the postwar period wore on, one of the main stories on the domestic front was the skyrocketing divorce rate and the concomitant decline of the "modern" family. The dominance of the nuclear family was now understood to have been only a (brief) historical stop in a more general historical process of familial fragmentation in the direction of absolute individualism.[17] In other words, the instability of the nuclear family indicated that "modernity" might not constitute the final historical expression of the family or of anything else. (A final ironic twist was that by the 1990s, demographers were describing the nuclear family as "traditional," whose ongoing decline we were supposed to lament.[18])

- New patterns of immigration and ethnoracial assimilation: Beginning with the 1965 liberalization of American immigration laws, a third great surge of immigrants began to enter the country, this time primarily from Latin America and Asia. Accompanying this surge was a decline in assimilationist ideologies and the emergence of movements for Native American rights, Black Power, and La Raza. These demographic and ideological trends would combine to make the United States a far more racially and culturally diverse (not to say dissonant) place, setting the stage for the "multiculturalism" of the 1980s and 1990s that celebrated diversity rather than (modernist) norms of universalism. If strife over integration in the 1960s and 1970s revealed that assimilation of African-Americans to the dominant cultural bloc was going to be difficult or even impossible, by the 1980s many would question whether such assimilation was even desirable.

- The return of religious fundamentalism: The emergence in the 1970s of a new generation of religious leaders in the United States, applying grass-roots fund-raising techniques to support their own reactionary causes, signaled the reemergence of politically active religious movements throughout the world. This reinjection of religion into political discourse reflected a movement away from the secularism of social modernism. This "fourth Great Awakening" in the United States mirrored the rise of fundamentalist Islam in other parts of the world. The apex of this movement was the 1979 overthrow of the Shah of Iran—a man who had cloaked himself in modernizing slogans while he despoiled his country for the benefit of himself and his cronies—by the Islamic radicals under the leadership of the Ayatollah Ruhollah Khomeini, who purported to hate everything associated with modernity.

- Economic stagnation and the crisis of Keynesian economics: A quintessential expression of social modernism, Keynesian economics held the view that governments should play an active role in both macroeconomic demand management and the microeconomics of allocating scarce resources. The end of the Keynesian economic system began in August 1971 with U.S. withdrawal from the gold standard, which led to the emergence of floating currencies and the arrival of money as pure signifier, untied to any specific, signified value holder. In 1973, for a variety of reasons, including American fiscal irresponsibility in the face of Vietnam War expenses and the Arab oil embargo following American support for Israel in the 1973 Middle East war, the world economy entered its worst downturn of the second half of the twentieth century. The particular form this crisis took, combining high persistent unemployment and high inflation rates—twin phenomena soon dubbed "stagflation"—was peculiarly resistant to demand-side macroeconomic Keynesian prescriptions of tax cuts and spending increases. The sorry state of the domestic economy in the 1970s muted the voices of those who wanted postcolonial countries to model themselves after the United States. With Keynesian economics in crisis, a number of alternative policies came to the fore, including monetarism and various forms of laissez-faire anti-interventionistic economic ideologies. All of these new economic doctrines shared a mistrust of technocratic rationalism—though often they gave lip service to "the rationalism of the market."

Finally, no discussion of the change in national mood would be complete without mention of the Vietnam War, an event that many perceived not just as revealing the inadequacies of the postwar liberal mind-view, but the direct causal result of that mind-view. And in this case, modernization theory was directly implicated. Despite Rostow's protestations to the contrary, everyone who knew him in his capacity as head of the policy planning staff under President Kennedy and later as national security advisor under President Johnson agrees that he was "one of the most persistent advocates of an active American intervention [in Vietnam] from the very beginning," so much so that Kennedy would refer to him behind his back as "the air marshal."[19] As Rostow moved up the Washington power ladder, he would become widely recognized as a "chief architect" of the Vietnam War. He himself would continually link his justifications for escalation in Vietnam to his academic theories, and if he was successful at nothing else, then he certainly managed to create a permanent link in the historical imagination between modernization theory and the policies the United States pursued in Vietnam. Laurence Grinter's 1975 appraisal of how Rostow's theories had informed American foreign policy provides a useful summation of the way the public connected modernization theory to the Vietnam War:

> The Rostow Doctrine was the most far-reaching American political-military doctrine/strategy employed in South Vietnam. It combined Cold War toughness with Western-style economic modernization. Rostowians saw the world locked in a communist-capitalist struggle whose outcome would be decided in the developing areas. South Vietnam was the linchpin in this struggle. Under Walt W. Rostow's guidance, the Doctrine became the primary tenet of American policy toward the developing areas in the 1960s and the principal rationale for U.S. intervention and conduct in Vietnam. . . . The international order depended on whether the developing areas could be "modernized"—a process Rostow equated with Western-style economic development.[20]

Regardless of the fairness of this assessment (and it was more fair than not), considering modernization theory as part of the intellectual edifice that had led the United States into Vietnam was a widely held belief. Perhaps the most moderate view was Dean Tipps's suggestion that, although modernization theory did not explicitly offer an apology for American expansionism, "there is little in the modernization literature that would seriously disturb White House, Pentagon, or State Department policymakers."[21]

It certainly did not help that people could point to Lucian Pye's advocacy of military dictatorship as a useful modernizing agent, or that Rostow and Pye's colleague at the Center for International Studies, Ithiel de Sola Pool, would publish statements like, "In the Congo, in Vietnam, in the Dominican Republic it is somehow clear that order depends on somehow compelling newly mobilized strata to return to a measure of passivity and defeatism from which they have recently been aroused by the process of modernization."[22] Though Samuel Huntington has been misidentified as a modernization theorist, that misidentification, combined with Huntington's advocacy of carpet bombing and "forced urbanization" in Vietnam, certainly did the theory no credit. The way the Vietnam War was fought caused some to question whether the elites in charge of the war were really rational, while others accepted the war as the sinister apotheosis of instrumental rationality. For Noam Chomsky, modernization theory would be Exhibit A in what he called "the double myth of the social sciences": the myth of political benevolence and the myth of scientific omniscience. If leftists led the charge in blaming liberals for the war, then such judgments were also congenial to the political right, which has always been eager to blame everything it could on liberalism.

Understanding what happened to modernization theory in the late 1960s and early 1970s cannot be separated from these wider phenomena, for these events and trends reflected and contributed to a fundamental shift in the mood of the country.[23] The result of these various crises was the emergence in the decade around 1970 of a deep sense of cynicism and pessimism about the future, the obverse of the paranoid optimism that prevailed in the 1950s. The self-confidence that America stood for virtue and had a mission in the world crumbled, and with it, the moral underpinnings that supported modernization theory. As sociologist David Riesman commented ruefully in 1980, the whole vision underpinning modernization theory had represented "the too easy grace of the winner."[24] As the reality of a consensual, liberal, rational, secular, technocratic, welfare-oriented United States broke down, so did the vision of a consensual, liberal, rational, secular, technocratic, welfare-oriented modernism as a model for third world development. The failure of liberalism to deal with the social and political crises of the 1960s and 1970s helped produce this psychological condition of pessimism and cynicism. If during the 1950s American liberals had lacked any nostalgia either for their own past—they venerated the American past by asserting that it remained alive in the present—or for the traditions that modernization was destroying in the post-colonial world, the new mood was marked by what Frederic Jameson described as "nostalgia for the present."[25]

These trends contributed to a growing incredulity about the very idea of development. In this "age of diminished expectations," a key target was the concept of "growth" as a desirable end for social and economic activity. The Club of Rome's 1972 manifesto *The Limits of Growth* claimed that the aim of societies should not be endless extension of man's domination and exploitation of nature, but rather an "equilibrium" between man and Earth. In a similar vein, *Daedalus* dedicated its fall 1973 issue to the subject of the "No Growth Society."[26] As Mancur Olson, who in the early 1960s had inaugurated the internal criticisms of modernization theory, noted in his introduction to the issue, the very "traditional" values that modernization theorists had decried as "obstacles to growth" might be appropriate and even necessary in a no-growth society. A rapid change in Americans' perception of reality and values, Olson intimated, had resulted in a profound change of consciousness and aesthetics. These new critics questioned modernism's desire to "master" nature; questioned the "myth" of continuous, linear history; questioned the very notion of progress and sometimes even the value of rationality. Often this led to a revaluation of "tradition," the category that had been the short-hand for everything that modernization theorists hoped to undo in bringing modernity to backward peoples. If TVA director and development enthusiast David Lilienthal spoke in the modernist voice of the 1950s and 1960s when he celebrated "the fruits of bigness,"[27] E. F. Schumacher captured the new spirit of the 1970s by arguing that *Small Is Beautiful.*[28]

The crisis of modernity, of modernism, of modernization theory was partial and uneven. If modernism was widely rejected, it was not always replaced by something else, as the processes of rationalization and globalization continued unabated. What was happening was a gut-level shift in opinion about whether benefits conferred by the process of rationalization and globalization offset the loss of community and the sacred that were its seemingly necessary by-products. What took place from the 1960s onward represented the return of an old dialectic in Western thought, which might be concisely described as a back and forth between Enlightenment and romanticism. Indeed, the quarrel that romantics had with the Enlightenment bears uncanny resemblance to the quarrel that many critics during the 1970s and 1980s would have with the liberal modernists. For both the romantics of the early nineteenth century and for the neo-romantic critics of the late 1960s through the 1980s, the problem was that their opponents had too much faith in rationality, too little appreciation of the sublime, too much fondness for uniformity, and too little appreciation for the losses entailed by the capitalist demolition of traditional lifeways. This explains claims that by the mid-1970s, modernization theory resembled warmed-over nineteenth-century social evolutionism,[29] bereft of any of the nineteenth century's skepticism about progress.[30] As Raymond Grew put it, the modernization concept was "doubly dated: old-fashioned *and* a product of the 1950s."[31] I propose that this debate over modernization theory can be seen as an opening salvo in the debate over modernism and postmodernism.

Just as the term "modernism" is powerful for its capacious polysemy, so, too, is the term "postmodernism" a useful way of capturing and describing a number of disparate intellectual movements, united mainly in their disdain for modernity. It is useful to see these various critiques of development and modernization theory—radical feminism, ethnoparticularism, fundamentalism, and environmentalism—as part of a wider intellectual shift that took place in the early 1970s, a shift that has been labeled by many scholars as "postmodern." What these emergent discourses shared was a dubiousness about the unity of mankind, a suspicion of master narratives, and a doubt that the state, especially the American state, was either the embodiment of human reason or a force for progress. In contrast to the modernist critiques of the dependency and world-systems theorists, these new critiques did not claim that modernization theory had been *insufficiently* rational, but rather that the very notion of a scientific-rational guidance was flawed. Critics began to question the desirability of a living in a "rational society"—the phrase took on a somewhat sinister ring. The intensifying ecological, urban, and social crisis in the first world seemed unsolvable, leading groups as diverse as the Reaganites and the Symbionese Liberation Army to doubt whether constructive collective social action was even possible. These new critics often celebrated the "local" over the "universal," seeing beauty in the differences of particular communities.

Feminists, gay rights activists, and advocates of racial and ethnic particularism would attack modernization theory for its deafness to questions of gender and color, calling instead for the recognition and celebration of particularity. In contrast to the collective notions of identity dominant in the 1950s, the 1970s and 1980s witnessed an increased "me-firstism." All of these discourses rejected the notion that "tradition" was something alien to modernity and to be overcome; generally, the years after 1970 witnessed a steady abatement of the conceptual tension between modernity and tradition.[32]

I do not want to give the impression that modernism was entirely eclipsed. However, rather than just representing the failure of modernism, the postmodern emergence also represented the disappointment over the success of modernism. The mood might be captured by the phrase "Is this all there is?" Postmodernists felt that the modernists had succeeded all too well in imposing modernism's forms on the contemporary social, aesthetic, political, cultural, and economic order. Confusingly, the most successful of these movements would be labeled neoliberalism—an ideology with decidedly hegemonic pretensions that was dedicated to the dismantling of state institutions in the attempt (always less than complete) to organize social activity as entirely as possible around markets. At the same time, neoliberalism would be forced to compete with antigrowth, antisecular, particularistic voices, which also had been all but silent in the first two postwar decades. Unreformed, welfare-state-oriented modernism became but one voice in a more mixed intellectual discourse on development that included conservative critics, neoliberals, Marxist modernists, and various postrational discourses such as ethnocultural movements, fundamentalism, feminism of various stripes, and environmentalism. Put another way, what emerged in the last quarter of the twentieth century in the United States was not a new hegemony of antimodernism, but a more polyvocal discursive scene in which no single strand of discourse dominated in the way that liberal modernism had in the decade straddling 1960. The prefix "post" indicates both the passing (the completion and the transcendence) of the modernist moment and the failure of intellectuals to formulate a viable hegemonic alternative. The high intellectual culture of the late twentieth century (which had become quite globalized by then) witnessed a melancholy sense of drift, a sense that a great project had passed but that nothing comparable had come to replace it.

Another reason why I wish to use the term "postmodern" is that the concept of postmodernity emerged as a direct consequence of thinking about the implications of the modernization idea. The first known social scientific usage of "postmodern" was C. Wright Mills's invocation of the term in *The Sociological Imagination* in 1959. "We are at the end of what is called The Modern Age," Mills proclaimed. "Just as Antiquity was followed by several centuries of Oriental ascendancy, which Westerners provincially call The Dark Ages, so now The Modern Age is being succeeded by a post-modern period. Perhaps we may call it: The Fourth Epoch." Mills went on to explain that the two climax ideologies of the modern age were liberalism and socialism, ideologies that "came out of the Enlightenment." Both shared certain traits such as the notions of progress by reason, a faith in science as an unambiguous good, a commitment to democracy in some form, and a belief in the inherent unity of reason and freedom. However, Mills claimed, these ideologies were now failing, with Marxism devolving into a dreary defense of bureaucracy and liberalism becoming merely irrelevant. "The ideological mark of The Fourth Epoch—that which set it off from the Modern Age," Mills concluded prophetically, "is that the ideas of freedom and of reason have become moot; that increased rationality may not be assumed to make way for increased freedom." Mills discerned an uneasiness in many modernist writers about this diremption between reason and freedom, but admitted that neither he nor anyone else had discovered a way to confront this conundrum. In other words, from its very first appearance in the social scientific literature, "the postmodern" appeared as a problem without a solution or even an adequate explanation.[33]

It is telling that Mills's reflections on this subject did not receive much attention until the late 1960s, when, half a decade after Mills's death, members of the New Left would claim him as a sort of martyred intellectual godfather to their own causes. Meanwhile, the modernization theorists themselves had begun to edge uneasily toward the same sorts of insights. In 1964 Robert Ward of the CIS noted that political modernization was an ongoing process and "probably unachievable in the ideal-type sense." He speculated about the emergence of new political systems that "bizarre though the semantics may be" would have "the characteristics of post-modern polities."[34] The modernization theorists were realizing, somewhat sheepishly, that something had to come after modernity—that American (and world) history, after all, had not stopped. One solution to this problem, as posed, for example, by James Coleman in his entry on "Modernization" in the 1968 *Encyclopedia of the Social Sciences,* was to suggest that modernization could be generalized into a theory of social evolution no longer burdened with the idea of the completion of modernity.[35] As Jürgen Habermas observed in the 1980s, the modernization theorists tried to separate the concept of modernity from its European origins to turn it into a model for the process of social development in general.

But this solution was inadequate even in the eyes of the modernization theorists themselves, in large measure because the congeries of events listed earlier were making it difficult to sustain the notion that what was happening to social modernism could possibly be considered progressive. By the early 1970s, even Talcott Parsons was admitting that "the superior adaptive capacity of modern societies does not preclude the possibility that a 'post-modern' phase of social development may some day emerge."[36] Likewise, in the introduction to *Beyond Belief,* a collection of previously published essays that appeared in 1970, Parsons's student Robert Bellah contrasted the mood of his papers from the late 1950s and early 1960s to those of the later 1960s. "The fundamental assumption" behind his earlier arguments, Bellah admitted, was "that modern Western society, especially American society, in spite of all of its problems, is *relatively* less problematic than the developing societies with their enormous difficulties in economic growth and political stability." Around 1967 his mood began to shift, however. He began to feel "dismay at the failure of society to move quickly and efficiently to correct racial injustice, distress at the growing turbulence . . . in the academic community, and above all horror at the profoundly immoral and unjustified war in Vietnam. These experiences have led me increasingly to feel that the problems of American society, not of the developing societies, are really the most serious ones today."[37] Bellah called it a transition from "pessimistic optimism" to "optimistic pessimism." Summing up the nature of this transition, Bellah referred to "post-modern man": "[T]his postmodern phase could not be seen simply as a continuous projection of the major trends of present relatively modernized societies. Theorists of modernization have been tempted to assume that once a certain degree of individualism, civic culture and industrial development were achieved the future of society was essentially non-problematic. It is hard in 1970 to make this assumption. . . . If modernization has brought far greater knowledge, wealth and power than men have ever had before, then, potentially at least, we are freer than men have ever been and our future is more open to make it what we will. But the same resources which can bring us freedom can also be used for oppression and control."[38]

By the 1970s modernization theory had clearly lost its momentum. Given that many modernization theorists were still in the prime of their careers, the collapse of this project meant that during the 1970s, many former modernization theorists began to pursue alternative projects.

Successor Movements

One direction in which some scholars turned in the 1970s was away from theory altogether. Ironically, this meant returning to the unstructured empiricism that modernization theorists in the 1950s had hoped to overcome. Luckily for the scholars wanting to go in this direction, the 1950s and 1960s not only had been an era of growth for theoretical approaches like their own, but also had witnessed the emergence of Area Studies programs. These programs, begun by the Social Science Research Council in 1943 in response to the obvious lack of knowledge about places where the United States was sending troops, resulted in the 1950s and 1960s in the establishment on scores of American university campuses of research centers defined not by a programmatic or theoretical agenda but by a focus on a particular postcolonial region such as the Middle East, Latin America, South Asia, Southeast Asia, or Africa.[39] Although these regions were themselves far from homogeneous, Area Studies programs did tend to focus on particularity more than modernization theory had. From 1953 to 1966, the Ford Foundation provided $270 million to thirty-four universities for area and language studies,[40] and had further funded the prestigious and well-endowed Foreign Area Fellowship Program. Former modernization theorists making this move tried to forget that during the 1950s and 1960s they had, as Immanuel Wallerstein unkindly pointed out, "relegated empirical work (especially about the past) to the position of hierarchical subordination to so-called theoretical work."[41] By the mid-1970s, Lucian Pye was claiming that the work of the Committee on Comparative Politics had always conceived of itself as operating in partnership with Area Studies programs.[42] Still, the return of many modernization theorists to Area Studies programs must have felt a bit like going back to the village after failing to secure a job in the big city.

On a policy level, development programs suffered the same constriction of ambition that was taking place on a theoretical level. As the high tide of modernism ebbed, development agencies in the 1970s propounded much more modest proposals than they had a decade earlier. The World Bank's reorientation away from grandiose infrastructure projects and toward "Basic Needs" typified this shift in emphasis. After the early 1970s, it would become hard to find development literature that claimed to be either providing or based on a master development blueprint. For the most part, the new mood signified the slow abandonment of activist efforts to improve the lot of the foreign poor. Problems at home were bad enough; who were we to go solving other people's problems? Whereas modernization theory had focused on nations and conceived of the state as a transparent instrument for nation building, new research focused on institutions and structural matters and suggested that postcolonial states had been responsible for creating many of the developmental disasters of the 1970s.[43] The activities of self-interested state actors came in for much of the blame for development failures, and by the late 1970s, antistatist ideologies and approaches were flourishing in every academic discipline. This change in attitude among sociologists and political scientists about the state dovetailed with changes taking place in the debate about development economics. Although the most vocal critique of development economics had come from the left, what ended up replacing welfare- and full-employment-oriented Keynesianism (in both the rich and the poor world) were monetarist and neoclassical economic policies. By 1980 development economist Raymond Bauer's neoclassical *Dissent on Development* (1971) had become mainstream development economics, and development economics itself would be dying as a separate subdiscipline. No longer were the problems of underdeveloped economies seen as structurally distinct from those of industrialized economies.

In terms of the ideological responses to the collapse of modernization theory, former modernization theorists tended to go either toward neoconservatism or toward communitarianism, depending on which of the fundamental assumptions of modernization theory they considered most flawed. Neoconservatism appealed to those who remained committed to the "values of modernity"—such as rationality, scientific authority, and orderliness—but who now doubted that modernization was capable of delivering a "technologically based, prosperous future that would obviate ideological conflicts."[44] As the belief in a postideological age crumbled, these intellectuals—including Seymour Martin Lipset, Lucian Pye, and Gabriel Almond—began to suspect that the *process* of modernization might be part of the problem rather than the solution. Instead of believing in a happy if boring modernity, these scholars now tended to agree with Daniel Bell in his 1975 assessment that capitalism contained certain fundamental "cultural contradictions"—in other words, that modernism's culture of rebellion undermined the work ethic and social stability necessary for society to run smoothly.[45] Mark Kesselman's acid judgment was that for neoconservatives, "[o]rder is not considered a prerequisite for achieving the highest political good but itself becomes the highest political good."[46] If earlier they had advocated establishing welfare states in the post-colonial world, they now hoped merely to maintain social and political order. In terms of the official U.S. policy toward underdeveloped countries, according to Donal Cruise O'Brien, neoconservatism resulted in a shift "from an initial and timidly reformist phase to one of undisguised conservatism and counter-revolutionary containment."[47] In other words, by the mid-1970s, many former liberal modernization theorists had come around to the position that Samuel Huntington had been advocating since the 1950s; ironically, people would read this new unity backward into time and conclude that Huntington and the new conservatives had always been ideologically aligned.

Whereas neoconservatism represented a "hard" reaction for disillusioned modernization theorists, communitarianism offered a "softer" response. It is no coincidence that many of the most influential works of communitarianism, from Robert Bellah's *Habits of the Heart* (1984) to Robert Putnam's *Bowling Alone* (1999), were written by former modernization theorists.[48] If neoconservatives continued to embrace rationalism and scientific authority as key values of modernity while rejecting welfare as a viable goal of social policy, communitarians made the opposite choice. While communitarians agreed with neoconservatives that modernity's "overemphasis on individual liberation" had led to a destruction of common moral tenets and produced an "ethical vacuum," communitarians argued that the blame for this error lay in the assumption that "rationality" was the decisive cognitive element of modernity. Exemplifying the rationale of those scholars who moved from modernization theory to communitarianism,[49] Amitai Etzioni lamented in *The New Golden Rule* (1996) that "after the forces of modernity rolled back the forces of traditionalism, these forces did not come to a halt; instead in the last generation (roughly, from 1960 on), they pushed ahead relentlessly, eroding the much weakened foundations of social virtue and order while seeking to expand liberty ever more." Communitarians argued that a successful welfare-oriented modernity had to be grounded in premodern values that would ensure social solidarity across social lines. Like other former modernization theorists, Etzioni believed that "order" ought to be given a new weight, reflecting his new sense that

American modernity was not the acme of freedom but instead licentious and disorderly. Promoting the same vision of social stability and increased welfare that had animated modernization theory, communitarians rejected the notion that rational technocrats using the instruments of the state could provide these goods. Instead, "communal values" had to be reemphasized so that communities themselves could supply these goods. The ideal of a community grounded in essential value consensus revealed Etzioni's continued reliance on a Parsonian framing of the "problem of modernity."

Globalization and Postmodern Developmentalism

A third successor movement to modernization, which emerged in the 1990s, was what would come to be known as *globalization*. While a thorough discussion of the intellectual roots of globalization discourse goes beyond the scope of this chapter, it is useful to consider the relationship between modernization theory and recent discussions about globalization. The first thing to observe is that globalization is a *phenomenon,* not a theory. Reduced to its most basic element, globalization is the result of what David Harvey has referred to as "time-space compression": as a result of improved transportation and communications technologies over the past two centuries, there has been a continuously accelerating reduction of the amount of time needed to move objects, ideas, and capital across space.[50] Driven by the possibilities for profit that result from bringing things and ideas together faster than ever before, the capitalist world economy has unleashed unimaginable possibilities for intellectual, cultural, economic, and human exchange—and at the same time destroyed older systems of power and knowledge unable to cope with the incursion of faraway things, ideas, and capital. For most of the postwar period, Marxism (under the influence of Lenin and Luxembourg) and modernization theory competed for this role of explaining the geohistorical implications of time-space compression. Globalization as a term arose in the 1990s to fill the discursive void left by the collapse of Marxism (some tried to revive modernization theory to fill this space), and globalization discourses have contrasted themselves both to modernization theory and to Marxist theories of globalization, while at the same time borrowing freely from both of these earlier discourses. In essence, theories of globalization differ from modernization theory (and Marxism) in four crucial respects:

1. A changed ethical tone: Globalization discourse contains both advocates and opponents of the process.
2. A changed view of the state: Whereas the state was the vehicle of modernization, globalization discourse sees the state as eroded by transnational forces and of growing irrelevance.
3. A heightened emphasis on culture: Globalization discourse makes cultural analysis grounds for both judging and explaining the globalization process.
4. A denial of convergence: Globalization discourse emphasizes geography and space as key variables for analyzing globalization.

As these distinctions suggest, contemporary discussions of globalization are thus bound up with the postmodern turn more generally. Let us examine each of these changes in further detail.

Modernization theorists were always cheerleaders for the process they described: reaching modernity was a good thing, and the only worry was whether all countries would make it as painlessly as possible. By contrast, globalization is a self-criticizing phenomenon. On the one hand, there are those who see globalization as an unabashed boon, and they often do so for many of the same uncritical reasons that modernization theorists celebrated modernity: advocates of globalization share with modernization theorists the idea that the human race is in the process of creating a "universal civilization." Particularly during the first world economic boom of the late 1990s, there were many who discussed globalization breathlessly as the triumph of the market and democratization, with capitalism delivering all things to all people as efficiently as possible. As Alan Ryan put it, "Where Marx envisaged a universal utopia founded on the common ownership of the means of production and exchange, globalization in this sense imagines a utopia built around a free market."[51] On the cultural front, likewise, some see globalization as opening new spaces for difference, diversity, hybridity, multiplicity, and localism. For advocates of the process, the solution to the problems caused by globalization is to have *more* globalization. On the other hand, as a hopeful vision of consumerism itself as liberation, no one has built a politically compelling ideology around globalization—even if its advocates defend it mostly as inevitable. Ironically, critics of globalization attack it for the same reasons its champions celebrate it: as the triumph of capitalism. In the eyes of many critics, who form a kind of twenty-first century New Left, globalization is a cipher for the decline of community, a disregard for the environment, and a simultaneous exacerbation of economic inequality and cultural homogenization. In sum, globalization spells the triumph of many aspects of liberal modernization (all except the welfare parts) but without the gusto and the passion. Both the International Monetary Fund (IMF) and the protesters in Genoa and Seattle at the turn of the century used the term "globalization" to refer to a more-or-less agreed upon phenomenon, despite differing sharply on whether they considered this process salutary.

The second way that contemporary discussions of globalization differ from modernization theory is in their conception of the role of the state. If the modernizing developmental state was the third world analog to the welfare state, then globalization sees the nation-state as withering away. Modernization theorist Lucian Pye defined modernization as "the diffusion of a world culture—a world culture based on advanced technology, and the spirit of science, a rational view of life, a secular approach to social relations, a feeling for justice in public affairs, and above all else, the acceptance in the political realm of the belief that the prime units of the polity should be the nation-state."[52] For Pye and other modernization theorists, the nation-state was the fundamental force for the diffusion of modernization, disrupting traditional societies on the way to building welfare states. But globalization theory suggests that state-led development may have been a historical anomaly of the twentieth century. Where nation-states and national economies were the subject-object of modernist development, globalization theorists posit that nation-states are declining in influence and that the causal agents of globalization are transnational extra-state organizations, especially multinational corporations, the IMF, the World Bank, and the World Trade Organization (WTO). The heroes (or villains) are international technocrats and swashbuckling entrepreneurs who push technological innovation and engage in "creative destruction." Even advocates of globalization concede that globalization involves a surrender of power to nonelected and technocratic, rationalistic transnational institutions. Inevitably, the decline of the state necessarily means the decline of the *welfare* state, which is a main reason for resistance to globalization in places like the European Union.[53]

The third important distinction between modernization theory and globalization discourse is that the latter has a heightened emphasis on culture.[54] Modernization theory focused on culture either as a dependent variable that would be transformed by modernization or as an "obstacle" to that transformation. Rostow was typical in reducing culture to "propensities" that were exogenous to his developmental model. On a cultural level, modernization theory often assumed that diverse local cultures were giving way to a single world culture; the destruction of these cultures, insofar as it was considered at all, was justified primarily on economic and political grounds. However, de-emphasizing the state as a developmental actor has opened a space to make culture a more determining variable in the analysis of globalization.[55] This theoretical opportunity has been seized in particular by anthropologists, who beginning in the 1980s began a desperate search for how to redefine their discipline as the last of their traditional subject matter ("indigenous peoples") disappeared under the pressure of globalization. By reinventing ethnography as the study of any local group, these scholars found a way to carry on the Boasian ethnographic tradition of assuming that culture is the primary determining variable in accounting for human difference. Continuing a tradition of protest anthropology, some globalization theorists have considered globalization's destruction of local cultures as an unquestionably bad thing, while others have seen it as opening new cultural possibilities. Some critics even try to do both things at once, castigating capitalism for homogenizing world culture while celebrating the fecund imaginations of postcolonials for inventing new hybrid forms of cultural expression off the ruins that capitalism has made of their "traditional" cultures.

The fourth way that globalization discourse differs from modernization theory is in its emphasis on geography and on the diverse impact of modernity/ globalization in different places. Edward Shils defined modernization as a "model of the West detached in some way from its geographical origins and locus." Daniel Lerner would reiterate the same point: "The modernization process . . . is (or should be) relatively geography free. Urbanization, industrialization, literacy, media participation and the rest work their main effects in *general* ways—with particular variations due to geography or culture as potentially important side effects."[56] Globalization theorists, by contrast, have drawn from world-systems theory to argue that globalization paradoxically both annihilates distance and at the same time creates increasingly differentiated outcomes in different locales. Globalization suggests that some regions will specialize in industrial labor (such as sweatshops), while other places will specialize in services (such as software and nouvelle cuisine). However, these spaces are not delimited along the lines of nation-states, nor can they be neatly divided either into three worlds or centers, peripheries, and semiperipheries. Instead, as

Frederic Jameson notes, "what used to be characterized as the Third World has entered the interstices of the First one."[57] In other words, the interdigitated world of high rollers has nodes not just in New York and London but also in Bombay and Panama City, while the "ghetto" spans the world from the slums of Brooklyn to the vast shanties surrounding practically every tropical metropolis. Modernization theory, by contrast, stated that all countries would be sites of "High Mass Consumption" with more or less equal access to consumer goods and with similar industrial mixes. When their work has been at its best, globalization theorists have moved beyond modernization theory by examining the microgeographic patterning of developmental processes—in other words, how modern cultural elements coexist in space and time with non-, or post-, or pre-, or antimodern ones.[58] Implicit in this new focus on differential geographic outcomes in the globalization process is a denial of a central tenet of modernization theory, namely the convergence hypothesis. Modernist development theories (in both Marxist and liberal guises) ignored geography, since they posited eventual convergence on a single model of modernity. Even though they admitted that some groups were temporary "losers in the modernization process," modernization theorists emphasized that everyone would be delivered to the golden future of modernity. Globalization discourse underscores the fact that even though liberal capitalism won the political battle against Communism, there is no necessary happy ending because the welfare state was not the final destination of modernity.

One important faction in the critical school of globalization discourse was the efflorescence in the 1990s of what I will refer to as the *postmodern school of development theory,* and which included writers like Arturo Escobar, Ali Mirsepassi, Serge LaTouche, Gilbert Rist, Wolfgang Sachs, Gustavo Esteva, and Timothy Mitchell. The arrival of the postmodern school can be dated from the 1992 publication of the collective polemic *The Development Dictionary: A Guide to Knowledge as Power,*[59] which, as the title suggests, pointed to a linguistic turn within development studies. Synthesizing ideas about Orientalism drawn from Edward Said, theories of power and discourse adapted from Michel Foucault, and the populist rage of the dependency theorists, scholars of the postmodern school spend their time reading and deconstructing what they refer to as development discourse. Modernization theory has been a preferred subject of attack, along with other programmatic schools of thought on development that the postmodernists grouped together under the heading "developmentalism." The poster child for the postmodern school has been anthropologist Arturo

Escobar, whose widely read *Encountering Development* (1995) purports to describe the "discursive construction" of the third world. According to Escobar, "the" discourse of development has taken place both in the literature on development and through development agencies in the postcolonial world. This "hegemonic" discourse has "essentialized" the third world through a "dominant paradigm" that has "privileged" economic narratives. Behind the humanitarian rhetoric, the real point of developmentalism has been to erode "poor people's ability to define and take care of their own lives." Instead of conceiving of development as a "cultural process," developmentalism reduces people and societies to "abstract concepts" and "statistical figures." Development economics, in particular, has historically "occupied the discursive space in such a manner that it precluded the possibility of other discourses." What other discourses? "A view of social change as a project that could be conceived of not only in economic terms but as a whole life project."[60] According to Escobar, development discourse is geared not toward improving the lives of the postcolonial poor but toward extending the power of the developmentalists (i.e., the modernist development authorities). "In the Third World, modernity is not 'an unfinished project of Enlightenment,'" Escobar explains. "Development is the last and failed attempt to complete the Enlightenment in Asia, Africa, and Latin America."[61] The postmodernists believe that modernism in unredeemable. Not only does modernism essentialize (always in a diminishing way) (post)colonial others, but indeed, according to Ali Mirsepassi, "[a]ll of the 'liberal,' 'enlightened,' and 'progressive' triumphs in Western modernity have had their interdependent counterpart in utterly illiberal, violently totalizing, and destructive assaults upon other people."[62] Postmodern skeptics decry the very notion of development as a power-knowledge regime for extending the scope of capitalism, as well as the World Bank and the IMF, institutions with classically modernist hopes for universalism. In the hands of Escobar, there is no sense that modernity itself is a fragmented experience, while for Mirsepassi, the emancipatory side of modernity is inseparable from its dimension of domination. Hostility to the Enlightenment and modernity (whether in liberal or Marxist form) is the unifying theme of the postmodern school of development.

In contrast to the monolithic views of modernists, Escobar claims to know what is happening in "real villages";[63] there, on the ground, "they have developed a hybrid model of sorts, ruled neither by the logic of modern farming nor by traditional practices."[64] Escobar detects a third world that is "manifold and multiple" and "increasingly illegible to any known idiom of modernity."[65] It turns out that contemporary Columbians (apparently the only postcolonials that Escobar has spent significant time with) have already erased all the modernist binaries of high and low, urban and rural, and so on. Always in a descriptive rather than prescriptive voice, Escobar claims that contemporary postcolonials, rather than succumbing to the modernist myth of economic growth, are embracing "a hybrid modernity characterized by continuous attempts at renovation, by a multiplicity of groups taking charge of the multi-temporal heterogeneity peculiar to each sector and country."[66] Their efforts at continuous cultural reconfiguration of modern and traditional elements resist efforts of development agencies to essentialize them. In the postmodern analysis, postcolonial cultural play becomes the only authentic form of resistance (yay!) to the hegemonic discourse (boo!) of economic development agencies.

The problem with all of this is not so much its analytical content—though in the case of Escobar, this too is often sloppy. The main problem is that postmodern discourse is guilty of the very thing for which it castigates developmentalism: it is not geared at improving the lives of the postcolonial poor. As Jonathan Crush points out, "To assert, like Esteva, that 'development stinks' is all very well, but it is not that helpful if we have no idea about how the odour will be erased."[67] Beyond cheering the supposed cultural habits of contemporary postcolonials, the postdevelopment school has no program. Indeed, Escobar calls on intellectuals to "resist the desire to formulate alternatives at an abstract macro level" and denies that alternatives can come from "intellectual or academic circles."[68] Having thrown out the social modernist baby with the developmental bathwater, these postmodernists find themselves incapable of imagining a plausible alternative on a policy level either to the modernist discourses of the 1950s and 1960s or to contemporary neoliberal discourses. Although I have spent a lot of time in this book showing how modernization theorists constructed their own national identity through the discourse of modernization, the idea that this is the *only* way that either the United States or modernity might define itself is merely wrong. (For most of this nation's history, Americans defined themselves mainly in contrast to Europe, not to any other part of the world—and it may yet happen again.[69]) Likewise, the conception that modernity *must* abject a (post)colonial other is an assertion rather than an argument. Celebrating "alternative ways of experiencing and knowing" is nice, but it fails to answer what thinkers as different as Kant and Lenin have emphasized is the most fundamental question, namely "What is to be done?"[70] This self-regarding refusal to advocate action-able programs for confronting postcolonial disempowerment represents not just an intellectual failure, but outright moral cowardice.

There is an almost neurotic quality to the way in which these scholars eternally return to attacking modernism. One suspects that what this school really represents is historionomic sour grapes: these writers are the intellectual offspring of the dependency theorists who considered socialism or Communism to be modernity's highest ambition, and the failure of that project has thus condemned all modernism in their eyes. On an intellectual level, the inability of these postmodernists to articulate any viable policy alternative to modernism consigns them to permanent parasitism vis-à-vis modernist development discourse—and irrelevance from the point of view of policy makers. All postmodernists can do is celebrate "multiplicity," "destabilize dominant modes of knowing,"[71] and tear down the shibboleths of modernist developmentalism. While pretending to iconoclastic radicalism, this amounts to conservatism: postmodernism undermines the national solidarities that have grounded North Atlantic welfare states from the late nineteenth century on, but proposes no alternative form of cosmopolitan or transnational solidarity in its place. It is corrosive, cynical, and decadent in a precise Nietzschean sense. Though modernism failed in many respects, refusing to think about how the aims of modernism might be realized in nondominating ways is an easy luxury for comfortable professors.

Modernization Theory in the 1990s and Beyond

As a formal theory, modernization had been discredited in nearly all quarters by the late 1970s.[72] If there is one way in which the postmodern school of development helps us, however, it is in reminding us how much modernist ideas about development are still (inescapably?) with us. As Craig Calhoun put it, after the 1960s, modernization theory lingered on, "its intellectual status deeply suspect but its theories . . . more critiqued than replaced."[73] Even as the main development debates turned toward structural adjustment and neoclassical economic analysis, and oppositional discourses focused on gender, ethnic, environmental, and linguistic concerns, most Americans' preconscious ideas about the differences between rich and poor countries did not change. In the collective view of most Americans (including intellectuals), poor countries and their peoples remained irrational, corrupt, inefficient, excessively fecund, technologically inadequate, incompetent, disease-ridden, superstitious, mired in age-old ways of doing things, and so on—always in implicit contrast to the happy success of our own country. As Björn Hettne commented, the idea of a radical distinction between modern and traditional societies, equated with "us" and "them," continued to inform the popular image of developing countries, regardless of the theoretical incoherence or political associations of this sort of thinking.[74] Furthermore, the postmodern prejudice against big narratives meant that no master narrative emerged (at least until the 1990s, with globalization theories) that could replace modernization theory's explanation for what was going on in the third world. Many intellectuals—to say nothing of less scholarly sorts—refused to accept the Marxian counternarrative but remained uncomfortable living in a world without a "big picture." As a result, modernization theory survived as the unstated, undefended, but nevertheless omnipresent vision of historical change, even as the content of the category "modernity" slowly evolved.

Given the dogged durability of the central images of tradition versus modernity, it is not surprising that sooner or later, modernization theory would come in for a more explicit rehabilitation. Predictably, the collapse of Communism provided the initial occasion for the rehabilitation of modernization theory. Some felt that the American victory in the cold war had "vindicated" modernization theory, as Lucian Pye among others claimed.[75] (Modernization theory would experience a boom in particular among bewildered former Sovietologists groping for a theoretical framework to explain the collapse of the Soviet Union—even though others pointed out that modernization theory did little to explain the dynamics of that collapse.[76]) Although the timing may have been miscalculated, and the correlation between economic and political growth not quite as tight as first supposed, the so-called third wave of democratization seemed to many to confirm that "in the long run,"[77] all good things do in fact go together. Furthermore, as Raymond Lee pointed out, the disintegration of Eastern European Communist regimes left "the First World as the only model of modernity to be emulated."[78] The person who would do most to try to put these self-congratulatory feelings on a firm pedestal of theory would be American philosopher Francis Fukuyama.

In his celebrated essay *The End of History*,[79] Fukuyama claimed that, though unacknowledged, modernization theory had continued to define the historionomic horizon for most American social scientists. Through the 1990s, Fukuyama's major intellectual project was to resurrect modernization theory by placing it on a firmer philosophical grounding. He was explicit in stating his debt to modernization theory and its technological determinism: because technology "guarantees an increasing homogenization of all human societies . . . all countries undergoing economic modernization must increasingly resemble one another."[80] Fukuyama claimed that only bashfulness prevented American intellectuals from admitting that modernization theory formed their basic philosophy of history. "It is striking," he has written, "that in all the rich literature on democracy and the democratic transitions published in recent years . . . it is difficult to find a single social scientist who will any longer admit to being a 'modernization theorist.' I find this odd because most observers of political development actually do believe in some version of modernization theory."[81] The time had come to discard the shame about modernization theory, for there was good empirical evidence, in Fukuyama's view, that modernization "is a coherent process than produces a certain uniformity of economic and political institutions across different regions and cultures," and that furthermore, this was a good and desirable thing.[82] Like Lucian Pye, Fukuyama felt that the history of the past thirty years had vindicated Seymour Martin Lipset's arguments about the correlation between democratic stability and rising per capita incomes.

Fukuyama sought to rehabilitate modernization theory by taking its historio-philosophical core, the convergence hypothesis, and grounding it in a Hegelian theory of history. "History" in Fukuyama's terms, consisted of the history of an ideological battle between conflicting visions of civilization and social order. Fukuyama's outré Hegelian claim was that the United States was standing at "the end of history," a fact that permitted American intellectuals (i.e., himself) to apprehend the meaning of the historical process, namely that "liberalism in the classical sense" was the historical calling of mankind. Rehabilitating modernization theory did not mean a return to the "simple-minded and overly deterministic formulation . . . that posited that all societies would, in effect, end up like suburban America in the 1950s."[83] On the contrary, standing at the end of history in 1989, we knew that the ideological outcome of the historical process was neoliberalism. Everyone in the world that mattered could agree, according to Fukuyama, that liberal democracy and unfettered capitalism had become accepted as the only viable, legitimate ways of organizing human societies. The reason for this universal embrace of liberalism and capitalism, he said, invoking Hegel, is that these systems are better suited than any others for allowing individuals to achieve the mutual social "recognition" that is the existential aim of human life. (Although he did not argue it explicitly, Fukuyama apparently felt that the welfare state did not give as much scope for "recognition" as unfettered neoliberalism.) Although Fukuyama admitted that there remained some who would resist liberalism and capitalism on ideological grounds, he dismissed them as resentful and ultimately irrelevant losers in the modernization process. Eventually these losers would realize, Fukuyama claimed, that the historical game is up and would recognize that the way of "the West" was the only way. If Talcott Parsons was the Marx of modernization theory and Rostow its Engels, then Fukuyama is its Lukacs.

Before we turn to discussing how the ideals of modernization theory have changed from the 1950s to the 1990s, let us examine one last intellectual figure, the inimitable Samuel Huntington, who through the 1990s has continued to do battle against the liberal (and now neoliberal) program of modernization theory. During the 1990s, both Huntington and Fukuyama made widely read big claims about the state of geopolitics, and the divisions between the two can be traced to their differing takes on modernization theory. Both Fukuyama and Huntington saw cultural difference as the distinguishing feature of contemporary societies, but they disagreed about how cultural difference operated on the historical stage. Following modernization theory, Fukuyama argued that economic pressures tended to push societies, insofar as they want to be economically successful, toward a convergence on a high-trust model of "modern" social organization in which the state was best left out. By contrast, Huntington argued that contemporary history was leading toward a clash of incommensurable and irreconcilable "civilizations," the latter term being defined in a Toynbean fashion.[84] Huntington separated the cultural characteristics of the West from the techno-scientifically driven process of human domination over nature. Late developers could adopt the technical advances first generated in the West without emulating the cultural particularities of the West. In Huntington's opinion, there was no reason to assume that material-economic convergence would lead to or even encourage cultural convergence.[85] Because economic convergence did not necessarily lead to cultural convergence, Huntington rejected the notion that modernization was either inevitable or a good thing. There was no basis, Huntington claimed, for saying that any one of these civilizations was "universal" in the sense either of moral superiority or of having history on its side. Huntington instead seemed content to argue that simply because one of these civilizations was "ours," we ought to fight like hell for it. Whereas Fukuyama adopted the neoliberal orthodoxy about getting the state out of social and economic affairs, Huntington continued to defend the conservative, militarist state as a requirement for keeping society in top fighting shape. Both Fukuyama and Huntington rejected multiculturalism and postmodernism—Fukuyama from a cosmopolitan-universalist perspective, Huntington from an authoritarian-centralizing perspective.[86]

Modernization Theory, Old and New

As the case of Fukuyama suggests, the 1990s witnessed the emergence of a new school of modernization, based on a philosophy of history spelling convergence on a universal, singular model of modernity. The idea of technologically driven historical convergence on single, interconnected, ideologically unified global modernity (curiously similar to the contemporary United States) has returned to popularity among American social scientists, policy makers, and pundits, providing theoretical credentials for a new agreement on U.S. development policy known in some circles as "the Washington Consensus."[87] Just as coeval ideas about the American national identity and mission grounded modernization theory in the 1950s, so, too, did contemporary conceptions of America's national identity and international mission encourage its return. As during the 1950s, the apparent economic success of the United States in the 1990s, in contrast to the stagnation or decline of other countries (Southeast Asia, Japan, the former Soviet Union), provided the emotional underpinning to these ideas. As during the 1950s, technology (this time information technology) appeared as the driving force of history, possessed of an immanent logic beyond human control, making technocratic prescriptions seemingly value neutral and above politics.[88] As during the 1950s, a global ideological challenge (this time from politicized Islam) galvanized efforts to market the virtues of modern civilization. Again, for a certain set of Americans, the definition of modernism came to resemble an idealized vision of the contemporary United States. And just as in the 1950s, bringing about organizational parallelism between rich and poor countries was the aim for post–cold war modernization theorists. The functional, epistemological aspect of the new modernization theory was nearly identical to the one in the 1950s, and with Fukuyama's Hegelian rereading of modernization theory, it was now on firmer historionomic footing.

Although the *function and cognitive operation* of this new modernization theory is remarkably similar to postwar modernization theory, the *substantive content of "modernity"* at the core of the new theory has changed considerably. Among post–Gulf War neoliberals (who sometimes, confusingly, call themselves neoconservatives), the definition of "modernity" has focused on the economic dimensions of American modernity. Reflecting the changes in the American economy from the 1950s to the 1990s, the old bottle "modernity" has been refilled with neoliberal wine. In the 1950s and 1960s, modernity signified New Deal ideals of collective action to achieve financial aid and social uplift. It signified the achievement of welfare states everywhere in the world that would more or less look the same. The postwar modernization theorists argued that modernizing states would impose a steeply progressive income tax, endorse social leveling, promote high-quality public education, sponsor industrial research, and intervene regularly to direct the economy. By contrast, neoliberals see not welfare guarantees but raw economic productivity as the United States' grandest achievement, often arguing that it was the basis for the American victory in the cold war and the cause of the United States' emergence as the unique global hyperpower. That productivity, they continue, is the result of deregulation, which has allowed corporations and nations to realize their full economic potential. The current vision of modernity promoted by the neoliberal elite jettisons the old postwar idea of a state-led (if not state-owned) economy in which union and corporate leaders collaborate to set policy and production goals. Instead, it is unfettered "turbo-capitalism" that is the essence of the new economic modernism.[89]

Because of the changed content of the category "modernity," there are crucial differences between what the new and the old versions of modernization theory have to say about change in the postcolonial world. Whereas the old version of modernization theory considered the state the vehicle for realizing modernity, the modernization theory promoted by Fukuyama and other neoliberals suggests that free markets lead to modernity. In economics, "structural adjustment" and trade liberalization policies dictated by the IMF have replaced the focus on state-directed heavy industrial production. In both cases the perceived economic engine in the United States—the state in the 1950s and the market in the post–Gulf War period—are assumed to be panaceas to underdevelopment. The World Bank justifies the evisceration of postcolonial state power by suggesting that the proper role for the state in the economy is to "steer not row."[90] In both the old and the new versions of modernization theory, the supposed agent of the growth process instead becomes the end in itself: development under the old modernization theory was equated with the penetration of the state into the social order, whereas development under the new theory has become synonymous with the penetration of market forces into an economy; "getting the institutions right" is the mantra of the new orthodoxy.[91]

As John Brohman has argued, however, the differences between Keynesian-based modernization theory and its neoliberal successors belie important continuities. Both share a disregard for indigenous knowledge and popular participation; both favor universal rules of economic development, developed originally to confront the domestic problems of the rich nations; and both elevate Western values and history to a normative position.[92] In politics, the new modernization theory is, of course, no longer motivated by the Soviet threat, but like old-school political development theory, it retains the notion of a transnationally comparable "transition" process, this time from "authoritarian" to "democratic" rather than from "traditional" to "modern."[93] Neoliberal modernization theory has found particular favor among the drafters of "transition programs" in Eastern and Central Europe, despite producing mixed results. Neoliberals assume that with the demolition of trade barriers and the encouragement of further global economic integration, economic benefits will accrue to all in the world economy—though they are conspicuously silent on how to ensure that these benefits get fairly distributed. Avoiding this question, they have instead quietly resurrected Lipset's hypothesis that economic liberalization "in the long run" leads to democratization. Leaving aside the issue of when the long run will arrive, or whether there is any tangible reason to believe that this linkage exists, it is certain that the 1990s ended with more global poor than it began with, and that even where democratization has proceeded, the vitiation of state power in the face of globalization in many postcolonial countries has made democratization a Pyrrhic victory. In sum, the neoliberal school takes on many of the worst assumptions of 1950s modernization theory— that what is good for the rich countries will be equally good for the poor, that modernization has the force of history behind it, that democratic accountability is unnecessary if scientifically trained elites (whether technocrats or entrepreneurs) run things, and that democracy is an inevitable epiphenomenon of economic liberalization.

So are the postmodernists right? In the face of this neoliberal vision of modernity, do we need to retreat into the purely critical stance? Must we lash ourselves to the mast of discursive theory to avoid the sirens of modernity? Were Horkheimer and Adorno right that modernity, as the highest realization of the Enlightenment, is inevitably fraught by a dialectic of domination? Or, to cite another angle of resistance to modernity, are conservatives everywhere right to decry modernity for its destruction of national sovereignty? What about Islamic radicals bent on imposing their own moral system on everyone they can get their hands on? What about unionized workers in rich regions who wish to preserve their protected markets and welfare benefits? Are all these diverse groups right to decry globalization and modernity as anathema?

The answer is no. The postmodernists and others may be right to decry the neoliberal vision of modernization, especially its naïve and often brutal ways of promoting modernity. But they are wrong to decry modernity *tout court*. It is the way the postwar generation and its neoliberal successors have executed their modernist dreams—not the content of the dreams themselves—that must be rejected. What we need is more modernity, not less; we need to realize the emancipatory promise of the Enlightenment, not scoff at modernity as either a moribund project or some sort of infernal machine that destroys identity, transcendence, locality, and meaning, giving nothing in return. Post- and antimodernists argue that fascism and Communism stand as indictments of the modernist project; and they are right to the extent that renewing a faith in modernity will require that we unflinchingly face the many earlier failures of modernist projects so as not to recapitulate them (as, for example, the Chinese are doing with the Three Gorges Dam).[94] We must not allow these failures of modernity to drive us into the cultural despair of postmodernism.

The main reason to reject postmodern hopelessness is that, in addition to the neoliberal version of modernization theory, there exists a more hopeful moment in the contemporary geopolitical discourse of modernity. This moment appeals not to the rationalizing and economizing aspects of the Enlightenment tradition, but instead to its emancipatory and ethical dimensions. It calls for human rights, whether Michael Ignatieff's modest form of respect for democracy, political expression, and the right to self-determination,[95] or Amartya Sen's more ambitious definition of human rights as the right to economic development.[96] These scholars consider modernity's most salutary feature to be not its economic productivity but its commitment to common, universal, inalienable rights. This human rights moment in the contemporary discourse on geopolitical modernity aims to build a moral order based on a transnational consensus against victimization, but without glorifying or sentimentalizing victimization. Interestingly, neoliberals often claim a natural association between their ideology and that of the more modest wing of the human rights movement: they claim that neoliberal economic institutions, by providing growth, will inevitably bring about democratization and greater respect for human rights.[97] And while it would be a mistake to assume, as the neoliberals too often do, that a natural or necessary connection exists between neoliberal economics and the advancement of human rights, the possibility of finding a synthesis between the neoliberal modernizers and the human rights modernizers does exist. This synthesis turns on global, transnational institutions and a new transnational cosmopolitanism. The emphasis on democracy and human rights, when combined with international economic institutions, provides the material and moral foundation for building welfare institutions on a global, transnational scale. Only the building of such institutions would realize the emancipatory dimension of the modernist project, without which modernity is scarcely defensible.

The neoliberals are right about one thing: it is a world economy, and retreat into autarky is the commercial equivalent of Luddism. In a globalized world economy, therefore, institutions must be built on a global level. One of the central failings of modernization theory was that its emphasis on building nation-states meant that little effort went into promoting the transnational solidarities necessary to sustain global institutions. Each country's modernization was a one-off affair, although foreign aid could be used to push these countries in the right direction. In the last thirty years, not only have few transnational solidarities been built (the European Union being a possible exception), but postmodern ideologies have eroded cross-class solidarities within nations, while globalization has eroded the power of states. Even more sadly, few voices in the ongoing globalization debate speak of the transnational solidarity that must go with efforts to build welfare policy on that scale. On the one hand, neoliberal advocates of globalization want no system of international taxation and redistribution to impede the individual pursuit of wealth. On the other hand, critics of globalization wish to slow or revise the process of globalization altogether. These two blocs collude in preventing the creation of welfare institutions on a global level. If they do not reject this vision explicitly, both at least believe that meliorism should be executed on a local scale, whether through entrepreneurialism, giving to the church or mosque, or protecting a local tract of old growth forest.

The way to promote a safer and more just world is not by retreating from globalization but by promoting more democratic forms of global governance. Between the World Bank, the World Trade Organization, and the International

Monetary Fund, financial institutions are the most elaborated of current transnational organizations, but these need to have their mandate both expanded and reformed so that social justice becomes an explicit goal. Debt forgiveness, international standards for financial institutions, and obligation sharing during financial catastrophes can be promoted by augmenting the power of the WTO and the IMF in ways that will let them investigate and enforce international transactions in much the same way that OECD countries regulate banking within their own borders today. International organizations are relatively well developed to fight criminal activity, though the legal infrastructure needs to be backed not just by national courts but by an International Criminal Court. To legitimate these and other new organizations will require the creation of global representative institutions, perhaps under the auspices of the United Nations, but perhaps with an altogether new institutional foundation. True international leadership will entail the creation of multilateral governing bodies that can help move us beyond the dangers inherent in the perception that globalization is really a code word for a hyperpower that sets and enforces all the rules in its own favor.[98]

Such transnational global institutions constitute the only way forward toward realizing the "good intentions" of postwar modernization theory, namely toward building social democracy on a global scale. To achieve this long-term goal will require recasting on a global level the kinds of national solidarities that emerged in the late nineteenth and early twentieth centuries in Europe, Japan, and some European immigrant societies. Such a cosmopolitan sense of identity must, in the words of Cora Bell, see "the individual as a citizen of 'the universal city'—that is, of a single worldwide community of humankind, all of whose members are deemed to be entitled to equal rights independent of what their existing national governments are prepared to allow them."[99] There is nothing natural about such cosmopolitan solidarity—it must be imagined and evangelized. But what may give us hope is the knowledge that such solidarities have been built before, in nation-states that before were often as divided among themselves as global communities are today. Furthermore, these national histories show that nations and national solidarities have most often *followed* the building of successful state institutions, not the other way around. Building transnational institutions and governance thus can be conceived as a step toward, rather than the result of, transnational solidarities and a transnational civil society. The success in building such a dynamic in the European Union (in a region that was the most violent in the world in the first half of the twentieth century) provides a model for moving forward in this direction. Transnational civil institutions such as Amnesty International, the International Chamber of Commerce, the International Committee of the Red Cross, and Greenpeace can be enlisted to support the creation of more formal rules-based activity across state boundaries.[100] The real challenge of globalization is how to build institutions that can be democratically inclusive and responsive on a planet in which there are seven billion voices to be heard, with a hundred thousand more arriving daily.[101]

One way that Fukuyama moves beyond anterior "end of ideology" arguments is that he defends liberalism *as an ideology* and seeks to uncover its social and cultural underpinnings.[102] Fukuyama realizes that if modern civilization is about nothing more soulful than letting some people have an opportunity to get rich, then it is difficult to defend it from the attacks of Zapatistas, to say nothing of the likes of Osama bin Laden. Some vision of a global welfare state remains the best defense of the Enlightenment as a global ideal. Recasting modernization around the aim of building transnational, welfare-providing institutions provides a much more compelling justification for the radical changes being wrought on the world than the banal encomiums to "efficiency" offered by *The Economist,* and a more realistic program than the neoimperialism being promoted by the regnant American foreign policy regime. The aim must be to actualize the best parts of 1950s modernization theory—its vision of a healthier, wealthier, more equal, and more democratic world. It is these benefits that the postcolonial poor want more than anything else, postmodern nonsense about cultural play and resistance notwithstanding. They want the Great Powers to live up to the positive side of the modernist promises that were made in the 1950s; equalitarian inclusion in global decision making on ecological, political, and economic policy; and an opportunity for economic improvement and access to a greater share of the world's riches. United Nations Secretary General Kofi Annan, in a speech on February 12, 2000, called on the rich nations not to use populist protestors against the WTO as an excuse for not fulfilling the promises of development. Calling for a "Global New Deal" that would spread goods, jobs, and capital among all countries, Mr. Annan asked, "Can we not attempt on a global level what any successful industrialized country does to help its most disadvantaged or underdeveloped regions catch up?"[103] The promise of a global Fair Deal enunciated by President Truman in his Point Four address remains the standard against which the achievements of justice on a global scale must be measured.

Notes

CHAPTER 1: Modernization Theory and American Modernism

Epigraph: David M. Potter, *People of Plenty: Economic Abundance and the American Character* (Chicago: University of Chicago Press, 1954), p. 135; Daniel Lerner, *The Passing of Traditional Society: Modernizing the Middle East* (New York: Free Press of Glencoe, 1958), p. 43. Though he makes no citation, Lerner probably took this Siegfried quote from Potter, who took it from Isabel Cary Lundberg ("World Revolution, American Plan," *Harper's Magazine* 197 [December 1948], p. 39). The wide circulation and reuse of this quote indicates how strongly it resonated with what the modernization theorists believed themselves to be doing.

1. Edward A. Shils, draft to "Political Development in the New States" (c. 1958), pp. 1–3, Folder 10734, Box 739, Series 1, Ammendum 8/96, SSRC Archives (Committee on Comparative Politics), Rockefeller Archive Center, North Tarrytown, New York (hereafter RAC).

2. Robert Bellah, *Beyond Belief: Essays on Religion in a Post-Traditional World* (New York: Harper and Row, 1970), p. xix.

3. "Economic, Social, and Political Change in the Underdeveloped Countries and Its Implications for United States Policy." A study prepared for the Senate Committee on Foreign Relations by the MIT Center for International Studies (March 30, 1960) by Francis Bator, Richard Blackmer, Richard Eckaus, Everett Hagen, Daniel Lerner, Max Millikan, Ithiel de Sola Pool, Lucian Pye, Paul Rosenstein-Rodan, and Walt Whitman Rostow, p. 4.

4. Lerner, *Passing of Traditional Society,* p. 438. Italics in original.

5. Jeffery C. Alexander, *Fin de Siècle Social Theory* (New York: Verso, 1995).

6. Karl Deutsch, "Social Mobilization and Political Development," *American Political Science Review* 55:3 (1961), p. 498.

7. Ibid., p. 495.

8. Clifford Geertz, *After the Fact: Two Countries, Four Decades, One Anthropologist* (Cambridge: Harvard University Press, 1995), p. 99.

9. Rupert Emerson, *Political Modernization: The Single-Party System* (Denver: University of Denver, 1964), pp. 4–5.

10. Frank Ninkovich, *Modernity and Power: A History of the Domino Theory in the Twentieth Century* (Chicago: University of Chicago Press, 1994), pp. xiii–xiv.

11. Daniel Joseph Singal, "Toward a Definition of American Modernism," *American Quarterly* 39:1 (1987).

12. Krishan Kumar, *From Post-Industrial to Post-Modern Society* (New York: Blackwell, 1995).

13. Daniel Bell, *The Cultural Contradictions of Capitalism* (New York: Basic Books, 1976).

14. Jürgen Habermas, *The Philosophical Discourse of Modernity,* trans. Frederick G. Lawrence (Cambridge: Massachusetts Institute of Technology Press, 1987), p. 2.

15. Michel Foucault, *The Archaeology of Knowledge and the Discourse on Language* (New York: Pantheon Books, 1972), p. 8.

16. Ithiel de Sola Pool, "The Necessity for Social Scientists Doing Research for Governments," *Background* 10:2 (1966), p. 111.

17. Clark Kerr et al., *Industrialism and Industrial Man: The Problem of Labor and Management in Economic Growth* (Cambridge: Harvard University Press, 1960), p. 1.

18. Gabriel A. Almond, "A Voice from the Chicago School," in *Comparative European Politics: The Story of a Profession,* ed. Hans Daadler (Washington, D.C.: Pinter, 1997), p. 61.

19. Paul Rabinow, "France in Morocco: Technocosmopolitanism and Middling Modernism," *Assemblage* 17 (1992), pp. 53–54.

20. Bert F. Hoselitz, "Main Concepts in the Analysis of the Social Implications of Technical Change," in *Industrialization and Society,* ed. Bert F. Hoselitz and Wilbert E. Moore (Mouton: UNESCO, 1966), p. 15.

21. Alex Inkeles, "Making Men Modern: On the Causes and Consequences of Individual Change in Six Developing Countries," *American Journal of Sociology* 75 (1969), pp. 208–225.

22. Samuel Huntington, "Paradigms of American Politics: Beyond the One, the Two, the Many," *Political Science Quarterly* 89:1 (1974), p. 17.

23. Arthur M. Schlesinger Jr., *A Thousand Days: John F. Kennedy in the White House* (Boston: Houghton Mifflin, 1965), p. 589.

24. Paul Rabinow, *French Modern: Norms and Forms of the Social Environment* (Chicago: University of Chicago Press, 1989), pp. 345–346.

25. James Ferguson, *The Anti-Politics Machine: "Development," Depoliticization, and Bureaucratic Power in Lesotho* (Minneapolis: University of Minnesota Press, 1994).

26. James C. Scott, *Seeing Like a State: How Certain Schemes to Improve the Human Condition Have Failed* (New Haven, Conn.: Yale University Press, 1998), quotes on pp. 5, 88–89.

27. Christopher Lasch, *The True and Only Heaven: Progress and Its Critics* (New York: W. W. Norton, 1991).

28. Paul A. Cammack, *Capitalism and Democracy in the Third World: The Doctrine of Political Development* (London: Leicester University Press, 1997).

29. Nils Gilman, "Modernization Theory, the Highest Stage of American Intellectual History," in *Staging Growth: Modernization, Development, and the Global Cold War,* ed. David Engerman et al. (Amherst: University of Massachusetts Press, 2003).

30. Robert E. Ward, "Political Modernization and Political Culture in Japan," *World Politics* 15:4 (1963), p. 570.

31. Francis X. Sutton, "Social Theory and Comparative Politics" [1954], in *Comparative Politics: A Reader,* ed. Harry Eckstein and David E. Apter (New York: Free Press of Glencoe, 1963), p. 79.

32. Minutes of CCP meeting October 30–31, 1959, SSRC Box 737, Folder 10687, Series 1, Accession 2, p. 3, RAC.

33. Hans-Ulrich Wehler, *The German Empire, 1871–1918*, trans. Kim Traynor (Providence, R.I.: Berg Publishers, 1985); Henry Ashby Turner, "Fascism and Modernization," *World Politics* 24:4 (1972), pp. 547–562; Hans Mommsen, "Nationalsozialismus als vorgetäuschte Modernisierung," in *Der historische Ort des Nationalsozialismus: Annäherungen,* ed. Walter H. Pehle (Frankfurt am Main: Fischer Taschenbuch Verlag, 1990); Manfred Rauh, "Anti-Modernismus im nationalsozialistischen Staat," *Historisches Jahrbuch* 107 (1987), pp. 94–121.

34. Yasushi Yamanouchi, J. Victor Koschmann, and Ryïchi Narita, *Total War and "Modernization"* (Ithaca, N.Y.: East Asia Program, Cornell University, 1998).

35. Anthony Woodiwiss, *Postmodernity USA: The Crisis of Social Modernism in the United States* (London: Sage Publications, 1993).

36. Reinhard Bendix, "Tradition and Modernity Reconsidered," in *Comparative Studies in Society and History* 9:3 (1967), p. 346.

37. Gøsta Esping-Andersen, ed., *Welfare States in Transition: National Adaptations in Global Economies* (London: Sage Publications, 1996).

38. Lerner, *Passing of Traditional Society,* p. 13.

39. Richard Hofstadter, *The Paranoid Style in American Politics and Other Essays* (New York: Alfred A. Knopf, 1965).

40. Paul Goodman, *Growing Up Absurd: Problems of Youth in the Organized System* (New York: Random House, 1960); Stanley Milgram, "Behavioral Study of Obedience," *Journal of Abnormal and Social Psychology* 67:4 (1963), pp. 371–378; Hannah Arendt, *The Origins of Totalitarianism* (New York: Harcourt, Brace, 1951); Hannah Arendt, *The Human Condition* (Chicago: University of Chicago Press, 1958); Michael Paul Rogin, *The Intellectuals and McCarthy: The Radical Specter* (Cambridge: Massachusetts Institute of Technology Press, 1967).

41. Edward A. Shils, *The Torment of Secrecy: The Background and Consequences of American Security Policies* (Glencoe, Ill.: Free Press, 1956), p. 14.

42. Ibid., pp. 154–155.

43. Bellah, "Meaning and Modernization" [1965], in *Beyond Belief,* p. 69.

44. Howard Brick, "The Reformist Dimension of Talcott Parsons's Early Social Theory," in *The Culture of the Market: Historical Essays,* ed. Thomas Haskell and Richard F. Teichgraeber (Ithaca, N.Y.: Cornell University Press, 1993).

45. Thomas W. Dichter, *Despite Good Intentions: Why Development Assistance in the Third World Has Failed* (Amherst: University of Massachusetts Press, 2003).

46. David E. Apter, *The Politics of Modernization* (Chicago: University of Chicago Press, 1965); Cyril E. Black, *The Dynamics of Modernization* (New York: Harper and Row, 1966).

47. CIS *Annual Report* (1957), p. 30.

48. Inter alia: Robert Packenham, *Liberal America and the Third World* (Princeton: Princeton University Press, 1973); Michael Latham, *Modernization as Ideology: American Social Science and "Nation Building" in the Kennedy Era* (Durham, N.C.: University of North Carolina Press, 2000); Kimber Charles Pearce, *Rostow, Kennedy, and the Rhetoric of Foreign Aid* (East Lansing: Michigan State University Press, 2001).

49. Ali Mirsepassi, *Intellectual Discourse and the Politics of Modernization: Negotiating Modernity in Iran* (Cambridge: Cambridge University Press, 2000).

CHAPTER 2: From the European Past to the American Present

1. Cyril Black, "Modernization Studies: Achievements and Problems," 1959, p. 2, Cyril Black Papers, Firestone Library, Princeton, Archive number C0676, box 2.

2. E. A. Wrigley, "The Process of Modernization and the Industrial Revolution in England," *Journal of Interdisciplinary History* 1:1 (1972).

3. Website, <http://cil.andrew.cmu.edu/projects/World_History/Modernization.html> (November 3, 1998).

4. Lucian Pye, *Politics, Personality, and Nation-building: Burma's Search for Identity* (New Haven, Conn.: Yale University Press, 1962), p. 33.

5. Gianfranco Poggi, "The Modern State and the Idea of Progress," in *Progress and Its Discontents,* ed. Gabriel A. Almond, Marvin Chodorow, and Roy Harvey Pearce (Berkeley: University of California Press, 1982), p. 342.

6. Karl Marx, "The Future Results of British Rule in India," in *Marx-Engels Reader,* 2d ed., ed. Robert Tucker (New York: W. W. Norton, 1978), p. 659.

7. Bernard S. Cohn, "History and Anthropology: The State of Play," *Comparative Studies in Society and History* 22:2 (1980), p. 212. Reinhard Kosseleck traces back to the ancient Greeks the European habit of projecting civilizational categories onto temporal categories and temporal categories onto geographic categories ("The Historical-Political Semantics of Asymmetric Counterconcepts," in *Futures Past* [Cambridge: Massachusetts Institute of Technology Press, 1989]).

8. Edward A. Shils, "Political Development of the New States (I)," *Comparative Studies in Society and History* 2:3 (1960), p. 267.

9. Frederick Cooper and Ann Stoler, eds., *Tensions of Empire: Colonial Cultures in a Bourgeois World* (Berkeley: University of California Press, 1997).

10. Enrique Dussel, "Beyond Eurocentrism: The World System and the Limits of Modernity," in *The Cultures of Globalization,* ed. Frederic Jameson and Masao Miyoshi (Durham, N.C.: Duke University Press, 1998), p. 3. Italics in original.

11. *Oxford English Dictionary,* vol. 13, p. 989. According to the *OED,* the word *modernization* first appears in English in the late eighteenth century, but before Thackeray the usage was limited to the sense of technical improvement. Thackeray was referring to Francis Bacon's technologistic paean to printing, gunpowder, and the compass: "For these three have changed the appearance and state of the whole world: first in literature, then in warfare, and lastly in navigation; and innumerable changes have been thence derived, so that no empire, sect, or star, appears to have exercised greater power and influence on human affairs than these mechanical discoveries" (quoted in Krishan Kumar, *From Post-Industrial to Post-Modern Society: New Theories of the Contemporary World* [Malden, Mass.: Blackwell Publishers, 1995], p. 76).

12. Karl Marx, *Capital,* vol. 1, ed. Ernest Mandel (New York: Vintage Books, 1977), p. 91.

13. Daniel Lerner, "Modernization: Social Aspects," in *Encyclopedia of the Social Sciences,* vol. 10, ed. David Sills (New York: Macmillan, 1968), p. 386.

14. David Engerman, Nils Gilman, et al., eds., *Staging Growth: Modernization, Development, and the Global Cold War* (Amherst: University of Massachusetts Press, 2003).

15. Frederick Cooper, *On the African Waterfront: Urban Disorder and the Transformation of Work in Colonial Mombasa* (New Haven, Conn.: Yale University Press, 1987).

16. Ithiel de Sola Pool memo on "Task Force on U.S.I.A. Part Three," to Lloyd A. Free of USIA, undated [c. 1960], Appendix 1, p. 2. Ithiel de Sola Pool Papers, Box 96, MC 440, MIT Archives.

17. Partha Chaterjee, *Nationalist Thought and the Colonial World: A Derivative Discourse?* (London: Zed Books, 1987).

18. James S. Coleman, "Nationalism in Tropical Africa," *American Political Science Review* 48:2 (1954), p. 410.

19. Precisely because it represents a promise of liberation, "modernization" also continues to be a rallying cry for indigenous dissidents, especially in China. As exiled astrophysicist Fang Lizhi claimed in 1998, "The basic principles of modernization and democracy are like those of science—universally applicable. In this regard there's no Eastern or Western standard, only the difference between 'backward' and 'advanced,' between 'correct' and 'mistaken.'" Quoted in Jonathan Mirsky, "Democratic Vistas?" *New York Review of Books* 45:13 (August 13, 1998), p. 28. See also Liu Kang, "Is There an Alternative to (Capitalist) Globalization? The Debate about Modernity in China," in *The Cultures of Globalization,* ed. Frederic Jameson and Masao Miyoshi (Durham, N.C.: Duke University Press, 1998).

20. Gabriel Almond, "The Development of Political Development," in *Understanding Political Development: An Analytic Study,* ed. Samuel Huntington and Myron Weiner (Boston: Little, Brown, 1987), pp. 438–439.

21. The first social scientist to equate modernization with nation building was Hans Kohn, "The Europeanization of the Orient," *Political Science Quarterly* 52:2 (1937), p. 267.

22. Daniel Lerner and James Robinson, "Swords and Ploughshares: The Turkish Army as a Modernizing Force," *World Politics* 13:1 (1960), p. 25. Francis Fukuyama celebrates Ataturk in "Has History Started Again?" *Policy* 18:2 (2002).

23. Hans Arndt, *Economic Development: The History of an Idea* (Chicago: University of Chicago Press, 1987), pp. 16–17.

24. See Charles S. Maier, "Some Recent Studies of Fascism," *Journal of Modern History* 48:3 (1976).

25. *American Economic Review* 2:3 (1912), p. 744.

26. E. J. Clapp, *Port of Hamburg* (New Haven, Conn.: Yale University Press, 1911).

27. Paul Streeten, "Development Ideas in Historical Perspective," in Albert O. Hirschman et al., *Toward a New Strategy of Economic Development* (New York: Pergamon Press, 1979).

28. Dankwart Rustow, "New Horizons for Comparative Politics," *World Politics* 9:4 (1957), p. 430.

29. Frederick Cooper, "Modernizing Bureaucrats, Backward Africans, and the Development Concept," in *International Development and the Social Sciences,* ed. Frederick Cooper and Randall Packard (Berkeley: University of California Press, 1997).

30. Mordecai Ezekiel, editor of *Towards World Prosperity through Industrial and Agricultural Development and Expansion* (New York: Harper and Brothers, 1947), quoted in Eugene Staley's review, *American Economic Review* 37:5 (1947), p. 961.

31. Arndt, *Economic Development,* p. 52.

32. Ira Kaznelson, "From the Streets to the Lecture Hall: The 1960s," in *American Academic Culture in Transformation: Fifty Years, Four Disciplines,* ed. Thomas Bender and Carl Schorske (Princeton: Princeton University Press, 1997), p. 337.

33. Marianna Torgovnick, *Gone Primitive: Savage Intellects, Modern Lives* (Chicago: University of Chicago Press, 1990).

34. Clive Bell, "Development Economics," in *The New Palgrave: Economic Development*, ed. John Eatwell et al. (New York: W. W. Norton, 1989).

35. Alexander Gerschenkron, "Economic Backwardness in Historical Perspective," in *The Progress of Underdeveloped Areas*, ed. Bert F. Hoselitz (Chicago: University of Chicago Press, 1952).

36. Colin Leys, *The Rise and Fall of Development Theory* (Bloomington: Indiana University Press, 1996), p. 7.

37. Karl Deutsch, "Social Mobilization and Political Development," *American Political Science Review* 55:3 (1961), p. 498.

38. Eugene Staley, "The Economic Implications of Lend-Lease," *American Economic Review* 33:1 (1943), p. 375.

39. J. B. Condliffe, "Mechanisms of Postwar Planning," *Annals of the American Academy of Political and Social Science* 228 (1943).

40. Quoted in Barry D. Karl, *Charles Merriam and the Study of Politics* (Chicago: University of Chicago Press, 1974), p. 245.

41. David E. Whisnant, *Modernizing the Mountaineer: People, Power, and Planning in Appalachia* (Knoxville: University of Tennessee Press, 1987).

42. Charles Maier, *In Search of Stability: Explorations in Historical Political Economy* (Cambridge: Cambridge University Press, 1987), p. 128.

43. For example, Herman Finer, *The T.V.A.: Lessons for International Application* (Montreal: International Labour Office, 1944). David Lilienthal, the director of the TVA, participated in numerous postwar overseas development projects. He was the main planner for the disastrous Dez Irrigation Project Plan in Iran in the 1950s and promoted a similar comprehensive valley development scheme for the Mekong Delta in the late 1960s. See Grace E. Goodell, *The Elementary Structure of Political Life: Rural Development in Pahlavi Iran* (New York: Oxford University Press, 1986).

44. David Lilienthal, *TVA: Democracy on the March* (New York: Harper and Row, 1953), p. 206.

45. Ezekiel, "Industrial Possibilities Ahead," in *Towards World Prosperity*, p. 28.

46. Arthur M. Schlesinger Jr., *The Vital Center: The Politics of Freedom* (New Brunswick, N.J.: Transaction Publishers, 1998 [1949]), p. 233.

47. Barbara A. Miller and Richard B. Reidinger, "Comprehensive River Basin Development: The Tennessee Valley Authority," World Bank Technical Paper No. 416 (1998).

48. James T. Patterson, *Grand Expectations: The United States, 1945-1974* (New York: Oxford University Press, 1996), p. 131.

49. John H. Backer, *Priming the German Economy: American Occupational Policies, 1945–48* (Durham, N.C.: Duke University Press, 1971); Bruce Kuklick, *American Policy and the Division of Germany: The Clash with Russia over Reparations* (Ithaca, N.Y.: Cornell University Press, 1972).

50. World Bank, *World Development Report 1997* (New York: Oxford University Press, 1997), p. 22.

51. In retrospect even Rostow acknowledged that the Marshall Plan inspired overconfidence: "Lessons of the Plan: Looking Forward to the Next Century," *Foreign Affairs* 76:3 (1997), pp. 210–211.

52. Robert E. Wood, *From Marshall Plan to Debt Crisis: Foreign Aid and Development Choices in the World Economy* (Berkeley: University of California Press, 1986), chap. 1.

53. Albert O. Hirschman, "The Political Economy of Import-Substituting Industrialization in Latin America," *Quarterly Journal of Economics* 82:1 (1968); Sylvia Maxfield and J. H. Holt, "Protection and Internationalization of Capital: U.S. Sponsorship of Import Substitution Industrialization in the Philippines, Turkey and Argentina," *International Studies Quarterly* 34:1 (1990).

54. David Engerman, "Modernization from the Other Shore: American Observers and the Costs of Soviet Economic Development," *American Historical Review* 105:2 (April 2000).

55. Holland Hunter, "Soviet Industrial Growth—The Early Plan Period," *Journal of Economic History* 15:3 (1955), p. 281.

56. Max Millikan, "Economic Policy as an Instrument of Political and Psychological Policy" [n.d.], p. 12, Millikan Papers Box 10, Folder 317.

57. Interoffice memo, Bryce Wood to Norman S. Buchanan and Joseph H. Willitts (director for the social sciences), March 18, 1948, Folder 332, Box 60, Series 900, RG 3.2, Rockefeller Foundation Archives, RAC.

58. Interoffice memo, Norman S. Buchanan to Dean Rusk, November 25, 1957, Folder 333, Box 61, Series 900, RG 3.2, Rockefeller Foundation Archives, RAC.

59. Samuel Z. Klausner, "The Bid to Nationalize American Social Science," in *The Nationalization of the Social Sciences,* ed. Samuel Z. Klausner and Victor M. Lidz (Philadelphia: University of Pennsylvania Press, 1986), p. 6.

60. Quoted in Frank Ninkovich, *Modernity and Power: The History of the Domino Theory in the Twentieth Century* (Chicago: University of Chicago Press, 1994), p. 269.

61. Max Millikan and Walt Rostow, *A Proposal: Key to an Effective Foreign Policy* (New York: Harper and Brothers, 1957).

62. Walt Whitman Rostow, with Richard Hatch, *An American Policy in Asia* (Cambridge: Massachusetts Institute of Technology Press, 1955), p. 52.

63. Deutsch, "Social Mobilization," p. 505.

64. See Frank Ninkovich, "The Rockefeller Foundation, China and Cultural Change," *Journal of American History* 70:4 (1983).

65. Robert McCaughey, *International Studies and Academic Enterprise: A Chapter in the Enclosure of American Learning* (New York: Columbia University Press, 1984), p. 147.

66. Ford Foundation Gaither Report, quoted in George Rosen, *Western Economists and Eastern Societies: Agents of Change in South Asia, 1950–1970* (Baltimore: Johns Hopkins University Press, 1985), p. 3.

67. Ronald L. Geiger, "American Foundations and Academic Social Science," *Minerva* 26:3 (1988), p. 316.

68. Rockefeller Foundation grant action to Richard S. Ekhaus of CIS, September 27, 1957, p. 3, SSRC Box 481, Folder 4112, Series 200S, RG 1.2, RAC.

69. Edward A. Shils, "Governments, Foundations and the Bias of Research," *Minerva* 18:3 (1979), p. 459.

70. Gabriel A. Almond, *The American People and Foreign Policy* (New York: Harcourt, Brace, 1950), pp. 138–139.

71. Joseph Schumpeter, *Capitalism, Socialism, and Democracy* (New York: Harper and Brothers, 1942). On the elite theory of democracy see Irene Gendzier, *Managing Political Change: Social Scientists and the Third World* (Boulder, Colo.: Westview Press, 1985), chap. 5.

72. Compare H. F. Gosnell, *Getting Out the Vote* (Chicago: University of Chicago Press, 1927) with Bernard Berelson, Paul Lazarsfeld, and William McPhee, *Voting* (Chicago: University of Chicago Press, 1954).

73. The word "democracy" did not appear in the index of David Easton's *The Political System* (New York: Alfred A. Knopf, 1953).

74. Gabriel Almond and Sydney Verba, *The Civic Culture: Political Attitudes and Democracy in Five Nations* (Princeton: Princeton University Press, 1963), p. 136.

75. Walt Rostow, "The National Style," in *The American Style: Essays in Value and Performance,* ed. Elting E. Morison (New York: Harper and Brothers, 1958), p. 310.

76. Walt Whitman Rostow, "Industrialization and Democracy" [c. 1960], p. 4, MIT Archives, Millikan Papers Box 10, Folder 317.

77. Edward A. Shils, *The Torment of Secrecy* (Glencoe, Ill.: Free Press, 1956), p. 154.

78. Raymond Aron, "Social Structure and the Ruling Class," *British Journal of Sociology* 1:1 (1949), p. 10.

79. John Higham et al., *History* (Englewood Cliffs, N.J.: Prentice-Hall, 1965), p. 221.

80. Alan S. Kahan, *Aristocratic Liberalism: The Social and Political Thought of Jacob Burckhardt, John Stuart Mill, and Alexis de Tocqueville* (New York: Oxford University Press, 1992).

81. Tom Bottomore, *Elites and Society* (Harmondsworth, England: Penguin Books, 1964), p. 117.

82. Raymond Aron, *The Opium of the Intellectuals* (Garden City, N.Y.: Doubleday, 1957), p. 322.

83. Edward A. Shils, "The Scientific Community: Thoughts after Hamburg," *Bulletin of the Atomic Scientists* 10 (1955), p. 109.

84. Almond, *American People,* p. 137.

85. Gabriel A. Almond, *Plutocracy and Politics in New York City* (Boulder, Colo.: Westview Press, 1998).

86. Almond, *American People,* pp. 145, 55, 139, 54. In his landmark essay, "Comparative Political Systems" (*Journal of Politics* 18:3 [1956]), Almond would "scientificize" the idea of national character into the concept "political culture."

87. Kent M. Beck, "What Was Liberalism in the 1950s?" *Political Science Quarterly* 102:2 (1987), p. 247.

88. Almond, *American People,* pp. 233, 235.

89. Daniel Bell, *The End of Ideology: On the Exhaustion of Political Ideas in the 1950s* (New York: Free Press, 1960), p. 312.

90. Edward A. Shils, "Daydreams and Nightmares: Reflections on the Criticism of Mass Culture," *Sewanee Review* 65:4 (1957), p. 593.

91. Edward A. Shils, "Mass Society and Its Culture," in *Mass Culture Revisited,* ed. Bernard Rosenberg and David Manning White (New York: Van Nostrand Reinhold, 1971), p. 68.

92. Shils, "Daydreams and Nightmares," p. 596.

93. Ibid., pp. 598–601.

94. Lucian Pye, *Guerrilla Communism in Malaya: Its Social and Political Meaning* (Princeton: Princeton University Press, 1956).

95. Shils, *Torment of Secrecy,* p. 226.

96. Sydney Verba, "The Kennedy Assassination and the Nature of Political Commitment," in *The Kennedy Assassination and the American Public,* ed. E. B. Parker (Stanford: Stanford University Press, 1965), p. 353.

97. Seymour Martin Lipset, "The End of Ideology and the Ideology of the Intellectuals," in *Culture and Its Creators: Essays in Honor of Edward Shils,* ed. Joseph Ben-David and Terry Nichols Clark (Chicago: University of Chicago Press, 1977), p. 17.

98. Raymond Aron, *L'Opium des Intellectuels* (Paris: Calmann-Levy, 1955), published in English as *The Opium of the Intellectuals* (Garden City, N.Y.: Doubleday, 1957).

99. Stuart L. Campbell, "The Four Paretos of Raymond Aron," *Journal of the History of Ideas* 47:2 (1986), pp. 290–292.

100. Aron, *Opium,* p. 324.

101. Raymond Aron, *18 Lectures on Industrial Society,* trans. M. K. Bottomore (London: Weidenfeld and Nicolson, 1967).

102. Aron, *Opium,* pp. 305, 315.

103. Christopher Lasch, "The Cultural Cold War: A Short History of the Congress for Cultural Freedom," in *Toward a New Past: Dissenting Essays in American History,* ed. B. J. Bernstein (New York: Pantheon Books, 1968).

104. Edward A. Shils, "The End of Ideology?" *Encounter* 5:5 (1955), pp. 52–58.

105. Seymour Martin Lipset, "The Changing Class Structure and Contemporary European Politics," *Dædalus* 93:2 (1964), p. 296.

106. Bell, *End of Ideology,* pp. 402–403.

107. Seymour Martin Lipset, *Political Man* (Garden City, N.Y.: Doubleday, 1960), p. 406.

108. Pierre Birnbaum, *La Fin du Politique* (Paris: Editions de Seuil, 1975).

109. Joseph LaPalombara, "Decline of Ideology: A Dissent and an Interpretation," *American Political Science Review* 60:1 (1966), p. 6.

110. Sheldon Wolin, "Political Theory as a Vocation," *American Political Science Review* 63:4 (1969), pp. 1062–1082.

111. David Easton, *A Framework for Political Analysis* (New York: Prentice-Hall, 1965), p. 8.

112. Bell himself would eventually repudiate this view explicitly in *The Coming of Post-Industrial Society: A Venture in Social Forecasting* (New York: Basic Books, 1973).

113. Edward A. Shils, *The Intellectual between Tradition and Modernity: The Indian Situation* (The Hague: Mouton, 1961).

114. Bell, *End of Ideology,* p. 403.

115. Lipset, *Political Man,* p. 417.

116. Seymour Martin Lipset, *The First New Nation: The United States in Historical and Comparative Perspective* (New York: Basic Books, 1963), p. 46.

117. Lipset, *Political Man,* pp. 416–417.

118. Lipset, *First New Nation,* p. 15.

119. Ibid., p. 3.

120. Seymour Martin Lipset, "A Changing American Character," in *The Culture and Social Character: The Work of David Riesman Reviewed,* ed. Seymour Martin Lipset and Leo Lowenthal (New York: Free Press of Glencoe, 1961).

121. John Higham, "The Cult of the 'American Consensus': Homogenizing Our History," *Commentary* 27:2 (1959).

122. John Higham, "Beyond Consensus: The Historian as Moral Critic," *American Historical Review* 67:3 (1962), p. 612.

123. Richard Hofstadter, *The Age of Reform: From Bryan to FDR* (New York: Alfred A. Knopf, 1955), pp. 59, 95, 92.

124. Ibid., p. 59.

125. Richard Hofstadter, *The Paranoid Style in American Politics and Other Essays* (New York: Alfred A. Knopf, 1966), p. 52.

126. Daniel Joseph Singal, "Beyond Consensus: Richard Hofstadter and American Historiography," *American Historical Review* 89:4 (1984), p. 987. Singal points out that by the mid-1960s, Hofstadter had overcome many of his antipopulist prejudices from the 1940s and 1950s, going so far as to march on Selma in 1965.

127. Richard Hofstadter, *The Progressive Historians: Turner, Beard, Parrington* (New York: Alfred A. Knopf, 1968), p. 439. Hofstadter also claimed that the notion that America was a "pervasively liberal-bourgeois" society stemmed from a fundamentally "Marxist" idea (p. 451).

128. Gene Wise, "'Paradigm Dramas' in American Studies: A Cultural and Institutional History of the Movement," *American Quarterly* 31:3 (1979).

129. Michael Denning, "'The Special American Conditions': Marxism and American Studies," *American Quarterly* 38:3 (1986).

130. Louis Hartz, *The Liberal Tradition in America: An Interpretation of American Political Thought since the Revolution* (New York: Harcourt, Brace, 1955), p. 285.

131. Walt Whitman Rostow and Max Millikan, *The Emerging Nations: Their Growth and United States Policy* (Boston: Little, Brown, 1961), pp. xi–xii.

132. Arthur M. Schlesinger Jr., *A Thousand Days: John F. Kennedy in the White House* (Boston: Houghton Mifflin, 1965), p. 589.

133. Robert Bellah, *Tokugawa Religion* (Glencoe, Ill.: Free Press, 1985 [1957]), p. xii.

134. Leonard Binder, "The Natural History of Development Theory," *Comparative Studies in Society and History* 28:1 (1986).

135. Daniel Boorstin, *The Genius of American Politics* (Chicago: University of Chicago Press, 1953), p. 1.

136. David M. Potter, *People of Plenty: Economic Abundance and the American Character* (Chicago: University of Chicago Press, 1954), p. 87.

137. Walt Rostow, "The Making of Modern America, 1776–1940: An Essay on Three Themes," 1960, CIS working paper no. C/60-6.

138. Potter, *People of Plenty*, pp. 116–117.

139. Ibid., p. 114.

140. Gilbert Rist, *The History of Development: From Western Origins to Global Faith*, trans. Patrice Camiller (New York: Zed Books, 1997).

141. Walt Whitman Rostow, "The National Interest" (September 1956), Folder 19, Box 2, RG V4A, Rockefeller Brothers Fund, Special Studies Project Collection, RAC.

142. Patterson, *Grand Expectations*, p. 84.

143. Report from One-Day Conference on Problems of Achieving an Adequate Overseas U.S. Information Program, December 17, 1954, p. 23. Ithiel de Sola Pool papers, Box 96, MC 440, MIT Archives.

144. D. W. Brogan, "Some Personal Reflections on Recent Changes in the United States," 1957, MIT CIS, working paper no. C/57-7, pp. 21–22.

145. Millikan and Rostow, *Proposal*, p. 8.

146. David Riesman, introduction to *The Passing of Traditional Society: Modernizing the Middle East,* by Daniel Lerner (New York: Free Press of Glencoe, 1958), p. 10.

147. CIS *Annual Report* (1955), p. 20.

148. Rostow, "National Interest," p. 13.

149. Rostow, "Modern America," p. 2/2.

150. Walt Whitman Rostow, *The United States in the World Arena* (New York: Harper and Brothers, 1960), pp. 531, 538, 539.

151. Truman Inaugural Address, January 20, 1949, *Public Papers of the President,* 1949, pp. 114–115.

152. David McCollough, *Truman* (New York: Simon and Schuster, 1992), p. 731.

153. "Point Four," Office of Public Affairs, Department of State, February 1949, p. 2.

154. John Lodewijks, "Rostow, Developing Economies and National Security Policy," in *Economics and National Security: A History of Their Interaction,* ed. C. D. Goodwin (Durham, N.C.: Duke University Press, 1991), p. 292.

155. "Act for International Development," quoted in W. L. Thorp, "Some Basic Policy Issues in Economic Development," *American Economic Review* 41:2 (1951), p. 407.

CHAPTER 3: The Harvard Department of Social Relations and the Intellectual Origins of Modernization Theory

Epigraph: International Development Advisory Board, *Partners in Progress: A Report to President Truman* (Washington, D.C.: Rockefeller Report, 1951), p. 4. Italics in original.

1. Pareto exercised an important influence at Harvard in the 1930s, promoted especially by the circle that formed around physiologist Lawrence Henderson, including Parsons, George C. Homans, Charles P. Curtis, Joseph Schumpeter, Bernard Devoto, Crane Brinton, and Elton Mayo. Explaining the appeal of Pareto, Homans wrote, "As a Republican Bostonian who had not rejected his comparatively wealthy family, I felt during the thirties that I was under personal attack, above all from the Marxists. I was ready to believe Pareto because he provided me with a defense" (quoted in Barbara Heyl, "The Harvard 'Pareto Circle'" [1968], in *Talcott Parsons: Critical Assessments,* vol. 1, ed. Peter Hamilton [New York: Routledge, 1992], p. 30).

2. Stephen Savage, *The Theories of Talcott Parsons: The Social Relations of Action* (New York: St. Martin's Press, 1981), p. 88.

3. See Talcott Parsons, "Department and Laboratory of Social Relations: The First Decade" (HUF 801.4156.2). For an institutional history of the DSR, see Patrick L. Schmidt, "Towards a History of the Department of Social Relations at Harvard University, 1946–72," B.A. honors thesis, Harvard 1978 (HU 92 78.769).

4. The reorganization kicked Pitirim Sorokin upstairs by giving him "extra-departmental status." For details see Barry V. Johnston, *Pitirim A. Sorokin: An Intellectual Biography* (Lawrence: University of Kansas Press, 1995), pp. 150–158.

5. "Allport Committee 1943," HUG (FP) 15.2, Box 1.

6. Charles Wagley, *Area Research and Training: A Conference Report on the Study of World Areas* (Columbia University and SSRC, 1947), p. 5.

7. Clifford Geertz, *After the Fact: Two Countries, Four Decades, One Anthropologist* (Cambridge: Harvard University Press, 1995), p. 100.

8. Robert Bellah, "The World Is the World through Its Theorists—In Memory of Talcott Parsons," *American Sociologist* 15:1 (1980), p. 60.

9. Charles Camic, "The Making of a Method: A Historical Reinterpretation of the Early Parsons," *American Sociological Review* 52:4 (1987), p. 423.

10. Marion J. Levy, *The Structure of Society* (Princeton: Princeton University Press, 1952), p. 224.

11. Talcott Parsons, "Social Science: A Basic National Resource," in *The Nationalization of the Social Sciences,* ed. Samuel Z. Klausner and Victor M. Lidz (Philadelphia: University of Pennsylvania Press, 1986), p. 74.

12. Talcott Parsons to Paul H. Buck, April 3, 1944, quoted in Johnston, *Pitirim A. Sorokin,* p. 152.

13. Walt Whitman Rostow, "The Historian and the Analysis of Economic Growth," [n.d.], p. 1, Millikan Papers Box 10, Folder 314.

14. Walt Whitman Rostow, "The Interrelation of Theory and Economic History," *Journal of Economic History* 17:4 (1957), p. 522.

15. "A Proposal to the Carnegie Corporation of New York," p. 1 [n.d.], signed by Edward A. Shils (chairman) and Harry Johnson (executive secretary) of the Committee for the Comparative Study of New Nations. University of Chicago Archives, Regenstein Library.

16. David C. McClelland, *Motives, Personality, and Society: Selected Papers* (New York: Praeger Publishers, 1984), p. 18.

17. Quoted in Camic, "Making of a Method," p. 428.

18. Parsons, "Department and Laboratory of Social Relations," p. 93.

19. Talcott Parsons and Neil Smelser, *Economy and Society: A Study in the Integration of Economic and Social Theory* (Glencoe: Free Press, 1956), p. 295.

20. Unpublished, undated manuscript, "The Role of Sociology among the Social Sciences," written after Parsons had retired in 1970, HUG(FP) 42.41, pp. 15–16, italics in original.

21. Parsons and Smelser, *Economy and Society,* p. 247.

22. Manuscript to "Natural Science, Social Science, and Values," HUG (FP) 15.70, p. 10.

23. Parsons, "Role of Sociology," pp. 13–14.

24. Neil Smelser and Talcott Parsons, "A Sociological Model for Economic Development," manuscript in HUG (FP) 42.45.4, p. 1, italics in original.

25. Benjamin Higgins, "The 'Dualistic Theory' of Underdeveloped Areas," *American Economic Review* 45:4 (1955).

26. W. Arthur Lewis, "Economic Development with Unlimited Supplies of Labour," *Manchester School of Economic and Social Studies* 22 (1954).

27. Lucian Pye, *Politics, Personality, and Nation-building: Burma's Search for Identity* (New Haven: Yale University Press, 1962), p. 297.

28. Talcott Parsons and Edward A. Shils, eds., *Toward a General Theory of Action* (Cambridge: Harvard University Press, 1951), p. 3.

29. Ibid., pp. 21, 24, 26.

30. Ibid., pp. 192–195.

31. Ibid., p. 82.

32. Ibid., p. 84.

33. Ibid., p. 90.

34. Walt Whitman Rostow, Review of "Toward a General Theory of Action," *World Politics* 5:4 (1953), p. 540.

35. Jeffery C. Alexander, "Formal and Substantive Voluntarism in the Work of Talcott Parsons: A Theoretical and Ideological Reinterpretation," *American Sociological Review* 43:2 (1978), p. 186.

36. Manuscript to "Comparative Studies and Evolutionary Change," 1971, HUG (FP) 42.45.4, p. 16. Italics in original.

37. Talcott Parsons, *Societies: Evolutionary and Comparative Perspectives* (Englewood Cliffs, N.J.: Prentice-Hall, 1966), pp. 109–110.

38. Jeffery C. Alexander, *Fin de Siècle Social Theory: Relativism, Reduction and the Problem of Reason* (New York: Verso, 1995), p. 14.

39. Parsons and Shils, *Toward a General Theory of Action,* p. 79.

40. Ibid., p. 353.

41. Talcott Parsons, "Evolutionary Universals in Society," *American Sociological Review* 29:3 (1964), pp. 340–341.

42. Robert W. Cox, "On Thinking about Future World Order," *World Politics* 28:2 (1976), p. 180.

43. Alexander, "Formal and Substantive Voluntarism," p. 185.

44. Parsons, "Evolutionary Universals in Society," p. 353.

45. Michael Adas, *Machines as the Measure of Man: Science, Technology, and Ideologies* (Ithaca, N.Y.: Cornell University Press, 1989).

46. Bert F. Hoselitz, "Karl Marx on Secular Economic and Social Development," *Comparative Studies in Society and History* 6:2 (1964).

47. Robert Bellah, "Meaning and Modernization," *Religious Studies* 4 (1968), p. 39.

48. Alex Inkeles and Raymond Bauer, *The Soviet Citizen: Daily Life in a Totalitarian Society* (Cambridge: Harvard University Press, 1959).

49. Alex Inkeles's theoretical position on modernization, the same in all its essentials as in 1974, can be found in "Social Stratification in the Modernization of Russia," in *The Transformation of Russian Society: Aspects of Social Change since 1861,* ed. C. E. Black (Cambridge: Harvard University Press, 1960).

50. Alex Inkeles, "Making Men Modern: On the Causes and Consequences of Individual Change in Six Developing Countries," *American Journal of Sociology* 75:2 (1969), p. 212.

51. Ibid., p. 210.

52. Alex Inkeles and David Horton Smith, *Becoming Modern: Individual Change in Six Developing Countries* (Cambridge: Harvard University Press, 1974), p. 87.

53. Ibid., pp. 6, 8, 5.

54. Inkeles, "Making Men Modern," p. 213.

55. Inkeles and Smith, *Becoming Modern,* pp. 10–11.

56. For more details on McClelland, see his autobiographical reflections, "Personal Sources of My Intellectual Interests," in McClelland, *Motives, Personality, and Society.*

57. Achievement meant "success in competition with some standard of excellence" (David McClelland, John W. Atkinson, Russell A. Clark, and Edgar Lowell, *The Achievement Motive* [New York: Appleton-Century-Crofts, 1953], p. 110).

58. *n* Ach was "presumably imposed on the child by the culture, or more particularly by the parents as the representatives of the culture" (Ibid., p. 275).

59. David McClelland, *The Achieving Society* (Princeton: Van Nostrand, 1961), p. 394. Italics in original.

60. Ibid., pp. 4, 422.

61. Ibid., p. 392.

62. David McClelland and David G. Winter, *Motivating Economic Achievement* (New York: Free Press, 1969), p. 2.

63. Manuscript to "Social Evolution and the Problem of Comparability," 1971, HUG (FP) 42.45.4, pp. 1–2.

64. William Form, "Comparative Industrial Sociology and the Convergence Hypothesis," *Annual Review of Sociology* 5 (1979), p. 22.

65. Walt Rostow, "The Making of Modern America, 1776–1940: An Essay on Three Themes," CIS working paper no. C/60-6, pp. 3/4–3/5.

66. Marion J. Levy Jr., *Modernization and the Structure of Society: A Setting for International Affairs* (Princeton: Princeton University Press, 1966), pp. 9–15, 35–38.

67. McClelland, *Achieving Society,* p. 403.

68. Max Millikan and Donald Blackmer, *The Emerging Nations* (Boston: Little, Brown, 1961), p. 143.

69. Robert E. Ward, "Political Modernization and Political Culture in Japan," *World Politics* 15:4 (1963), p. 571.

70. Black, *Transformation of Russian Society,* p. 8.

71. Edward Shils, "The Military in the Political Development of the New States," in *The Role of the Military in the Underdeveloped Countries,* ed. John J. Johnson (Princeton: Princeton University Press, 1962), p. 67.

72. Arnold S. Feldman, "The Nature of Industrial Societies," *World Politics* 12:4 (1960).

73. Quoted in Alexander, *Fin de Siècle,* p. 8.

74. David Riesman, *The Lonely Crowd: A Study of the Changing American Character* (New Haven, Conn.: Yale University Press, 1951).

75. Frank W. Notestein, "Population: The Long View," in *Food for the World,* ed. Theodor Schultz (Chicago: University of Chicago Press, 1945); Irene B. Taeuber and Frank W. Notestein, "The Changing Fertility of the Japanese," *Population Studies* 1:1 (1947). Adolphe Landry coined the term *demographic transition* in *La Révolution Demographique* (Paris: Librarie du Recueil Sirey, 1934).

76. Warren S. Thompson, "Population," *American Journal of Sociology* 34:6 (1929), pp. 959–975.

77. Dudley Kirk, "Demographic Transition Theory," *Population Studies* 50:3 (1996), 361–387; Susan Greenhalgh, "The Social Construction of Population Science: An Intellectual, Institutional, and Political History of Twentieth-Century Demography," *Comparative Studies in Society and History* 38:1 (1996), pp. 26–66; Simon Sretzer, "The Idea of Demographic Transition and the Study of Fertility: A Critical Intellectual History," *Population and Development Review* 19:4 (1993), pp. 659–701.

78. Irene B. Taeuber, "Population Increase and Manpower Utilization in Imperial Japan," *Modernization Programs in Relation to Human Resources and Population Problems* (New York: Milbank Memorial Fund, 1950), p. 139.

79. Eric B. Ross, *The Malthus Factor: Poverty, Politics, and Population in Capitalist Development* (London: Zed Books, 1998), pp. 87–95.

80. Taeuber and Notestein, "The Changing Fertility of the Japanese," p. 2.

81. Walt Whitman Rostow with Richard Hatch, *An American Policy in Asia* (Cambridge: Massachusetts Institute of Technology Press, 1955), p. 50.

82. Riesman, *Lonely Crowd,* pp. 11, 15.

83. Clark Kerr et al., *Industrialism and Industrial Man: The Problem of Labor and Management in Economic Growth* (Cambridge: Harvard University Press, 1960), p. 1n. Although Kerr collaborated officially with John T. Dunlop, Frederick Harbison, and Charles A. Myers on this volume, I attribute this work to Kerr, whose influence over the *Industrial Man* project mirrored that of Talcott Parsons in the formulation of the theory of social action.

84. Ibid., pp. 278–279, 296, 267, 284, 285.

85. Clark Kerr, *The Uses of the University* (Cambridge: Harvard University Press, 1963).

86. Daniel Bell, *The Coming of Post-Industrial Society: A Venture in Social Forecasting* (New York: Basic Books, 1973), p. 342.

87. Kerr et al., *Industrialism and Industrial Man*, p. 283.

88. Max Weber, *The Protestant Work Ethic and the Spirit of Capitalism*, trans. Talcott Parsons (New York: Scribner's, 1930), p. 182.

89. Clark Kerr and Abraham Siegel, "The Structuring of the Labor Force in Industrial Relations: New Dimensions and New Questions," *Industrial and Labor Relations Review* 8:1 (1955), p. 163.

90. James L. Cochrane, *Industrialism and Industrial Man in Retrospect: A Critical Review of the Ford Foundation's Support for the Inter-University Study of Labor* (New York: Ford Foundation, 1979), p. 117.

91. Quoted in Pierre Birnbaum, *La Fin du Politique* (Paris: Editions de Seuil, 1975), p. 26.

92. Kerr et al., *Industrialism and Industrial Man*, p. 9.

93. Daniel Bell, *Post-Industrial Society*, pp. 75–76.

94. Ibid., p. 365.

95. Kerr, *Uses of the University*, p. 125.

96. Millikan and Blackmer, *Emerging Nations* (Boston: Little, Brown), p. 102.

97. Kerr et al., *Industrialism and Industrial Man*, p. 12. Italics in original.

CHAPTER 4: The Rise of Modernization Theory in Political Science

1. Hans Daadler, introduction to *Comparative European Politics: The Story of a Profession* (Washington, D.C.: Pinter, 1997), p. 4.

2. Barry Karl, *Charles Merriam and the Study of Politics* (Chicago: University of Chicago Press, 1974); Herbert A. Simon, "Charles E. Merriam and the 'Chicago School' of Political Science" (University of Illinois, 1987); Mark C. Smith, *Social Science in the Crucible: The American Debate over Objectivity and Purpose, 1918–1941* (Durham, N.C.: Duke University Press, 1994), chap. 3.

3. Robert A. Dahl, "The Behavioral Approach in Political Science: Epitaph to a Successful Protest," *American Political Science Review* 55:4 (1961), p. 762.

4. Karl W. Deutsch, "A Path among the Social Sciences," in *Journeys through World Politics: Reflections of Thirty-Four Academic Travelers*, ed. Joseph Kruzel and James N. Rosenau (Lexington, Mass.: Lexington Books, 1989), p. 18. Adumbrating Deutsch's view were Albert Somit and Joseph Tanenhaus, *The Development of American Political Science* (Boston: Allyn and Bacon, 1967), p. 183. Deutsch is incorrect to suggest that the behavioral approach in political science had "nothing to do" with behaviorism in psychology.

The term arrived in political science via psychology (e.g., Horace Kallen, "Political Science as Psychology," *American Political Science Review* 17:2 [1923], pp. 181–203; or Charles E. Merriam, "The Significance of Psychology for the Study of Politics," *American Political Science Review* 18:3 [1924], pp. 469–488), and psychological methods were an essential part of the focus on the "individual," as evidenced by the work of Lucian Pye (see chap. 4).

5. Gabriel Almond, *A Discipline Divided: Schools and Sects in Political Science* (Newbury Park, Calif.: Sage Publications, 1990), p. 40.

6. Raymond Siedelman, *Disenchanted Realists: Political Science and the American Crisis, 1884–1984* (Albany: State University of New York Press, 1985), pp. 152–153. Although the criticism of behavioralism as a form of naïve scientism may have been fair as it related to the study of American politics, behavioralist methodology unquestionably represented a step forward in the understanding and methodology of studying postcolonial politics. With ascendant domestic conservatism preventing experimentation on Americans, postwar behavioralists redirected their technocratic, reformist desires to the postcolonial "laboratories." Many postwar American liberals believed that the postcolonial world constituted a "laboratory" in which "experiments" could be conducted. For example, in reference to the great political liberties available in South Vietnam, John F. Kennedy suggested in 1956 that the "United States is directly responsible for this experiment—it is playing an important role in the laboratory where it is being conducted" (quoted in James T. Fisher, "The Vietnam Lobby and the Politics of Pluralism," in *Cold War Constructions: The Political Culture of the United States Imperialism, 1945–1966* [Amherst: University of Massachusetts Press, 2000], p. 236).

7. Quoted in Dahl, "Behavioral Approach in Political Science," p. 764.

8. David Truman, "The Implications of Political Behavior Research," *Items* 5:4 (1951), p. 37.

9. *Items* 7:4 (1953), p. 47.

10. Joseph LaPalombara, "Decline of Ideology: A Dissent and an Interpretation," *American Political Science Review* 60:1 (1966), p. 6.

11. E. Pendleton Herring, *Group Representation before Congress* (Baltimore: Johns Hopkins University Press, 1929).

12. Carl J. Friedrich, *Constitutional Government and Politics* (New York: Blaisdell, 1937); later retitled *Constitutional Government and Democracy* (Boston: Ginn, 1946); Klaus von Beyme, "A Founding Father of Comparative Politics," in Daadler, ed., *Comparative European Politics*, pp. 7–14.

13. Herring memo dated December 3, 1951, SSRC Box 735, Folder 10655, Series 1, Accession 2, RAC.

14. Roy Macridis, "Interuniversity Summer Research Seminar, 1952: Comparative Politics," *Items* 6:1 (1952), p. 7.

15. Robert Hall, *Area Studies: With Special Reference to Their Implications for Research in the Social Sciences* (New York: SSRC, 1947); Charles Wagley, *Area Research and Training: A Conference Report on the Study of World Areas* (New York: SSRC, 1948); Julian Steward, *Area Research: Theory and Practice* (New York: SSRC, 1950); Wendell C. Bennett, *Area Studies in American Universities* (New York: SSRC, 1951).

16. Robert K. Merton, *Social Theory and Social Structure* (Glencoe, Ill.: Free Press, 1949); Charles Crothers, *Robert K. Merton* (London: Tavistock Publications, 1987); Piotr

Sztompka, *Robert K. Merton: An Intellectual Profile* (Basingstoke, England: Macmillan Education, 1986).

17. Roy Macridis, "Comparative Politics: Method and Research," *Items* 6:4 (1952), p. 48.

18. Roy Macridis and Richard Cox, "Research in Comparative Politics," *American Political Science Review* 47:3 (1953), p. 648.

19. Macridis, "Comparative Politics: Method and Research," p. 47.

20. Dwight Waldo, comment on "Research in Comparative Politics," *American Political Science Review* 47:3 (1953), p. 675.

21. Report to Carnegie Corporation, August 16, 1954, SSRC Box 735, Folder 10658, Series 1, Accession 2, RAC.

22. Rupert Emerson, *State and Sovereignty in Modern Germany* (New Haven, Conn.: Yale University Press, 1928); Rupert Emerson, *Malaysia: A Study in Direct and Indirect Colonial Rule* (New York: Macmillan, 1937); Rupert Emerson, *The Netherlands East Indies* (Boston: World Peace Foundation, 1942).

23. Emerson memo, October 18, 1953, SSRC Box 735, Folder 10655, Series 1, Accession 2, RAC.

24. Herring to Pye, October 21, 1953, SSRC Box 735, Folder 10655, Series 1, Accession 2, RAC.

25. Ibid.

26. Macridis to Kenneth Thompson, December 30, 1953, SSRC Box 735, Folder 10655, Series 1, Accession 2, RAC.

27. Marion Levy, *The Structure of Society* (Princeton: Princeton University Press, 1952), p. vii.

28. The participants in this seminar published their collective findings as D. F. Aberle, A. K. Cohen, A. K. David, M. J. Levy Jr., and F. X. Sutton, "The Functional Prerequisites of a Society," *Ethics* 60:2 (1950), pp. 100–111.

29. Princeton *Alumni Weekly* (September 26, 1952).

30. Marion Levy, "Contrasting Factors in the Modernization of China and Japan," *Economic Development and Cultural Change* 2:2 (1953), pp. 174–175, 179, 182, 190.

31. Marion J. Levy Jr., *Modernization and the Structure of Society: A Setting for International Affairs* (Princeton: Princeton University Press, 1966), pp. 14, 83–84, 19.

32. Herring to Almond, January 21, 1954, SSRC Box 735, Folder 10656, Series 1, Accession 2, RAC.

33. Almond, *The American People and Foreign Policy* (New York: Praeger Publishers, 1960 [1950]); and Almond, *The Appeals of Communism* (Princeton: Princeton University Press, 1954).

34. Gabriel Almond, "A Voice from the Chicago School," in Daadler, ed., *Comparative European Politics*, pp. 54–67.

35. Gabriel A. Almond, "Research in Comparative Politics: Plans of a New Council Committee," *Items* 8:1 (1954), p. 2.

36. Ibid.

37. Roy Macridis, *The Study of Comparative Government* (Garden City, N.Y.: Doubleday, 1955).

38. Ibid., p. 35.

39. Ibid., pp. 68, 72.

40. Ibid., p. 66.

41. The CCP was a tight-knit group of scholars who, over their many years of collaboration, came to see themselves as a community. It is a profound challenge for the historian to convey this elusive sense of community. How is the historian to present the quotidian chumminess that appears in the use of nicknames on memos addressed to certain but not other members of the CCP? Herb (Herbert Hyman), Lennie (Leonard Binder), Joe (Joseph LaPalombara), Jim (James S. Coleman), Sam (Samuel Huntington), Sid (Sydney Verba), Mike (Myron Weiner), Gay (Gabriel A. Almond), Dave (Apter), Lu (Pye), Dan (Dankwart Rustow), and the two Bobs (Robert E. Ward and Robert A. Dahl) all tended to address each other in intimate terms. What does it mean that Roy Macridis remained forever "Macridis" and never became "Roy"? Were Macridis's arguments shunted aside because he was "a difficult person" (to quote several former members of the CCP), or was he considered difficult because he refused to go along with the intellectual agenda of the other members? How can the historian illustrate the sense of self-satisfaction pervading the correspondence among the members, the smug sense that those who disagreed with them had been vanquished once and for all? (By the mid-1960s, one could imagine from reading the internal correspondence of the CCP that the academic world outside the committee scarcely existed, except as a recruiting ground for like-minded young scholars.) How can the historian convey his intuitively certain but textually intangible sense that this clubby mentality on the CCP contributed to the polemical—indeed vituperative—quality of many of the critiques of modernization theory that began to emerge in the late 1960s?

42. The following pages rely heavily on the minutes of meetings of the CCP. Unfortunately, the minutes are written in the passive voice and rarely record exactly who said what at the meetings. Still, as I hope what follows makes clear, it is not difficult to make an educated guess at who was making which comments.

43. Minutes of CCP meeting, 19 February 1954, SSRC Box 736, Folder 10681, Series 1, Accession 2, p. 2, RAC.

44. Ibid., p. 6.

45. Roy Macridis, "The Role of Organized Labor in French Politics," April 22, 1954, SSRC Box 739, Folder 10719, Box 739, Series 1, Ammendum 8/96, RAC.

46. Minutes of CCP meeting, May 8, 1954, SSRC Box 736, Folder 10681, Series 1, Accession 2, p. 2, RAC.

47. Ibid., p. 9.

48. Almond memo, June 10, 1954, SSRC Box 735, Folder 10656, Series 1, Accession 2, RAC.

49. George M. Kahin, Guy Pauker, and Lucian Pye, "Comparative Politics in Non-Western Countries," *American Political Science Review* 59:4 (1955), p. 1022.

50. Ibid., p. 1041.

51. Given how often early development theory in general and modernization theory in particular have been accused of a sort of neocolonial "Eurocentrism," it is important to emphasize that using the West as a model for development was demanded by the spokespersons of postcolonial countries themselves. If the members of the CCP were guilty of anything, it was not so much Eurocentrism as a somewhat naïve acceptance that the statements of the current generation of (largely European-educated) postcolonial elites necessarily spoke for the majority of the population or represented the strongest political forces in these emergent countries.

52. Gabriel A. Almond, "Comparative Political Systems," *Journal of Politics* 18:3 (1956), p. 392.

53. Almond to Macridis, December 18, 1957, SSRC Box 735, Folder 10660, Series 1, Accession 2, RAC.

54. Almond remarks to CCP meeting, March 26, 1955, SSRC Box 736, Folder 10682, Series 1, Accession 2, RAC.

55. Francis X. Sutton, Seymour Harris, Carl Kaysen, and James Tobin, *The American Business Creed* (Cambridge: Harvard University Press, 1956).

56. This view would later be echoed by Gabriel Almond, who stated that "[c]ontemporary comparative politics is a *movement* rather than a subfield or subdiscipline" ("Comparative Politics," in *The Encyclopedia of the Social Sciences,* vol. 12, ed. David Sills [New York: Macmillan, 1968], p. 331).

57. Ibid., p. 71.

58. Robert Redfield, "The Folk Society," *American Journal of Sociology* 52:4 (1947), pp. 293–308.

59. Francis X. Sutton, "Social Theory and Comparative Politics" (1954), in *Comparative Politics: A Reader,* ed. Harry Eckstein and David E. Apter (New York: Free Press of Glencoe, 1963), p. 72. Sutton said that Parsons's was "the system of social theory I grew up on" (p. 80, n. 2).

60. C. S. Whitaker Jr., "A Dysrhythmic Process of Social Change," *World Politics* 19:2 (1967), p. 192.

61. Interviews with Gabriel A. Almond, July 9, 1999, and Lucian Pye, July 18, 1999.

62. Gabriel A. Almond, "The Seminar on Comparative Politics, June 1956," *Items* 10:4 (1956), p. 46.

63. Almond memo, September 2, 1964, SSRC Box 738, Folder 10705, Series 1, Ammendum 8/96, p. 8.

64. Almond, "Comparative Political Systems."

65. Ibid., pp. 398, 401, 408.

66. Almond memo, December 1955, SSRC Box 736, Folder 10682, Series 1, Accession 2, RAC.

67. Almond, "Comparative Political Systems," p. 394.

68. Macridis proposal, November 30, 1955, SSRC Box 735, Folder 10658, Series 1, Accession 2, RAC.

69. Almond to Merillat (of the Ford Foundation), December 29, 1955, SSRC Box 735, Folder 10658, Series 1, Accession 2, RAC.

70. Memo, Almond to Herring, February 11, 1957, SSRC Box 737, Folder 10683, Series 1, Accession 2, RAC.

71. Gabriel A. Almond, "Research Note," *American Political Science Review* 52:1 (1958), p. 270.

72. Minutes of CCP meeting, May 11, 1957, SSRC Box 737, Folder 10684, Series 1, Accession 2, p. 5, RAC.

73. CCP *Annual Report,* 1956–57.

74. Almond to Herring, June 9, 1958, SSRC Box 735, Folder 10661, Series 1, Accession 2, RAC.

75. Roy Macridis, *Comparative Politics: Notes and Readings* (Homewood, Ill.: Dorsey Press, 1971).

76. Minutes of CCP planning session, May 4-6, 1958, SSRC Box 737, Folder 10685, Series 1, Accession 2, p. 4, RAC.

77. Daniel Lerner, "The Middle East: The Human Meaning of Modernization," *Foreign Policy Bulletin,* March 1, 1959, p. 92.

78. Minutes of CCP meeting, November 15, 1958, SSRC Box 737, Folder 10685, Series 1, Accession 2, p. 3, RAC.

79. S. N. Eisenstadt, "Edward Shils," *Proceedings of the American Philosophical Society* 141:3 (1997), p. 368.

80. Peter Coleman, *The Liberal Conspiracy: The Congress for Cultural Freedom and the Struggle for the Mind of Postwar Europe* (New York: Free Press, 1989), pp. 176–177.

81. For useful and succinct biographical background on Shils, see Philip G. Altbach, "Edward Shils and the American University," *Society* 36:3 (1999), pp. 68–73. In 1996 *Minerva,* the Anglo-American journal of science policy that Shils founded in 1962, published a commemorative issue with reflections on Shils the man (*Minerva* 34:1), the sociologist, and the critic by various contributors, the best of which is Joseph Epstein's tribute, "My Friend Edward."

82. Michael Shattock, "Edward Shils, the Intellectuals and Minerva," *Minerva* 34:1 (1996), p. 4.

83. Jean Floud, "Edward Shils (1910-1995)," *Minerva* 34:1 (1996), p. 85.

84. Joseph Epstein, "My Friend Edward," *Minerva* 34:1 (1996), p. 109.

85. Gabriel A. Almond, interview with the author, July 9, 1999.

86. Shils preferred Aleksandr Solzhenitsyn, Sidney Hook, Hilton Kramer, James Q. Wilson, and Edward C. Banfield. See Epstein, "My Friend Edward," pp. 108–109.

87. Quoted in Harold Orlans, "Edward Shils's Beliefs about Society and Sociology," *Minerva* 34:1 (1996), p. 24.

88. Edward A. Shils, "The Culture of the Indian Intellectual," reprint by the University of Chicago Committee on South Asian Studies, p. 21. Originally published in *Sewanee Review* (1958).

89. Ibid., p. 27.

90. Edward A. Shils, "Political Development of the New States (I)," *Comparative Studies in Society and History* 2:3 (1960), pp. 265–267.

91. Edward A. Shils, "Political Development of the New States (II)," *Comparative Studies in Society and History* 2:4 (1960), p. 387.

92. Shils, "Political Development of the New States (I)," pp. 274–275, 278.

93. Ibid., p. 267.

94. Shils, "Political Development of the New States (II)," p. 379.

95. Minutes of CCP meeting, November 15, 1958, SSRC Box 737, Folder 10685, Series 1, Accession 2, pp. 3–4, RAC.

96. SSRC Box 733, Folder 10626, Series 1, p. 3, RAC. We owe the marvelously detailed notes from this meeting to CCP amanuensis Bryce Wood.

97. Ibid., p. 40.

98. Ibid., p. 8.

99. Ibid., p. 30.

100. Ibid., p. 72.

101. Ibid., p. 71. In 1965 Apter would later reverse this argument, claiming that modernization was a special case of development—defined as structural differentia-

tion—and that industrialization was the technical and economic dimension of modernization (*The Politics of Modernization* [Chicago: University of Chicago Press, 1965], p. 67).

102. Ibid., p. 50.

103. Ibid., pp. 11, 16, 36, 53.

104. Ibid., pp. 70, 39, 53.

105. Ibid., pp. 8, 39, 73.

106. Lerner, "The Middle East," p. 91.

107. SSRC Box 733, Folder 10626, Series 1, pp. 21–22, 11 (italics in original), 41, RAC.

108. Ibid., pp. 66, 73, 72.

109. SSRC Box 733, Folder 10626, Series 1, p. 11, RAC.

110. Minutes of CCP meeting, October 30–31, 1959, SSRC Box 737, Folder 10687, Series 1, Accession 2, p. 3, RAC.

111. Ward memo, November 1959, SSRC Box 735, Folder 10661, Series 1, Accession 2, RAC (italics in original).

112. SSRC Box 733, Folder 10626, Series 1, p. 20, RAC.

113. Gabriel A. Almond, "Introduction: A Functional Approach to Comparative Politics," in *The Politics of Developing Areas,* ed. Gabriel Almond and James S. Coleman (Princeton: Princeton University Press, 1960), p. 64.

114. David Easton, *The Political System: An Enquiry into the State of Political Science* (New York: Alfred A. Knopf, 1953).

115. Almond, "A Functional Approach," in *Politics of Developing Areas,* pp. 19, 27, 16.

116. Ibid., pp. 11, 12.

117. SSRC Box 735, Folder 10662, Series 1, p. 2, RAC.

118. Ibid., p. 4.

119. Committee on Comparative Politics, *Report on the Activities of the Committee* (New York: SSRC, 1971), p. 70.

120. Bernard E. Brown, "The French Experience of Modernization," *World Politics* 21:3 (1969), p. 366.

121. Gabriel A. Almond, "Political Theory and Political Science," *American Political Science Review* 60:4 (1966).

CHAPTER 5: Modernization Theory as a Foreign Policy Doctrine

Epigraph: Walt Whitman Rostow keynote address to a conference held at West Point on "The New Nations and Their Internal Defense," April 18, 1963, p. 2, Ithiel de Sola Pool Papers, Box 96, MC 440, MIT Archives. In attendance at this conference were Leonard Binder, Clifford Geertz, Dankwart Rustow, Ithiel de Sola Pool, and Lucian Pye. The picture of Rostow and President Lyndon Johnson on the cover of this book was taken exactly five years later, providing graphic illustration of the results of modernization theory in action.

1. Allan Needell, "Project Troy and the Cold War Annexation of the Social Sciences," in *Universities and Empire: Money and Politics in the Social Sciences during the Cold War,* ed. Christopher Simpson (New York: New Press, 1998), p. 22.

2. Walt Whitman Rostow, *The Dynamics of Soviet Society* (New York: W. W. Norton, 1953).

3. Donald Blackmer, *The MIT Center for International Studies: The Founding Years, 1951–1969* (Cambridge: Massachusetts Institute of Technology Press, 2002).

4. Walt Rostow, interview with the author, April 12, 1999.

5. Christopher Simpson, *Science of Coercion: Communication Research and Psychological Warfare, 1945–1960* (New York: Oxford University Press, 1995), p. 82.

6. *The Center for International Studies: A Description* (MIT, July 1955), p. 7, italics in original.

7. Rostow, *Dynamics of Soviet Society;* Walt Whitman Rostow, *Prospects for Communist China* (Cambridge: Massachusetts Institute of Technology Press, 1954); Walt Whitman Rostow with Richard Hatch, *An American Policy in Asia* (Cambridge: Massachusetts Institute of Technology Press, 1955).

8. General statement from the CIS *Annual Report,* reprinted unchanged from 1957 to 1960, p. 33.

9. Walt Whitman Rostow, *The Process of Economic Growth,* 2d ed. (New York: W. W. Norton, 1962), pp. iii–iv.

10. Walt Whitman Rostow, "The National Interest" (September 1956), Folder 19, Box 2, RG V4A, Rockefeller Brothers Fund, Special Studies Project Collection, RAC, pp. 106–107.

11. General statement from the CIS *Annual Report,* reprinted unchanged from 1957 to 1960, p. 1.

12. Ibid., p. 5.

13. Rostow, *Process of Economic Growth,* p. 49.

14. Ibid., p. 12.

15. Michael Haas, *Polity and Society: Philosophical Underpinnings of Social Science Paradigms* (New York: Praeger Publishers, 1992), p. 24.

16. Rostow, *Process of Economic Growth,* p. 91.

17. Ibid., p. viii.

18. Ibid., p. 104.

19. Ibid., p. 108.

20. P. N. Rosenstein-Rodan, "Problems of Industrialization of Eastern and South-Eastern Europe," *Economic Journal* 53 (1943), pp. 202–211.

21. See John L. Love, *Crafting the Third World: Theorizing Underdevelopment in Rumania and Brazil* (Stanford: Stanford University Press, 1996).

22. Rosenstein-Rodan, "Problems of Industrialization," pp. 202–211.

23. Paul N. Rosenstein-Rodan, "International Aid for Undeveloped Countries," *Review of Economics and Statistics* 43:2 (1961), p. 108.

24. Ron Robin, *The Making of the Cold War Enemy: Culture and Politics in the Military-Intellectual Complex* (Princeton: Princeton University Press, 2001).

25. Harold Lasswell, *Psychopathology and Politics* (Chicago: University of Chicago Press, 1930).

26. Fred I. Greenstein, introduction to Lasswell, *Psychopathology and Politics* (Chicago: University of Chicago Press, 1977 [1930]), p. xx.

27. Raymond Seidelman, *Disenchanted Realists: Political Science and the American Crisis, 1884-1984* (Albany: State University of New York Press, 1985), p. 135.

28. Simpson, *Science of Coercion,* p. 21.

29. Mark C. Smith, *Social Science in the Crucible: The American Debate over Objectivity and Purpose, 1918–1941* (Durham, N.C.: Duke University Press, 1994), p. 213.

30. John G. Gunnell, *The Descent of Political Theory: The Genealogy of an American Vocation* (Chicago: University of Chicago Press, 1993), p. 123.

31. James C. Scott, *Seeing Like a State: How Some Schemes to Improve the Human Condition Have Failed* (New Haven, Conn.: Yale University Press, 1998).

32. Harold Lasswell, "The Policy Orientation," in *The Policy Sciences,* ed. Harold Lasswell and Daniel Lerner (Stanford: Stanford University Press, 1951).

33. Ibid., p. 11.

34. Donald L. M. Blackmer, "Introduction: An Appreciation of Lucian W. Pye," in *The Political Culture of Foreign Area and International Studies: Essays in Honor of Lucian W. Pye,* ed. Richard J. Samuels and Myron Weiner (Washington, D.C.: Brassey's, 1992).

35. Gabriel A. Almond, *The Appeals of Communism* (Princeton: Princeton University Press, 1954), pp. 234, 380.

36. John Higham, "The Cult of 'American Consensus': Homogenizing Our History," *Commentary* 27:2 (1959), p. 95.

37. Lucian Pye, *Guerrilla Communism in Malaya: Its Social and Political Meaning* (Princeton: Princeton University Press, 1956).

38. Erik Erikson, *Young Man Luther: A Study in Psychoanalysis and History* (New York: W. W. Norton, 1958), p. 14, quoted in Lucian W. Pye, *Politics, Personality, and Nation-building: Burma's Search for Identity* (New Haven, Conn.: Yale University Press, 1962), p. 187.

39. Lucian W. Pye, "Personal Identity and Political Ideology," in *Political Decision-makers,* ed. Dwaine Marvick (Glencoe, Ill.: Free Press, 1961), p. 309.

40. Ellen Herman, "The Career of Cold War Psychology," *Radical History Review* 63 (1995), p. 72.

41. Pye, "Personal Identity and Political Ideology," in *Political Decision-makers,* p. 310.

42. Gabriel A. Almond and G. Bingham Powell, writing in 1966, compared the prospects of postcolonial countries to those of a "young high school graduate" (Gabriel A. Almond and G. Bingham Powell, *Comparative Politics: A Developmental Approach* [Boston: Little, Brown, 1966], p. 301).

43. Seymour Martin Lipset, *The First New Nation: The United States in Historical and Comparative Perspective* (New York: Basic Books, 1963), p. 16.

44. Quoted in Ian Buruma, "MacArthur's Children," *New York Review of Books* 46:16 (October 21, 1999), p. 33.

45. Simpson, *Science of Coercion.*

46. Daniel Lerner, *The Passing of Traditional Society: Modernizing the Middle East* (New York: Free Press, 1958).

47. Ibid., p. 50.

48. David Riesman, *The Lonely Crowd: A Study in the Changing American Character* (New Haven, Conn.: Yale University Press, 1950).

49. Daniel Lerner, "The Middle East: The Human Meaning of Modernization," *Foreign Policy Bulletin,* March 1, 1959, p. 92.

50. "This observational standpoint," Lerner claimed, "implies no ethnocentrism. . . . The Western model of modernization exhibits certain components and sequences whose relevance is global. . . . The same basic model reappears in virtually all modernizing

societies on all continents of the world, regardless of variations in race, color, [or] creed" (*Passing of Traditional Society*, p. 46).

51. Ibid., p. 398.

52. Ibid., pp. 398–399.

53. Ibid., p. 46.

54. Ibid., p. 401.

55. Karl Deutsch, "Social Mobilization and Political Development," *American Political Science Review* 55:3 (1961), pp. 493–514.

56. Lerner, *Passing of Traditional Society*, p. 47.

57. Ibid., p. 405.

58. Ibid., p. 407.

59. Simpson, *Science of Coercion*, p. 90.

60. See Eugene Castle, *The Great Giveaway: The Realities of Foreign Aid* (Chicago: H. Regnery, 1957).

61. James T. Patterson, *Grand Expectations: The United States, 1945–1974* (New York: Oxford University Press, 1996), p. 133.

62. Walt Whitman Rostow, *Eisenhower, Kennedy and Foreign Aid* (Austin: University of Texas Press, 1985), p. 96. Also attending the meeting were the president of Associated Universities Lloyd Berkner, George Baldwin of the CIS, and Harvard economist (and future World Bank president) Edward Mason; assistant secretary of commerce Samuel Anderson, assistant secretary of the treasury Chapman Rose, CIA director Allen Dulles, director of the Office of Defense Mobilization Arthur Fleming, and presidential assistant General Robert Cutler; *Time* vice president Charles Stillman, *Time's* C. D. Jackson, and *Time's* Robert Jessup; Thomas McKittrick of Chase National Bank and World Bank vice president Robert Garner; and United Steel Workers president David McDonald.

63. "Objectives of United States Economic Assistance Programs." A study prepared by CIS for the Senate Special Committee to Study the Foreign Aid Program (January 1957), prepared by Max Millikan, Donald Blackmer, James E. Cross, Richard Ekhaus, Everett E. Hagen, Charles Kindleberger, Lucian W. Pye, Paul N. Rosenstein-Rodan, and Walt Whitman Rostow, p. 4 (hereafter "Objectives").

64. Ibid., p. 5.

65. Ibid., p. 15.

66. Rostow with Hatch, *American Policy in Asia*, p. 42.

67. "Objectives," p. 25.

68. Max Millikan and Walt Whitman Rostow, *A Proposal: Key to an Effective Foreign Policy* (New York: Harper and Brothers, 1957).

69. Walt Whitman Rostow, *The Diffusion of Power: An Essay in Recent History* (New York: Macmillan, 1972), pp. 87–88.

70. Millikan and Rostow, *A Proposal*, p. 4.

71. Ibid., p. 151. Rostow loved this quote. He first used it as early as 1946, as the coda to *The American Diplomatic Revolution* (Oxford: Clarendon Press, 1949), and as late as 1967 in a speech entitled "The Great Transition: Tasks of the First and Second Postwar Generations," *Department of State Bulletin*, March 27, 1967.

72. Ragnar Nurkse, "Some International Aspects of the Problem of Economic Development" (1952), in *The Economics of Underdevelopment*, ed. A. N. Agarwala and S. P. Singh (New York: Oxford University Press, 1963).

73. Millikan and Rostow, *A Proposal*, p. 71.

74. Ibid., pp. 68–69.

75. Ibid., p. 85. On the significance of the postwar dollar shortage, see chapter 2.

76. Ibid., pp. 63, 4, 6.

77. Arthur M. Schlesinger Jr., *A Thousand Days: John F. Kennedy in the White House* (Boston: Houghton Mifflin, 1965), p. 589.

78. Russell Edgerton, *Sub-Cabinet Politics and Policy Commitment: The Birth of the Development Loan Fund* (Syracuse, N.Y.: Inter-University Case Program, 1970), pp. 77, 80, quoted in Rostow, *Eisenhower, Kennedy and Foreign Aid*, p. 42. Rostow modestly comments about this quote that "Edgerton's evaluation proves nothing, of course, about the correctness of CIS' views."

79. "Economic, Social, and Political Change in the Underdeveloped Countries and Its Implications for United States Policy." A study prepared for the Senate Committee on Foreign Relations by the CIS (March 30, 1960), by Francis Bator, Donald Blackmer, Richard Eckaus, Everett E. Hagen, Daniel Lerner, Max Millikan, Ithiel de Sola Pool, Lucian W. Pye, Paul Rosenstein-Rodan, and Walt Whitman Rostow. (Hereafter "Economic, Social, and Political Change.")

80. Eugene Burdick and William Lederer, *The Ugly American* (New York: W. W. Norton, 1958).

81. Jonathan Nashel, "The Road to Vietnam: Modernization Theory in Fact and Fiction," in *Cold War Constructions: The Political Culture of United States Imperialism, 1945–1966*, ed. Christian Appy (Amherst: University of Massachusetts Press, 2000).

82. "Economic, Social, and Political Change," p. 1.

83. Ibid., pp. 13–14, 59, 20, 47.

84. Ibid., pp. 9, 4.

85. Ibid., pp. 17, 28.

86. Ibid., p. 23.

87. Ibid., pp. 36–37.

88. Ibid., p. 35.

89. Ibid., p. 3.

90. Ibid., p. 47.

91. Ibid., p. 34.

92. Seymour Martin Lipset, *Political Man* (Garden City, N.Y.: Doubleday, 1960), p. 46.

93. Daniel Lerner and James Robinson, "Swords and Ploughshares: The Turkish Army as a Modernizing Force," *World Politics* 13:1 (1960).

94. Hans Speier, preface to *The Role of the Military in Underdeveloped Countries*, ed. John J. Johnson (Princeton: Princeton University Press, 1962), p. v.

95. Lucian W. Pye, "Southeast Asia and American Policy," address to the National War College March 6, 1959, CIS working paper no. C/59-8, p. 19.

96. Lucian W. Pye, "Military Development in the New Countries," a report submitted to the Research Group in Psychology and the Social Sciences, Smithsonian Institution, December 1961, CIS working paper no. C/62-1, p. 12.

97. Pye, "Southeast Asia and American Policy," p. 18.

98. Pye, "Military Development," pp. 12, 22, 13, 22.

99. Pye, "Southeast Asia and American Policy," p. 19.

100. Lucian W. Pye, "Armies in the Process of Political Modernization," in *The Role of the Military in Underdeveloped Countries*, ed. John J. Johnson (Princeton: Princeton University Press, 1962), p. 70.

101. *The Center for International Studies*, p. 11.

102. Rostow, *Process of Economic Growth*, p. 106.

103. "Economic, Social, and Political Change," p. 78.

104. Pye, "Military Development," p. 10.

105. Ibid., p. 30.

106. Pye, "Political Modernization," p. 76.

107. Pye, "Southeast Asia and American Policy," p. 19.

108. Pye, "Military Development," p. 40.

109. Ithiel de Sola Pool memo on "U.S. Information Efforts," to Lloyd A. Free of USIA, December 23, 1960, p. 5. Ithiel de Sola Pool Papers, Box 96, MC 440, MIT Archives.

110. David Halberstam, *The Best and the Brightest* (New York: Random House, 1972), p. 159.

111. M. M. Postan, "Walt Rostow: A Personal Appreciation," in *Economics in the Long View: Essays in Honor of W. W. Rostow*, vol. 1, ed. Charles P. Kindleberger and Guido di Tella (New York: New York University Press, 1982), p. 10.

112. Walt Whitman Rostow, *The Stages of Economic Growth: A Non-Communist Manifesto*, 3d ed. (Cambridge: Cambridge University Press, 1990), p. xviii.

113. CIS *Annual Report* (1957), p. 32.

114. Rostow, *Stages of Economic Growth*, pp. 10, 11, 77, 88, 79.

115. "Objectives," p. 70.

116. Rostow, *Stages of Economic Growth*, pp. 7–8, 58.

117. Ibid., pp. 18–19

118. Ibid., p. 26.

119. Ibid., p. 27.

120. Walt Whitman Rostow, *The View from the Seventh Floor* (New York: Harper and Row, 1964), p. 26.

121. Rostow, *Stages of Economic Growth*, p. 28.

122. Millikan and Rostow, *A Proposal*, p. 141.

123. Rostow, *View from the Seventh Floor*, p. 89.

124. Robert Langbaum, "Totalitarianism: A Disease of Modernism?" *Commentary* 19:5 (1955), p. 494.

125. Walt Whitman Rostow, "Guerrilla Warfare in the Underdeveloped Areas," *Department of State Bulletin* (August 7, 1961), p. 236.

126. Rostow, *View from the Seventh Floor*, p. 85.

127. Pye, *Guerrilla Communism*, p. 8.

128. Almond, *Appeals of Communism*, p. 183.

129. Walt Whitman Rostow, *The United States in the World Arena: An Essay in Recent History* (New York: Harper and Brothers, 1960), p. 431.

130. Walt Whitman Rostow, "Guerrilla Warfare," p. 234.

131. Ibid., p. 237.

132. Ibid., p. 236.

133. Deborah A. Straub, "Walt Rostow," in *Contemporary Authors, New Revision Series*, vol. 8, ed. A. Evory and L. Metzger (Detroit: Tower Books, 1983), p. 429.

134. Walt Rostow Oral History interview by Dick Neustadt, April 11, 1964, Kennedy Library, sent to the author by Rostow, October 4, 1999, pp. 3, 25–26.

135. Halberstam, *Best and the Brightest*, p. 160.

136. Ibid. What motivated this comment (contempt? jealousy?) is unclear. On July 9, 1999, I asked Pye about the import of his comment, but he declined to provide any elaboration.

137. Joseph G. Bock, *The White House Staff and the National Security Assistant: Friendship and Friction at the Water's Edge* (New York: Greenwood Press, 1987), p. 71.

138. John K. Lodewijks, "Rostow, Developing Economies, and National Security Policy," in *Economics and National Security: A History of Their Interaction*, ed. C. D. Goodwin (Durham, N.C.: Duke University Press, 1991).

139. Rostow, *Stages of Economic Growth*, p. xlvii.

140. Quoted in Kimber Charles Pearce, *Rostow, Kennedy and the Rhetoric of Foreign Aid* (East Lansing: Michigan State University Press, 2001), p. 12.

141. Rostow, *Process of Economic Growth*, p. 9.

142. Lipset, *Political Man*, p. 68.

143. Daniel Bell, *The Coming of Post-Industrial Society: A Venture in Social Forecasting* (New York: Basic Books, 1973), p. 56.

144. Walt Whitman Rostow, *Essays on a Half-Century: Ideas, Policies, and Action* (Boulder, Colo.: Westview Press, 1988), p. 77.

145. "It is certainly the case that Marx and Engels had some second thoughts about economic determinism, in its simple form" (Rostow, *Process of Economic Growth*, p. 42 n).

146. Rostow, *Stages of Economic Growth*, p. 162.

147. Rostow, *Dynamics of Soviet Society*, pp. 21, 24–25.

148. Rostow, *Process of Economic Growth*, p. 43 n.

149. Rostow, *Dynamics of Soviet Society*, p. 85.

150. Rostow, *Process of Economic Growth*, p. 329. Rostow felt that this was a sufficiently important point that he also included this sentence in a footnote of *Stages of Economic Growth*, p. 146.

CHAPTER 6: The Collapse of Modernization Theory

1. C. A. Doxiadis and J. G. Papaioannou, *Ecumenopolis: The Inevitable City of the Future* (New York: W. W. Norton, 1974), p. 240.

2. Daniel Yergin and Joseph Stanislaw, *The Commanding Heights: The Battle between Government and the Marketplace That Is Remaking the Modern World* (New York: Simon and Schuster, 1998).

3. *World Development Report: Workers in an Integrating World* (New York: Oxford University Press, 1995).

4. Max Millikan, preface to *The American Style: Essays in Value and Performance*, ed. Elting E. Morison (New York: Harper and Brothers, 1958), pp. vii–viii.

5. Elting E. Morison, "The Course of Discussion," in *American Style*, p. 411.

6. Walt Rostow, "The National Style," in *American Style*, pp. 247, 256, 258, 259, 305.

7. Ibid., pp. 198, 292, 307.

8. David Riesman, "Commentary: The National Style," in *American Style*, pp. 358, 360, 361, 362, 367.

9. "Subcommittee Reports Presented at the Final Meeting of the CSG," April 28, 1957, MIT Archives School of the Humanities and Social Science, Office of the Dean, Records 1933-1983, AC 20, Box 1, Folder 27, p. 9.

10. Robert Haddow, *Pavilions of Plenty: Exhibiting American Culture Abroad in the 1950s* (Washington, D.C.: Smithsonian Institution Press, 1997), pp. 98, 100, 174.

11. Walt Whitman Rostow, "Some Unfinished Business of the American Community," MIT Archives School of the Humanities and Social Science, Office of the Dean, Records 1933–1983, AC 20, Box 1, Folder 27, p. 1.

12. Walt Rostow, "The National Style," in *American Style*, p. 290.

13. James Plaut interview with Walt Rostow, January 10, 1957. Max Millikan papers 1946-1964, Box 4, Folder 119, MC 188, MIT Archives.

14. "Subcommittee Reports Presented at the Final Meeting of the CSG," April 28, 1957, MIT Archives School of the Humanities and Social Science, Office of the Dean, Records 1933-1983, AC 20, Box 1, Folder 27, p. 10.

15. Report on a one-day conference on "Problems of Achieving an Adequate Overseas U.S. Information Program." Held on December 17, 1954, at MIT, which argued that the *Brown* decision should be represented as meaning that "despite conflicts, growth is taking place in the right direction. The information service should present this as a basic trend in the country" (p. 15).

16. Haddow, *Pavilions of Plenty*, p. 175.

17. Ibid., p. 181.

18. Ibid., p. 180.

19. SSRC Box 731, Folder 10595, Series 1, Accession 2.

20. Draft in ibid. Published in slightly revised version as "Toward the Study of National-International Linkages," in *Linkage Politics: Essays on the Convergence of National and International Systems*, ed. James Rosenau (New York: Free Press, 1969).

21. Ibid.

22. Daniel Lerner, "Survey Research on Political Modernization," MIT-CIS working paper no. C/63/40, pp. 5–6.

23. Mancur Olson, *The Logic of Collective Action: Public Goods and the Theory of Groups* (Cambridge: Harvard University Press, 1965).

24. Mancur Olson, "Rapid Growth as a Destabilizing Force," *Journal of Economic History* 23:4 (1963), pp. 529–552.

25. Reinhard Bendix, "Tradition and Modernity Reconsidered," *Comparative Studies in Society and History* 9:3 (1967), p. 323.

26. Lloyd I. Rudolph and Susanne Hoeber Rudolph, *The Modernity of Tradition: Political Development in India* (Chicago: University of Chicago Press, 1967).

27. Joseph Gusfield, "Tradition and Modernity: Misplaced Polarities in the Study of Social Change," *American Journal of Sociology* 72 (1967), p. 361.

28. Ian Weinberg, "The Concept of Modernization: An Unfinished Chapter in Sociological Theory," in *Perspectives on Modernization: Essays in Memory of Ian Weinberg*, ed. Edward B. Harvey (Toronto: University of Toronto Press, 1972), pp. 8–9.

29. Ian Weinberg, "The Problem of Convergence of Industrial Societies: A Critical Look at the State of a Theory," *Comparative Studies in Society and History* 11:1 (1969), p. 9.

30. Joseph LaPalombara, "Decline of Ideology: A Dissent and an Interpretation," *American Political Science Review* 60:1 (1966), p. 13.

31. Ibid., p. 14.

32. Dean Tipps, "Modernization Theory and the Comparative Study of Societies: A Critical Perspective," *Comparative Studies in Society and History* 15:2 (1973), p. 206.

33. A. K. Cairncross, "Essays in Bibliography and Criticism: The Stages of Economic Growth," *Economic History Review* 13:2 (1961), pp. 451–452, 458.

34. Leonard Binder et al., *Crises and Sequences in Political Development* (Princeton: Princeton University Press, 1971).

35. Ibid., p. viii.

36. Charles Tilly, ed., *The Formation of National States in Western Europe* (Princeton: Princeton University Press, 1975), pp. 609, 616, 617, 620.

37. Raymond Grew, ed., *Crises of Political Development in Europe and the United States* (Princeton: Princeton University Press, 1978).

38. Keith Thomas, "The United Kingdom," in *Crises of Political Development*, p. 41.

39. Robert Nisbet, "Knowledge Dethroned," *New York Times Magazine*, September 28, 1975.

40. Max F. Millikan, "The Political Case for Economic Development Aid," in *Why Foreign Aid?* ed. Robert A. Goldwin (Chicago: Rand McNally, 1962), pp. 94, 99.

41. Edward C. Banfield, "American Foreign Aid Doctrines," in *Why Foreign Aid?* pp. 12, 16, 27.

42. Hans J. Morgenthau, "Preface to a Political Theory of Foreign Aid," in *Why Foreign Aid?* p. 70.

43. To clarify the ideological nature of the axe he was grinding, Nisbet sounded the Hayekian theme that welfarism was the road to serfdom by claiming that Rostow's *Stages of Growth* argued "in the clear direction of an almost despotic form of political centralization" (Robert A. Nisbet, *Social Change and History: Aspects of the Western Theory of Development* [New York: Oxford University Press, 1969], pp. 262, 296, 253).

44. Samuel Huntington, *The Soldier and the State: The Theory and Politics of Civil-Military Relations* (Cambridge: Harvard University Press, 1957).

45. Samuel Huntington, "Conservatism as an Ideology," *American Political Science Review* 51 (1957), pp. 454–473.

46. Donal Cruise O'Brien, "Modernization, Order, and the Erosion of the Democratic Ideal," *Journal of Development Studies* 7 (1971), p. 368.

47. Samuel P. Huntington, "Political Development and Political Decay," *World Politics* 17:2 (1965), pp. 387–393.

48. Samuel P. Huntington, *Political Order in Changing Societies* (New Haven: Yale University Press, 1968), pp. 1, 6.

49. Ibid., p. 8.

50. Colin Leys, *The Rise and Fall of Development Theory* (Bloomington: Indiana University Press, 1996), p. 76.

51. John Gretton, "The Double-Barreled Character of Professor Huntington," *Times Educational Supplement* (June 29, 1973), p. 10.

52. Leys, *Rise and Fall of Development Theory*, p. 76.

53. Quoted in Theda Skocpol, *States and Social Revolutions* (Cambridge: Cambridge University Press, 1979), p. 206.

54. Michael Schaller, "TVA on the Mekong: LBJ, the New Deal, and the Tragedy of the Vietnam War," *Reviews in American History* 24:4 (1996).

55. Samuel Huntington, "The Bases of Accommodation," *Foreign Affairs* 46:4 (1968), pp. 647, 652.

56. Arthur Schlesinger Jr., *A Thousand Days: John F. Kennedy in the White House* (Boston: Houghton Mifflin, 1965), p. 589.

57. Eqbal Ahmad, "Revolution Warfare and Counterinsurgency," in *National Liberation: Revolution in the Third World,* ed. Norman Miller and Roderick Aya (New York: Free Press, 1971), p. 198.

58. Samuel P. Huntington, "The Change to Change: Modernization, Development and Politics," *Comparative Politics* 3:3 (1971), p. 304.

59. Ibid., p. 292.

60. Michel S. Crozier, Samuel P. Huntington, and J. Watanuki, *The Crisis of Democracy: Report on the Governability of Democracies to the Trilateral Commission* (New York: New York University Press, 1975).

61. Paul Baran, *The Political Economy of Growth* (London: Penguin, 1957).

62. Andre Gunder Frank, "The Development of Underdevelopment," *Monthly Review* 18:4 (1966), pp. 17–31.

63. Andre Gunder Frank, "The Sociology of Development and the Underdevelopment of Sociology" *Catalyst* 3 (1967).

64. Immanuel Wallerstein, "Modernization: Requiescat in Pace," in *The Uses of Controversy in Sociology,* ed. Lewis A. Coser and Otto N. Larsen (New York: Free Press, 1976), pp. 131–132.

65. Edward Shils, *Center and Periphery: Essays in Macrosociology* (Chicago: University of Chicago Press, 1975).

66. Daniel Chirot and Thomas D. Hall, "World-System Theory," *Annual Review of Sociology* 8 (1982), p. 85.

67. Immanuel Wallerstein, *The Modern World System,* vol. 1–2 (New York: Academic Press, 1974, 1980).

CHAPTER 7: The Postmodern Turn and the Aftermath of Modernization Theory

Epigraph: Clark Kerr et al., *Industrialism and Industrial Man: The Problem of Labor and Management in Economic Growth* (Cambridge: Harvard University Press, 1960), p. 288.

1. Jean-François Lyotard, *The Postmodern Condition: A Report on Knowledge,* trans. Geoff Bennington and Brian Massumi (Minneapolis: University of Minnesota Press, 1984), p. 11.

2. John Kenneth Galbraith, *The New Industrial State* (Boston: Houghton Mifflin, 1967).

3. Immanuel Wallerstein, "The Eagle Has Crash Landed," *Foreign Policy* (July 2002), www.foreignpolicy.com/issue_julyaug_2002/wallerstein.html.

4. Michael Latham, *Modernization as Ideology: American Social Science and "Nation-Building" in the Kennedy Era* (Chapel Hill: University of North Carolina Press, 2000), chap. 3.

5. Frederick Ward Frey, "Political Attitudes in Development," CIS working paper no. C/64-31, p. 2.

6. Rachel Carson, *Silent Spring* (New York: Fawcett Crest, 1962).

7. James P. Pinkerton, "Enviromanticism: The Poetry of Nature as a Political Force," *Foreign Affairs* 76:3 (May/June 1997), pp. 2–7.

8. Marc Reisner, *Cadillac Desert: The American West and Its Disappearing Water* (New York: Penguin, 1993).

9. Luc Ferry, *The New Ecological Order* (Chicago: University of Chicago Press, 1995).

10. J. R. McNeill, *Something New under the Sun: An Environmental History of the Twentieth-Century World* (New York: W. W. Norton, 2000), pp. 201–203.

11. Marshall Berman, *All That Is Solid Melts into Air: The Experience of Modernity* (New York: Penguin, 1988).

12. Jane Jacobs, *Death and Life of Great American Cities* (New York: Random House, 1961).

13. Robert Venturi, Denise Scott Brown, and Stephen Izenour, *Learning from Las Vegas* (Cambridge: Massachusetts Institute of Technology Press, 1972).

14. Mike Davis, *Magical Urbanism: Latinos Reinvent the American City* (New York: Verso, 2000).

15. Jane S. Jaquette, "Women and Modernization Theory: A Decade of Feminist Criticism," *World Politics* 34:2 (1982), pp. 267–284; Catherine V. Scott, *Gender and Development: Rethinking Modernization and Dependency Theory* (Boulder, Colo.: L. Rienner Publishers, 1995); Nirmala Bannerjee, "Whatever Happened to the Dreams of Modernity? The Nehruvian Era and Women's Position," *Economic and Political Weekly* 33:17 (April 25, 1998), pp. WS2–WS7.

16. Edward A. Shils, "The Concentration and Dispersion of Charisma: Their Bearing on Economic Policy in Underdeveloped Countries," *World Politics* 11:1 (1958), p. 17. This "hypothesis" was then asserted as fact by the United Nations Statistical Office, *Handbook of Population Census Methods*, vol. 3, *Demographic and Social Characteristics of the Population, Studies in Methods*, Series F 5:1 (New York: United Nations, 1959), p. 76; and finally was "proven" by Irma Adelman and Cynthia Taft Morris, "A Factor Analysis of the Interrelationship between Social and Political Variables and Per Capita Gross National Product," *Quarterly Journal of Economics* 79:4 (1965), pp. 555–578.

17. Christopher Lasch, "The Emotions of Family Life," *New York Review of Books* (November 27, 1975), and the April 15, 1976, exchange in *New York Review* between Lasch and Fred Weinstein and Gerald M. Platt, whose book *The Wish to Be Free: Society, Psyche, and Value Change* (Berkeley: University of California Press, 1969) was the original subject of Lasch's review.

18. See Barbara Vobejda, "Traditional Families Hold On, Census Says," *Washington Post*, May 28, 1998, p. A02.

19. Frank Ninkovich, *Modernity and Power: A History of the Domino Theory in the Twentieth Century* (Chicago: University of Chicago Press, 1994), p. 267.

20. Laurence E. Grinter, "How They Lost: Doctrines, Strategies and Outcomes of the Vietnam War," *Asian Survey* 15:12 (1975), pp. 1123–1124.

21. Dean Tipps, "Modernization Theory and the Comparative Study of Societies: A Critical Perspective," *Comparative Studies in Society and History* 15:2 (1973), p. 210.

22. Ithiel de Sola Pool, "The Public and the Polity," in *Contemporary Political Science*, ed. Ithiel de Sola Pool (New York: McGraw-Hill, 1967), p. 26.

23. For further evidence of this periodization, see David Harvey, *The Condition of Postmodernity: An Enquiry into the Origins of Cultural Change* (New York: Blackwell, 1989).

24. David Riesman, "Commentary: The National Style," in *The American Style: Essays in Value and Performance*, ed. Elting E. Morison (New York: Harper and Brothers, 1958), p. 367.

25. Frederic Jameson, *Postmodernism, or the Cultural Logic of Late Capitalism* (Durham, N.C.: Duke University Press, 1991), pp. 279–296.

26. *Daedalus* 102:4 (1973).

27. David Lilienthal, *Big Business: A New Era* (New York: Harper and Brothers, 1952).

28. E. F. Schumacher, *Small Is Beautiful* (New York: Harper and Row, 1973).

29. Ali A. Mazrui, "From Social Darwinism to Current Theories of Modernization," *World Politics* 21:1 (1968), pp. 69–83.

30. Christopher Lasch, *The True and Only Heaven: Progress and Its Critics* (New York: W. W. Norton, 1991).

31. Raymond Grew, "Modernization and Its Discontents," *American Behavioral Scientist* 21:2 (1977), p. 291. Emphasis added.

32. Jameson, *Postmodernism*, esp. pp. 309–311.

33. C. Wright Mills, *The Sociological Imagination* (New York: Oxford University Press, 1959), pp. 165–167.

34. Robert E. Ward, "Political Modernization and Political Culture in Japan," *World Politics* 15:4 (1963), p. 571.

35. James Coleman, "Modernization," *Encyclopedia of the Social Sciences*, vol. 10 (New York: Macmillan, 1968), p. 397.

36. Talcott Parsons, *System of Modern Societies* (Englewood Cliffs, N.J.: Prentice-Hall, 1971), p. 3.

37. Robert Bellah, *Beyond Belief: Essays on Religion in a Post-Traditional World* (New York: Harper and Row, 1970), pp. xvi–xvii.

38. Ibid., p. xx.

39. Immanuel Wallerstein, "The Unintended Consequences of Cold War Area Studies," in Noam Chomsky et al., *The Cold War and the University: Toward an Intellectual History of the Postwar Years* (New York: New Press, 1997).

40. Bruce Cumings, "Boundary Displacement: Area Studies and International Studies during and after the Cold War," in *Universities and Empire: Money and Politics in the Social Sciences during the Cold War*, ed. Christopher Simpson (New York: New Press, 1998), p. 163.

41. Immanuel Wallerstein, "The Rise and Future Demise of World-Systems Analysis," <http://fbc.binghamton.edu/iwwsa-r&.htm> (November 25, 2001).

42. Introduction to *Political Science and Area Studies: Rivals or Partners?* ed. Lucian W. Pye (Bloomington: Indiana University Press, 1975), p. 15.

43. P. T. Bauer, *Dissent on Development* (London: Weidenfeld and Nicolson, 1971).

44. John Ehrman, *The Rise of Neoconservatism: Intellectuals and Foreign Affairs, 1945–1994* (New Haven, Conn.: Yale University Press, 1995), p. 3.

45. Daniel Bell, *The Cultural Contradictions of Capitalism* (New York: Basic Books, 1975).

46. Mark Kesselman, "Order or Movement? The Literature of Political Development as Ideology," *World Politics* 26:1 (1973), p. 142.

47. Donal Cruise O'Brien, "Modernization, Order, and the Erosion of the Democratic Ideal," *Journal of Development Studies* 8:4 (1972), p. 352.

48. Robert Bellah went from *Tokugawa Religion: The Values of Pre-industrial Japan* (Glencoe, Ill.: Free Press, 1957) to *Habits of the Heart: Individualism and Commitment in American Life* (Berkeley: University of California Press, 1985); Robert Putnam went from *The Comparative Study of Political Elites* (Englewood Cliffs, N.J.: Prentice-Hall, 1976) to

Bowling Alone: The Collapse and Revival of American Community (New York: Simon and Schuster, 2000).

49. Amitai Etzioni went from *Modern Organizations* (Englewood Cliffs, N.J.: Prentice-Hall, 1964) via *An Immodest Agenda: Rebuilding America before the 21st Century* (New York: New Press, 1983) to *The Spirit of Community: Rights, Responsibilities, and the Communitarian Agenda* (New York: Crown Publishers, 1993) and *The New Golden Rule: Community and Morality in a Democratic Society* (New York: Basic Books, 1996).

50. David Harvey, *The Condition of Postmodernity: An Enquiry into the Origins of Cultural Change* (Cambridge: Blackwell, 1989), esp. chap. 15.

51. Alan Ryan, "Live and Let Live," *New York Review of Books* (May 17, 2001), p. 55.

52. Lucian W. Pye, "The Political Context of National Development," MIT Archives, CIS working paper no. C/62-3, p. 3.

53. Pierre Bourdieu points out that there are actually two distinct visions for the European Union. The first is a neoliberal vision of the EU as a vehicle for greater integration and globalization, and not much more. The second vision "asserts its commitment to the ethics of solidarity, to solidarity with the Third World, and to a welfare state" (*Le Monde Libertaire* [April 12, 2001], no. 1240, p. 2). This second vision of the European Union provides a model for recasting the modernist development practices, as discussed at the end of this chapter.

54. Frederic Jameson and Masao Miyoshi, eds., *The Cultures of Globalization* (Durham, N.C.: Duke University Press, 1998).

55. See Frederick Bell, *National Culture and the New Global System* (Baltimore: Johns Hopkins University Press, 1994); see also Edward Said, *Culture and Imperialism* (New York: Alfred A. Knopf, 1993).

56. Daniel Lerner, "Survey Research on Political Modernization," CIS working paper C/63-40.

57. Frederic Jameson, *The Cultural Turn: Selected Writings on the Postmodern, 1983–1998* (New York: Verso, 1998), p. 62.

58. Vicente Rafael comments that "[i]t is the uncanny quality of the regional that emerges when modernity is unmoored from theories of modernization." Vicente Rafael, "Regionalism, Area Studies, and the Accidents of Agency," *American Historical Review* 104:4 (1999), p. 1210. Edward Soja highlights the importance of the spatial for contemporary social theory in *Postmodern Geographies* (New York: Verso, 1989).

59. Wolfgang Sachs, *The Development Dictionary: A Guide to Knowledge as Power* (London: Zed Books, 1992).

60. Arturo Escobar, *Encountering Development: The Making and Unmaking of the Third World* (Princeton: Princeton University Press, 1995), pp. 39, 83.

61. Ibid., p. 221.

62. Ali Mirsepassi, *Intellectual Discourse and the Politics of Modernization: Negotiating Modernity in Iran* (Cambridge: Cambridge University Press, 2000), p. 35.

63. Escobar, *Encountering Development*, p. 49.

64. Ibid., p. 51.

65. Ibid., p. 215.

66. Ibid., p. 218.

67. Jonathan Crush, "Imagining Development," in *Power of Development*, ed. Jonathan Crush (London: Routledge, 1995), p. 19. The Esteva phrase comes from "Regenerating People's Space," *Alternatives* 10:3 (1987), p. 135.

68. Escobar, *Encountering Development,* p. 222.

69. Timothy Garten Ash, "Anti-Europeanism in America," *New York Review of Books,* February 13, 2003.

70. "Small may be beautiful," Crush concludes, "but it does not mean power" ("Imagining Development," p. 42).

71. Ibid., p. 219.

72. Dwight Hoover, "The Long Ordeal of Modernization Theory," *Prospects* 11:4 (1986), pp. 407–451.

73. Craig Calhoun, "Modernization and Other Modes of Producing Muddled Thinking," *Contemporary Sociology* 11:1 (1982), p. 29.

74. Björn Hettne, *Three Worlds of Development,* 2d ed. (London: Longman Scientific and Technical, 1995), p. 64.

75. Lucian Pye, "Political Science and the Crisis of Authoritarianism: The Vindication of Modernization Theory," *American Political Science Review* 84:1 (1990), pp. 3–19.

76. Any notion that modernization theory could be said to have "predicted" the fall of Communism can be refuted by citing one of the few attempts to use modernization theory during the 1980s, Zehra F. Arat's "Democracy and Economic Development: Modernization Theory Revisited," *Comparative Politics* 21:1 (1988), which after careful quantitative analysis concluded that the Soviet Union was among the ten most stable countries on earth in terms of its likelihood of shifting "between relatively more authoritarian and democratic systems" (p. 31).

77. Howard J. Wiarda, "Toward the Future: Old and New Directions in Comparative Politics," in *New Directions in Comparative Politics,* ed. Howard J. Wiarda (Boulder, Colo.: Westview Press, 1991), p. 241.

78. Raymond L. M. Lee, "Modernization, Postmodernism and the Third World," *Current Sociology* 42:2 (1994), p. 38.

79. Francis Fukuyama, *The End of History and the Last Man* (New York: Free Press, 1992).

80. Francis Fukuyama, "On the Possibility of Writing a Universal History," in *History and the Idea of Progress,* ed. Arthur M. Melzer, Jerry Weinberger, and M. Richard Zinman (Ithaca, N.Y.: Cornell University Press, 1995), p. 16.

81. Francis Fukuyama, "The Illusion of Exceptionalism," *Journal of Democracy* 8:3 (1997), p. 146.

82. Ibid.

83. Ibid.

84. Samuel Huntington, *The Clash of Civilizations and the Remaking of World Order* (New York: Simon and Schuster, 1996).

85. Samuel P. Huntington, "The West: Unique, not Universal," *Foreign Affairs* 75:6 (1996), p. 37.

86. September 11, 2001, reinvigorated interest in Fukuyama's and Huntington's opposing visions, bringing the debate into the popular press. See, for example, Joel Aschenbach, "The Clash: Two Professors, Two Academic Theories, One Big Difference," *Washington Post,* December 16, 2001, p. W17. Fukuyama defended his theory against Huntington's in a lecture given in Melbourne, Australia, on August 8, 2002, entitled "Has History Restarted since September 11?" in which he summarized his

unabashed position this way: "The 'end of history' hypothesis was about the process of modernisation. . . . My hypothesis was that there was such a thing as a single coherent modernisation process, but that it led not to socialism or to a variety of culturally-determined locations, but rather to a liberal democracy and market-oriented econom-ics as the only viable choices. The modernisation process was, moreover, a universal one that would sooner or later drag all societies in its train. . . . September 11 represents a serious detour, but in the end modernisation and globalisation will remain the cen-tral structuring principles of world politics" (Center for Independent Studies, <www.cis.org.au/Events/JBL/JBL02.htm> [August 13, 2002]). As Stanley Kurtz noted in June 2002, "Ultimately, it is impossible to adjudicate the Fukuyama-Huntington debate without a well-grounded theory of modernization" ("The Future of 'History,'" *Policy Review* 118 [2002]).

87. John Williamson, "Democracy and the Washington Consensus," *World Development* 21:8 (1993).

88. Andrew Feenberg demolishes this view of technology in *Alternative Modernity: The Technical Turn in Philosophy and Social Theory* (Berkeley: University of California Press, 1995).

89. Edward Luttwack, *Turbo-Capitalism: Winners and Losers in the Global Economy* (New York: HarperCollins Publishers, 1999).

90. World Bank, *World Development Report* (New York: Oxford University Press, 1997).

91. Marcella Miozzo and Andrew Tylecote, "'Getting the Institutions Right': Corporate Governance and Technological Capability in East Asia and Latin America," paper delivered at DRUID Nelson Conference, June 2001, Aalborg, Denmark; Rob D. van den Berg, "Problems in Evaluating Partnerships: Suggestions on a Policy Level" (Washington, D.C.: World Bank Publications, 2001).

92. John Brohman, "Universalism, Eurocentrism, and Ideological Bias in Develop-ment Studies: From Modernisation to Neoliberalism," *Third World Quarterly* 16:1 (1995), pp. 121–140.

93. Modernization theorist Dankwart Rustow pioneered this literature in "Transitions to Democracy: Toward a Dynamic Model," *Comparative Politics* 2:3 (1970), pp. 337–363.

94. The contemporary Chinese Communist regime is the last of the classic authori-tarian high modernist regimes. It continues to envision remaking the Chinese social order through large-scale, state-led industrial engineering projects, which they refer to, tellingly, as "modernization." Perhaps the most monumental of these projects is the soon to be completed Three Gorges Dam, which will displace more than a million peas-ants from their riparian homes. Interestingly, however, opposition intellectuals in China also invoke "modernization" as a means to criticize what they perceive to be their country's political failings.

95. Michael Ignatieff, *Human Rights as Politics and Idolatry* (Princeton: Princeton University Press, 2001).

96. Amartya Sen, *Development as Freedom* (New York: Alfred A. Knopf, 1999).

97. See Williamson, "Democracy and the Washington Consensus."

98. Joseph S. Nye Jr. and John D. Donahue, eds., *Governance in a Globalizing World* (Washington, D.C.: Brookings Institution Press, 2000).

99. Cora Bell, "Normative Shift," *The National Interest* 70 <http://www.nationalinterest.org> (January 10, 2003).

100. Larry Diamond, *Promoting Democracy in the 1990s: Actors and Instruments, Issues and Imperatives* (Carnegie Commission on Preventing Deadly Conflict, Carnegie Corporation of New York, December 1995).

101. Alice Amsden, "Why Are Globalizers So Provincial?" *New York Times,* January 31, 2002.

102. Francis Fukuyama, *Trust: The Social Virtues and the Creation of Prosperity* (New York: Free Press, 1996).

103. *New York Times,* February 13, 2000, p. A12.

Essay on Sources

The line between primary and secondary sources on modernization theory is not clear-cut. Many who have written about the theory in a historical mode have themselves been development theorists, and in this sense their criticisms continue a debate about "development" that modernization theory helped to inaugurate. Initial efforts to historicize the theory emerged in the 1970s as part of the attack on modernist development practice, as detailed in the last two chapters of this book.

Focused on "development" rather than "modernization" but nonetheless the first significant attempt to historicize the modernization idea, Robert Packenham's *Liberal America and the Third World: Political Development Ideas in Foreign Aid and Social Science* (Princeton: Princeton University Press, 1973) stands up remarkably well after thirty years. Packenham explains the postwar efforts at development in terms of "American values and ideology," though he does not appreciate how much the American national identity he accurately depicts as underpinning postwar policy making was itself not a timeless artifact but rather a peculiar postwar product. A turning point in the recognition of modernization theory as a distinct body of thought was Samuel Huntington's "The Change to Change: Modernization, Development and Politics" (*Comparative Politics* 3:3 [1971], pp. 283–322), which was also a demolition of the theory, as we saw in chapter 6. Carl E. Pletsch ("The Three Worlds, or the Division of Social Scientific Labor, circa 1950–75," *Comparative Studies in Society and History* 23 [1981], pp. 565–590) notes that modernization theory required the invention of the concept of the third world, and that the popularity of both the theory and the concept of three distinct worlds of development in turn supported postwar redefinitions of the disciplinary boundaries within the social sciences. Michael Latham's *Modernization as Ideology: American Social Science and "Nation Building" in the Kennedy Era* (Durham, N.C.: University of North Carolina Press, 2000) describes the theory as an *ideology,* in the Geertzian sense, with valuable case studies of the impact of modernization theory on Kennedy-era programs like the Alliance for Progress in Latin America, the strategic hamlet program in Vietnam, and the Peace Corps. He interprets the theory as a reformulation of older American ideologies of Manifest Destiny and imperialism in more inclusive terms.

Recent historians have considered the impact of modernization theory not just on American ideas and policy but on wider global audiences as well. Jeffery Alexander's *Fin de Siècle Social Theory: Relativism, Reduction, and the Problem of Reason* (New York: Verso, 1995) describes modernization theory not so much as a social scientific theory but as a symbolic system, or metalanguage, that provided its audience with a sense of meaning and purpose in a chaotic, decolonizing world. Gilbert Rist's *The History of Development: From Western Origins to Global Faith* (New York: Zed Books, 1997) considers "development" an element of the global "religion of modernity" that seeks to obviate debate regarding economic growth as the solution to all social and political problems. James

Ferguson's *Expectations of Modernity: Myths and Meanings of Urban Life on the Zambian Copperbelt* (Berkeley: University of California Press, 1999) argues that modernization has operated as a "mythology," not just in the West but also at a popular level in postcolonial countries, where it has survived even as it has declined in significance among Western intellectuals and policy makers. Yasushi Yamanouchi et al.'s *Total War and "Modernization"* (Ithaca, N.Y.: East Asia Program, Cornell University, 1998) examines how modernization ideas supported the Allies' view of the causes of the Second World War and its aftermath in Japan, the United States, and Germany. More dispassionate is David Engerman, et al., eds., *Staging Growth: Modernization, Development, and the Global Cold War* (Amherst: University of Massachusetts Press, 2003), which shows how America's allies and enemies alike shared an enthusiasm for modernist ideas about achieving increased production and higher standards of living. Several of the essays in this book look at the diffusion of the idea of modernization into the wider popular culture, a theme also taken up by Jonathan Nashel's discussion of *The Ugly American:* "The Road to Vietnam: Modernization Theory in Fact and Fiction," in *Cold War Constructions: The Political Culture of United States Imperialism, 1945–1966,* ed. Christian Appy (Amherst: University of Massachusetts Press, 2000).

The "postdevelopment" coterie has taken a prominent role in historicizing midcentury approaches to the postcolonial world. The unifying themes of postdevelopment are an incredulity toward the very idea of "development" or "progress," and a methodology usually heavy on textual analysis and light on historical context. Wolfgang Sachs, ed., *The Development Dictionary: A Guide to Knowledge as Power* (London: Zed Books, 1992) and Arturo Escobar, *Encountering Development: The Making and Unmaking of the Third World* (Princeton: Princeton University Press, 1995) are the most widely cited postdevelopment texts, though James Ferguson, *The Anti-Politics Machine: "Development," Depoliticization, and Bureaucratic Power in Lesotho* (Minneapolis: University of Minnesota Press, 1994) and Ali Mirsepassi, *Intellectual Discourse and the Politics of Modernization: Negotiating Modernity in Iran* (Cambridge: Cambridge University Press, 2000) are more thoughtful. Much of this scholarship reflects a search for alternative bases for opposition to current modes of global organization in the wake of post-1989 disillusionment with Marxist theory. Tom Brass argues in "Old Conservatism in 'New' Clothes" (*Journal of Peasant Studies* 22:3 [1995]) that these post- Marxist celebrations of "difference," "diversity," and "choice" merely replay timeworn claims in the name of populism. Taking the postmodernists to task for their lack of historical sense rather than their ideological nonsense are many of the essays collected in Jonathan Crush, ed., *Power of Development* (London: Routledge, 1995). One convoluted effort to analyze the historical roots of development discourse can be found in M. P. Cowen and R. W. Shenton's *Doctrines of Development* (London: Routledge, 1996). More circumspect is Michael Watts, in "A New Deal in Emotions: Theory and Practice and the Crisis of Development" (in Crush, above), who argues that modernity is a negotiated process whose origins cannot be located simply in the West. Watts, along with Frederick Cooper in "Modernizing Bureaucrats, Backward Africans, and the Development Concept," in *International Development and the Social Sciences: Essays on the History and Politics and Knowledge,* ed. Frederick Cooper and Randall Packard (Berkeley: University of California Press, 1997), connect development discourse in the colonial and postcolonial worlds and welfare state norms and forms in the industrialized states. On the impact of postmodernism theory on the social sciences generally, see Pauline Rosenau, *Post-Modernism and the Social Sciences* (Princeton: Princeton University Press, 1992).

In the wake of the cold war, there have been a number of efforts to rehabilitate modernization theory, beginning with Francis Fukuyama, whose reformulation of modernization theory in neo-Hegelian terms remains a touchstone for contemporary policy debates: *The End of History and the Last Man* (New York: Free Press, 1992). See also Peter Berger, *The Capitalist Revolution: Fifty Propositions about Prosperity, Equality, and Liberty* (New York: Basic Books, 1986); Lucian Pye, "Political Science and the Crisis of Authoritarianism: The Vindication of Modernization Theory," *American Political Science Review* 84:1 (1990), pp. 3–19; K. N. Waltz, Ted Gurr et al., "America as a Model for the World?" in *PS: Political Science and Politics* 24:4 (1991), pp. 658–670; Edward Tiryakian, "Modernisation: Exhumetur in Pace," *International Sociology* 6:2 (1991); Joel Barkan, "Resurrecting Modernization Theory and the Emergence of Civil Society in Kenya and Nigeria," in *Political Development and the New Realism in Sub-Saharan Africa,* ed. David Apter and Carl Rosberg (Charlottesville: University Press of Virginia, 1994); Ronald Inglehart, *Modernization and Postmodernization: Cultural, Economic, and Political Change in 43 Countries* (Princeton: Princeton University Press, 1997). In "Neo-Modernization? IR and the Inner Life of Modernization Theory" *(European Journal of International Relations* 8:1 [2002], pp. 103–137), David Blaney and Naeem Inayatullah suggest that modernization theory can be partially salvaged by recasting the object of liberal modernization as the world rather than individual nation-states.

David Engerman argues that modernization theory emerged out of interwar American efforts to understand the prototypical backward land, Russia: "Modernization from the Other Shore: American Observers and the Costs of Soviet Economic Development," *American Historical Review* 105:2 (2000), pp. 383–416. The 1990s witnessed a recrudescence of modernization theory among former Sovietologists scrambling to understand what took place in Eastern Europe at the turn of the 1990s. For two withering critiques, from opposite ends of the political spectrum, of the post–cold war return to modernization theory among former Sovietologists, see Martin Malia, *The Soviet Tragedy: A History of Socialism in Russia, 1917–1991* (New York: Free Press, 1994) and Michael Burawoy, "The End of Sovietology and the Renaissance of Modernization Theory," *Contemporary Sociology* 21:6 (1993), pp. 774–785. Homegrown Eastern European critics of post-Soviet applications of modernization theory include Boris Kagarlitsky, *The Mirage of Modernization* (New York: Monthly Review Press, 1995) and Ilana Shapiro, "Beyond Modernization: Conflict Resolution in Central and Eastern Europe," *Annals of the American Academy of Political and Social Science,* vol. 552 (1997), pp. 14–27.

Of all the figures covered in this book, only Talcott Parsons has a significant literature dedicated to his work, though most of it has taken place within the sociology profession rather than among historians (who, one suspects, have long been repelled by his notoriously crookbacked prose). The connections between Parsons's work and modernization theory have been more acknowledged than explained, and the influence of his work outside his own discipline has yet to receive systematic attention. Uta Gerhardt's intellectual biography *Talcott Parsons* (Cambridge: Cambridge University Press, 2002) promises to fill some of these historiographical gaps. My own interpretation of Parsons's work relies on the work of his student Jeffrey Alexander, cited earlier, as well as Roland Robertson and Bryan Turner's edited volume of essays, *Talcott Parsons* (London: Sage Publications, 1991). The transformation of Parsons's social engineering ambitions in the 1930s to a conservative domestic ideology is explained in Howard Brick, "The

Reformist Dimension of Talcott Parsons's Early Social Theory," in *The Culture of the Market: Historical Essays*, ed. Thomas Haskell and Richard Teichgraeber (Ithaca, N.Y.: Cornell University Press, 1993); Brick dates Parsons's attempt to counter the rising might of economics to the late 1930s in "Talcott Parsons's 'Shift Away from Economics,' 1937–1946," *Journal of American History* 87:2 (2000), pp. 490–514. Despite its formidable presence at the United States' most storied educational institution, the Department of Social Relations (DSR) as an institution has been little studied. A useful narrative that tracks the formation but not the dissolution of the DSR is Patrick Schmidt, "Towards a History of the Department of Social Relations Harvard University, 1946–72" (B.A. honors thesis, Harvard University, 1978). No other systematic historical account of the DSR exists, though various alumni have written memoirs recounting their own involvement in the department.

The most detailed narrative of the history of the Committee on Comparative Politics (CCP) is Fred Riggs, "The Rise and Fall of 'Political Development,'" in *The Handbook of Political Behavior*, vol. 4, ed. Samuel Long (New York: Plenum Press, 1981). Riggs focuses on the rise of the term "political development" after 1960 and separates it from the concept of "modernization," which he dismisses as an altogether different idea (though he does not rigorously distinguish the two). Paul Cammack in *Capitalism and Democracy in the Third World: The Doctrine of Political Development* (London: Leicester University Press, 1997) claims that the CCP aimed above all to block postcolonial democratic advances, and in his polemical haste continues the unfortunate habit of conflating the views of Samuel Huntington with liberals like Gabriel Almond or Lucian Pye. For a revealing look at Huntington's personal ideology, see John Gretton, "The Double-Barreled Character of Professor Huntington," *Times Educational Supplement* (June 29, 1973), p. 10. Quite a bit more discussion of the CCP is likely now that its papers have been made available by the Rockefeller Foundation Archives in Tarrytown, New York. (The Rockefeller Foundation should be commended for rescuing the papers of the Social Science Research Council, which had been literally moldering in a Manhattan warehouse. Marvelously organized, the papers should prove a rich source for intellectual historians of the twentieth-century United States.)

The first retrospective look at MIT's Center for International Studies (CIS) came from George Rosen, *Western Economists and Eastern Societies: Agents of Change in South Asia, 1950–1970* (Baltimore: Johns Hopkins University Press, 1985), which gave especial attention to the center's activities and travails in India. CIS veteran Donald Blackmer's institutional history of the center's early years, *The MIT Center for International Studies: The Founding Years, 1951–1969* (Cambridge: Massachusetts Institute of Technology Press, 2002), gives Max Millikan his proper due as the spiritual leader of the center, while downplaying the role and influence of Walt Rostow. On Project Troy and its relationship to the foundation of the CIS (and many other things), see Allan Needell's *Science, Cold War and the American State: Lloyd V. Berkuer and the Balance of Professional Ideals* (London: Routledge, 2000). Quite a bit has been written on Walt Rostow, but the best character profile remains David Halberstam, *The Best and the Brightest* (New York: Random House, 1972). Kimber Charles Pearce's analysis of Rostow's rhetorical skills shows why he became the leading popularizer of modernization theory: *Rostow, Kennedy, and the Rhetoric of Foreign Aid* (East Lansing: Michigan State University Press, 2001). Two recent dissertations deal with the role of modernization ideas in Rostow's Vietnam policies: Mark Haefele, "Walt Rostow, Modernization, and Vietnam: Stages of Theoretical

Growth" (Ph.D. diss., Harvard University, 2001) and David Armstrong, "The True Believer: Walt Whitman Rostow and the Path to Vietnam," (Ph.D. diss., University of Texas, Austin, 2001).

There is a growing literature on the connections between the academy and the darker sides of the American cold war apparatus. For a crisp overview of the development of the American propaganda machine, see Christopher Simpson, *Science of Coercion: Communication Research and Psychological Warfare, 1945–1960* (New York: Oxford University Press, 1995). Ron Robin's *The Making of the Cold War Enemy: Culture and Politics in the Military-Intellectual Complex* (Princeton: Princeton University Press, 2001) considers modernization theory part of the behavioralist movement, unaware of ideology and disinclined to think about power. He takes the Project Camelot scandal to be a cause rather than an effect of the changing mood about quantifying social science in the late 1960s. Ellen Herman dissects how modernization theorists such as Gabriel Almond, Harold Lasswell, and Daniel Lerner contributed to the short-lived Psychological Strategy Board ("The Career of Cold War Psychology," *Radical History Review* 63 [1995], pp. 52–85). Noam Chomsky et al., *The Cold War and the University: Toward an Intellectual History of the Postwar Years* (New York: New Press, 1997) allows a number of prominent senior scholars to reflect on how the university's place in American society changed during the cold war. In the same ideological vein but less autobiographical in method are the essays in Christopher Simpson, ed., *Universities and Empire: Money and Politics in the Social Sciences during the Cold War* (New York: New Press, 1998), which argue that postwar social science evolved to help justify the peculiar form of American cold war internationalism. Mark Solovey argues that social scientists adopted the natural science model in order to mask their ideological agenda: "The Politics of Intellectual Identity and American Social Science" (Ph.D. diss., University of Wisconsin, Madison, 1996). On the postwar changes to the American university system more generally, see Thomas Bender and Carl Schorske, eds., *American Academic Culture in Transformation: Fifty Years, Four Disciplines* (Princeton: Princeton University Press, 1997), especially Charles Lindblom's essay, "Political Science in the 1940s and 1950s."

This book's original blueprint included a fourth case study, on the University of Chicago's Committee on the Comparative Study of New Nations, set up in 1959 by Edward Shils, Clifford Geertz, David Apter, and Lloyd Fallers. This institution, while somewhat more heterodox than the three discussed in this book, belongs alongside them as a key player in the story of modernization theory. Unfortunately, the committee's papers have not yet been made public by the University of Chicago Archives, nor have Edward Shils's personal papers, which at Shils's request are off-limits until 2045. Including the New Nations group would have had several benefits. First, it would have further underlined the importance of Edward Shils in the intellectual history of modernization theory. Second, it would have provided a context to discuss Apter's work. Third, it would have provided a forum for discussing the quasi-modernizationist work being done at the University of Chicago by Robert Redfield, Bert Hoselitz, and others. Finally, it would have provided a place to discuss the early work of Clifford Geertz. On the influence of modernization theory on Geertz, see Nils Gilman, "Involution and Modernization: The Case of Clifford Geertz," in *Economic Development: An Anthropological Approach*, ed. Jeffrey Cohen and Norbert Dannhaeuser (Walnut Creek, Calif.: Altamira Press, 2002). For Geertz's own account of the committee's history, as well as his student experience as a member of the DSR and CIS, see Clifford Geertz, *After the Fact: Two*

Countries, Four Decades, One Anthropologist (Cambridge: Harvard University Press, 1995), chap. 5. Like the other modernization theory institutions, the New Nations committee dissolved amid disillusionment in the early 1970s.

The first work to attempt to place modernization theory within the wider intellectual milieu of the 1950s was Irene Gendzier's *Managing Political Change: Social Scientists and the Third World* (Boulder, Colo.: Westview Press, 1985), which connected modernization theory with other intellectual movements of the 1950s, such as the elitist theory of democracy, antipopulism, and the end of ideology debate. Alan Brinkley, *The End of Reform: New Deal Liberalism in Recession and War* (New York: Alfred A. Knopf, 1995) recounts the emergence of a "conservative liberalism" in the 1940s, in which holding the line on New Deal programs replaced the desire to advance the reformist agenda. A similar perspective on the dominant ideology of the 1950s appears in Richard Pells's intellectual history, *The Liberal Mind in a Conservative Age: American Intellectuals in the 1940s and 1950s* (New York: Harper and Row, 1985). For an overview of the end of ideology debate, see Job L. Dittberner, *The End of Ideology and American Social Thought, 1930–1960* (Ann Arbor: UMI Research Press, 1979). Robert Collins ("David Potter's *People of Plenty* and the Recycling of Consensus History," *Reviews in American History* 16:2 [1988], pp. 321–335) and Daniel Rodgers ("Republicanism: The Career of a Concept," *Journal of American History* 79:1 [1992], pp. 11–38) provide helpful contextualizations of consensus history. On the cold war role of the USIA and the U.S. Chamber of Commerce, see Robert Haddow, *Pavilions of Plenty: Exhibiting American Culture Abroad in the 1950s* (Washington, D.C.: Smithsonian Institution Press, 1997). For a survey of 1960s intellectual history, see Howard Brick, *Age of Contradiction: American Thought and Culture in the 1960s* (New York: Twayne Publishers, 1998).

For the modernization theorists, "the modern" represented a total social vision that encompassed scientific norms of rational inquiry, as well as an underarticulated yet omnipresent formalist aesthetic of straight lines, clarity, and transparency. Frank Ninkovich observes in *Modernity and Power: A History of the Domino Theory in the Twentieth Century* (Chicago: University of Chicago Press, 1994) that the modernization theorists participated in the conceptual revolution of modernity just as fully as avant-garde artists, writers, and musicians did. Jürgen Habermas's *The Philosophical Discourse of Modernity: Twelve Lectures* (Cambridge: Massachusetts Institute of Technology Press, 1987) argues that "good" modernization requires equal emphasis on both the instrumental and the emancipatory democratic-egalitarian dimensions of Enlightenment reason. More ambivalent about modernity is Zygmunt Bauman, who (ironically) defines modernism as a quest to overcome ambivalence: *Modernity and Ambivalence* (Ithaca, N.Y.: Cornell University Press, 1991). This definition helps to explain the modernization theorists' "rage for order." Daniel Singal ("Toward a Definition of American Modernism," *American Quarterly* 39:1 [1987], pp. 7–26) notes how historians have tended to erect a wall between economic, social, and technical modernization and cultural modernism. This unfortunate habit forecloses interesting questions about the interconnections between modernity and modernization, such as the ones explored by Daniel Bell in *The Cultural Contradictions of Capitalism* (New York: Basic Books, 1976). Dealing mainly with the prewar period, Emily Rosenberg's work has pioneered the notion of "liberal" modernist development as elite-guided welfarism: *Spreading the American Dream: American Economic and Cultural Expansion, 1890–1945* (New York: Hill and Wang, 1982) and *Financial Missionaries to the World: The Politics and Culture of Dollar*

Diplomacy, 1900–1930 (Cambridge: Harvard University Press, 1999). Paul Rabinow's *French Modern: Norms and Forms of the Social Environment* (Chicago: University of Chicago Press, 1989) argues that the real target of the civilizing mission was the French themselves, and the colonies were used as laboratories for developing effective civilizing techniques for use back at home. Likewise, the modernization theorists' object of study was always already not just the third world but also the United States itself.

As what comes "after" modernism has come into clearer light, the contours of modernism have become more intelligible. Writing in 1979, Jean-François Lyotard's *The Postmodern Condition: A Report on Knowledge* (Minneapolis: University of Minnesota Press, 1984) was among the first to use the word "postmodern" to describe the outcome of the early 1970s crisis of the welfare state, the lowering of trade barriers, the breakdown of American economic hegemony, and the decline of the socialist alternative—all of which were redefining global relationships between states, markets, and civil society. David Harvey expands Lyotard's insights into a muscular neo-Marxist theory of globalization in *The Condition of Postmodernity: An Enquiry into the Origins of Cultural Change* (New York: Blackwell, 1989). Anthony Woodiwiss develops the idea of "social modernism" as a way of characterizing pro–New Deal postwar intellectual culture in *Postmodernity USA: The Crisis of Social Modernism in the United States* (London: Sage Publications, 1993). Harvey's interpretation of modernism also influences James C. Scott's *Seeing Like a State: How Certain Schemes to Improve the Human Condition Have Failed* (New Haven, Conn.: Yale University Press, 1998), which describes much of twentieth-century development practice as a series of "authoritarian high modernist" attempts to impose linear order on mainly peasant societies. Georges Canguilhem's brilliant work of medical history, *The Normal and the Pathological* (New York: Zone Books, 1991), provides an inspired way to understand the way efforts to define pathology (for example, Communism) always rest on unstable definitions of normalcy.

The global macroeconomic underpinnings of the world-historical break in the early 1970s are explained with reference to Eastern Europe in Charles Maier's *Dissolution: The Crisis of Communism and the End of East Germany* (Princeton: Princeton University Press, 1997) and Stephen Kotkin's *Armageddon Averted: The Soviet Collapse, 1970–2000* (New York: Oxford University Press, 2001), which together suggest that the crisis of modernity in the early 1970s affected not just the liberal-democratic modernity of the West but also Soviet modernism. Both forms of modernity found themselves challenged by global economic stagnation and rising commodity prices (which, not coincidentally, made the 1970s the golden age of the third world). The way that the liberal and Communist forms of modernism responded to this crisis in large measure determined their futures: the United States jettisoned the full employment part of the Fordist compromise in favor of radical technical transformation of the economy (i.e., the decimation of the manufacturing sector of the American economy), while the Soviet Union and its satellites attempted to stay their ossified modernist course, setting the stage for their catastrophic collapse in the late 1980s. The locus classicus for understanding the cultural reverberations of that radical technical transformation of the American economy remains Frederic Jameson's *Postmodernism, or the Cultural Logic of Late Capitalism* (Durham, N.C.: Duke University Press, 1991).

Index